# GILMOUR DOBIE

## PURSUIT OF PERFECTION

## LYNN BORLAND

Gilmour Dobie: Pursuit of Perfection / Lynn Borland
www.gilmourdobie.com

ISBN: 0615400841
EAN-13: 9780615400846
Library of Congress Control Number: 2010907638

Title page photograph: University of Washington Libraries, Special Collections, Neg. No. UW 21826

Cover design: Bryan Coopersmith, Group 22
Cover art: Bill Garland
Printed in the United States of America.

For my all-girls' team
Vicki, Laurie, Christine, Angie,
Devin, Jenna, Quinn, Caroline

# CONTENTS

# ACKNOWLEDGEMENTS

My wife Vicki and granddaughter Devin worked long hours for days at a time over two years in researching archival records from museums and libraries across the country. Many of these were extremely fragile requiring protective cotton gloves. They discovered several of the gems included here that added depth and substance to Dobie's life that have never been included in any prior written account. They applied organizational skills vastly superior to mine, had copies made, digitized and catalogued the massive stacks of data, sorted them into logical order, and filed them to enable ready access. Some of us are blessed with such skills and I, falling far short of competence in this area, am fortunate to have two in my family circle that are. Daughter Christine taught me timesaving technical shortcuts (as expected from the younger generation) for transferring data from drafts into the fixed digital format required for my editor to review. Daughters Laurie and Anjanette (Angie) read portions of the manuscript and provided encouragement and critical reviews that aided in moving the project forward.

Special thanks go to grandchildren, Margaret Eva Zayha and Gilmour Dobie Howatt and wife Chelle, who shared family photographs, letters and memorabilia that were extremely helpful in revealing personal insights on Gilmour Dobie, his wife Eva, and their children. These family collections have preserved important documentation of the acclaim Dobie received during his lifetime from his players and members of his profession. Genealogist Patricia Matzke contributed greatly in sharing her interpretive skills and research on Dobie and his family in the pre-1900 era.

The original inspiration to embark on this in-depth look into the life of Gilmour Dobie and his players came from Richard Linde. As a football fan I did know of the coach and from a few articles I read had an idea of this guy that caused me to dismiss him as some sort of loner who was universally disliked. It was an article that I read on Rich's website www.4malamute.com titled "A Plaque For Gil Dobie" that piqued my interest. Rich was saying that instead of deserving dismissal to the backwaters of history, he deserved to be exalted. He made the case that because of his greatness as a coach that a substantive remembrance of his and his players' contributions to Pac-12 and Washington football was warranted. I did not agree with this from a quick internet search I undertook of modern-day articles on the coach. However, I began to find contradictions, obvious errors of fact and downright misrepresentations—all of these having the appearance of credibility. The common thread running through these poorly sourced writings demonstrated that purported facts came from long held myths rather than original accounts dating back to Dobie's time. It was Rich Linde who opened this line of inquiry in my mind and aroused my interest sufficiently to embark on this quest. For this I am ever thankful.

The Special Collections Division of the University of Washington Libraries could not have been more accommodating in suggesting resources and aiding us in locating rare documents that form the foundation for this work. In particular Nicolette Bromberg was most outreaching in accessing hard to find writings and photography in archival scrapbooks. The Museum Of History And Industry (MOHAI) in Seattle also proved to be a rich resource. There, Librarian Carolyn Marr opened up her vast reservoir of photographs and was extremely helpful in guiding us in selecting several pearls from her collection.

# INTRODUCTION

Pursuit of Perfection is about a man widely celebrated as one of the greatest practitioners of his craft, that of coaching young men in the game of college football. Despite humble beginnings he was able to climb to the highest rungs of nationwide acclaim during his day. We first explore the historical record extolling his gifts as a master of psychology. During his coaching career, this facility was oft-acclaimed as the reason for his success, but was not understood at the time. Gilmour Dobie said himself that football was nothing more than psychology; here we discover how he came to be of this opinion.

Why did he coach the way he coached? Why did he act the way he acted? Over the past century, hundreds of writers have speculated on these questions. In this biography, for the first time in history, the answers are revealed. As a child, both of his parents had died by the time he was eight years old. He spent his next nine years as an orphan and ward of the state of Minnesota. This remarkable event shaped the man he was to become. In Chapter 2 the struggles he faced proved formidable but through his own pluck, internal fortitude and a fascinating set of circumstances, he was saved from a life of deprivation.

In his years at Washington he gained his greatest success and his national identity became the stuff of legend. It is this identity that we deal with throughout the book. When he began at Seattle in 1908 he brought a resume of some achievement, but nothing to give a hint of what was to follow. Here he was lionized by his many fans, and for good cause, he never lost a game for the nine years he coached there. And yet he became known as "Gloomy Gil" during this time. How could someone who rose to such national renown be branded a doomsayer? The answer proves to be quite surprising, as we delve into first hand reports of his behavior and discover just how this happened. There were times he did appear gloomy, however, the key to understanding the man is not through quick snapshots, but by surveying his life in its overall context as set out within these pages.

Just as with any strong personality who attracts wide media coverage, information regarding the coach became distorted over time. For this work hundreds of eye witness accounts were reviewed to get the original perspective on events. Dobie proved easy to caricature, being eminently quotable and one who always spoke his mind. There is a wide divergence from original accounts and the more sensationalist writings done decades later. Dobie did make mistakes and these are covered here but he learned and matured from his missteps. The fact that he shortly overcame his errant behavior is most often left unreported.

Dobie's nine years at Washington (1908-16) cover football's most critical years as the great collegiate game progressed into how it is played today. The rules changes of 1910,'12 and '14 brought about the shift from the old power game of brute force to one requiring speed and tactical skill. Contrary to many accounts stating that Dobie was stuck in the past and solely depended on the off-tackle line buck, we discover that from his earliest days he adapted his style of play as the game advanced. In his own words, he admits that he learned this lesson years before as an assistant at Minnesota where he had been stubbornly uncompromising.

The center of the football world in the early 1900s was the East Coast. Before Dobie, the Far West received scant media coverage. As his string of undefeated games grew year-after-year, this changed dramatically. The record reflects that his unbeatable reputation was the impetus that raised the level of competition far beyond Dobie's Pacific Northwest Conference. The dramatic climax of events that brought the University of Washington and the University of California together on the football field on November 6, 1915 set the wheels in motion that led to the creation of what became the Pac-10/Pac-12 Conference. In this writing we connect these events with the people who made it happen. At the heart of the movement, Gilmour Dobie and his outstanding athletes played a pivotal role.

W = Won Letter, H = Honorary Letter, C = Captain, S = Substitute, No Letter

| NAME | No. | POS | WT | HOMETOWN | 06 | 07 | 08 | 09 | 10 | 11 | 12 | 13 | 14 | 15 | 16 | 17 |
|---|---|---|---|---|---|---|---|---|---|---|---|---|---|---|---|---|
| Abel, (Don) Donald | 24 | RE | 165 | Hoquiam, WA | | | | | | | | | W | S | W | |
| Abel, George | · | LH | | Hoquiam, WA | | | | | | | | | W | S | | |
| Abel, (Bob) Robert | · | LH | 155 | Aberdeen, WA | | | | | | | | | | S | S | |
| Anderson, (Andie) Arthur | · | LT | 183 | Portland, OR | | | | | | | | | | S | | W |
| Anderson, (Andy) Herman | · | RT | 201 | La Conner, WA | | | | | | W | W | C | W | | | |
| Babcock, (Bull Moose) Frank | · | RG | 210 | Everett, WA | | | W | | | | | | | | | |
| Baker, Tracy | 22 | FB | 178 | Pendleton, OR | | | S | W | | | | | | | | |
| Bantz, (Admiral) Burwell | · | LT | 195 | Juan de Fuca, WA | W | W | W | | | | | | | | | |
| Beck, (Bruce) Broussais | · | C | 166 | Seattle, WA | | W | S | S | | | | | | | | |
| Bliss, (Jack) Bernard | · | RT | 174 | Seattle, WA | | | | S | S | W | W | | | | | |
| Bronson, (Dick) Deming | · | QB | 5'7" | Fairbault, MN | | | | | | | S | S | S | H | | |
| Bruce, James | · | RT | 180 | Seattle, WA | | | | | | | W | | | | | |
| Cahill, William | · | FB | 165 | Wenatchee, WA | | | | | W | S | | | | | | |
| Calkins, (Spaghetti) Julius | 14 | T | 180 | Seattle, WA | | | | | | | | | | S | W | |
| Chapman, (Mike) Myers | · | RH | 201 | Kirkland, WA | | | | | | | S | | W | | | |
| Clark, Arthur | · | RE | 150 | Centralia, WA | W | | S | | | | | | | | | |
| Clark, (Click) Earle F. | · | LE | | Everett, WA | | | | | | | | W | W | | | |
| Cook, (Deacon) William | · | LH | 162 | Seattle, WA | | | | S | S | W | | | | | | |
| Coyle, (Wee) William | 16 | QB | 151 | Seattle, WA | | | W | W | W | C | | | | | | |
| Cushman, (Tom) Thomas | · | C | | Seattle, WA | | | | | | | | | | W | | |
| Devine, Richard | · | RG | 205 | Pendleton, OR | | | | | | W | S | | | | | |
| Dieter, Louis | · | FB | 176 | Lewistown, ID | | | S | W | | | | | | | | |
| Dorman, Harry | · | LH | 161 | Everett, WA | | | | | | | W | W | | | | |
| Eakins, (Eak, Max) Maxwell | 14 | RT | 181 | Gary, SD | | | W | W | W | | | | | | | |
| Faulk, (Ted) Theodore | 11 | LE | 168 | Hoquiam, WA | | | | | | | | | | S | W | |
| Flaherty, Guy | · | LG | 165 | Sed.-Wooley, WA | W | W | S | | | | | | | | | |
| Gardner, (Ray) Raymond | 14 | RH | 6'11" | Spokane, WA | | | | | | | | | | S | S | W |
| Gellatly, (Shoes) Lester | · | C | 170 | Wenatchee, WA | | | | | | | | | W | | | |
| Griffiths, Burke | · | LG | 180 | Seattle, WA | | | | | | S | S | W | S | | | |
| Griffiths, (Tom) Thomas | 12 | RG | 186 | Seattle, WA | | | | W | W | W | C | | | | | |
| Grimm, (Polly) Huber | 15 | E/LT | 210 | Centralia, WA | | W | | W | C | | | | | | | |
| Grimm, (Wedge) Warren | 21 | LE | 189 | Centralia, WA | | | | W | W | W | W | | | | | |
| Grimm, (Bill) William | 22 | T/LG | 170 | Centralia, WA | | | | | | | | | | W | W | |
| Hainsworth, (Bill) William | 25 | FB | 170 | Seattle, WA | | | | | | | | | S | S | W | |
| Hardy, (Mike) Warren M. | · | RG | 175 | Seattle, WA | | | | | S | S | S | W | | | | |
| Hazelet, Calvin | · | LH | 164 | Cordova, AL | | | | | | S | W | | | | | |
| Hosely, Rex | · | LH | 160 | Nielsville, WI | | | | | W | | | | | | | |
| Hunt, (Mike) Raymond | 1 | LE | 181 | North Yakima, WA | | | | | | | W | W | W | C | | |
| Husby, (Pete) Peter | · | RE | 180 | Stanwood, WA | | | | | W | W | | | | | | |
| Jaquot, (Jake) Frank | · | RH | 178 | Tacoma, WA | | | | | | | W | W | | | | |
| Jarvis, Paul | · | LG | 190 | Seattle, WA | W | S | W | | | | | | | | | |
| Johnson, (Ching) Clark | 29 | QB | 154 | Tacoma, WA | | | | | | | | | | S | W | |
| Leader, (Ed) Edward | · | RE | 165 | Portland, OR | | | | | | | W | W | S | S | | |
| Leader, Elmer | 2 | LT | 174 | Portland, OR | | | | | | | W | W | W | W | | |
| Logg, (Dave) David | 23 | C | 175 | Rolling Bay, WA | | | | | | | | | S | W | S | |
| MacKechnie, (Mac) Ross | 11 | C/RH | 175 | Port Angeles, WA | | | | | | | | | S | W | | |
| Markham, (Mark) John | 20 | RT | 5'11" | Centralia, WA | | | | | | | | S | | W | | |
| Mattson, (Bill) William | 19 | RE | 164 | Tacoma, WA | | W | W | W | | | | | | | | |
| Mayfield, (Ben) Benjamin | · | RT | 175 | Chehalis, WA | | | | | | | | | S | S | W | |
| May, (Charlie) Charles | 18 | LG/C | 187 | Ithaca, NY | | | S | W | | | | | | | | |
| McPherson, (Andy) Andrew | · | LG/T | 171 | Bellingham, WA | | | | | | | | | W | | | |
| Miller, (Hap) Cedric | 19 | LH | 198 | Vancouver, WA | | | | | | | W | W | W | W | | |
| Moran, (Mal) Malcolm | · | FB | | Rosario, WA | | | | | | | | | | | S | W |
| Morrison, (Vic) Clarence | 6 | RG | 182 | Seattle, WA | | | | | | | | | S | S | W | |
| Mucklestone, (Muck) Melville | 20 | RH | 176 | Gary, SD | | | W | C | | W | | | | | | |
| Murphy, (Tramp) Ernest | 26 | T/LH | 186 | Wallace, ID | | | | | | | | | S | W | W | C |
| Noble, (Cy) Elmer | 27 | RH | 177 | Centralia, WA | | | | | | | | W | W | W | W | |
| Patten, (Jack) John | · | RT | 181 | Seattle, WA | | | | | | W | W | | | | | |
| Pike, Roscoe | · | RH | 177 | Ballard, WA | | | | S | W | | | | | | | |

| Name | # | Pos | Wt | Hometown | | | | | | | | | | | | |
|---|---|---|---|---|---|---|---|---|---|---|---|---|---|---|---|---|
| Presley, BeVan | • | C | 176 | Seattle, WA | | | | | W | W | W | W | | | | |
| Pullen, (Pink) Royal | • | RG/T | 182 | Skagway, AL | | | | S | W | W | | | | | | |
| Savage, (Tony) Anthony | • | RE | 172 | Roslyn, WA | | | | | | S | S | W | | | | |
| Seagrave, (Louie) Louis | 24 | RG | 187 | Spokane, WA | | | | | | | W | W | W | C | | |
| Schively, (Pitt) Hugh | • | E | 130 | Olympia, WA | | | | S | S | S | H | | | | | |
| Shiel, (Walt) Walter | 10 | FB | 190 | Spokane, WA | | | | | | | W | W | C | W | | |
| Smith, (Charley) Charles | • | QB | 165 | Auburn, WA | | | | | S | S | W | W | | | | |
| Smith, (Snake) George | 32 | RE | 165 | Seattle, WA | | | | | | | | W | W | S | | |
| Sparger, Fred | • | FB | 173 | Seattle, WA | | | | W | W | W | | | | | | |
| Sutton, (Sut, Pete) Wayne | • | RE | 176 | Seattle, WA | | | | | | | W | W | W | W | | |
| Swarva, (Guy, Pete) George | • | RG | 180 | Seattle, WA | | | S | S | W | | | | | | | |
| Taylor, (Scrappy) Leonard | 17 | LH | 148 | Massachusetts | | | W | W | | | | | | | | |
| Tegtmeier, (Pete) Fred | 11 | C | 190 | Everett, WA | W | W | C | W | | | | | | | | |
| Tidball, (Ben) Benjamin | 34 | LT | | Bellingham, WA | | | | | | | | | S | W | | |
| Wand, (Tom) Thomas | • | QB | 147 | Seattle, WA | | | | S | S | S | H | | | | | |
| Wand, Walter | • | LH | 168 | Seattle, WA | | | S | W | W | W | | | | | | |
| Westover, (Penny) Ralph | • | FB | 175 | Seattle, WA | | | W | | | | | | | | | |
| Wick, (Sandy) Sanford | 4 | C | 178 | Arlington, WA | | | | | | | | | S | W | S | |
| Willis, Hart | • | FB | 175 | Seattle, WA | W | W | S | | | | | | | | | |
| Winn, Grover C. | • | RT | 175 | Seattle, WA | | | | S | S | W | | | | | | |
| Wirt, (Harry) Harold | 3 | LG | 186 | Yakima, WA | | | | | | | | S | S | W | W | |
| Young, (Bud) Allan | 8 | QB | 162 | Seattle, WA | | | | | | | W | W | W | | | |

*There were more than 200 non-lettermen who served under Coach Dobie deserving of honor. Records are not adequate to accurately include their names.

| FOOTBALL STAFF | | | | | | | | | | | | | |
|---|---|---|---|---|---|---|---|---|---|---|---|---|---|
| NAME | HOMETOWN | 06 | 07 | 08 | 09 | 10 | 11 | 12 | 13 | 14 | 15 | 16 | 17 |
| Cutting, (Joe) Joseph | Minneapolis, MN | | | x | x | x | | | | | | | |
| Eakins, Maxwell | Gary, SD | | | | | | x | x | | | | | |
| Fancher, Jack | Spokane, WA | | | | | | | | | | x | x | |
| Hall, David C. Dr. | Seattle, WA | | | x | x | x | x | x | x | x | x | x | |
| Hartman, (Bob) Robert | | | | | | | | | | | | | |
| Hurr, Ralph | | | | | | | | x | x | | | | |
| Grinstead, Loren | Cheney, WA | x | x | | | | | | | | | | |
| Miller, (Hap) Cedric | Vancouver, WA | | | | | | | | | | | x | |
| Sieler, Herbert | | | | x | x | x | x | | | | | | |
| Sutton, Wayne | Seattle, WA | | | | | | | | | x | x | x | |
| Rasmussen, (Bill) William | | | | x | | | | | | | | | |
| Wand, Thomas | | | | | | | | | x | | | | |
| Younger, (Jesse) J. Arthur | | | | | | | | | | x | x | | |
| Zednick, (Vic) Victor | Seattle, WA | | | x | x | x | x | | | | | | |

| Date | Team | UW | OP | Date | Team | UW | OP |
|---|---|---|---|---|---|---|---|
| | NCAA Record – 1917* 60 – 0 – 4 | | | | | | |
| | **1908** | | | | **1913** | | |
| 9-26 | Lincoln HS | 22 | 0 | 9-27 | Everett HS | 26 | 0 |
| 10-3 | Washington HS | 23 | 5 | 10-11 | All-Navy | 23 | 7 |
| 10-17 | Whitworth | 24 | 4 | 10-18 | Whitworth | 100 | 0 |
| 10-24 | Whitman | 6 | 0 | 10-25 | Oregon State | 47 | 0 |
| 11-7 | Washington State | 6 | 6 | 11-1 | Whitman | 41 | 7 |
| 11-14 | @ Oregon | 15 | 0 | 11-15 | @ P Oregon | 10 | 7 |
| 11-28 | Oregon State | 32 | 0 | 11-27 | Washington State | 20 | 0 |
| | **1909** | | | | **1914** | | |
| 10-9 | Queen Anne HS | 34 | 0 | 9-26 | Aberdeen HS | 33 | 6 |
| 10-16 | USS Milwaukee | 39 | 0 | 10-3 | Washington Park AC | 45 | 0 |
| 10-23 | Lincoln HS | 20 | 0 | 10-10 | Rainer Valley AC | 81 | 0 |
| 10-30 | @ S Idaho | 50 | 0 | 10-24 | Whitman | 28 | 7 |
| 11-6 | Whitman | 17 | 0 | 10-31 | @ A Oregon State | 0 | 0 |
| 11-13 | @ Oregon State | 18 | 0 | 11-14 | Oregon | 10 | 0 |
| 11-25 | Oregon | 20 | 6 | 11-26 | Washington State | 45 | 0 |
| | **1910** | | | | **1915** | | |
| 10-8 | Lincoln HS | 20 | 0 | 10-2 | Ballard Meteors | 31 | 0 |
| 10-15 | @ Univ. of Puget Sound | 51 | 0 | 10-9 | Washington Park AC | 64 | 0 |
| 10-22 | Whitman | 12 | 8 | 10-23 | @ S Gonzaga | 21 | 7 |
| 11-5 | Idaho | 29 | 0 | 10-30 | Whitman | 27 | 0 |
| 11-12 | @ S Washington State | 16 | 0 | 11-6 | @ California | 72 | 0 |
| 11-24 | Oregon State | 22 | 0 | 11-13 | California | 13 | 7 |
| | | | | 11-25 | Colorado | 46 | 0 |
| | **1911** | | | | **1916** | | |
| 10-2 | Lincoln HS | 42 | 0 | 9-30 | Ballard Meteors | 28 | 0 |
| 10-14 | Fort Worden | 99 | 0 | 10-14 | Bremerton Naval Team | 62 | 0 |
| 10-21 | Univ. of Puget Sound | 35 | 0 | 10-28 | Whitman | 37 | 6 |
| 10-28 | @ S Idaho | 17 | 0 | 11-4 | @ Oregon | 0 | 0 |
| 11-4 | Oregon State | 34 | 0 | 11-11 | Oregon State | 35 | 0 |
| 11-18 | @ P Oregon | 29 | 3 | 11-18 | @ California | 13 | 3 |
| 11-30 | Washington State | 30 | 6 | 11-30 | California | 14 | 7 |
| | **1912** | | | | | | |
| 9-28 | Everett HS | 55 | 0 | | | | |
| 10-12 | Univ. of Puget Sound | 53 | 0 | | | | |
| 10-19 | Bremerton Naval Team | 55 | 0 | | | | |
| 10-26 | Idaho | 24 | 0 | | | | |
| 11-9 | @ P Oregon State | 9 | 3 | | | | |
| 11-16 | Oregon | 30 | 14 | | | | |
| 11-28 | Washington State | 19 | 0 | | | | |

@S = Played in Spokane     @P = Played in Portland   @A = Played in Albany

*NCAA undefeated streak includes Dobie's teams' record of 59-0-3 plus a 1907 last game Idaho tie and a 1917 first game win over Whitman. California broke the streak with a Nov. 3, 1917 win at Berkeley in a shutout 27-0.

# COACHING COMPARISON

## Dobie Versus the League

The NCAA record for undefeated games of 60-0-4 at the University of Washington still stands. Coach Gilmour Dobie having coached 97% of these games is singularly responsible for the record as his streak of 59-0-3 over nine year's accounts for virtually all of this unprecedented accomplishment.

In that era of sparse population density and long distance travel challenges, college teams scheduled their preseason games with athletic clubs, military bases, high schools, all-star teams and semi-pro squads. This practice was commonplace in the early 1900s and lasted into the 1920s. As such, the records of those days include competition with much weaker teams as colleges prepared for league play. Under today's NCAA rules both teams must be college level but the same strategy applies of scheduling weaker teams in preparation for tougher games within the conference.

Because of the wider disparity between the bonafide NCAA teams and their preseason opponents compared to today some will discount the records of the early twentieth century. However, since from conference to conference each team within a particular league played each other and had comparable preseason schedules, a record such as Dobie's should be evaluated based on how well his teams stacked up within the Pacific Northwest Intercollegiate Conference (Big 6). During his nine years at Washington the other five teams had a total of twenty-four coaches. Not all teams played a round robin schedule every year from 1908-1916, but their total head-to-head records do serve as a valid standard of comparison. Recruiting was primarily limited to the Pacific Northwest with all teams getting the vast majority of their players from the same talent pool.

Here is the comparison of the six league teams for all games played within the Big 6:

| College | Winning Percentage |
|---|---|
| Oregon | .680 |
| Washington State | .645 |
| Oregon State | .580 |
| Idaho | .464 |
| Whitman | .222 |
| Total For Five Teams | .538 |
| **Washington** | **.976** |

The Big 6 teams for the nine years Dobie coached Washington competed head-to-head for a total of 203 league games. His undefeated record of a winning percentage of 98% as compared to the conference's 54% is clear evidence of his coaching supremacy when viewed against his peers.

The Big 6 won 78% of Division 1 level teams when they competed outside their conference. They played against the likes of USC, California, Colorado, Nebraska, Michigan State, Utah and Pennsylvania. This record calls into question claims of Northwest football from 1908 to 1916 being an inferior product.

# CHAPTER ONE

# Football as Psychology

"After all football is mostly psychology."
*Gilmour Dobie*

F. A. Churchill, who personally knew and frequently wrote of Gilmour Dobie in his time, gave this description of the tall lanky Scotsman: "Far above usual stature, with a figure whose leanness is the continual joy of the sporting slang artist, Dobie looms gauntly among even the massy men who surround him. He has a head worth studying. It rests alert on a wiry neck, is small, and well-shaped. Straight, crisp, black hair tends, in intense moments, to flare out over a brow which bears the short, vertical line of irascibility between the eyes. When that line deepens with a twitch, and the bright, dark eyes begin to snap like a slave-driver's lash, and the short lips disappear in a foreboding white line, the squad looks for trouble. Dobie always means what he says, and rarely says it. As a result, the squad accepts his words in the attitude of a gang of Platos surrounding a Socrates."

Dobie carefully orchestrated his manner and dress on the sidelines to emphasize his role as coach and supreme commander of the team. Being over six feet tall and of slender build, he would always wear a long, usually black overcoat to further accentuate his linear frame. His outfit included a suit, white shirt with tie and either a slouch hat or, more often, a stylish black derby to add a commanding look of authority as he paced the sidelines barking orders. As with all aspects of his persona, Dobie perfected this look to uniquely set himself apart. He deliberately sought to stand out, not to blend into the background. William "Wee" Coyle, the star quarterback on Dobie's inaugural team of 1908, described him as being totally engaged during the games. "He works just as hard as his players, running back and forth in a position parallel to the action of the game, waving his long arms excitedly, biting his ever-present cigar, kneeling to pick up pebbles only to throw them down again—more in earnest than his men, for his gaze never loses the ball nor the movement of any player on the field." Coyle compared him to General Ulysses S. Grant in that both always smoked a heavy black cigar when in charge of their "fighting men."

Emil Hurja, writing in 1914 in *Sunset, the Pacific Monthly*, also describes Dobie's sideline behavior as being quite intense. "If one can picture thousands of cheering spectators banked, tier upon tier, about a gigantic quadrangle keenly watching a gridiron battle, and then place upon the sidelines, crouching low, a tall, silent, raincoated figure, one may be able to get the relation of Gilmour Dobie to football. To observe Dobie on a gridiron, where his name is on the lips of thousands, young and old alike, one hardly knows what to think. He is so quiet, yet apparently absorbed mind and soul in the game. There is an uncanny mysteriousness about him sometimes when he moves along the chalk-marked edge of the field, following the advance of the players. He is an enigma when college yells start to ring out, short and snappy or prolonged and wailing, and the teams trot out on the field. But when one sees him after a game, calm and cool and undisturbed, quiet though receiving congratulations from hundreds of staid graduates and enthusiastic, admiring undergraduates, one cannot help wonder whether this unassuming demeanor is but a mask for an acutely active mind and an energetic body, wrapped up in the business of football."

He was an early adherent of physical fitness and athletic conditioning. There were many games where the other team would be running out of gas but Dobie's men seemed to gain a second wind. They practiced hard with heavy running in order to play hard. The Eastern style of play was based on a theory of identifying the best athletes in the early season, focusing on building up their talents to their peak, and, as the season progressed, bringing the team together as a single unit. From his Minnesota playing and assistant coaching background, he was an adherent of the Middle West style and came to Washington with this attitude of how to develop the team. He was an apostle of teaching the players to run their plays off quickly in an effort to tire the opposition. His strategy was excessively weighted towards teamwork first, with the development of the individual star later.

Since Dobie's teams won with such overwhelming dominance, the question can be asked whether Dobie was totally ruthless and showed no element of mercy in pursuit of winning. It is correct that many players on all teams played the entire game with very little or no substitution. But it is a mistaken impression to assume that coaches of the early 1900s purposely overextended their players with too much playing time. Teams of the conference typically had eighteen to twenty-two men in the primary squad, some of whom did not get enough playing time to earn letters. This was in an era where men performed triple duty on offense, defense, and special teams. To reduce expenses traveling squads were typically eighteen athletes. Players, of necessity, were generalists rather than the highly trained specialists of today. In 1908 Washington had twelve men who earned letters and ten more nonlettermen substitutes who, in other years, earned a letter. The entire team, including men who never saw game time, was thirty-five strong. There were many dedicated athletes who practiced in the trenches with no glory other than the love of sport. By 1915 the team consisted of fifteen lettermen plus Deming Bronson, who got an honorary **W** for his four years of service without earning a letter, and eleven nonlettermen who, in other years, did qualify. The entire team, with those high enough in ranking to make it out for picture day, totaled twenty-nine men. In 1916, the first year freshmen were excluded from varsity league play, the freshman team alone totaled seventeen men. This marked the beginning of the large composition squads seen today, as by 1917 there were fifty-seven men on the team, twenty-nine being freshmen. Of this group fourteen earned letters.

But it wasn't just the smaller squads and players working triple duty. Dobie's players were on the field for what may seem to be excessive time (considering the lopsided scores.) The rules of the day forced coaches to leave their front line in the game beyond what merciful conduct would dictate. Up until 1910, when a player was removed from the game he was not allowed to return. In 1910 this rule was amended to allow removal of a player, but he could not return until the next quarter. The player could only come out and return once per game. Game stats gradually reflected an increase in the number of players, with as many as ten substitutes coming in off the bench.

Whether Dobie's personal style was being described in his early days as a rookie coach or thirty years later at his last head coaching position at Boston College, the one word most often used to describe this complex man was pessimism. "Gloomy" had such alliterative charm when attached to Gil that headline writers of his time found it hard to resist. "Doom" and "dour" likewise blend beautifully when wed to his last name. Before the game coming up for that week, he could often predict imminent disaster. The opposition was stronger, more athletic, better skilled, better conditioned, healthier, or his players just weren't committed to the task at hand. He certainly didn't invent the strategy of setting low expectations with his coachspeak gimmicks, as many other coaches of the day did exactly the same thing—as do many today. One reason Dobie gained such notoriety for his pessimism was his relentless consistency in its application. No matter how weak the "dopesters" predicted the other team to be, Dobie would invariably announce to the world that his boys didn't have a chance. He also could be counted on for a colorful quote, and the obvious contradiction of a coach who quite often predicted loss but always won made for rich copy. Reporters reveled at mocking him for this puffing or would set up story lines that "perhaps the wily master" was onto something this time. His sharp tongue would forever endear him to the press.

He honed his skill for projecting pessimism to a fine art. This became the centerpiece of his strategy in the pregame jousting between opposing sides for next Saturday's contest. The dark cloud of gloom and doom, while overplayed in the press, became a trademark, and the phenomenal results Washington enjoyed demonstrate that it worked. As his popularity with the press increased, it became hard to find a sports story that didn't devote some angle to his pessimistic slant. If he didn't offer one in his interview, the lack of a glum stance would often be highlighted as news. As his legend spread far and wide with season after undefeated season, this grew into the popular conception of his identity. The tag inexorably stuck with him throughout his life, as if this was all there was to the man. In closely surveying his lifetime of accomplishment on the football field, his family life, and the descriptions of him from those who knew him, it's apparent there was much more to the coach than a cynical outlook towards next week's game. In actuality, his outward aspect of dour countenance masked an intelligent, well-spoken man of high standards and compassion. Why, then, was the glass always half empty when sizing up his chances against the competition? He was astoundingly successful over a long career; could he really believe his team would never win? Deep down inside, was he a pessimist? To find the answer to these questions, we need to take a broader look at many other driving forces that define the man.

There was a definite system to Dobie's approach to football. William "Wee" Coyle, starting quarterback on the team for 1908-11, writing in 1913, paid homage to this important aspect of Dobie's coaching skills: "The football secret of the Dobie plan is an efficient system. Dobie's business is football." The system didn't require a large variety of complicated resources to succeed; in fact, it was just the opposite. The coach was creative but was not known as an innovator breaking new ground with exotic formations or glamorous plays. His bread-and-butter play was the off-tackle line buck designed to get 3 to 4 yards per carry. He used the forward pass, but this was a supplement to the far more important power football of the running game. There are reports that Dobie did not believe in the forward pass under any circumstances, but these are not correct. When conditions were right, he would often use the pass to great advantage.

Discussing how he won the league championship in his first year at UW, Dobie said, "Straight football was very essential to win, yet I spent twenty minutes every night of practice developing Washington in the forward pass formation, which play, I emphatically declare, won for us the season's honors." He attributed the win over Oregon and the team's showing in the tightly contested tie against Washington State in the 1908 season to the forward pass. Dobie's skill at preparing his teams in the execution of the forward pass was further attested to in the Seattle *Post-Intelligencer* description of Washington's victory over Oregon State to clench the championship of 1910: "Three touchdowns were the result of the use of the forward pass, the play which has, more than any other strategic feature, gained first place for the varsity. Dobie has developed this play with all possible variations, in all its intricacies. Sometimes the tackle throws the ball, sometimes a punter, Max Eakins, sometimes the quarterback, end or tackle. But always they know where they are to toss it and who is to receive it."

The *Seattle Times*, in reviewing the 1912 game against the University of Idaho that virtually everyone expected to end in resounding defeat for Washington, emphasized Dobie's skill of motivating the players just as they go into a game. "He has the faculty of sending his men into battle to fight as if for their lives.

He coaches them in football in the right way; he pays strict attention to detail and leaves nothing to chance but right at the last moment he fires his men with some of his own fighting spirit and they simply tear all opposition to tatters. The Washington boys hit Idaho so hard in that first half that the boys in the red shirts simply could not stand up before the onslaught."

In writing an account of Dobie's system, George Pfann, who was an All-American wingback on Dobie's national champion teams at Cornell in the early 1920s, attributed his success there to the same techniques he employed at Washington. "Aside from insistence on careful execution of fundamentals and careful attention to detail, I think that the factors which made Dobie an outstanding coach were: (1) His ability to select a team. (2) His ability to keep a team in top condition mentally and physically. (3) Obtaining an extremely high degree of coordinated team play. (4) Getting the best performance of which they were capable out of the team."

While Dobie reached the height of his gridiron accomplishments at Washington, where he was known as a master of detail and brilliant teacher of fundamentals, these attributes were also acknowledged during his later years at Cornell. In 1923, the *Cornell Daily Sun*, reporting from an Associated Press account, attributed his success to the same principles. "Dobie's coaching method, or rather the style of play that he develops, has the peculiar quality of absolute precision that goes with definite cadence, not unlike that of a crack drill squad going through the manual of arms. The marvelous thing about it is that it goes ahead unerringly in the midst of the confusion of charging lines and strenuous physical combat. On a given play each member of the team has definite duties to perform in a perfect routine and he takes his three steps in one direction and two in another as infallibly and accurately as if there were no one else on the field." Dobie summed this up himself in this explanation of his standards: "In fact any play is merely the performance of fundamentals by eleven men working in perfect unity." The way to achieve this ideal, as he explained, depends on the team's "complete mastery of fundamentals."

Dobie's system centered on him as the master and the players as obedient servants. His players soon grew to understand that Dobie allowed no margin for error. He was an obsessive/compulsive taskmaster who demanded not just best efforts, not just excellence, but perfection. Setting this unattainable standard was how he got his athletes to stretch to their full potential. His season would start with introducing only a few simple plays and not advancing to anything more complex until these were learned to the smallest detail of footwork, body position, timing, and use of arms. When a new play was introduced, the players would feel they had it down, but it would never be to Dobie's satisfaction. If a player was a few inches out of place, he would have to suffer the wrath of the exacting instructor. It's not quoted to be from Dobie's lips, but Coyle stated the tall Scot's motto as "I am always right—you are always wrong." His record shows that he turned average players into good, and good players he elevated to greatness. They could hate his harsh methods, but, over time, admitted they respected his ability to squeeze everything possible out of the team.

The Dobie system required total compliance to his will and a dedication to hard work that would take his men right up to the breaking point. When sensing he had pushed one of his athletes too far, the coach could turn on a dime and reach an arm out to show comforting, fatherly support. This characteristic of his nature was not often deployed, and because it was used with such discrimination, its effectiveness was greatly magnified. As for the team as a whole, there were few such fatherly expressions. Dobie believed in creating a fighting spirit, and this could only come from hard work and perseverance from both players and coach. He inspired a love for hard work by his own example. At season's end, Wee Coyle said that even if the last game was won by a large score, there was no congratulatory speech from the coach. He would address the team with words to this effect: "You are a fine lot of football players. Why, you should have licked that gang a hundred to nothing. They'll get you next year for sure! How many of you dubs are going to be back next year?" Self-doubt would set in and the players would ask themselves if they could have played a better game. Maybe the team could do better, and it's possible Dobie was right after all. Not being content to link his coach to just one Civil War general, Coyle also compared Dobie's brand of football to General Sherman's famous quote, "War is hell."

Biddy Bishop, sports editor for the *Tacoma News Tribune* from 1906-16 tells of Dobie's earliest head coaching days at North Dakota State. The players wanted to test the coach to assert their manhood and were said to "rag" him. This was attributed to his youth and his tall, slender frame. Seeing that he had to take drastic steps to establish himself as boss, Dobie turned the tables and physically challenged the entire squad. "Now you fellows have got it into your head that I'm not a fighter. I'm going to show you that you have made one big mistake." He pulled off his coat and sweater and, from the middle of the football field, dared every player to fight him one-on-one. There were no takers. The point was made, and after that the players held him in the highest regard. Dobie's toughness and ability for psychological maneuvering came early in his career. This vignette from his earliest head coaching days in 1906 offers the perfect illustration of his attitude of command and control.

Players were kept on edge by Dobie in that they were never totally sure of their status, this being done to get them to practice their hardest right up to game day. Stars from the year before would quite often be relegated to practicing with the second team as a way of Dobie exercising his authority. This wasn't intended to demean, but was a tactic to assure that they didn't get too full of themselves. The coach had a mortal fear of inflated egos and felt that individual expression was the surest route to collective failure. He knew that self-importance could lead to a player branching out on his own, and such creative license would end in disaster. His plays were exacting, and the apparatus broke down if every part didn't operate with machinelike precision. To accomplish this end required obedience and subservience. All that remained to get the players to buy in was to prove the system on the field of battle.

When the numbering of players was first used on the West Coast in the Thanksgiving game at Washington against Oregon, played on November 25, 1909, Dobie resisted this innovation because of the fear that his players would showboat with their easily distinguishable identities. He also felt that when opposing teams scouted him, numbering would make it too easy to pinpoint just how his plays were run. Many coaches of the day selected all-star teams, and Dobie philosophically objected to this because of his concern for the damaging effects of star power. By 1911 he grudgingly made selections. He acceded because if didn't select a team, the other coaches would obviously bypass his players and Dobie would look like a bad sport in the end.

In sizing up his competition, Dobie would scout the opposition to identify its best players, which was particularly important if the captain was a standout. The Washington mentor would train his men to double- or triple-team him early in the game. He knew that average players depended on the star to carry the biggest load. As the star's spirit would break, the rest of the team would weaken. This was another side to Dobie's insistence that his players perform as a unit and give up any attitude of individual stardom. Too much reliance on one person meant that others on the team would possibly slack off. In Dobie's system, every responsibility, whether it was ball carrying, blocking, passing, pass reception, kicking, interference (blocking for the ball carrier), or tackling, was of equal weight. Each player's role was on par with that of any other player on the field. Knowing that opposing players who depended on a star would lose confidence when the star couldn't fully contribute gave Dobie's men a decided advantage. There was one player on Dobie's teams, however, who did have absolute authority. He was the play and signal caller, who was usually, but not always, the quarterback. The coach gave this man absolute authority, and even the captain was subordinate. This was all the more important because the coach was prohibited from signaling plays, and even a player coming in off the bench was not allowed to share any instructions he may have gotten while on the sidelines.

Dobie was a master of human psychology. Throughout his professional life he exhibited great skill in gaining the upper hand over an entire team or an individual player. This talent was evident in the very earliest days of his tour of duty and only improved as he matured in his coaching tactics. He knew how to get into a player's head or how to gain advantage over the group psyche of the entire team. More than any other aspect of the ample bag of tricks he used to gain control over those he set his sights on, his mastery of psychology was his greatest tool. This can be seen in his ability to get his own players to compete at their best and to psych out the opposition to compete at less than their best. Sportswriters, fans, his players, University of Washington presidents Thomas

Kane and Henry Suzzallo, and opposing coaches would consistently bring up Dobie's grasp of psychology and his skill in its deployment to win games. As we observe his game strategies in the pages to follow, this attribute will be abundantly evident. Victor Zednick, the graduate manager of student affairs for 1908-11 (essentially the title of athletic director today), worked closely with the coach for four years and, in addition to lauding what he termed his wonderful attention to detail, singled out his command of psychology as a secret to his success. "He takes nothing for granted. He works night and day and dreams of football. It is the power of mind over matter. A psychologist, too, Dobie knows how to handle men. His personality is powerful, irresistible. He has a mastery of every position. Wiry, keen, magnetic, he drives his men to victory."

An essential characteristic that defined his teaching skills as a coach was his commitment to detail. To call him a mere stickler for detail is to understate this critical aspect of what made him a great coach. Seven decades later this same quality was universally ascribed to Washington's Coach Don James as being a key to his remarkable leadership skills. Dobie triumphed far out of proportion to other teams in the league, and his painstaking nature was largely behind this success. Back then teams didn't conduct widespread multistate recruiting drives like today; they had to rely primarily on local talent. Victor Zednick said this in sizing up Dobie's insistence on covering all bases: "Every student can learn a lesson from his attention to the most minute detail and his consistent application. No matter how weak his opponents, he worries that he has overlooked something and when the teams meet, you can wager Dobie has forgotten nothing." This was well before full-ride scholarships were offered at West Coast universities to attract the best players. The league drew its athletes from the same pool of prospects, so the end result depended much more on each coach's ability to impart basic skills.

George Varnell was a sports reporter for the *Spokane Tribune* and a football referee who later became sports editor for the *Seattle Times*. As a friend of Dobie's, he enjoyed a close-up vantage point to assess the coach's methods. "He was a wonderful friend. However, in his coaching work he was a driver of the first water. He was a perfectionist in the truest since of the word. I saw him in practice when he worked virtually the entire afternoon on a single play. He believed in fundamentals, and he worked on them like a beaver building a dam. He brooked no talk from his players. He was the *word* and his players were the listeners and doers." This relentless insistence of breaking down each player's role to its basic steps defined how he taught principles. Dobie stressed that it was the little things that count, and he insisted that his men strive for perfection in seemingly minor details in order to be successful in the larger goal of teamwork. Repeat drills of running each player through his assignment *ad nauseam* assured that he could carry out his job under game conditions. The monotony of repeating the play for an entire afternoon also nailed down for each player how his teammates were to interact. Dobie's teams were described as "machines" for good reason. His insistence on perfection became a distinguishing characteristic every bit as much as the reported pessimism that commanded the headlines. Reporting on seemingly mindless and repetitious drilling was not nearly as catchy as a headline claiming "Gloomy Gil Predicts Team To Get Crushed."

Dobie did not believe in a wide arsenal of plays because his strategy depended on precise execution of every play. With perfection as the standard, a dazzling array of plays just would not work. Too many plays would lead to mistakes. Since the coach approached his job much as a dance choreographer who demands exacting footwork, the system required flawless performance but fewer steps to learn. The 1914 Thanksgiving Day game with Washington State was anticipated to be more competitive than in recent years, even though UW had dominated the series over the easterners the past four years, allowing them only six points to the westerners' eighty-five. Somehow Dobie in analyzing the circumstances of the contest predicted his team could not win this one, but nevertheless his boys managed to eke out a 45-0 victory. That evening Dobie and his fiancée, Eva Butler, were dining with George Varnell and his wife at the Butler Hotel (no relation to Eva) when John Bender, the Washington State coach, happened on their party. Varnell reported their discussion: " 'I can't understand that licking. Why Gil, we had a hundred and five plays to work on your team,' said Bender. 'Maybe that was your trouble,' Dobie responded. 'We had only nine plays; but coach, we sure knew them all well.' "

The Washington mentor was a rough talker, devoid of nuance, who never held back his feelings. He would resort to crude, insulting, and seemingly demeaning name calling to make a point or call out a player. When his tongue lashings are taken out of context or interpreted to represent his true beliefs, an objective observer would judge them as flat-out unacceptable. With his strong personality, those in earshot of one of his verbal assaults had to know that here was a person who meant business. When he used tough language, it was not to berate, but to deflate. After a big win, in getting his players ready for next Saturday, Dobie felt he had to let some air out of the swelled heads that inevitably built up after a crushing victory. There was no subtlety of expression when Dobie wanted to drive a point home. Purposeful overkill and sarcasm were tools of his trade, and this must be considered when we judge just what motivated his behavior. Over his career he didn't reserve his caustic remarks for just his players. He could be just as generous with derogatory observations of fans, faculty members, sportswriters, and game officials who ruled on a play other than how he saw it. The public outbursts almost got him fired when he first came to Washington, as we will see in chapter 2, so he did learn to rein in this behavior.

As will often happen with strong personalities a trait such as Dobie's penchant for coarse language can serve as a principal marker to define the individual. This is certainly fair, but it can result in overshadowing other less-dramatic but relevant aspects of personality. As a biographer, I seek to place such characteristics of his nature into a broader framework so that the reader can better reach his or her own understanding of the man. To do otherwise paints a more sterile picture of someone who is far deeper than the outward impression left only by words with no context. I sought the opinions of those who were there and either witnessed or were the recipients of the coach's flights into verbal overkill.

Dobie's own accounts of these episodes are also reported here to add more dimension to the question. One particularly enlightening incident is given with his answer to a question about what was the hardest situation he ever had to face as a football coach. His explanation involved how he handled replacing four-year, all-everything quarterback Wee Coyle upon his graduation with Bud Young, who was in many respects a better athlete, only to have him suffer a terrible knee injury landing him on the bench for the season. We will hear Dobie's description of how, in one week, he had to turn Charles "Chunky" Smith, who was described as short, stocky, and bowlegged, into his starting quarterback. All he did was to take a player who, in his prior two years, had not earned a letter and turn him into the starting quarterback for a game won by Washington, 100-0.

At the University of Minnesota, Gil Dobie graduated with a degree in law. Throughout his career he was described by those who knew him personally as well spoken, very intelligent, and a good conversationalist. As a head coach he practiced his profession for thirty-three years, had a lifetime winning percentage of .784, had fourteen undefeated college seasons, never lost a game in nine years at Washington, was elected by his peers as the third president of the American Football Coaches' Association, had teams who three times were voted national champions, is a member of the Hall of Fame at every college where he coached, and, among many other honors, was inducted as a charter member into the National Football Hall of Fame. The obvious question is, given his overbearing temperament, how is that he could succeed to the very highest level of accomplishment in his field? In a job where your every coaching move is covered as the headline story of four metropolitan newspapers' sports sections, with many articles being picked up by national news services, he clearly wasn't surviving on smoke and mirrors. In looking for answers to the contradictory nature of the man, there is one singular aspect of his makeup that stands out. The answer lies in his ability to command respect through sheer force of personality. We have pointed out that his greatest strength in dealing with people was his mastery of psychology. With this innate skill, he manipulated virtually everyone in his sphere of influence to alternately love him or hate him.

There are two primary examples of this. His practice techniques of working his men right up to the edge but knowing where to ease back made him a target at that moment for his players' wrath. Their great success resulting from these torture sessions made it all worthwhile and earned their lasting respect. Time after time, and long after their playing days had ended, his players returned to pay tribute to their mentor. When Dobie was invited back to Seattle in 1940 by a committee of his players to be feted at a banquet held in his honor at the Washington Athletic Club, Royal Brougham of the *Post-Intelligencer* gave an account of this. In his early days as a reporter, he knew of standout fullback Walt Shiel's succession of feelings for his coach. Dobie would later single him out after leaving Washington as the greatest fullback he ever coached. "There is something fine about the loyalty of football men for the Simon Legree who lashed and scolded and drove them until they dropped from exhaustion. 'I used to hate that guy Dobie until I could have killed him,' Walt Shiel used to tell me. Today, a quarter century later, the tall Scot is his idol."

His rough and biting language was another tool in his psychological arsenal. He told you how he felt and where you stood with him. His was not a condescending anger. It is wrong to describe his behavior as brooding contempt for those who did not act or think like him. This was vintage Gil Dobie. It's only from a position of strength that someone can hazard to publicly rebuke another and expect to maintain his respect. Dobie could accomplish this rare feat since he knew that the sting of his words would cause only short-term damage but long-term gain. Let's examine a few instances of his vocal combat:

Fred "Pete" Tegtmeier, Center—One of the greatest players to put on a uniform for Dobie. He was a four-year letterman; captain of the 1908 team, Flaherty Medal winner in 1909, and, for three years, a unanimous All-Northwest selection. In the very earliest days when the new coach had taken over the team, the players hadn't adjusted to Dobie's harsh methods, and the talented Tegtmeier was having particular trouble. In a textbook demonstration of reverse psychology, Dobie cut his center low with this shot: "Why, you great big yellow-haired bum, you've got a yellow streak up your back as yellow as your dirty yellow hair." One can only imagine the other players' reaction to hearing such a rebuke of a standout team member and, at 190 pounds, one of the largest players on the squad. Wee Coyle, a witness to the oral mugging, had this reaction: "Pete took it as every other player took it…You wonder why? It was because Dobie was a student of psychology and understood men. He would go right up to the breaking point and then leave you out on a limb." The treatment Dobie gave to this famously talented player falls into that category of psychological tools used by the coach to knock a star's ego down to manageable proportions.

Museum of History and Industry
William "Wee" Coyle, Quarterback 1908

Museum of History and Industry
Melville Mucklestone, Right Halfback 1908

Tegtmeier truly was a great athlete, and everyone knew it, including Dobie. While his methodology here is certainly perverse, and those on the receiving end of such an attack would initially take it as a personal insult, the approach did work for Dobie. He didn't use such crude language with the intent of driving the player away, but to let him know the coach was the boss and to solidify the star's commitment to hard work. Dobie knew all too well the dangers of such talents falling in love with their celebrity. Such intense methods can only work in the hands of a strong personality, and everyone who ever described Dobie was unanimous in this portrayal of the coach. In his hands, these well-aimed assaults worked.

Ralph "Penny" Westover, Fullback—He played only one year under Dobie on the 1908 team. He wasn't a highly gifted player but, through hard work, did earn his letter. In learning the fundamentals, he drew Dobie's wrath by getting confused on his role on basic plays. Dobie, not being one to praise in public and criticize in private, laid into the mild-mannered Westover: "Get out of here, you poor numbskull, go turn in your suit and never show yourself again." The dejected Penny left the field, and that night, after thinking it over, was still hot. "Oh, if I had only hit him; oh, if I had only hit him." For the next practice Penny was the first man on the field and was called out for the first drill, determined to prove himself. Dobie's instincts told him that pride would draw him back, which is exactly what happened. Penny doubled down and became a dependable journeyman on the team.

Melville "Muck" Mucklestone, Halfback—One of the all-time great athlete's names, and likewise one of Dobie's all-time great players: All-Northwest for 1908, '09, and '11, and captain of the 1909 team. In 1911, going into the third game of the season against Idaho, it appeared to all the world that Washington should make easy work of this weaker team. As circumstances unfolded, Mucklestone unwittingly played right into Dobie's hands, giving him just what he needed to deflate some pumped-up egos. The Purple and Gold hadn't been scored upon for six games going back to the prior year, and Mr. Gloom's dire predictions for defeat were being called into question. Prior to the game in Spokane, the coach had assembled the team at their hotel and, as he was going over pre-game strategy, a loud snore from Mucklestone interrupted Dobie's address. He couldn't have done worse had he set off a stink bomb. "I hope you get licked! You cowards! You! You! You! I'm through with you!" Those were the last words from Dobie before or during the game; he didn't even speak to the team at halftime. A drastic measure, to be sure, but an unmistakable point was made: the coach was in supreme command.

In winning by the narrow margin of 17-0, the team could plainly see that their leader did make a difference. Cunning staging by Dobie to drive home a point, or a reckless coach who lost control for the moment? The reader can draw his or her own conclusion. Opinions from those of the time who judged the coach's behavior are split. This brought an end to inattention at team meetings and proved to the superstars that they weren't quite as hot as they thought they were. Taking advantage of this opportunity to use Mucklestone as his public foil worked for Dobie, but regardless of the way the coach went about delivering his lessons to his young charges, the players held him in high regard. Going into the 1909 Oregon game for the championship, Mucklestone was quoted in the *Seattle Times* saying, "We feel we have the best coach in the country and intend to show him our appreciation by winning."

William "Wee" Coyle, Quarterback—This great athlete is in the Washington Hall of Fame in football, baseball—and track. He was captain on the 1911 team, served as an officer and was wounded in World War I, served as Washington state lieutenant governor for 1921-25, and lettered in all four years as quarterback in football, never losing a game. There was no mistaking his all-around athletic prowess, certainly not to someone with as keen an eye for talent as Coach Dobie. Given Dobie's constant struggle to impress the imperative of teamwork over individuality, a star of this magnitude posed a particularly difficult challenge. The record shows that Dobie was entirely consistent in his treatment of

Coyle. He did not place him on a pedestal; quite the contrary, despite Coyle's record of 27-0-1. Clark Squire, writing in the *Washingtonian*, declared, "Dobie says that Coyle gave him a fight every year, and it was necessary to tie him and whip him before he would do his work." Leaving no game details to chance, Dobie called Coyle to his house at 4738 Fourteenth Ave NE (today University Avenue) in Seattle for both pregame preparation the night before the game and a postgame critique the night after. Coyle described the sessions as totally one-sided, with Dobie doing all the talking. "I have been grilled by school teachers, by high-ranking army officers, by the general public, and even my wife, but nothing ever so intense as those endless...private conferences with Dobie." Dobie gave the complete schedule of plays to follow, and Coyle admitted that he always followed them to the letter. Paraphrasing Dobie's parting words as the evening came to a close, Coyle recalls that the coach "probably" said something like, "Coyle, you're a rotten quarterback, and if I didn't have so many cripples you'd be sitting on the bench. You've played your last two games like a man devoid of brains." Taken at face value, a player on the receiving end of such a harsh rebuke was obviously doing a lousy job. The record is abundantly clear that this was not the case.

Despite the seeming disrespect, Coyle didn't just go through the motions from these "pep talks"; to the contrary, he was impelled to greatness. If we seek an answer as to how this could be, the great quarterback resolves the quandary for us. He goes to great lengths to explain that Dobie cast a spell over the team through the severe treatment he inflicted on players from the first day of practice. He admits, "The terrorizing tactics of Gilmour Dobie will remain with me until my dying day." It was never possible to perform up to his standards. "We couldn't pass, we couldn't run, we couldn't kick, we couldn't tackle, we couldn't block—in fact, to use his own words, 'You are the dumbest, clumsiest, rankest collection of so-called football excuses I have ever seen.' " Coyle unabashedly concludes that after four weeks of practice, the entire team was eating out of Dobie's hand. In chapter 2 we look into the challenges and life experiences Dobie faced as a small child. From this we gain a thorough understanding of why and how he came to adopt the severe methods he used in teaching his men the game of football.

The players grew to trust the coach as they saw personal improvement in their own skills, with great strength and unity in the team as a whole. This growing bond, in Coyle's opinion, was consistent with so many other observers of the time. He resolved that it sprang from Dobie's brilliant command of human psychology. Over his lifetime Coyle shared many laudatory remarks he held regarding his former coach. Perhaps his highest tribute came in his ten-part series in the *Seattle Times*, "The Spell Of Gil Dobie": "I still have to meet one of his former players who would fail to say that he was glad to have played under Dobie, and at the same time was glad when he was through playing. He was held in the highest respect and admiration by the men over whom he held his mailed fist, because he was honest and fair. He was a natural leader of men."

Here is Dobie's take on his interaction with Penny Westover and Wee Coyle, as reported in the *Seattle Times* November 29, 1908. "Then, the grim humor lines deepening in his face, the Washington coach takes up a bit of gossip that all will appreciate. 'Yes, there was trouble with Westover and with Coyle at the beginning of the season. They did not fall kindly to the submissive spirit of team organization. It is a condition that comes to every coach in the history of football. It was a question as to who was to be boss. The two boys and I came to a perfect understanding in a short time and I do not believe I have any better friends than Coyle and Westover.' "

The attitudes expressed by Washington players were shared by Cornell men who played under Dobie in the 1920s. George Lechler, a Cornell player going back to see Dobie after graduating, gave this observation of players' reactions: "They go to see Dobie gratefully, as disciples return to a teacher who gave them helpful lessons in character building and in ability to understand their fellow men. They are unanimous in their praise of his fairness and sense of justice. And though their mentor has a caustic speech, there is no one whose favorable opinion they would rather have; therefore they play the game not alone for love of Alma Mater but for the gold of his approval, which is not carelessly bestowed."

George M. Varnell, Football Referee and Sports Reporter—"Varnell I never did trust you. You're a rotten referee. If you don't watch for a certain play today, I'll do something I might later regret." Wee Coyle was in the room and gave a firsthand account of this put-down as being just before the Oregon game of November 4, 1911, when Dobie was making sure that the referee was aware that he intended to call a trick play in the game. Since Dobie, in giving the referee of the game a heads-up on the play, was asking for his assistance, he obviously wouldn't insult the man. Varnell happened to be a close personal friend of Dobie's and a referee that he would often recommend to officiate his games. If Dobie's remarks are just taken at face value without knowing the circumstances within which they were made, even a charitable observer would conclude he was off his rocker.

There are many instances of latter-day reporting on Dobie's conduct that did just that: drew a conclusion that Dobie had a serious personality disorder because of such caustic language. There certainly are instances where he does go over the top, but to accurately assess his purposes and mind-set when going into such seeming rages, we must look deeper into what made him tick. Clearly here, it can be seen that Dobie must have been taking dramatic license with his feigned insults directed at his good friend George Varnell. Dobie's choice of words and tone of delivery were calculated for maximum effect and were not the ravings of a man in despair. This is further underscored by the fact that Dobie would want this ally to judge him fairly in calling the game. Dobie was too smart and knew too much about human psychology to talk down to the very official who held his championship hopes in the balance.

We've found that he was vastly successful at his chosen occupation, was intelligent, well-spoken, driven, detail minded, a perfectionist, strong willed, held a gifted mastery of human psychology, and feared individualism as destructive to teamwork. Given his many talents, there is one additional trait that also stands out: the predictability of his behavior. He held such rigid standards that he brought a set of beliefs to his work and stuck to them. To some degree he could just about always be counted on to play down his team's chances of winning their next game. He likewise spoke his mind and, judged by any standard of normal human interaction, was much too strict. He was extremely sparing of compliments to players for doing a good job. His attention to detail and insistence on perfection could be viewed as obsessive. Now, given all of these very predictable behaviors, he still excelled far above his competitors. In his thirty-three-year career, he won more than 78 percent of his games, placing him at the highest echelon among the winningest college coaches of history. It can only be concluded that he succeeded because of his behavior, even though much of his conduct certainly can be called into question.

I found through volumes of documents drawn from firsthand Dobie observers that his greatest motivating force for dealing with players was his fear of success going straight to their heads. His view that winning demanded teamwork was wired into his DNA. Great accomplishment through superior athleticism was an ideal, and he always encouraged his athletes to do their best, but he felt that he needed to tamp down bloated egos. Winning could only come by his constant efforts to assure that his players had no room to improvise. The one prerequisite for success was teamwork. In guarding against a player wandering off the ranch, he kept praise to a minimum, and since he carefully courted each player's trust, could aim overly critical language in his direction at just the right time. In the earliest experiences of this rough treatment, the player would feel that Dobie was directing the assault at him personally, but he soon learned that this was Dobie's style in critiquing his performance, not criticizing his character. This magnified response to the mistake served its purpose, since this was what the players grew to expect from the coach. There was no room left for the player to pat himself on the back since he quickly learned that playing time came by keeping in Dobie's good graces.

Dobie himself traced his deep-seated fear of overconfidence to the days he started as quarterback at Minnesota. Emil Hurja, in asking him for the key to his success, stated, "Instantly he will reply. 'Pound out overconfidence from your men and you'll win most any time.' " Dobie went on to give this account of a very early coaching lesson he had learned thirteen years before. "Our greatest rival was Wisconsin. We skinned 'em one year with comparative ease, and the next season we thought we'd have a snap. We trained and we practiced, more from routine than otherwise. When we met the Badgers we were surprised.

Somehow they seemed to have the jump on us all around. We couldn't see how it was possible, but it was. We were licked. I learned my lesson right there." Soon after this bitter experience Dobie launched his collegiate coaching career.

There is a reason this made such an impact on this impressionable twenty-two-year-old. In 1900, with Dobie quarterbacking Minnesota, their record was 10-0-1, including a win over archrival Wisconsin. Next year Minnesota's record was 9-1-1, with the sole blemish being the Wisconsin loss. During his three playing years, he started at end in 1899 and quarterbacked the team in 1900 and 1901. He was an excellent player and had a reputation as being fiercely competitive. In chapter 7 we will delve into Dobie's deep-seated anguish over just his *fear* of losing. From this it can be seen that an *actual* loss, such as the 18-0 shutout at the hands of Wisconsin, was pure torment. It is little wonder that he singles out this loss as the root cause for his great fear of overconfidence. The lesson Dobie learned back on November 16, 1901, formed the foundation for what guided him for as long as he mentored men in the game of football.

The question still remains as to how Gil Dobie came by his most identifiable characteristic as being a gloomy pessimist. We earlier asked this question and concluded that it could only be answered by taking a broader look at the other driving forces that define his nature. Dobie's ever-so-constant predictions of impending doom coming at the hands of his next opponent is also a product of the coach's obsessive belief in team solidarity over self-expression. By predicting that his team would lose, he was (in his mind) just being consistent that you can't risk complacency by signaling to your players that they are going to win. Predict doom, and even if the odds are enormously in the team's favor, the coach has gone public that his machine can possibly lose. Each player, being one piece in the overall process, might be that one weak link that could cause the system to fail. As the Purple and Gold climbed to twenty, thirty, forty, fifty and sixty-plus games without a loss and won so consistently over a span of years, Dobie's pessimism obviously wore thin. He was nothing if not a creature of habit, so he stuck with it. With as much press as his pessimism attracted, many are shocked to discover that upon closer analysis—Dobie often did not go dark. This reveals a pattern of predictable behavior that exposes the real purpose behind his foretelling disaster ahead, a toss-up game, or oftentimes victory. It's a core principle; his predictions weren't so much based on what the rest of the world was saying but what he needed to get on the street to suit his purposes. To do otherwise would expose his team to that most dreaded of all diseases to afflict a football team, a fat ego.

Hurja, being such a close observer of Dobie, included his penchant for gloomy predictions as one more way he influenced his players to do their best. "Every fall, when the football season approaches, one will hear and read on every hand reports of Dobie's team. The men are out of condition, mere dubs, unfit to battle with the other conference elevens, sure to lose, with no possible chance of winning. He has been styled 'Gloomy Gil' by the sport writers of the

Northwest. They acknowledge that Dobie has no equal as a dispenser of hard-luck tales. When critics think his machine is working at its best he will point out the poor, unstable condition of the team; he will parcel out news of overtraining, undertraining or disorganization. And when the referee blows the final whistle and the score board shows unmistakable victory, he will start to tell about the injuries his men suffered in the game, preparing, as it were, for the next contest. Throughout the season his men are ever on edge, fighting to show him that they are in the running, and that his pessimism is unwarranted.

"Dobie, idol coach of Washington, has solved the puzzle of football science. He has seen what needed to be done, and he has done it, consistently, for nine years. He has made pessimism pay." But this is only one side of the man. It takes his entire nine-year career at Washington to fully understand just how pessimism fit into the overall makeup of the man. It is not correct to strictly label him as "Gloomy Gil," the "Apostle of Grief," the "Sad Scot," or any one of several appellations that headline writers so readily branded him with. He was far deeper than such a superficial tag could describe. A writer needs a headline, and the sports pages love to theme their heroes or anti-heroes, but in the full account of his life given here, you will discover that he did not always predict disaster ahead. Of course not. The fascinating back story, however, is just how much it reveals about Dobie's real intent behind his message when he does not broadcast a gloomy prediction. The complete man cannot be conveniently bundled into a couple of catchy words.

Away from his self-imposed obsessiveness in game preparation, daily practice, and on-field behavior, he was another man entirely. It was natural for a Scot to take up golf, which he did while at Washington. When on the golf course or gathering with friends over a cigar and a beer, he was described as convivial, relaxed, and a good conversationalist with broad-ranging opinions. In these pages we have the opportunity to observe the great coach on and off the field. His widely reported gloomy nature can be seen as an affectation that springs to life when he puts on his overcoat and derby, lights his cigar, and goes to work. When a reporter wants to know his take on that week's game, he can be riddled with doubt, but as we will see—not always. The doubt is real and not a put-on but springs from a deep well within his complex nature that requires him to place every ounce of his wit and intelligence into winning. To Dobie, losing, after all his intensity of preparation, is the most feared aspect in life. He seeks perfection, and by this standard there is no room for a loss. Take the man away from the game and we see a husband, father, and mentor who won the near unanimous respect of the hundreds of players who grew as men under his leadership.

# CHAPTER TWO

## *Off to a Shaky Start—1908*

"The prospects are not bright. They are fairly good but nothing more. There has been, in the past years, too much of such talk here, too much four-flushing and bragging, too little work. Last year Oregon beat Washington. So did Whitman and Pullman. Idaho tied Washington, and little Whitworth played her a 5 to 0 game. What possible right have we to talk of a championship team? Take these five teams. If they were exactly evenly matched, by the cold figures of arithmetic, we could only expect to win one out of the five games. We must work, I tell you. But do not get the idea I am a pessimist."

*Gilmour Dobie, address to team, September 15, 1908*

Robert Gilmour Dobie was born January 31, 1878, on the outskirts of Minneapolis/St. Paul on Ashland Street, Hastings, Minnesota, the son of Robert Dobie, a well digger and later machinist, and homemaker Ellen (Black) Dobie, both natives of Scotland. He had two older sisters, Ellen (b1874), and Jane (b1876), and a younger brother George (b1880). Dobie's mother died in 1882 of consumption and the next year his father married Jane Ford, another Scottish immigrant. Two half-brothers were added to the family with the birth of Alexander in 1884 and Robert in 1886. Family tragedy struck again when they lost their father in 1886 leaving Jane with 5 children. She was also pregnant at the time, with Robert. The father died of what was suspected to be an overdose of laudanum, a widely available patent medicine at the time that combined alcohol and opium. Some accounts list the cause of death as suicide and others as an accidental overdose.

It was a difficult struggle for a thirty-five year old woman to be suddenly thrust into the role of breadwinner for this large family. She decided that it would be best for Gilmour, age 8, and George, age 6, to be sent to the Minnesota State Public School for Dependent and Neglected Children as wards of the state. This orphanage in Owatonna, sixty miles south of Hastings, had just opened and her two step-sons were among the first ten children admitted. Coming from the hardscrabble life they now led, both boys surveyed the newly-built orphanage and deemed it a considerable upgrade over their current miseries. This would soon change when they came to grasp the reality of institutional living and its strict controls over every aspect of their life. To add to the shock of adjustment, most communications with the outside world were cut off, even letters from the family.

Over his many years as a "state schooler" Dobie's life was intermittently under the stern control of a matron who, of necessity, given the hardened backgrounds of many of her wards, had to rule with an iron hand. The state public school was a self-sufficient working farm with the goal of teaching their young charges the value of hard work, obedience and scholarship. Classes were in session 11-months of the year. Demanding activity and rigid discipline were high on the school's list of objectives. At this most impressionable time in his life, Dobie had a perfect model to teach him the elements of leadership by authoritarian rule. It is little wonder that Dobie would adopt such traits himself when he set out to mold a young band of recruits into the disciplined brand of football he insisted on.

During the nine year period from December 1886 to September 1895, that Dobie was under the auspices of the school, there were four contracts made with outside families to take him into these households for indentured labor. The agreement essentially required work from the child for room and board, but the education requirement was reduced to only four months per year. It was just six months later, in June 1887 that Dobie was sent out to his first home. The aim of indentured contracts was for the guardians to keep the child until he or she reached the age of 21. However, young Dobie and this first family's six year old son didn't get along, and since the contract allowed a 60-day right to cancel without penalty, he was sent back to the orphanage after only one month.

Dobie spent the next year at the orphanage and in August of 1888 he was again indentured out, this time to a childless couple. After one year the guardian couple saw that the arrangement wasn't working and negotiated an early cancellation of the contract. The young orphan, barely ten years old met rejection wherever he went. He already had endured more hardships than most people encounter in a lifetime, but even more trying times were ahead.

In August of 1889 Dobie was indentured to yet a third farming couple, this time a husband and wife whose children had left home. The state school agent's report for the first two years offered no hint of trouble in the home. If this was correct, matters suddenly turned for the worse in the spring of 1892. Dobie ran away from his contracted home and in May showed up with his sisters in Hastings who were now living with Mrs. Anna Bollis. The desperate orphan revealed that he had been beaten, worked dreadfully long hours, was deprived of proper schooling and only had one suit of clothes and nothing adequate for the harsh Minnesota winters. On hearing of this treatment Bollis immediately sent a letter to the state school agent pleading to take Dobie into her home "as he has already found a warm place in my heart." Also, no less than Probate Judge Michael H. Sullivan, who originally heard the case and approved the court order committing Dobie to the state school, wrote a letter to the school superintendant complaining that the child must be removed from his indentured home or "it will result in the moral ruin of the boy."

Anna Bollis was the sister of William Reed, a wealthy and prominent local merchant, who himself immediately began a letter writing campaign to the school advocating for Dobie's release from his present situation. He concluded, if this was not done "the place he is now in will make a criminal of him." Lest she be accused of harboring a runaway ward of the state, Bollis sent young Gilmour back to the host family. But wasting no time and exhibiting considerable spunk (especially for a woman in the 1890s) she wrote a scathing letter of indictment against Dobie's guardian to Minnesota Governor William Merriam. The governor immediately interceded by issuing a request that the superintendent investigate and report his "final conclusions as to the matter." It was only a few days following this ever-so-polite nudging by the governor that Dobie was back in safekeeping at the orphanage.

It must be noted that the host family mounted a rebuttal to the charges lodged against them. They conducted a letter writing blizzard of their own making the case that they loved the boy like a son and yes, "I corrected him again yesterday [May 22, 1892] for a trifling matter that perhaps has caused him to go away." The campaign put on by them in their defense was a well orchestrated attempt to make their case but the letters all seemed to have been too coordinated to make a convincing argument that the young boy would be better off returning to their farm. The state agent's report didn't help their position as it was now at odds with those of two and three years earlier. "Gilmour has not the same spirit. He is saucy, restless and discontented. Says he will not stay."

It took the balance of the year for the legal process of gathering a quorum of the state school board to cast their vote on the matter and to complete the indenture agreement with William Reed. The agreement was effective January 18, 1893. The massive campaign to rescue young Dobie, reaching as high as the governor's office, most assuredly turned his life around. The years of hardship and rejection were now behind him. Dobie's life as a pauper was now transformed to one of princely comforts. He enjoyed the motherly love of Anna Bollis, the security of privilege provided by the wealth of his benefactor, William Reed, a return to family and most significantly to be in close proximity to his older sister Ellen. Her positive influence, due to her love, intelligence and the example she set for her younger brother cannot be overstated. She was now teaching in the local school and had the reputation of a young woman of amazing talent. This would be proven out, first as she graduated Phi Beta Kappa from the University of Minnesota and throughout her long life of accomplishment.

The young Dobie's record with previous guardians showed that often the labor expected of him meant that his school year was shortened even below the required four months set out in the contract. The state school was to be paid $75.00 per year for this labor. Reed's priority was education so he placed the school on notice that this arrangement was a "very bad policy" since it deprived the child school time. It took a man of stature such as Reed to buck a system such as this. Of course, the school superintendent would be ever mindful that the governor had interceded on this orphan's behalf, so contractual modifications, were the least of his concerns.

The state agent's report now said the guardian's treatment was "as that of an own son," the home was considered "excellent," and his clothing now was "very nice." When Dobie first arrived in his new home his interest in schoolwork was lackluster, at best. This was soon to change according to Reed in reporting to the superintendent "while not as remarkably bright as Nellie [Ellen] he is as good as the average." Dobie showed that he was making up for lost time in a later report from Reed: "Dobie went to the head of his class scoring 100 in arithmetic and in his other studies has become interested and doing well."

In the last state agent's report issued on August 29, 1895 Dobie was in such good care that the agent recommended that he be released from the contract of indenture and be declared self supporting. This was agreed to by the school and made effective on September 9, 1895, when Dobie was seventeen.

It was on the banks of the Mississippi in the small town of Hastings when Dobie had returned home that his football career began as a 150-pound end and halfback on the local high school team. His younger brother George was also on the team and in the spring Dobie played catcher on the baseball team. With his orphanage background and having reached age twenty in high school, he was a target for teasing but rose above this and proved to be a highly talented athlete. He soon developed friendships and blended into life outside his regimented past. The very first game in 1898 of his senior year, the team lost 35-0 to St. Paul Central High but they quickly turned the tables on the competition and swamped the remaining five teams on their schedule by a combined score of 221-0.

In 1899 he joined his sister Ellen at the University of Minnesota and graduated with a Bachelor of Laws degree in 1904. He played end on the varsity in 1899 and quarterback in 1900 and 1901 on teams coached by Dr. Henry L. Williams. Financial difficulties prevented him from turning out for the team in his senior year. In 1900, as quarterback, he led the team to its first Western Conference (later to become the Big 10) championship. He was selected on the 1900 All-Western team at quarterback and received honorable mention on the Walter Camp Foundation (WCF) All-American squad. *Outland* magazine described him as being a quick and accurate passer and a swift runner. His greatest strengths were described as catching and running back punts, and he was deemed to have no equal in the West, if not the whole country. He was regarded as "second to none" in kicking punts. He also distinguished himself in baseball.

He began his coaching career as an assistant at Minnesota for 1903-04-05, and while there he was also the head coach of the Minneapolis South High School team. He led them to two undefeated seasons. In 1903 his high school team won the state championship, winning all six games and outscoring their opponents 320-5. For many years, football authorities considered this to be Dobie's greatest coaching accomplishment. South High enjoyed a good reputation in football, but internal squabbling and troubles with their head coach led to them withdrawing from the league. Being ridiculed by the other teams in the conference, they later reversed this decision, but by that time there were nine veterans who had quit the team and never returned. Dobie pulled a rag-tag team of second stringers and assorted lightweights together. To everyone's astonishment, this band of no-names won their first game, then somehow pulled off a second win and kept on winning all season. They came back the next year and again went undefeated.

Collection of Dobie's granddaughter, Eva Zayha, Thomas Swem photo
Gilmour Dobie, circa 1906

His first college head coaching job was at North Dakota Agricultural College (today North Dakota State), where he went undefeated in his eight games for the 1906-07 seasons. He also coached the basketball team for two years with a record of seventeen wins and four losses. Dobie benefited greatly being a novice football coach in these formative years as the sport transitioned from its primitive rugby like roots into the modern game. He grew as a coach by being a dedicated student of the fundamentals as football invented itself. He knew that he had to learn the details of the game to be successful. Detail study came naturally to this student of the law.

Clearly the young coach offered great promise, and, as an undeniable winner, he caught Washington's eye, taking over its program for the 1908 season. It was this year that Washington, Washington Agricultural College (today Washington State University), Oregon, Oregon Agricultural College (today Oregon State University), Idaho, and Whitman (the Big 6) established the area's first formal league, the Pacific Northwest Intercollegiate Conference. College athletic programs in this turn-of-the-century era were managed by a Student Board of Control that answered to a Faculty Athletic Committee. Common practice was to assign a graduate of the university as a graduate manager who was in charge of the business of managing the athletic programs. Loren Grinstead as graduate manager in 1907 was one of the key people at Washington responsible for hiring Dobie. The position of graduate manager was held by Victor "Vic" Zednick for 1908-11. In 1910 he assumed the role of president of the Northwest Conference.

Grinstead arranged for a gathering of some of the incoming freshmen to meet their new coach. The men knew nothing of Dobie or his coaching style. The coach was quick to launch his campaign to manipulate their impressionable natures as only he could do. Freshman Wee Coyle, straight from his summer job as a longshoreman in Nome, Alaska, soon to become his starting quarterback, had a vivid recollection of the meeting. "No smile, no handshake, no slap on the back, no 'How are you?' 'How do you feel?' No 'Glad to see you at Washington'—nothing but a pair of black eyes peering coldly out of a dark face that was hidden partially by a slouch hat drawn loosely over a head of mussed black hair. Nobody said a word after the brief introduction, which didn't seem to interest him in the least. He began to unfold himself from his lounging position. He seemed to mount into sections until his six feet or more of black overcoat had assumed an upright position. Those eyes still were working on us." The meeting was described as seemingly endless, but in actuality the freshmen made their getaway in two or three minutes. Dobie had no great speech; the get-to-know-you session was all theatrics. The most important bit of information the coach wanted to impart was, "Remember, all you fellows, practice starts Monday at 2 p.m. One thing I demand is promptness." As a coach, Dobie hit the ground running in that the first practice was a full-on workout. No period to stretch out the kinks from summer jobs or a gradual buildup to heavier exercises. Coyle was impressed, though, and knew that the team was in good hands. "Just one day on the practice field convinced us that the tall angular genius was the boss. He quickly brought us to our senses, and we became as docile as babes in arms."

Dobie's coaching style of exercising total control over his players was quickly established. This was at first met with natural resistance until those he brought into his circle of influence learned to understand his strong personality. He was demanding to the point of intolerability, but when his methods brought positive results, he made converts. Graduate Manager Victor Zednick tells of having the same type of superior/subordinate relationship with Dobie as did the players in relating a story reported by Wee Coyle in a *Seattle Times* article forty-one years later.

He said the players only had Dobie on their necks in the afternoon at practice, but Zednick had him morning, noon, and night. It seemed he couldn't do anything right. He recalled that during his four years as graduate manager, "Dobie said whom we played, where we would play and when we would play." In actuality the coach was entirely consistent in his relationship with just about everyone: players, management, sports reporters, and, to a lesser extent, faculty.

As an example of Dobie's uber-controlling manner of dealing with people, Zednick related his practice of hiring young boys before games to clear the field of loose rocks that continually worked up to the surface of Denny Field. "If one small rock was found on the field after the cleanup, Dobie would come at me like a wild man, intimating that I deliberately put it there," Zednick recalled. This is a vignette that has been widely reported over the years by those bent on exposing the "real Gil Dobie." Interestingly in these tellings, the story ends here, leaving the reader to conclude that Dobie's only way of dealing with those around him was to go into unrestrained fits of temper. However Zednick goes on to sum up his overall opinion of the man with whom he worked so closely over many years. "Despite all the heartaches Dobie gave me, he was one of the finest men I ever had the pleasure of knowing. He was a builder of men and one of the few real coaches the game of football has had."

University of Washington Libraries, Special Collections,  Neg. No. A. Curtis 13444          1908 Team
Top Row: (L to R) Joe Cutting (Ass't Manager), William Rasmussen (Athletic Manager), Bill Mattson,  George Swarva, Walter Wand, Paul Kaylor, Warren Grimm, Louis Diether, Coach Gilmour Dobie, Keisling Thayer

Middle Row: Arthur Clark, Maxwell Eakins, Frank Babcock, Captain Fred Tegtmeier, Paul Jarvis, Burwell Bantz, Hart Willis

Bottom Row: Guy Flaherty, Broussais Beck, Melville Mucklestone, Ralph Westover, William Coyle, Leonard Taylor, Ernest Wells.

## Preseason

Teams in these early days of college football selected who to play in the preseason, as is done in modern times. Then as now, softer preseason games for major football schools were chosen to pad the win/loss record of the stronger program. Staying at home and playing a weaker opponent was widely accepted. The stronger school got to put its team through a real game situation without too much risk of loss or concern for injury. The weaker school got the financial rewards that go along with playing a more prestigious team that draws a big gate—even though defeat on the field was the most likely outcome. Long-distance travel offered major challenges, and with fewer colleges playing football, teams of this era often scheduled preseason contests with club/semi-pro teams, military teams, high schools, and all-star teams.

Dobie's inaugural preseason games at Washington were anything but impressive. The team looked like a continuation of earlier years, displaying a very ragged brand of football. Despite the lanky Scot's promise, his teams definitely did not show any signs that he was about to launch a nine-year stand of invincibility. Based on the weak performances in playing warm-up games against Lincoln High and Washington High, even competing for the league championship in this first year looked out of the question. The team showed none of the synchronized efficiency of the Dobie machine that was to follow. As for flawless execution, it didn't seem this team would ever reach this Dobie standard.

The Purple and Gold front line barely held their own, a very real concern given the competition. The backfield did somewhat better but didn't show consistent strength. The one aspect of the Varsity's performance that did attract attention was the successful passing game. (Since the Husky team mascot was not adopted until after Dobie left Washington, many writers of his day chose to refer to the team as the "Varsity." This convention is used throughout in *Pursuit of Perfection*). The forward pass was looked down on by many as not "real" football. It had only been formally approved by the Intercollegiate Athletic Association (forerunner to the NCAA) in 1906. Considered cheap yardage in this game of high contact, it took time for it to become widely accepted. Much of the reportage of Gil Dobie has been written of his supposed scorn for the forward pass. In actuality, the facts are just the opposite. He favored the off-tackle line buck, but, being a student of strategic football, he most definitely did not proscribe use of the forward pass. In this very first game, the *Post-Intelligencer* observed, "the football season was notable for the best exposition of the forward pass ever seen in this city." George Varnell witnessed Dobie's use of the pass in many games and knew how he instructed his backs. "Never pass when inside your 30. Never pass inside your own half of the field unless two touchdowns to the good. Seldom pass between the center of the field and the opponents' 35. Use the pass when threatening the opponent's line, but use it with care." By 1912 Dobie would abandon these principles as rules changes allowed for broader opportunities of using the pass.

The forward pass, being such a major innovation, was cautiously introduced with restrictions. Considering that the football itself was more round than oblique, the rule makers could not possibly have foreseen the exciting future ahead for football that would follow their controversial decision to allow heaving the ball downfield instead of players head butting their way to the goal. This groundbreaking rule still came with strings attached, serving to reduce its effectiveness. A straight downfield pass was not allowed. The ball had to be passed at a diagonal to the line of scrimmage that had to be at least 5 yards on either side of the center.

In a very early interview of Dobie's in the first months of his arrival in Seattle, he stressed that the perception among potential recruits in the league was that Washington "didn't count in football." Coming into his job, he felt it was his responsibility to silence all such talk. He issued a challenge "that the huskies come out, and if they do not, that the rest of you get them out." It's doubtful that he foretold the team's mascot becoming *Huskies* fully fourteen years before the choice was official, but the important point is that he challenged the student body to get fully behind the team. He spoke of developing a fighting spirit, as he correctly saw that lacking on campus. The team's preseason performance wasn't a clarion call of inspiration, but, however low-key the start, Dobie was laying the groundwork for the great days ahead. There was reason to believe that the new coach could reverse UW's fortunes, but no one could have imagined the spectacular journey about to unfold.

Despite inexcusable fumbles, poor blocking up front, spotty defense, inconsistent ball carrying, and inspired play by weaker opponents, the Varsity did post lackluster wins of 22-0 over Lincoln and 23-5 over Washington. In the first game against Lincoln, Dobie wasted no time in giving the team a dose of his coaching technique with what was described as a "scorching talk" at halftime as he made wholesale substitutions. Wee Coyle described a similar verbal blast from the coach at game's end. "Dobie packed us into one corner of the gym and started giving us the works. You would have thought that the worst crime in the world had been committed and that all was lost. He told us we were the worst bunch of fumblers he had ever seen; we all needed baskets; we should all go to an old women's home; we were a hopeless bunch of misfits, and if we won any games at all it would be just luck." Coyle attributed the coach's ability to fixate on errors, such as fumbling, and his way of drilling this into the players' heads as the reason they were noted for so few miscues in handling the ball.

Dobie never revealed to any public source that he had been orphaned at eight years of age and certainly did not divulge that his childhood included working as an indentured laborer. For his own reasons throughout his life, he maintained this veil of secrecy. Had the players he mentored and the many writers of his time who analyzed his every move known of his stern upbringing, they would have better understood behavior such as the scorching talk that stood out in Coyle's mind. Dobie spent his formative years being subjected to the strictest of authoritarian rule. By his experience this was how the world worked. His brand of leadership came naturally since he didn't learn top down command and control from a military textbook—he lived it.

### Whitworth College

The stage was now set for higher-level competition, with a nonleague game scheduled on Denny Field for October 17, 1908. The opponent was Whitworth College, located in Tacoma. As game day drew closer, the outlook didn't look any too good for the Purple and Gold. Let's take a closer look at the serious trouble the Varsity faced leading up to this historic game. As late as the week before, matters looked grim. Burwell "Admiral" Bantz, Paul Jarvis, and Frank

"Bull Moose" Babcock, who were strong interior linemen from the year before, had not committed to the team because of their concerns that football would interfere with their heavy academic loads. Left guard Guy Flaherty, who had played every minute of every game the previous two years, was suffering from a serious case of boils but did see his first action in this game. This would be the only game he was able to compete in until the final game against Oregon State.

The late commitment of the trio of Bantz, Jarvis, and Babcock caused a citywide recruiting campaign to see if they could be sweet-talked into coming out. All three were outstanding and experienced athletes in football and track who were essential to that year's success. They were also honor students in the classroom and had planned to focus on their studies for their senior year. Dobie growled and fumed over their reluctance and put out the word that he flatly had to have these stars on the team. Soon the honor societies, fraternities, Men's Club, the *UW Pacific Daily Wave*, and the downtown sportswriters all began a concerted effort to win them over. There was even reported mention that the faculty weighed in as favoring their return. The crusade finally worked, with all three reporting, but too late to be in shape for the first league game just a couple of weeks away. Their decision altered the course of Washington football, for if they had not come out, Dobie would not have gone undefeated in his inaugural year.

Left end Warren "Wedge" Grimm, right tackle Maxwell Eakins, right halfback Melville Mucklestone, quarterback Wee Coyle, left halfback Leonard "Scrappy" Taylor, and fullback Penny Westover were first-year Washington players who were highly touted recruits but had to adjust to Dobie's methodical tactics and learn to mesh as a unit. The high school transcript for Eakins hadn't been received, making him ineligible for league competition. As the last nonleague game he could play, this rendered him questionable for next week's league opener. Westover was limping and had to use a cane because of a bad knee, and fullback Hart Willis was not practicing that week because of a serious charley horse. And, to add insult to (pun intended) injury, star center and Captain Pete Tegtmeier was questionable with a sprained knee!

Two hundred fans came out for an open practice. Consensus held that unless the line was somehow strengthened, the team would stand absolutely no chance of winning even half their games. The passing game was not working at all, even being played against the second team. Pulling no punches in its description of the Varsity's tackling, the *Daily Wave* described it as "rotten." In the scrimmage, the second team drew first blood with a touchdown, and it wasn't until the second half that the Varsity was able to score. With all of their injuries and organizational problems, the offense wasn't clicking, and unfortunately this also held for the defense. As for talent, the dopesters placed that year's team as one of the best ever at Washington, but their showing in practice and their preseason record didn't bear this out. Word on the street was that Dobie was failing and his team was out of shape.

Teams of the day were composed of the eleven-man varsity, who played offense, defense, special teams, usually four to six substitutes, and ten to fifteen "scrubs," who practiced with the team. Scrubs, a wholly unacceptable description today for a hard-working athlete, was common practice back then. At year's end Coach Dobie paid homage to these second-team players, who were under the direct guidance of Assistant Coach Joe Cutting. Joe Cutting played for Dobie at North Dakota State and followed him to Washington. In singing the praises of the second team, he stated, "It was through these exponents of true sport that Washington had a winning team in 1908, through men who, for the true love of the sport and from purely patriotic motives, loaned their valuable services that their college might be represented by a team which could uphold the honor and dignity entrusted to them when put to the test." In putting them to the test, with the injuries and other problems he had, it must have been the Whitworth game that Dobie had in mind.

"Too little speed, too much fumbling, and a weak line" was the assessment of the team quoted in the *Daily Wave*. In practice, play after play was spoiled by fumbling because the men handling the ball were consistently out of place. Men who the team counted on for strong performances were still not in condition. Pessimistic reports were being put out before the game with the obvious intention of misleading the competition as to just how strong Reuber's team really was. Yes, Coach Arthur Reuber of Whitworth didn't think much of his team's chances. But hold it, haven't we always heard that pessimism and downplaying his team back then was the exclusive province of our very own Gloomy Gil? What is this, can anyone other than their own coach really predict disaster when facing Washington?

Now that we have over one hundred years of history to look back on and analyze this brilliantly complex man, a clearer picture comes into focus. Was he really a negative thinker? Personal opinions of those close to him respond emphatically, no. Did he make frequent negative assessments of his team's abilities in stacking up against the competition? Frequently yes, but not at every opportunity as sports writers delighted in claiming. His colorful personality, winning ways, and penchant for off-the-cuff remarks brought him widespread fame with reporters throughout the country. Sportswriters jumped at the chance to put out copy on Dobieisms, the print equivalent of today's sound bites in that era devoid of electronic media; great to catch attention, but scarcely relevant in getting to the real story. Since he lost his mother at age four, his father at eight and spent six years as a ward of the state subject to bouts of indentured servitude, this also must be considered for its profound impact on his behavior.

The Purple and Gold was forty-five minutes into the game on Denny Field and neither team had any points on the board. With all of the conditioning and eligibility problems the Varsity was having, desperate measures were called for. At this point Coach Dobie pulled a risky move, sending Bantz, Jarvis, and Babcock into the game. These men were lacking in preparation but were tagged by Dobie to become the future beef and strength of the line. As noted, Dobie is often declared to be an exclusively power, off-tackle strategist who abhorred the forward pass. Here myth is confused with fact. The *Seattle Times* was quite impressed with the aerial game: "Mucklestone's reception of the forward pass at times was little short of remarkable." The play that got the game off dead center was a pass from freshman Coyle to Mucklestone (of the reported sprained knee), placing the ball on the 2-yard line. Hart Willis, who had been out of practice all week with his charley horse, carried the ball over for the first touchdown. Whitworth couldn't score on its possession and gave up the ball to Washington.

Maxwell Eakins proved he was a star in the making if his school transcript problems could be straightened out. For this game the *Times* reported his punting "was the best seen here in years." On the Varsity's next possession, Coyle punted over the head of receiver Colbert, who picked up the ball at the goal line and was tackled beyond the line by UW's Bill Matson for a 2-point safety. At this time the field was 110 yards long with no end zone, and the goal posts were hazardously mounted on the goal line. Touchdowns counted five points in 1908, with one point scored for the point after. Washington's total scoring was made up of three touchdowns with an extra point added for each, one safety and one field goal. The Varsity's other three TDs came by a Coyle pass to fullback Hart Willis that went for 20 yards, a Coyle-to-Mucklestone pass from the 5-yard line, and left end Warren Grimm running in a fumbled punt. The deciding factor of the game was players who, only days before, were either unknown quantities, uncommitted, out of condition, or injured. In the end, they all delivered. For the remainder of the game, Washington was well in control on both sides of the ball. The visitors' only score came on a dropkick by left end Tanner late in the game from the 30-yard line. Under rules of the day, this kick scored four points. Final score, Washington over Whitworth, 24-4.

### Whitman College

This marked the season's first conference game. The promise of the great first-year men assembled for that year's team and any indicator that the high expectations for Dobie would bear out were nowhere in sight. Judging by the sorry performance against Whitworth, it looked by all reasonable standards that neither the team nor the coach was destined for greatness. It was characteristic of Dobie's teams to come out vulnerable in the early going, but when his system had time to get the players into rhythm, this would all change. The year 1908 was no exception.

The continuing controversy regarding Eakins' eligibility was coming into better focus, but now, in the fourth game, right halfback Mucklestone had been added to the mix. Both players attended North Dakota State the prior year and played football there but entered Washington as freshmen. In an investigation that wouldn't be resolved until the next year, it turned out that they were attending high school prep classes at the university but did play for one year on the football team. For a time, and through a complaint brought by Oregon trainer Bill Hayward, it appeared that both players' eligibility would expire at the conclusion of the 1909 season. Due to Washington's dominance, this news was met with considerable delight within the league. The investigation confirmed that both had competed in only one year at North Dakota State and thus were eligible for three years at Washington.

Were it not for Whitman's captain and right halfback, Vincent "Nig" Borleske, stepping out of bounds on a sure touchdown run, a dropped pass by the Missionaries with the receiver having an open field to the goal line, and a tackle by Wee Coyle on a blocked punt that would have been an easy touchdown, Washington could well have lost the game. Borleske's mistake of missing the sideline was uncharacteristic for one of the all-time greats of Northwest football, who many say was robbed in not being declared a WCF All-American. He later coached the team, and in 1926 their football stadium, named Borleske Field, was opened.

The team was still waiting for Eakins' transcript, so he watched this league opener from the sidelines. Captain Tegtmeier was still out with his injured knee, so the substandard play could partially be blamed on missing two of their stars. It was late in the game when Coyle, on a great punt return, placed the ball near the 5-yard line. On the third down, Mucklestone carried it in for the lone touchdown of the day. The extra point completed the only scoring of the game. Final score: Washington 6, Whitman 0.

"His Actions…Will Not Be Tolerated Longer," read the headline in the *Argus* of November 7, 1908, the very day of the Washington State game. Being only thirty years old when he arrived at Washington and having never lost a game in his four years of coaching, Dobie possessed more than his share of youthful hubris. His brand of rough language, public outbursts, rude behavior, and immaturity were drawing the attention of "the good people of Seattle." As we've seen, Dobie's teams had shown moments of brilliance in their four games up to this time, but there were enough ragged edges that he had not yet assumed the position he was to eventually hold—the sage of Northwest football.

He was walking on thin ice when a career-saving event occurred: an open letter of complaint written by Bobby Boyce, sporting editor of the *Argus,* dated November 2 and addressed to none other than Dr. Thomas F. Kane, president of the University of Washington. He flatly stated that Dobie was one of the best football coaches at Washington in years and that he had an excellent opportunity to win the championship. He didn't appear to have it in for Dobie, but publishing an open letter to your boss featuring a litany of complaints was hardly a love note.

The embarrassing charges leveled were posted before the world, with Boyce pulling no punches in his criticism:

"However there are certain things about Dobie's conduct during the progress of a game that must be done away with and if not, then you will certainly miss the sympathy and support of 'the old guard' downtown, and after all it is the downtown people who make football a paying institution.

"My charges may be found as follows:

(1) Coaching from the sidelines; purely unprofessional and more than disheartening to visiting players. Let us win our games on the square or lose them in the same manner.
(2) Swearing at officials because of an adverse decision. For proof of this I can cite you to a graduate and old football player from your own institution.
(3) The use of language in addressing spectators that would hardly be tolerated in a barroom.

"Of course, the last charge is the most serious of all. The Offense was committed during the progress of the Whitman game. One of the best men in Seattle happened to say something to Dobie whereupon the coach turned with a remark that cannot be placed in this letter, simply because Uncle Sam has made postal laws that forbid. The remark was not only loud enough for every man in the party to distinctly hear, but there was certainly nothing to prevent women who were in that vicinity from also hearing.

"And again, when the coach is in a fit of temper, his tongue frequently gets the better of his judgment, and the oaths he hurls upon the more or less rain-soaked atmosphere falls upon the ears of the grammar school youngsters."

It was a matter of only three days before President Kane replied:

"I write at this time simply to acknowledge your kind and very thoughtful and considerate letter in regard to our athletic situation. You may feel assured that this situation is as humiliating to us as to our loyal friends in the city.

"Previous to the last game our committee had done all that in reason seemed necessary to do to correct the faults which were so galling to all of us. Seems hardly possible that we shall have further trouble in the matter but you may rest assured that whatever remedy is necessary will be applied.

"Nothing could have revealed to me more clearly than this situation the genuine loyalty of the men in the city and of whom have deplored the situation and practically all of whom have been very considerate in registering their disapproval and humiliation. You may feel assured in your own case your communication will be regarded just as all of our pleasant communication have been on matters pertaining to the University interests."

The parties to the well-deserved public flogging of Coach Dobie quite obviously had their eye on the football schedule in bringing resolution to what Dr. Kane described as causing "disapproval and humiliation." In the *Argus'* November 14 issue, the publication promised it would print the president's response to the charges leveled against his football coach, but would hold it until November 28. That just happened to be the date of the last game of the season, the big Thanksgiving showdown against Oregon State. During this time, Dr. Kane took the matter to the faculty committee, where Dobie was roundly rebuked for his bad conduct. The president himself took his immature charge to the woodshed, which must have been difficult for a man of Dobie's makeup to endure. Used to being the one who gave orders and expected complete obedience, Dobie now found himself on the receiving end of a shape-up-or-ship-out lecture. He dug the hole he found himself in, and with so many witnesses to his unacceptable conduct, he had no choice but to alter his behavior, and to start comporting himself in keeping with the highly visible public position he held before the sporting world.

This saved Dobie's job. Had there not been such a communitywide display and public airing of Dobie's intolerable behavior, circumstances would have undoubtedly led to his firing. This was such a seminal event in his career that Dobie spoke of it seven years later in a speech he delivered to an assemblage of three hundred of the "old guard" dignitaries, former players, alumni, faculty, and students gathered to honor him at a going-away luncheon for the coach. President Henry Suzzallo and others convinced Dobie to retract his resignation, but he chose this august forum and conceded that in those early days, he indeed had exceeded any bounds of propriety with his juvenile behavior.

On February 3, 1939, long after the coach and president had moved beyond these trying times, Thomas F. Kane, wrote a letter to Dobie from his Florida winter home. He shared words of high praise for the coach who so many years before had placed him in a position he deemed "humiliating." In seeing how Dobie had grown beyond the immaturity he showed in his early coaching days the president now expressed glowing admiration.

"Few men have a better or more consistent record of coaching. A coache's [sic] work, I have always felt, is the most trying work about a university. If the members of the faculty had the same severe tests of their work that the coach has every season, many of them would have a shorter term of service than they now have. Coaches often have unfair treatment. They have to win, regardless of material or circumstances.

"It has been a pleasure to me a number of times to see you put in a very short list of the best coaches in the country, by writers who understand football." He advised Dobie to put aside the unfair things he had been dealt and treasure the memory of the tireless service he gave to his men and to the schools he served.

The November 28 article in the *Argus* gave a journalistically honest account of the messy situation. The article reported that there had been much pressure applied by "influential members of the faculty and alumni with the request that we back down and quit—'all for the good of the order.'" Despite this sycophantic attitude from the win-at-any-cost crowd, the end result of this chaotic ordeal was for the better. It was reported in the write-up that Dobie was to be retained for two more years, and in an editorial remark it was added, "It is hoped the plan goes through." The newspaper was even willing to advance an opinion as to how strongly the message had been delivered to Dobie, offering the supposition that he would be cleaning up his act. "There can be no question, so we have been informed, but that Dobie thoroughly understands the situation and that it will never again be necessary to repeat the charges we made on November 7." Dobie did learn a lesson, as after this he tempered his rude public outbursts. He would draw on a good bit of rough language in private but eliminated the boorish public spectacles that placed his career in jeopardy hardly before it began.

There were three charges in the *Argus'* original complaint: coaching from the sidelines, swearing at game officials, and a verbal dust-up with spectators at the Whitman game. In the Dobie era, the established sentiment towards collegiate athletics was that on the field of play, amateurism reigned. The coach's job was to prepare his team at practice, but when the game was under way, the contest was to be decided by the pure athleticism of the competing squads. There was to be no signaling from the professional coaches to taint the outcome. Since that time, the game has come full circle, where today every manner of sideline coaching and signaling of plays is not just encouraged but has become an imperative to competitive play. But did Dobie actually employ a system of signals? The *Argus*, on December 5, just after everyone thought the public pillorying of Dobie had ended, brought a claim against both the coach and Oliver Cutts, the head referee of the Oregon State game. They complained that Dobie was coaching from the sidelines and Cutts failed to penalize him for "a flagrant violation."

It would be expected that a player would defend his coach during his time on the team. But often there's the case of players who come out with the real inside scoop after they hang up their cleats. The case of Wee Coyle, who starred on Dobie's teams for four years and, in addition to all of his other accomplishments, later coached Gonzaga football for one year, would appear to have considerable credibility in reporting on the subject. Throughout his life,

Coyle was adamant that Dobie did not coach from the sidelines. In an article he wrote in the *Olympian* on September 23, 1914, while Dobie was still coaching, he stressed that there was no signaling from the sidelines. The charges claimed that the lanky Scot used certain movements of his ever-present black cigar to call for a line buck, end run, or forward pass. Other movements of his long arms were to direct the team to go for a touchdown. Quoting Coyle, "All such talk is nonsense, and is used only to detract from Dobie's ability as a coach and from the machine-like movement of his team. In the four years during which it was my pleasure to serve under Washington's incomparable coach, he at no time gave signals while walking up and down the sidelines." Thirty-four years later, Coyle, having the opportunity to set the record straight if indeed Dobie had violated the rules, chose not to do so. In fact, his written account in the *Seattle Times* in 1948 was entirely consistent with his article from 1914. There are no instances of players coming forward neither to dispute either of Coyle's accounts nor to register a complaint themselves, and since officials never called a penalty for such an infraction, it can be concluded that Dobie was not guilty of the violation.

As to the second complaint lodged by the *Argus* about Dobie "swearing at officials" in disputing referees' calls, this, from all accounts, did happen. Based on the young coach's weak skills of socialization so clearly demonstrated in these early days, it would have been shocking for this grievance not to have been lodged. The newspaper reported this was witnessed by a UW graduate and former player, and, beyond this, the coach was well known for the use of barroom language. In his speech at the going-away banquet in 1915, given in Dobie's honor, he also brought up his penchant for using off-color language. While he did learn in President Kane's spanking not to be so crude in public, when he was not in the spotlight the coach was not hesitant to call up a vocabulary unacceptable in polite society.

The third complaint brought to bear against Dobie of getting into a verbal row with "one of the best men in Seattle" at the Whitman game was the worst of all the offenses. For this there is no dispute that it happened, and if he hadn't been able to rein in such deplorable conduct, this surely was grounds for termination. No matter the circumstances, a public representative of a major institution in the glare of the spotlight, and with newspaper reporters ever at the ready for a juicy story—a coach cannot behave as happened in this case.

The incident was not exaggerated in Bobby Boyce's account of the fracas between Coach Dobie, Hiram C. Gill (a city councilman who was elected Seattle mayor two years later), and Seattle Postmaster George Russell. Gill was hardly the upstanding citizen and certainly not one of the "best men" in Seattle, as he was constantly embroiled in one scandal or another throughout his long public career. He would be recalled in 1911 for massive corruption in office amidst charges of civic indecency, open gambling, thuggery, and graft. Many years later he regained his office after two tries, but this time hired a crooked police chief who served prison time for official misconduct. And, through illicit law practices, Gill was disbarred from the practice of law.

The coach was quite animated on the sidelines and walked up and down the field with the movement of the football. Denny Field in 1908 was not the elevated arena of today's major stadiums. In 1910, due to the success of the football program, a modern grandstand was built that raised the seating level four feet above the gridiron. Being tall, always wearing a hat, and with the stands close to the field of play, Dobie definitely would block spectators' views of the action. Demonstrating an obstinate lack of appreciation for ticket-buying fans, Dobie didn't heed polite requests that he not block their view, so the situation quickly escalated. Wee Coyle, who played in this game, reported in the *Seattle Times* that a less-than-polite demand came from the stands: "Sit down, you big bum." There being no response from the offending coach, these two members of Boyce's "old guard downtown" resorted to throwing a fusillade of peanuts as a more direct means to perhaps elicit the recalcitrant coach's cooperation. It took a few more volleys to finally break the ice, whereupon Dobie's verbal tirade erupted. It was undeniably the coach's fault in allowing the situation to boil over to such a level that it ended up as an open letter addressed to his boss. But given Dobie's iron will, it took just this sort of public embarrassment to get through to him. While he demanded that his players follow his commands, he was smart enough to see that he had to respect the commands of President Kane. In the end, it can be seen that Bobby Boyce performed a great service in driving it into Dobie's head that maturity, polite behavior, and good judgment were prerequisites for his job. While he fell short of choirboy standards, this brought an end to verbal tiffs with the fans and protests lodged in his direction from the paid seats.

Because this episode occurred in the very earliest months of Dobie's long tenure as Washington head coach and was told and retold, it grew into exaggerated legend. Some writers more interested in tabloid journalism than accurate reporting wrote that fans throughout his career would shell the coach with peanuts and his own student-fans would openly boo and throw rocks at him. While it makes for sensationalist reading, all of these stories were concocted several generations after Dobie left Washington, and the actual record shows no evidence that they are true. The fact that Dobie redeemed himself as a result of this episode never made it into print.

One year after the great peanut-throwing incident, the *Argus* asked Victor Zednick to give an update on just how Dobie was doing after he had been called on the carpet. "He is the most popular coach Washington has ever had. The students almost worship him and the faculty praises him for his sterling worth. This is the truth about Dobie's standing at the University." Zednick can be viewed as a bit too close to the subject for a completely unbiased opinion, but considering that he was employed by the students as their graduate manager and served at the pleasure of the faculty, such a public statement as this could not stand unless it had some basis in fact. Sports Editor Bobby Boyce, proved by his own actions, to be an honest purveyor of facts regarding Dobie, no matter that they placed his job in jeopardy. In later years he would give further insights into how the coach's career progressed. In chapter 7 we will look into a surprising twist to the relationship between Boyce and Dobie.

### Washington State

A game had been scheduled to follow the battle with Whitman against the University of Puget Sound, but it was called off by Washington's Manager Bill Rasmussen because he said the team needed a rest. This left an open date, but the rest didn't do much good since there were several injuries coming from scrimmages that weakened the team. There was some good news, though, on the long-standing controversy over Max Eakins' eligibility. When his preparatory school transcript finally arrived from North Dakota State, he was three classes short of being qualified to enter UW as a freshman. He took examinations after the Whitman game, passed them, and that week was cleared to play. Most sources were giving the advantage to State, particularly because they were much heavier than the Purple and Gold. The weight differential was even greater than it looked on paper, as insiders reported selective tweaking by the easterners. "Chub" Cherry, their center, showed the biggest spread at 190 pounds on paper, but his actual weight was much more—some sources reporting it to be 315.

The game's overall review as to comparative performance was weighted in favor of Washington. This prevailed until the last ten minutes, when WSU's heavier team wore on the lighter Varsity. The backfield for UW of Wee Coyle, Leonard Taylor, Melville Mucklestone, and Ralph Westover was all freshmen playing against the more experienced visitors. This foursome outgained Pullman 273 yards against 122 and performed remarkably, playing offense and defense for the full seventy minutes. Linemen Warren Grimm, Paul Jarvis, and Bill Mattson were playing injured. With a crippled line and the inexperienced backfield, this gave added credence to the majority predicting defeat for the Varsity. The return of Eakins, a strong punter, was a huge asset since in 1908 only one pass was allowed per scrimmage. An incomplete pass of less than 5 yards turned the ball over to the other side. This meant that punting was much more prevalent, even on first and second downs, should a team be buried deep in its own territory.

Scoring for the game came in uncharacteristic fashion, with neither team recording a touchdown. Scores were made via a four-point field goal and a two-point safety for each team. Washington made a habit of picking up good yardage and threatening to score but fizzled near the goal line. Within just the first five minutes, largely on the strength of a pass completion from Coyle to Warren Grimm for 40 yards, Washington made it to the 3-yard line but couldn't punch the ball over. Washington State racked up the first points on a brilliant fake punt by left guard Joe Halm, who gained 25 yards. Halm scored the field goal from the 23-yard line. Washington's first score came when Halm juggled the ball trying to punt from beyond his goal and was tackled for the safety. Shortly into the second half, Washington took the lead off Maxwell Eakins' field goal from 35 yards out. This placed the home team in front, 6-4. Washington, while executing a first-rate running game, had a miserable 1 out of 7 in booting the ball through the uprights. Coyle didn't make a single place kick and the lone field goal by Eakins was the only effort saving him from total embarrassment. Definitely not the outcome expected from a team coached by Dobie, the master of fundamentals.

The four thousand fans in attendance was the largest crowd ever assembled on the university gridiron, and even with the close score, the partisan home crowd was getting the sense that momentum was leaning in their boys' direction. There was more excitement than Washington had seen in years, with a beautiful sunny day, the brass band, obnoxious cowbells, clanging gongs, colorful streamers, and fired-up rooters. A contingent of expatriate rooters from Minnesota had made special preparations to come out and root for Dobie, their native son. They had a particular interest in seeing Washington prevail, as WSU's Coach Walter Rheinschild hailed from the Gophers' bitter rival, Michigan. Seeing the promise of Dobie, they launched a Seattle-led movement of Minnesota alums to woo him back home, but Washington aggressively fought to retain him. Though vastly outnumbered, the crimson-and-gray-clad visitors did manage to project, even though the ramped up locals were especially animated.

With both teams pulling out long runs at midfield, only to be cut short after heroic goal-line stands, and defenses continually stretched to the limit, there was widespread acclaim that this was one of the best games ever played in the Northwest. The supreme compliment came from Oregon's Coach Robert Forbes, who was in attendance to scout the game for next week's matchup with his boys. "Today's game was the best I have ever seen played in the Northwest." Forbes knew football; he was a two-year All-American end at Yale and came to Oregon after serving as head coach of the Army eleven.

The hopes of the home crowd for a victory would soon be dashed. The game would end up in a controversial call that took the edge off an exciting and tightly contested defensive struggle. A midfield punt late in the game by WSU's Joe Helm sailed low and wide toward the east goal line, out of reach of receiver Wee Coyle. Substitute right end Arthur Clark, the fastest man on the squad, ran the ball down, falling on it at what many reported to be just inches short of the goal line. Here is where the hullabaloo erupted. Depending on where Clark recovered the ball, the rules then and now are clear as to only two possible calls that can be made. If he fell on the ball inches short of the goal line, Washington would gain possession with a first down and 99 yards facing them. If Clark had fallen on the ball beyond the goal, rules declared this to be a touchback. The touchback rule of 1908 required that the ball be kicked out from beyond the goal line and must be kicked into the field of play. The ball would not have been placed on the 20-yard line as done today.

As it happened, there was a pile-up of players on top of Clark, and when referee Johnny Bender (WSU coach 1906, '07, '12, '13, '14) and umpire W. S. Kleinholtz (WSU coach 1909) sorted things out, the ball was inches beyond the goal line; some observers declared that the momentum of the pile pushed Clark together with the ball over the line. If this was the case, it didn't matter, as the ball is dead at the point of possession. The officials became confused and mistakenly declared this a safety, awarding two critical points to Washington State. As stated above, UW, in the overall game, had outplayed the visitors, but in the last ten minutes the tide shifted in favor of the eastern visitors. There is no predicting how the game would have played out if not for this incorrect call. Either team could have won, but odds are the contest would not have ended in a tie. Final score: Washington 6, Washington State 6. After this game Washington would go undefeated and untied for six more years. It was not until October 31, 1914, that the Varsity would again conclude a game with a tie.

A controversy erupted over Washington State's playing ineligible "ring-ers" in this game. The Faculty Athletic Committee, Registrar Condon and General Manager Rasmussen all advocated severing athletic relations with the state college. When Washington State finally admitted to the transgressions claimed by the rest of the league, Washington, Oregon, and Oregon State all refused to compete against them in football for 1909. Professor Carpenter of the Washington State Athletic Committee admitted in a letter that star punter and center Joe Halm, highly acclaimed guard Deaner, and fullback Bryan were not eligible. The stated justification for this action was their "assumption" that Washington would waive the question of eligibility. This naturally was not the case. There had been the earlier claims lodged against Washington for playing Mucklestone and Eakins, which, to the league's satisfaction, had been settled. They were indeed eligible, and this was cleared up in a letter received from President A. H. Parrott, of North Dakota State, and reported in the *Argus*. He verified their status as preparatory students not enrolled at the collegiate level. The tie game of 1908 goes down in the record books with not just one but two asterisks.

### University of Oregon at Oregon's Kinkaid Field

Fullback Dudley Clarke for Oregon had a reputation as one of the best punt-ers in the country and definitely was considered the best on the West Coast; this in an era where punting was of much greater importance than would be the case with later rule changes. Right tackle and Captain Fred Moullen was a highly touted and dangerous placekicker with a record of scoring as far out as the 45-yard line. The kicking advantage decidedly favored the southerners. Oregon had lost a shocker to Whitworth, partially explained since three starters were out of the game with injuries. With this embarrassing loss, the team had something to prove: that they could beat Washington.

Arriving at the field, the Washington coaching staff and team discovered that the field had been covered with four to six inches of sawdust, making for slippery and uneven footing. Oregon's explanation being that this would benefit footing in the event of heavy rain. This happened to be a clear day with no rain in sight, so Dobie seized on this opportunity to turn the tables on Oregon. This epitomizes his skill for deploying psychology to gain advantage in game-day strategy. The bad footing would have affected both teams, but Dobie had a freshman-dominated squad, and he knew they could have panicked. Through a theatrical performance on his part, he placed the team into a mind-set that the sawdust was put down as an insidious plot to place them at a disadvantage.

That morning Dobie instructed the players to be on the field and suited up by 1:00 pm for a game scheduled for 2:30. Game-day jitters are bad enough, but this could just make matters all the worse. The second string stayed behind in the dressing room, and the first team took the field ready for pregame instructions. As the team just began their drills, Wee Coyle, as reported in the *Seattle Times*, stated that Dobie lodged a protest: "Look at what they've done, put a foot of sawdust on the field so you can't run. Did you ever hear of such a thing? They've licked you before you've started." He centered his anger towards Bill Hayward, Oregon's legendary track coach. As the trainer for the football team, he was singled out by Dobie as the culprit of this dastardly scheme. Dobie's claim was for unsportsmanlike conduct, but Coyle said that the players, while seeing this as a "terrible handicap," would go out and do the best they could. No one caught on to the psychological gamesmanship at play by this master of the craft.

As the afternoon wore on, Dobie commanded the stage, not letting anyone else talk. He turned some of his ardor back on the team, calling them quitters and saying he wouldn't let them play against the deadbeats that were pulling this stunt. The sympathies of the team started to turn in favor of Dobie since, as their leader, he did have their best interests at heart. He worked them into a frenzy, and with the team thinking he was going to order them to take off their uniforms and quit the game, he said, "Boys, you're going out and get licked, and I can't help you, but I'll be ashamed of you if you don't go out and fight 'em and fight 'em hard!" Coyle gave all of the credit for Washington's performance to Dobie in directing the team's passions against Bill Hayward. Dobie had masterfully characterized this as a destructive ploy to gain unfair advantage.

In a speech given in 1915, Dobie looked back on this game and gave his take on the sawdust episode. "That same year we went down to Oregon, and when I presumed so much as to complain about the foot-deep sawdust on Multnomah field [editor's note: actually Kinkaid Field] Bill Hayward scorned my protests, wanted to know who I was to question the condition of the field, and informed me that Oregon considered us a second-rate team anyhow, and had the sawdust on the field because they didn't want their men to get hurt for some of the bigger, more important games to follow. We beat them 18-0 [actually 15-0], and for a year they called it an accident." Dobie, never one to pass up an opportunity, would certainly have complained about the sawdust-covered field to his players in any event. But with such dismissive remarks coming from Hayward, this gave the master strategist all the ammunition he needed to turn this into a battle royal. From Bill Hayward's own lips, the players' manhood was called into question. This is all it would take for Dobie to light a fire under the team, and that he did.

Game statistics reflect that Oregon's strategy was to challenge Washington by relying on its talented kicking duo of Clarke and Moullen. They only ran eight plays from scrimmage, one being a fumble, and only three of these were successful in making first down. Being more familiar with the footing problems of the dry sawdust, this was probably a purposeful strategy, but this may have led to their downfall. Washington continually had trouble in making cuts and gaining footing but through repeated attempts was successful in making good yardage. Wee Coyle, in receiving punts, was the standout player of the game, catching them on the run and making excellent yardage. Except for one very long punt of Clarke's, the hometown boys were never closer to the northerners' goal than the 25-yard line. While the ball was in their possession, Oregon never crossed the midfield stripe with the ball. In the punting arena, Eakins won the battle and was said to have "wrested the Northwest championship for punting from the famous Clarke of Oregon."

Washington's scoring all came in the second half. Moving from his right guard position into the backfield, Frank "Bull Moose" Babcock, on long gainers, advanced the ball well down the field to aid in setting up the first score. With the ball on the 1-yard line, Mucklestone carried it in. Neither this extra-point try nor the next one attempted by Eakins was successful. Shortly after, Coyle got in a 24-yard run. A few plays later he connected with Warren Grimm on a 23-yard pass, and Grimm bulled over the goal, carrying two tacklers as he placed the oval just in bounds at the corner of the field. The final score came when Clarke, in trying to kick out of danger, couldn't handle a bad pass from center and was tackled on his 1-yard line. On a strong goal-line stand by Oregon, Mucklestone couldn't get the touchdown until the third and final try. Coyle took over extra-point kicking duty, but with the unfamiliar footing, he too missed this last attempt.

Dobie was quite effusive in his praise of his freshman quarterback's performance as quoted to a *Seattle Times* reporter: "Coyle's game against Oregon could not have been bettered by any man living. He had more difficult chances than I have ever seen one man get in a football game, and he accepted every one of them. He improved from game to game and the climax of his work was reached when he displayed the greatest generalship in the O.A.C. game, Thanksgiving Day. Coyle is cool. He rises to the occasion in a manner that dazzles not only his teammates and the public but it causes his coach, who sees things that the players are not expected to see in the heat of the battle, to marvel at the boy's intuition and marvelous grasp of the situation. He has been a source of unending pleasure to me and to everybody connected with the game at Washington."

The Oregon fans exhibited great sportsmanship in showing their appreciation for a good performance, no matter which team made the play. At the end of the game, the fans carried both teams off the field on their shoulders. Washington students and a few players also rewarded Coach Dobie with an on-shoulder escort off the field. The game ended with Washington over Oregon, 15-0. This marked the beginning of Washington's forty-game win streak that would hold as the NCAA record until broken by Oklahoma's forty-seven-game winning run from 1953-57. The scoreless tie against Oregon State in 1914 brought an end to the six-year unblemished stretch by Dobie's men.

## Oregon State

The earliest seeds of doubt from Gil Dobie as to the upcoming contest were now being sown. He saw this as a cat-and-mouse game, with his team being on the receiving end of the marauding cat from Oregon State. He did have some reasonable justification, since the kicking game played such a prominent role in a team's strategy in this three-down era and Max Eakins, his strongest punter, was laid up with a badly twisted ankle. His right tackle slot would be filled by Guy Flaherty who hadn't played since the Whitworth game. Kicking duty would be taken over by Coyle. Dobie had scouted Washington State's loss the week before against Oregon, and he was convinced that Oregon only won because of Dudley Clarke's superior toe. Oregon State was the defending league champ, and there was some evidence that they could prevail, but Dobie's fears did seem inflated. He was particularly convinced of the visitor's chances should the weather be clear for Thanksgiving Day.

In reporting on Oregon State, the *Times* was still having trouble with the game against Washington State. In their subhead announcing this win, the newspaper referenced the "Host of Ineligibles" from the earlier 6-6 deadlock. In this game, the writer described Washington's performance as wonderfully classy, excellent team work, a magnificent machine, and glorious. Tribute was paid to Dobie, noting that there was a clear-cut trend showing consistent development from game to game. This is the mark of a good coach; do the players show improvement under his tutelage? It wasn't just in the case of this season, but it was a frequent accolade describing the Scottish mentor throughout his career. The *Times* stated, "He has had wonderful influence over the players, all of whom like him and will do their best when he gives the word." Such glowing tribute must be put into context with the reality that Dobie was about to bring a championship to Seattle, and some giddiness is understandable.

The game was played on a muddy field, and according to Dobie's pregame analysis; the sloppy conditions should favor his boys. The Varsity ran the ball at will and, once they overcame early-game fumbling, spread the scoring across several players. Left end Warren Grimm accounted for two TDs, right end Bill Mattson scored one, fullback Penny Westover had a touchdown, and there was one more contributed by substitute fullback, Hart Willis. Quarterback Wee Coyle was successful in kicking three of the five extra points and made one field goal. The final score was a lopsided Washington 32, Oregon State 0. A record crowd of six thousand was in attendance.

A cash surplus was discovered in the '08 class treasury, and Chairman Thomas Latimer, along with Ned Pugsley, decided to donate the money for an award to be designated by a faculty committee. The committee was made up of President Thomas F. Kane, Registrar Herbert T. Condon, and Physical Director Dr. David C. Hall. They chose to set aside the award for the player whose contributions to the football team for the previous year were deemed most inspirational to his teammates' performance. The inscription on the medal reads, "In recognition of service to U.W. football." Guy Flaherty last saw action in the Whitworth game and had been suffering a severe case of boils, which prevented him from playing until this last game of the season. Despite his painful infection, he showed up for practice every week and volunteered as a student assistant coach. It was for this selfless contribution that the team's choice for this first award went to him. This "Most Inspirational Player" award, now named after Guy Flaherty, was the first collegiate award of its type in the country.

# CHAPTER THREE

## *My Best Team—1909*

"As stated to Associated Press Reporter Steve O'Leary: "Most fans would say Dobie's greatest teams were the Cornell elevens of the early '20s. 'I'd say my best team was in 1909 at Washington and the 1914 team there was pretty near as good. Those Cornell teams with Kaw and Pfann were fine but not quite as good as the other two.'"

*Gilmour Dobie, 1941*

That year the incredible Alaska Yukon Pacific Exposition was held on the university campus from June to the middle of October. School didn't open until October 4, with football practice not starting until September 20. Some of the players, for financial reasons, couldn't leave their summer jobs just for football and waited for school to open to come out for practice. Dobie rightly complained this could give his opponents an advantage of more practice time. But he had more serious reasons for concern with the loss by graduation of left tackle Burwell Bantz, left guard Paul Jarvis, right guard Frank Babcock, left guard Guy Flaherty, fullback Ralph Westover, and fullback Hart Willis. Of these, Jarvis and Babcock had made the All-Northwest team.

For some time that year, a dialogue had been under way between UW and teams outside the Northwest. Washington was seeking a contest against competitive non-conference teams, such as the University of Denver or the University of Utah. As events played out, the University of Southern California, even though its football team was only a shadow of what it was to become, turned out to be the likeliest shot for setting up an intersectional game. Dobie was on board, and Manager Zednick was making arrangements to get faculty approval for a game in Los Angeles on either Christmas or New Year's Day. These dates had already been approved by Thomas Clay, USC's graduate manager. However, Clay came back suggesting dates of Thanksgiving, which conflicted with the Varsity's Oregon contest, or December 4, which wouldn't work because the long trip came right at the semester break for Washington. Clay gave as a reason that he had made a "mistake" for not sticking with the agreed-upon dates. One can only imagine the great rivalry that could have been born of such a matchup coming as it did in this early day of West Coast football. Alas, it was not to be, as USC even went backwards in its program, dropping football altogether for the years 1911, '12, and '13.

Dobie never left anything to chance. Players, no matter whether they were stars in previous years or first-year unknowns, were treated as if they had never stepped on a football field before. He scrutinized every detail of every player. More than any other quality, he looked for speed. It was Dobie who was the earliest western advocate of this focus on speed over force. Of course, over the years this became the standard. He also expected his players to not only know their own position, but also to be fully aware of the on-field responsibilities of their teammates. Practices in the early part of the season would begin with a light workout in the afternoon followed by a blackboard lecture. The lecture was treated by the coach no differently than if this were a university class. There was a quiz in the evening, and this wasn't just for show; answers were graded by the great disciplinarian as his way of gauging each player's progress. Dobie's focus and attention to detail were fully in play. There was nothing he did that didn't have a purpose. When he and the players stepped onto the field for drill (practice), there was only one purpose in mind: get ready to win that week.

It was required that every man on the squad must perfect himself in charging, tackling, blocking, interference (blocking for the ball carrier), throwing the ball, catching the ball, and assisting the man carrying the ball. It wasn't until his men mastered these fundamentals to his satisfaction that he would even begin lessons on unified offensive play. Observers of Dobie's practice methodology describe it as an almost painful attention to the details of preparation. There were no stars on his teams, and every player was constantly reminded of the value of teamwork. When the word "perfect" is used in context with Dobie and his means of drilling each man on learning his assignment, it means the individual is to subordinate himself to the greater glory of the team. It is only through going over every fundamental of each assignment and breaking these down into their constituent parts of footwork, timing, ball position, teammates' positions, play objective, opposition reaction, and each player's response to this opposition that Dobie would feel some modicum of satisfaction. An entire afternoon practice session could be made up of Dobie lining up each player in his position and walking through two or three plays for hours on end. What seemed like mindless repetition became so well drilled into each player that it became rote behavior in the game. Even when the competition was familiar with Dobie's play selection, the plays were executed with such remorseless efficiency, they were virtually unstoppable. Dobie speaks of seeking men who "stand high in their classes," and with this emphasis he describes his outcome as ensuring hard and intelligent workers.

Game strategy was to wear down the opposition, not with any aim to pick up large chunks of yardage but to methodically eke out steady and consistent shorter gains. In this era of eleven men playing offense, defense, and special teams Dobie masterfully executed a game plan where the other team spent far more time in the early going on defense than offense. With defense being much more wearing on the player than offense, the opposition was quicker to tire or be forced to bring in less-skilled players as the game wore on. His strategy would also include singling out the other team's stars and keying on them with directed plays to diminish their effectiveness and wear those players down. As their greatest players were getting heavy in the legs and frustrated, the psychological balance of play shifted to Washington. Unlike Dobie's methodology, the other teams of the era often elevated the captain to a position of total generalship when the game was under way. In the early going, Dobie would single out the captain with double-teaming tactics or other attempts to reduce his effectiveness. In describing this tactic, Dobie stated, "Their players, in believing in their captain, were demoralized by our success in attacking this point on their line. After all, football is mostly psychology."

There is abundant evidence for psychology as being the hallmark of Dobie's craft. Newspaper headlines would trump up his very quotable pessimistic forecasts of the upcoming game, and eventually those close to him were well aware that this was all for show. Pregame write-ups were a fright to behold. Gloom and doom and terrible outcomes were often ahead for the team, but not universally, as the popular conception would have it. His players were not up to par because of injuries, bad attitudes, puffed-up egos, lack of team play, or the unquestioned strength of the great squad on tap for that weekend. With lopsided scores, as was often the case, these tactics eventually become less effective, but Dobie, nevertheless, would still try to slip by some reason for his team's imminent demise. His belief held that not every player on the other side was onto this brand of gamesmanship. He knew that the opposing coaches, while using a lot of the same psychological ploys, were not able to control the mind-set of every one of their players. With his success, Dobie's every utterance got banner headline treatment. A new player for the other team or a new coach or new assistant might read his dire predictions and think "maybe, just maybe" we have a chance of beating this guy.

Dobie was also a master of getting inside his own players' heads. He believed in eleven-man teams, not ten men and a captain, or nine men and two stars. The captain was not the automatic on-field leader of the team. His program called for a field general who, on offense, was the quarterback. The coach would not tolerate any type of divided leadership during a game. The field general was in charge, and that was the end of the story. Dobie made a point of going to his captain at the start of the season to make sure that it was clearly understood as to what his captaincy meant in the Dobie system. He feared the destructive power of a big ego and was ever vigilant in guarding against this dreadful malady. He would sit a player down if he attempted to showboat and even threatened to kick players off the team who got too self-important. The players always got the message and came back having learned that the master was right after all.

### Preseason

Dobie was heartsick at his miserable chances for the season ahead and, playing the part of the deprived coach to the hilt, met his players at the opening of practice with tears in his eyes. The theatrics were his way of getting the players to double down if they had any hope of salvaging a game or two for the season. By Dobie's account, there was no celebrating last year's championship as the team's time in the sun had passed; for now there was little chance of defending the title. The preseason games would be tough enough, but he described it as a disgrace to go into the conference games as shorthanded as they were. There was no notice given to the fact that superb players such as future Captain Wee Coyle, Maxwell Eakins, Warren Grimm, Bill Mattson, former Cornell star Charles May, '09 Captain Melville Mucklestone, Leonard Taylor, '08 Captain Pete Tegtmeier, and Walter Wand were back. Not to mention that the star high school fullback Fred Sparger had joined the team. Future captain Tom Griffiths showed tremendous early-season promise, and Warren's brother, Huber "Polly" Grimm, was now back from last year's baseball tour of Japan. He would become captain of the 1910 team and was the first-ever selection from Washington on the WCF All-American team (albeit a third-team choice for 1910 at tackle).

Bringing up these riches of talent wouldn't suit Dobie's purpose. The team was coming off an undefeated championship year, and he knew full well that the players loved all the attention they were getting. He felt it was his primary and most urgent duty to let some air out of their swelled heads. Young men getting their egos charged up being his greatest fear, he set about to chop them down a few notches. At this he was the undisputed master. As quoted in the *Argus*, he was thoroughly disgusted. "I simply can't get that bunch to work. They won't buckle down and fight. They are too easy going. They think they have the championship ready for them on a platter. It is a mistake. We have a fighting chance, but the men have got to fight, that's all there is to it." His PR moves weren't just to draw attention to himself or the team—such tough talk in the public forum was calculated to get the players' attention.

The three preseason games, all won by Washington, were with Queen Anne HS on October 9 with a score of 34-0; a club team with the crew of the USS *Milwaukee* on October 16, 39-0; and Lincoln HS on October 23, 20-0. In the game with the USS *Milwaukee*, the coach took the unusual step of pulling quarterback Coyle out of the game on a play that resulted in a touchdown. It was Dobie's assessment that his quarterback used poor judgment in calling for a pass with 18 yards to go. The preseason was unusually weak in this critical title-defending year because Washington cancelled a more competitive game scheduled with Whitworth. Whitworth was not a member of the league, but the conference did require that competing teams field only players eligible to play under league residency rules. There were, according to Washington, several players not eligible and three that were particularly a problem. For this reason, the game was cancelled, resulting in the Varsity going into league play without benefit of sharpening their skills against Whitworth. Washington and other league members, going back to last year, as we have seen, were not satisfied with WSU's progress towards clearing its roster of ineligible players. The Board of Control decided not to hold a game against the cross-state rival for that reason.

### University of Idaho at Spokane

Without doubt the squad was a strong collection of players, but injuries were mounting in the weeks leading up to the league opener with Idaho. There were mounting questions as to Washington's ability to defend its title. In the three weeks prior to the Idaho game, this was the injury list: Bill Mattson, muscle bruise; Tracy Baker, lame shoulder; Melville Mucklestone, lame shoulder; Fred Tegtmeier, sprained wrist; Bruce Beck, crushed foot; Max Eakins, wrenched knee; Louis Diether, wrenched back; Polly Grimm, charley horse; and Charles May, lame back. There is no way to avoid injury in football; it's a part of the game. In that day of smaller squads playing with such primitive equipment, it was a much greater factor. When one key player went down, it more likely meant the difference between winning and losing. Dobie and his men were all too aware of this.

To a master strategist of Dobie's caliber, there was no passing up this opportunity. Thus far in the preseason, the team hadn't been scored upon, but this had no effect on the coach's plan to further press the case that in losing so many stars to graduation and with the epidemic of injuries, they were sure to get beaten by Idaho. Wee Coyle reported that on the train to Spokane, "Dobie howled, yelled and carried on like a wild man. All was lost." With the made-to-order opening of injuries dropped in his lap, the much ballyhooed gloom of Gil Dobie came to full flourish. Coyle described the trip to Spokane as being "like a nightmare. The 'Old Man' was on the warpath for fair. We were going to be slaughtered." The players believed him. Having methodically woven his web, the coach had the team under his control, be it physical or mental.

The Idaho coach, John Grogan, and Dobie were personal friends going back to the days when they were on opposite sides as coaches in North Dakota. Dobie had put in a favorable word for Grogan when he came up for consideration at Idaho. "I appreciate that so much that I'd like to beat Dobie's team about 20 to 0," Grogan said going into the game. These two teams had more of a friendly rivalry due largely to the coaches' kinship. This contrasted sharply with the animosity between the Varsity and WSU or Oregon. The Idaho games over the years usually had Washington as the favorite but would often end up as sensational battles with spectacular plays.

The 1909 game, though, was short on drama. Washington took it to Idaho from the start. If a game MVP had been picked, the unanimous choice would have been Wee Coyle. He ran the team, called plays, scored a touchdown on a punt reception, scored a goal from a dropkick, and did an outstanding job running the ball from scrimmage. At halftime the score was 21-0 in the visitor's favor, with Washington ending the game with the largest score ever racked up against an opponent in the league, putting 50 points to zero on the board. In pulling no punches, Idaho was described as being "deplorably weak." Washington's smothering defense had a great deal to do with that assessment. Dobie was complimentary of his team's performance but, despite the lopsided win, couldn't pass up the chance to cast a shadow over upcoming games. He gave this assessment to the *Daily Wave* in his postgame wrap-up: "By defeating Idaho by such a large score Washington is not a bit closer to the championship. The game with Whitman this Saturday will be our real test." Of course, Dobie hadn't held any great hope that his chances of winning against Idaho were any too good either.

## Whitman College

Dobie hadn't yet settled into the life of a championship football coach. Since his days as coach of the Minneapolis South High School team and on into his second year at Washington, his teams hadn't yet tasted defeat. In this, the year that he had turned thirty-one, he didn't fully appreciate his coaching ability. He began to have self-doubt as to his staying power in the coaching profession. His obsessive work ethic, which his followers viewed as all there was to the man, wasn't well received in these early days, and signaled to him his accomplishments weren't fully appreciated. Football loyalists hadn't yet caught on to the reality that Dobie's all-engrossing coaching style was far different from the more refined persona he would express away from football. To Dobie's surprise, he discovered that the faculty at times was not totally behind him; the newspapers could find fault with his behavior, the downtown business community would voice discontent, his student fans weren't out full force for every game, and his players wouldn't always kowtow to his demanding practice regimen. With his limited life experience, his expectation for perfection, and his low threshold of tolerance for those not viewing the world as he saw it, there's little wonder that in this second year of his Seattle tour, his life went drastically off track. This couldn't rationally be justified, but it can be explained because we are dealing with the early-days Gil Dobie, a man that had not yet come to terms with the reality that he didn't rule the universe. He could buck the system only so far. In taking his intractable stands he would eventually, but slowly, learn that moderation also had a place. Most of us learned this earlier in life but we are dealing with the strongest of strong-willed characters in Coach Dobie, for whom it takes more outside force to set his mind on the right path.

It was on November 5, 1909, just one day before the game against Whitman, that Dobie announced that "under no circumstances would he coach the team next year." It should be noted that this was not an official resignation. Some historians have taken the position that Dobie was somewhat flaky and quit every year. While this was not the case, he most definitely did create great concern in his early years that he was on the brink of leaving football altogether. With the huge success he enjoyed and with the attractive salary he was paid, his on-again, off-again public statements could hardly be viewed as sensible. And they most definitely were not. He was the sole cause of his own self-doubt. However, in a strange twist of irony, if it weren't for his unjustified, almost paranoid behavior, this driven man probably could not have achieved what he did. His self-generated personal demons were in reality what elevated him to greatness. This realization would only come later.

The Whitman game was played on November 6, 1909, hardly allowing enough time for Dobie's announcement of his intended resignation to make the rounds. To further fuel the flames and to most likely cement Dobie's decision in his own mind, the Faculty Athletic Committee passed a cryptic note to the coach just before this second league game of the season. Whether justified or not, there was serious doubt raised that Dobie had done anything wrong, but the note indicated that the committee was still after Dobie to clean up his act on the sidelines. He had been publicly rebuked the year before and was brought before President Kane, who denounced his behavior and swore that any untoward conduct would be corrected, or else. But it seems the faculty felt there was still room for improvement. The note had to do with an accusation against Dobie for sideline coaching in the Idaho game. This charge was strongly denied by other observers stating that the committee letter writer "had been misinformed that he had coached during the progress of the Idaho game at Spokane." It would seem that the charge could be called into question, as it was just twelve days from the date of the note that Dobie was unanimously reelected to extend his contract for another year by both the Student Board of Control and the Faculty Athletic Committee.

Because of pressing circumstances, Dobie's response would have to be put aside; there were more urgent matters of the moment, an all-important conference game to be played. This wasn't just any game, but a game against the team of captain and superstar halfback Vincent Borleske. Around the league he was universally recognized as the Northwest's greatest player. Gil Dobie was quite vocal in proclaiming that if there was one player on the West Coast who deserved recognition on the annual WCF first team All-American squad that would be Vincent Borleske. Before a game the coach would rarely make such a declaration about one of his own players, but he had no hesitation in singing the praises of his opponent's star.

---

The game turned out to be a rough contest for both teams. There were penalties aplenty and constant warnings issued by the officials after nearly every play. In this matchup, however, the earliest game-day example of Dobie's genius was given public display. With the growing awareness of the other coaches in the conference that this new kid on the block, Gil Dobie, just may be up to something, all sent a scout to the Idaho game. The crafty Scot, catching on to their inquiring presence, made sure that he didn't display all of the cutting-edge football tricks in his arsenal. The forward pass being a recent innovation to the game, and Dobie having been exposed to the open game in its formative years from Minnesota, he knew that these teams were there to learn from him. He had perfected eight different styles of the forward pass but, knowing this game was a clinic for the rest of the league, he only allowed Wee Coyle to call two of the formations. He knew that despite his prediction of disaster against Idaho, Whitman would be more of a challenge. He would have to dig deeper into his playbook if he was to merge victorious.

Going into the game, the weather turned Denny Field into a sea of mud, making it appear that the best strategy would be to keep the ball on the ground. The Varsity had difficulty practicing on any level, let alone putting in the time to burnish their passing game to a winning standard. Finally it looked like the rash of injuries was behind them, opening the door, perhaps, to a rosier outlook from the head coach. Alas, this was not to be, as the coach looked into his crystal ball and did not see a win. Dobie was far from optimistic and let everyone who would listen know that he was deathly afraid of Borleske. It should be noted that the Washington coach has not gone down in history as projecting a positive outcome for his teams, but this was only his second year in the Northwest. His gamesmanship in setting up the opposition wasn't widely known quite yet. His constant pumping up of the indomitable Borleske, however well deserved, just may have been for another purpose: an objective such as to inflate the confidence of the other team. Later, being more familiar with his methods, his competitors wouldn't be so quick to go for the bait.

Dobie's game preparation extended well beyond just sending out signals that the Whitman powerhouse captained by Vincent Borleske was too much for the Purple and Gold. He devised a way to turn all of the PR behind the Borleske machine into an opportunity in his favor. He devised a mock-up dummy of Borleske and set up this ersatz ball carrier to constant assault by his defense as they prepared for Saturday. Dobie's practices often were an endless series of repetitions of just one play. With Borleske being the chief threat to Washington's chances, painting a figurative bull's-eye on his back in practice was the ideal motivation.

The crafty coach had a difficult test coming up. It did appear the Whitman game was definitely a challenge, but if his team was to repeat as champions, he was facing even tougher struggles ahead with Oregon State and Oregon. With his success preceding him and with the coterie of scouts from the other schools sitting in the stands, the question most everyone had on his mind was: is this guy for real? The game went much easier in Washington's favor than the dopesters had predicted, so Dobie adjusted his game strategy to best prepare his team for the upcoming game with OSU. It did seem that he was the genuine article and not the flash in the pan as reported from enemy camps.

"Whitman was licked because Whitman had built its play around one man—Borleske—and every time that man shrugged a shoulder or winked an eyelash, a Washington man crashed into him." This wasn't by accident; Dobie knew that when a team had a superstar in its ranks, keying on him (if successful in taking the star out of the play) would serve to debilitate the rest of the players. A player such as this great halfback could do more than his share under ordinary circumstances, but with a countervailing influence posed by the likes of Gil Dobie, Borleske was doomed. Dobie had his men double- and triple-teaming the team captain at his every move, soon wearing him down to the level of just another struggling man on the other side of the line. The above quote from the *Seattle Times* of November 7, 1909, summed up the aptitude that the mentor from Minnesota had for picking a line of attack sure to bring home a win.

As the game unfolded, it was apparent that the Varsity had their way against the Missionaries. Dobie felt the eyes of the scouts in the stands taking their notes and was able to stick with his plan to hold back and never unleash his full arsenal. The scouts didn't get the clinic on Washington's strengths they were looking for. Wee Coyle held back on what were considered "trick plays" of the day, and Washington easily held its own with straightforward line bucks mixed in with a few forward passes. The team scored two touchdowns, plus both extra points and an Eakins field goal in the first half for a 15-0 lead. Whitman was able to tighten its defense in the second half, holding Washington to its lone second-half score, a safety, to complete the scoring at Washington 17, Whitman 0. The tighter struggle put up in the second half posed no real threat as the local boys had an answer.

## Oregon State at Corvallis

A football rally is hardly the place for a show of objectivity, its charter being to unashamedly support its own. With just two games left in the season, however, it seemed that university-sanctioned boosterism had now been elevated to entirely new heights. No one could remember when, or if, President Kane had ever attended a pregame rally. But here he was alongside yell king Ki Ram Winn, delivering a glowing tribute to the team. He told the crowd that every year he received compliments on the creditable conduct of "our representatives," thus deftly choosing a word that didn't identify either coach or players. This unprecedented pep talk didn't seem to stem from mere desire to rev up the emotions of this already committed crowd. Dobie was still undeclared on renewing his contract, even though near unanimous support was being expressed from all quarters: students, alumni, sports reporters, downtown business interests, players, and faculty. A speaker at the rally even expressed an impassioned plea to show appreciation to Dobie in an effort to win him over to return next year. While this forum was the very locus for all things positive concerning the team, it did appear that an extra effort went into broadcasting the fact that not just the student fans but the official university position was to retain Dobie.

As game day neared, the Portland *Oregonian* was expressing serious doubt as to Oregon State's chances at winning, and reports were received that there were injuries to two key men, making them doubtful for the game. There also were reports of not just rain forecast for the game, but a serious storm, threatening to turn the poorly draining field into a quagmire. On the bright side for the visitors, Washington's men were in excellent shape, with no limiting injuries of any kind. With a team that hadn't been scored on that year Dobie was hard put to come up with an angle to project doubt on his chances for a win, with the tepid observation: "It will be a hard game."

The football field, as described by the *Daily Wave,* was "a windswept, mud-oozing pasture. The surface was one stretch of mud, broken here and there by standing pools of water." The difficulties the teams had to play under were monstrously severe. On top of pounding rain, heavy winds, and bone-chilling cold, the host team hadn't set up adequate facilities for the teams to protect themselves from the brutal elements. Conditions were so bad that coaches Metzger and Dobie agreed to shorten each half by ten minutes. If it had been known to Dobie that not even proper locker rooms were set up for the players' comfort and safety under the horrible circumstances of the weather, he would have called off the game and rescheduled it for a better day.

The weather and the three-down rule turned this into a punting contest. Max Eakins being the league's strongest punter gave the edge to Washington. The first fifteen minutes were an evenly matched, scoreless, and heroic struggle for both teams, but Bill Mattson managed a touchdown shortly thereafter, with Coyle kicking the extra point. The Varsity was on the eve of another touchdown, but as they approached the goal, the game was stopped for a weather-related problem. Fierce winds had blown down the goal crossbar, and the game was held in suspense until the referees had the bar replaced. The football was positioned within inches of the goal line for first down with Washington again knocking on the door. Before the team could make their try, the timer called for the halftime break, much to the surprise of observant fans. It wasn't known to most of the crowd that the half had been shortened, so it wasn't clear until later just why Washington hadn't been given a chance to put the ball into play before the half.

With the players caked in mud and half-frozen, they were placed in tents at either end of the field. The only heat was supplied by a wholly inadequate oil stove. The team could only huddle around for what limited heat was available and wring the water out of their uniforms. The Varsity was supplied with dry socks, and a few of the home team came out wearing a change of dry uniform tops.

Somehow, despite the appalling conditions, Washington seemed to pick up energy in the second half and played with greater resolve. Right halfback Walter Wand, coming in for Leonard "Scrappy" Taylor, scored at the six-minute mark, with Coyle again making the kick for the extra point. The score now had Washington in the lead, 12-0.

With the terrible north wind in his face, Eakins couldn't place his team too far down the field, no matter how formidable his leg. Wee Coyle found an inner strength despite the conditions and, on three back-to-back quarterback keepers, netted 50 yards. The third carry resulted in the play of the game. As he was tackled, the slippery pigskin squirted out of his grasp, and the always dependable Pete Tegtmeier was right there to grab the ball before it hit the ground. The big blond with the "yellow streak" who by now greatly admired his coach made another 25 yards before being brought down. It was Captain Mucklestone who assumed ball-carrying duties at that point and scored the third and final touchdown, with Coyle again coming through with the point-after kick. The southerners could only make short gains and managed to squeeze out minor yardage on forward passes. This was their only resort, as the running game was stopped dead in its tracks by the interior front line of Tom Griffiths and Charles May at guard, Max Eakins and Warren Grimm at tackle, and Pete Tegtmeier at center. No matter that they found themselves wallowing in mud throughout the afternoon, this rock wall formed an impenetrable barrier that Oregon State could not break. As this most horrendous of games came to an end, Washington extended its streak of holding its opponents scoreless to eight games with a final tally of Washington 18, Oregon State 0. For all those who paid attention to the developing strength of Dobie's teams, it didn't go unnoticed that he hadn't been scored upon in one year going back to the Washington State contest on November 7, 1908. Washington held its competition scoreless for eight straight games, while the denizens of Denny Field racked up a commanding total of 241 points.

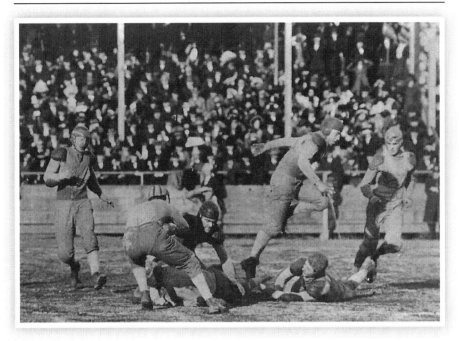

Museum of History and Industry, UW vs. Oregon, Nov. 25, 1909     Wee Coyle, Far right
Note face guard on player to the left to protect his broken nose.

## University of Oregon

On the brink of the last game of the season and for the league championship no less, there were still lingering signs of resentment towards the undefeated Washington coach. The *Seattle Times* often treated Dobie quite fairly, but if there was any sign of discontent or rumors that "he was up to his old ways," reporters were quick to stir the pot. There may have been an attitude of competitive pressure involved, as it was the much smaller *Argus* that scooped the *Times* the previous year with the big story of Dobie's sideline misbehavior. That soap opera sensationally ended up with the open letter to President Kane, forcing his hand to come out with the public *mea culpa* on Dobie's behalf. In advancing a story intended to diminish the coach a full year later, it would not be wholly cynical to suspect the newspaper's motives. It was on November 15, 1909, that the *Times* came out with a story described rather unflatteringly by the *Daily Wave* as, "Times Froths At The Mouth Again."

The *Times* headline was clearly meant to agitate: "Dobie Quits Washington After This Year." Dobie had not turned in his resignation, so this was just talk. The subhead was sensationalist to the max: "No One at Station to Greet Varsity Team Coming Home From Victorious Trip." There's more on this later. Conceding that the team had an excellent chance to repeat as champions, it was posited in the article that student support for the team was so anemic that fewer than five fans were on hand to root for the team, both for the departure to and return from Spokane for the Idaho game. This was tied to Dobie's declaration that he would not be returning to coach next year and, in the same paragraph, reporting on the faculty letter supposedly "warning him to behave while on the sidelines." As for what behavior was meant—swearing, coaching, or some other brand of misconduct—it was not stated. A reporter who had the facts would have included this to validate and punch up his story. Since no facts were given, his intention was to leave the impression that student fan support had totally evaporated. It also made for a juicy article to upstage the *Argus*, in that the faculty letter must mean that Dobie was still out of control during the games. He hadn't learned anything from his sit-down with Dr. Kane. As noted, Dobie had already been hired with a unanimous vote by the Faculty Athletic Committee. So while the student newspaper can certainly be viewed as pro-Dobie, in attacking the *Times* for its coverage, it appears the evidence falls in favor of the *Daily Wave*.

The *Times* article even got through to the taciturn coach, who broke his public silence on such matters to tell his side of the story. He adamantly refuted any disharmony with the university as the cause and said that "if" he were to leave his position, it would be to enter business. He had either played or coached for eight years, and he was having thoughts that it might be time to move on. He did have a law degree, and later in life, he became wealthy investing in the stock market. So leaning towards a career change was not out of the question.

A crowd of two hundred students, with shouts of "We want Dobie!" marched to his house just over a week before the Oregon game. Always a straight talker, he characterized the claim that the students weren't supportive of the team as ridiculous. He explained that since there was no way to know when the team train from Spokane was to arrive, no one expected a crowd to greet them. He also addressed the issue of his spotty relations with the faculty. "What I want you boys to know is that I don't care what the people downtown think, or the people in other colleges, as long as I have the students and faculty back of me. Any trouble I have had with the faculty was started through false rumor downtown, and those have always been settled in a few minutes." This hearkens back to the claim in the *Argus'* open letter that Dobie, against rules of the day, sent coaching signals to players on the field. As we have seen, Dobie always denied this, and Wee Coyle, writing on the subject during Dobie's time at Washington and forty years later, was adamant that Dobie did not violate this rule. No one connected with the team, whether player, staff, or assistant coach, ever made such an accusation, so Dobie's calling it a false rumor would appear to stand up. Victor Zednick, who was a constant overseer of just about every move of the team, offered his take on the controversy: "The Faculty Committee wrote Dobie a letter that he be careful not to coach on the sidelines because they had been misinformed that he had coached during the progress of the Idaho game at Spokane. Dobie's conduct, on the contrary, at Spokane was exemplary, and this same Faculty Athletic Committee heartily approves of Dobie's work this season and is agreeable to his reelection."

Dobie, in the meantime, was declaring to be fearful of Oregon, which came as no great surprise. The opponents did have a ten-pound weight advantage and, considering the Varsity had been heavier than all their rivals this year, however tenuous, this was a point. Not much of a point, but he needed something to hang his hat on, never mind that it was trivial.

He was becoming a believer in telling what were termed "bear stories" in those days to everyone who would listen, believing if he told the story often enough, someone would buy it. When he gave his speech to the students gathered at his house, he told them, "Oregon has been training for a year with this game in view. They have heavy men, as a whole, and on the average faster men, and if they don't beat us they ought to be ashamed." He also slipped in a reminder that overconfidence can cost the team the game, just to be entirely consistent on all of his favorite themes. In straining to make his case, Dobie added, "I have been accused of sending out stories, but in every case I have been giving out what was true." One can only imagine that fans reading such Dobieisms back in those days, even given that they were Dobie supporters, could only take a deep breath and say to themselves—sure!

The week before the big Thanksgiving game, the vote showing unanimous support for renewing Dobie's contract came in from both the student authorities and the faculty. There were no other candidates even under consideration. When given the news, the coach had this to say: "I will quit football coaching for good after the close of the present season. I have been in the game eight years now and intend to do something else besides coach football teams all my life."

In a deft display of student entrepreneurship, Wee Coyle and Captain Melville Mucklestone landed a contract to create and produce the fifty-two-page souvenir program for the game, including twenty-three pages of revenue-generating full-page ads. These enterprising businessmen were up to the challenge, creating a very good product that offered exciting, behind-the-scenes details and insider perspectives on the teams. This matchup represented another milestone in that it was the first game on the West Coast where players were numbered. As added incentive to buy the program, advance promotion touted it as the fans' source for matching number with player. In this day before one-hundred-foot-wide television monitors and the announcer's only broadcasting aid being a non-electronic megaphone, it was nigh on impossible for the hapless spectator to consistently tell who was doing what on the field. Even newspaper postgame reports gave conflicting accounts of the same play. Official stats were often a best guess. Numbering the players met with universal support from the appreciative fans, but Dobie was stubbornly opposed. He feared the players would grandstand with such ease of identification and that the opposing team could too readily identify the role of his players on set plays. This would make it too easy for the opponent to defend on the play the next time he saw a similar formation.

Here is the number assignment for each starting player as given in the program. Because of communication challenges of the day, advance printings of rosters invariably were incorrect. The actual starting lineup for Oregon showed Hickson at LE, Kellogg at C, Stone at RG, Scott at RT, Kiltz at RE, Sullivan at LH, and Clarke at FB. Because Washington was the home team with a direct line to the coach, there was only one change in its starting roster, with Sparger starting instead of Baker at FB.

|  |  |  |  |  |  |  |
|---|---|---|---|---|---|---|
| 4 | 3 | 2 - Capt |  |  |  | **Oregon** |
| Taylor | Walker | Clarke |  |  |  |  |
| RH | FB | LH |  |  |  |  |
|  | 1 |  |  |  |  |  |
|  | LaTourette |  |  |  |  |  |
|  | QB |  |  |  |  |  |

| 6 | 8 | 10 | 0 | 9 | 7 | 5 |
|---|---|---|---|---|---|---|
| Hickson | Main | Giles | Mitchell | Bailey | Pinkham | Michael |
| RE | RT | RG | C | LG | LT | LE |

| 21 | 15 | 12 | 11 | 18 | 14 | 19 |
|---|---|---|---|---|---|---|
| W.Grimm | H. Grimm | Griffiths | Tegtmeier | May | Eakins | Mattson |
| LE | LT | LG | C | RG | RT | 19 |

|  |  |  |
|---|---|---|
|  | 16 |  |
|  | Coyle |  |
|  | Q |  |

|  |  |  |  |
|---|---|---|---|
| 17 | 22 | 20 - Capt | **Washington** |
| Taylor | Baker | Mucklestone |  |
| LH | FB | RH |  |

| Oregon Average Weight . . . . . . . . . | Team . . . 179 | Line . . . 184 | Backs . . . 172 |
|---|---|---|---|
| Washington Average Weight . . . . . . | Team . . . 176 | Line . . . 185 | Backs . . . 161 |

Oregon subs as given in program: Kellogg, Storie, McKinley, Dodson, Kiltz

Washington subs as given in program: Cook, Deither, Sparger, Beck, Swarva, Pullen, Hawley, Wand, Ohn

If there was anyone left who gave any credence to the *Seattle Times* article of the previous week that the students had deserted Dobie, a giant rally on Tuesday just before the Thanksgiving Classic put all such talk to rest. The student body presented a gold watch to the coach in appreciation of his work, and as he approached the stage to receive the gift, the crowd rose to their feet and for several minutes gave him a thunderous ovation, not allowing him to speak. When they finally quieted down, he surprised everyone and even treated them to a (somewhat) positive statement that "if the luck breaks even, we will win." It doesn't sound like much, but the tall Scot was obviously softened up by the showering of gratitude he was given. But the students weren't through yet. The women, whose loyalty to football was often questioned, raised the money within their ranks to buy a gold engraved pin displaying each player's initials and the year. This brought out another roof-rattling ovation as the students made sure the team knew they were appreciated along with their coach.

On the eve of the game, the *Times* was taking a positive direction after its fleeting attempt to stir up controversy. For game week, its reporters sought out both teams' coaches and captains for their slant on the game. The captains were predicting wins for each of their crews, but the coaches were decidedly reserved. Coach Robert Forbes brought his impressive All-American Yale credentials to the contest but was guarded in assessing his chances. He declared, "If we lose, it will not be because we lack the fighting spirit…The struggle will be a close one." Dobie couldn't let all the accolades heaped on his players go to their heads, so he decided to come out with one of his textbook quotes. "If Washington wins it will be the greatest victory in its history…The team is in pretty good condition although the feeling of overconfidence has not yet left them." Not yet, as he says, but the team can rest assured Doble will be doing everything he can to make sure the "feeling" that has him so worried exits their collective psyche well short of kickoff.

It's not known whether the *Times* was trying to go out of its way to make amends for straying off the ranch with its catty article the previous week or if its lead in the paper's game wrap-up was just a bit of hometown boosterism. The editor was overly generous in devoting three large early paragraphs to a conflict between the two teams' official timers that ended in a decision to take a TD off the scoreboard for Washington. Considering the final outcome of the game, and having no way to determine which timer was correct, we are left to wonder if this was an unspoken makeup to Dobie for the prior week's attacks.

Once the *Times* had dispensed with the silliness of the disputed touchdown, the real story came out. "Washington used the powerful right leg of Max Eakins and the best forward passing ever put on display on this coast, to win the biggest game of the year, and the combination was a winner." The passing game that Dobie developed was a far cry from the drop-back technique of the modern game. His style in this game was designed to confuse and place the defense into a guessing game as to just who would be passing the ball. Today a halfback pass is a rarity, pulled out most often in desperate situations. Not so in the schemes that thrilled the crowds in the 1909 Thanksgiving contest. On their second touchdown, the Varsity's coach, known famously for an up-the-middle power game, pulled some razzle-dazzle that caught the Oregon team totally off guard: a triple pass play, where the ball was passed by means of a lateral from quarterback Coyle to halfback Taylor to halfback Mucklestone, who then threw it downfield to Warren Grimm, who ran it in for the touchdown. So much for the apocryphal tales that Dobie claimed the forward pass wasn't real football!

As a repeat of the previous year's Oregon game, line bucks weren't working for either team, even though this year they weren't playing under the infamous sawdust handicap. Again both coaches resorted to the punting game, with the league's two stars, Maxwell Eakins and Dudley Clarke, battling it out with their toes. In 1908, game stats showed that the Washington man won this competition, and for 1909 repeated the task. Eakins outkicked the highly touted Clarke, gaining advantageous field position. Eakins got a lucky break in the first half with the wind at his back, with several kicks traveling 70 yards. He faced off across the line with one of the West Coast's strongest tackles in Louis Pinkham, who came out on the short end of this duel. Time-out was called several times for Oregon trainer Bill Hayward to work out soreness inflicted on his players from the tough hand-to-hand combat of these warriors. Comparing the scars of battle, a reporter observed that after the game, Eakins raced from the field appearing robust, but Pinkham was bloodied about the face and was in a hunched-over position as he lumbered slowly to the locker room. Sportswriter E. R. Hughes ranked Max Eakins above Dan Pullen, the great Washington tackle who lettered in 1903-04-05 and, after transferring to West Point, was named a WCF All-American. Pullen was largely a powerhouse strength player, while Eakins doubled as both strong interior lineman and exceptionally gifted kicker. In his year-end overview of the season, Coach Dobie made this flat-out declaration, underscoring it with uncharacteristic emphasis: "And put this down for me: Max Eakins is the best football player in the Northwest."

For all appearances, it looked to the shocked home crowd that Oregon would draw first blood. The usually reliable Wee Coyle fumbled a Clarke punt with Oregon's Kiltz running at full speed on an open field, attempting to scoop an errantly bouncing ball but was unable to get it contained. Fortunately, Washington's speedy halfback, Leonard Taylor, with a headlong dive as if sliding into second base, grabbed the ball. It was moves like this that earned him the well-deserved nickname "Scrappy." With nothing ahead of him but the goal, Kiltz had a definite five points were he able to match Taylor's athleticism. Following this close escape, the first score fell to Washington at eight and one-half minutes, with Captain Mucklestone plunging across the line. Today's description for the extra point wasn't in usage; it was called the "kicking goal," with Wee Coyle serving up the honor.

It was at the midway point of the first half (in 1909 the game was still two thirty-five-minute halves; quarters wouldn't come until next year) that Oregon would have the distinction of being the only team in the league to post a touchdown on the board since Dobie came to Seattle. At this point with the ball first and goal, center Pete Tegtmeier in his last game for UW, fought off opposing center Kellogg twice bringing down the ball carrier. On the final try,

Latourette on a pass play finding all of his men covered took a long route to the corner of the field for the score. With the kicked goal, this tied the score at six apiece. Out of an abundance of concern to fully report what he observed, or in a gesture of hometown outreach, the *Times* in reporting the play, said that Latourette "would have been stopped had not an Oregon man held Coyle in a loving grasp." According to this Washington-friendly witness, the referees didn't see the penalty (if indeed there was one.) This would be the lone touchdown scored against Washington for all of 1909 and broke the opponents' scoreless streak going back to last year's Oregon game.

With the situation exactly reversed, Washington soon found itself on Oregon's 5-yard line with three downs to score. The southerners stood strong and with three line bucks straight up the middle could not shove the pigskin across the goal line. On their possession, Captain Clarke punted very short from behind the goal and Coyle brought it back to the ten. Making up for his weak kick Clarke intercepted a Coyle pass. The game in seeming gridlock, Clarke kicked again from behind goal, with Washington again unable to score. Eakins moved into the backfield and attempted a failed pass. It must have seemed to the large crowd that this could go on forever, as Clarke immediately kicked the ball out of danger. The ball fell in the middle of several players, with Warren Grimm jumping high above the mass and coming down with the prize.

Sophomore end Warren Grimm was the undisputed star of the game. He seemed to have transferred his flair for handling the ball in baseball to receiving passes in football. Rather than the safer and more conventional means of grasping a pass into his arms and drawing it next to his body he had the hand-eye coordination to catch the oval baseball style, pulling it out of the air above his body. It was on this possession that Washington totally confounded Oregon, with Warren Grimm going in for the touchdown off the triple pass. Coyle missed the point after, possibly because he was groggy most of the opening half from being kicked in the head. The *Argus* reported that at one point he said to Leonard Taylor, "Get that ball, I can't see it." He did recover his senses late in the half as time was running out. Coyle made what was described as a beautiful dropkick, bringing the scoring to 14-6 in favor of the home team.

In the second half, Coach Forbes was freely substituting with the intention of wearing Washington down, but instead Dobie's well-conditioned players only seemed to grow stronger. This is particularly impressive considering that there were no substitutions made by the locals. Every starter for Washington played the full seventy minutes of the game. Oregon used six substitutes.

Washington's strategy shifted to a conservative kicking game in the second half, with Eakins twice attempting what were termed "place kicks" (field goals today), missing both. Coyle also tried another dropkick for a score, but this also was unsuccessful. Oregon continued its kicking strategy with the sure-footed Clarke often punting on first down. Coyle was having an uncharacteristically bad day on punt receptions, so the Oregon hope was to gain much better field possession on recovered fumbles. This effort did not pan out. Eakins was also kicking effectively for Washington and gave his team the edge in field possession.

All of this emphasis on kicking may have lulled Oregon into a false sense of confidence, as field general Coyle called for the triple pass a second time. With Oregon substituting players, this also provided a chance to pull this razzle-dazzle against players who hadn't defended it earlier—the same backfield criss-cross of Coyle to Taylor to Mucklestone standing well back of the line, then muscling the ball downfield on a perfect strike to Warren Grimm on the run. With his brother, Polly, trailing the play, the younger Grimm had to block out three defenders on his race to the score. Coyle made a successful kick for the extra point to complete the day's scoring at 20-6. With the game still in reach, Oregon hadn't given up and continued a strong effort but was not able to threaten Washington's goal for the rest of the game. This convincingly wrapped up the Varsity's defense of the league championship before the largest crowd to ever witness a football game in the Northwest, with seven thousand in attendance. In looking back on the year, Dobie summed up why his team came out on top once again: "We won because we had players who were good in every department." A modest assessment, but most certainly accurate.

There was one overarching matter still outstanding as the season drew to its triumphant close: the issue of Coach Dobie's job status. It was less than a month before that the *Seattle Times* broke the news that Dobie had quit. In the article, it was reported that "Coach Dobie gives it out positively that under no circumstances will he coach the Washington team next year." The article referenced a "reliable source" saying that he could take his pick of coaching jobs at either Wisconsin or Minnesota. Intent on turning the story into something that Dobie wasn't really saying, later events proved the *Times* to be off base. What Dobie actually said at the time was that he was burned out on coaching and wanted to go into business. The other misdirected angle of the story tried to advance the theory that somehow Dobie had no base of support at the school from either faculty or students.

At season's end, the *Times* was making a complete about-face as to where matters stood. Now the headline blared: "Washington Students Banking On Dobie." The article listed no less than ten reasons for his return: (1) Great influence has been brought upon him, making it the hardest thing he has ever done to refuse the job; (2) Manager Zednick's very good hunch. (3) Practically all of the football stars at the year-end banquet hailed him as the greatest coach in the United States. (4) This unstinted praise was seconded by alumni representatives on the Board of Control. (5) The Student Body president, Edward Brown, members of the faculty, and Postmaster George Russell (of last year's peanut-throwing incident) offered that all opposition to Dobie and his methods had been swept away by the triumphant season. (6) Intimately acquainted friends of Dobie's were of the opinion that he wouldn't leave and would make his announcement after visiting his relatives in Berkeley. (7) He told a friend that if he wasn't going to return, he would sell his overcoat. He still had the overcoat. (8) He was given a tip on a good high school recruit by a student, with Dobie showing deep interest in following up on the lead. (9) The tentative game schedules and arrangements for the new squad for next year had been drawn up with Dobie's involvement and approval. (10) The 1910 team would enjoy the return of nearly all of its players, only losing Fred Tegtmeier and Charlie May to graduation. This can be viewed as a mass stampede for the bandwagon, but hometown crowds have always exalted their winners—warts and all.

It was at a farewell smoker the night of December 16, 1909, that Dobie made it final: he would return to coach another year. All assembled could breathe a sigh of relief. The *Times*, not able to scoop the story via an advance tip precluded by their attempted trashing of him the month before, was there to report on the scene. "Dobie's announcement coming definitely and authoritatively from himself, caused the greatest enthusiasm among the players, and every one present believed that Washington's chances for a third victorious season have been brightened fourfold by the announcement." The news was met with great jubilation on campus now that the issue, after the long travail and uncertainty, was finally put aside. To make sure history recorded that those attending were well cared for, it should be noted that, "Smokes, sweet cider, and refreshments were served to the guests."

The *Washington Alumnus*, which in actuality held an editorial opinion in favor of student coaches, made no bones about its approval of Doble as the right professional, despite its opposition to professional coaches:

"The prayers of the righteous prevaileth and Washington has a championship football team. It is a team, a fighting machine, and a thing of beauty to see in action. Whatever else may be said, no one disputes the fact that Washington has a team, which, to use that pregnant Americanism, can deliver the goods.

"One man has made the team what it is, and that man is Gilmour Dobie. Handicapped in the beginning by lack of material, badgered by men who should have been his assistants, hampered by self-appointed advisers and sideline coaches, and embarrassed by a press which found his practice rules too exacting, the unassuming man from Minnesota has said not a word but has sawed several cords of knotty wood. He has faults; he uses expletives when someone rolls the log; he declines to sit in the grandstand and read from a Book of Common Prayer while his team is fighting for an inch of territory; and last and greatest crime of all, he refuses absolutely to assimilate that gratuitous advice on making a football team which floats so unconcernedly over our beautiful campus.

"Coach Dobie should be retained, not for one, but for two or three years."

Many theories can be advanced as to just why such a melodrama occurred in the first place. Dobie could have felt wronged; he may have believed his efforts weren't appreciated; he could have done it for effect to drum up attention for the team; he may have wanted to punish his detractors; he might have attempted this ploy to gain sympathy; he might have seized the opportunity to manipulate events; and it is also within the realm of possibility that he did intend to quit and, as the spectacle unfolded, had a change of heart. This last consideration is not given any credence by the author. Over his career Dobie's complex personality did not lend itself to ease of analysis. He could be a loner and then a gregarious friend. He could appear bitter towards those he deemed unsupportive and unappreciative of those who supported him. He could as easily show indifference for good work as disdain for bad work. He was hardly ever satisfied with a win; no matter how convincing, it could have been better. He was ferociously loyal to those on his side and combative towards those not aligned with him. He was meticulous and exacting to a fault. To those who sang his praises, such attention to detail was hailed as a great personal asset.

He elevated his players to higher achievement by all sorts of psychological skills at which he was the master. This trait came naturally to Dobie and just about always garnered such impressive results that when needed, he never hesitated to call on it. It was with great ceremony that he announced he was quitting football and then abruptly altered course. The man dedicated his life to football and devoted the next twenty-nine years to coaching the sport. Since he was so effective in maneuvering his players one-on-one, he used the same tactics when going up against a larger audience. The *Times* was on his back and assessing how he often overreacted when under fire by using some means of shock treatment, here was the perfect opportunity to announce he was leaving Washington. If this was his line of defense, it worked. Everyone soon rallied to his cause, and even the *Times*, when it saw the tide of public opinion shifting against the paper, was quick to sing his praises. In the end Dobie accomplished his objective; the king was now back on his throne.

# CHAPTER FOUR

## *Redemption—1910*

> "In building up a football team the first attention must be given to the fundamentals of the game. Without a thorough knowledge of these no team, no matter how brilliant potentially, can be successful. For the same reason, the success of a team, week in, week out, depends to a very great measure on its complete mastery of fundamentals. In fact, any play is merely the performance of fundamentals by eleven men working in perfect unity."
>
> *Gilmour Dobie*

The highway to acceptance was now wide open to Dobie. He had gone through the public spectacle of being called out for his uncompromising behavior, and here, two years later, he was still left standing. Not just with a routine contract extension; he ended the year with an outpouring of forgiveness. His contract for 1908 had been renewed with a whopping 50 percent increase in salary, and for 1909 he received a boost of another 39 percent, bringing his pay to $2,500 for this year. It appeared to his fan base that he had now turned the corner and understood that civility was not just an option. He had won two consecutive championships and, not by default, he had yet to lose a game. With this record in the books, everything was set for the coach to assume his station at the top of the Northwest sporting world. But to get there, he would also be judged by the standards of the real world. For Dobie, the latter was the greater challenge.

Despite his widespread public acclaim, there was nevertheless a deep hole that Dobie had dug for himself. Since his abrupt manner and sometimes caustic behavior were difficult to understand, many detractors held a wait-and-see attitude. In this writing, we dig more deeply into the man, his motivations, and the events that shaped his behavior. We do present a clearer picture of his sometimes confounding but most certainly complex makeup. Human nature does grant wide latitude to a winner, and the tall Scot most definitely had this going for him. As rough a game as football is, the coach is also rewarded for being tough—up to a point. This is the fine line that Dobie had to walk. His players were the first to admit they hated his practices but loved the results. Dobie's fans ran the gamut from cautious followers to wild-eyed boosters. His detractors were outspoken in their criticism, primarily because Dobie's personality was a bundle of behaviors very rarely, if ever, encompassed within one human being. There were so very many facets to his conduct that it is understandable why so many could find fault one day but admiration the next.

Dobie was paid more than the average professor, so this raised eyebrows at a time of theoretical amateurism in college athletics. Sports reporters did need a story other than "Dobie Wins Again," so exposing any on- or off-the-field peccadilloes would guarantee above-the-fold banner headlines. Then there were those who just flatly did not accept crude behavior and felt this set a bad example for impressionable youth. So no matter if Dobie's methods of running the team were just personal quirks, a perverse way of showing his good intentions, or derived from some base motive—he must change his ways. The harsh judgment of the spotlight was unavoidable. It is not overstating the case to say that the future was in his hands.

College football's wide popularity which only accelerated year by year, placed even more attention on the team and its leadership. Along with increased interest in the game came a public outcry to create more humane conditions for the athletes. The "Flying Wedge" and interlocking of arms on defense were a thing of the past, but the more open passing game to follow was still in its infancy. To his credit, Dobie embraced this trend towards lessening the brutality and placing more emphasis on skill, strategy and athleticism.

Football in 1910 took a giant step in its evolution towards the modern game. A new set of rules—called radical by some, essential by others, and instilling doubt in all—was enacted. The primary goal was to open up play and reduce the tragic number of injuries suffered because of the emphasis on brute force in the old game. The new rules were designed to promote more creative plays, liberalize passing rules and reward resourcefulness. They were aptly described as a transition away from a focus on beef and brawn to one of cleverness and speed. In 1900, by outlawing the Flying Wedge, the number of men that could mass on the line was limited, but it was only in 1906 that the forward pass was made legal. It was President Roosevelt's threat in 1905 that he would bring down the full weight of federal regulation on the game unless it was made safer that forced the effort to address the issue of player safety.

These were the significant rules placed into effect that year:

1. Players removed from the game except for disqualification could return at the beginning of the subsequent period. This was allowed only once during the contest. Previously when a player

was removed from the game, he could not return. This meant players would stay in games to the point of exhaustion, which too often led to inevitable injury.

2. The game was now divided into four quarters of fifteen minutes. A three-minute break was allowed between quarters but to prevent coaching assistance during the game, players could not leave the field. Only trainers or medical personnel were allowed on the field. This rule would come to the forefront in 1914, leading to one of Coach Dobie's most famous quotes, still widely repeated to this day. At the fifteen-minute halftime the teams could gather off the field with the entire coaching staff as before. At the beginning of the second and fourth quarters the teams change goals. When a score is made, the side scored upon has the option of kicking off or receiving the kickoff.

3. Seven players must now remain on the line of scrimmage at the point of putting the ball in play by the center. In the earliest days of the game there was no limitation, leading to the dangerous mass rushing plays that injured so many men. The game also had evolved away from the era of line shifts. Shifting was initiated as an offensive strategy to keep the defense guessing as to how the play would progress. Tackles would line up in the backfield and then move forward at the snap. Other variations were practiced involving ends and guards. The Minnesota Shift left the guards and center on the line and the rest of the team in the backfield. At the snap, everyone shifted into his correct position. The rule in place prior to the changes of 1910 required six men up front, but when only six were on the line, one man must be outside the last man on the end, limiting his effectiveness.

4. The first man in the backfield to receive the ball from center may advance the ball across the line at any point. The prior rule required that when the quarterback received the pass from center, he must first run out 5 yards before turning up the field.

5. The flying tackle was made illegal. This dangerous maneuver had been lessened by an earlier requirement that the defensive man must have at least one foot on the ground when contacting his opponent. It was now abolished altogether, adding an even greater element of safety to the game.

6. When punting, the kicker must be in position a minimum of 5 yards behind the line of scrimmage, and the ball must be punted a minimum of 20 yards to be an "on side kick." In this reference, an on side kick is that point when the ball becomes a free ball and available to both sides. When the ball had gone beyond 20 yards, it was deemed live and available to both teams, even before the receiving team

touched it. The prior rule allowed a kicker to quickly boot the ball a short distance, causing a mad scramble for the ball and resulting in many injuries. If there was a situation where the defense suspected a quick kick, they would set well back of the line while the entire offensive line would make a mass charge against the undermanned defense, again causing undue injury.

7. The offense on a running play was now prohibited from pushing or pulling the runner. Under the old rules, a premium was placed on the heavy runner who could be given an added boost by strong teammates. The line buck usually consisted of this offshoot of the old mass play, and now this too was rendered obsolete. This was seen as greatly opening the game up and placing an emphasis on athleticism over strength. Here the rulemakers took a critical step in advancing the game to the way it is played today.

8. A forward pass can only be caught by a player on the end of the scrimmage line or at least one yard behind the line. Any player, whether he is a center, tackle, guard, or back, can receive a forward pass as long as he is one yard back of the line. The offensive captain, if he wishes, can switch either the tackle or guard into the end position, making him eligible to receive a downfield pass.

9. Only one forward pass per scrimmage is allowed. The forward pass must be made from a point 5 yards behind the line and at any point along the line; it cannot be passed for longer than 20 yards downfield, and the receiver cannot be interfered with in any way except on a bona fide attempt to catch the ball. These rules were put in place to assist the defense in spreading its manpower to more team members in defending against the pass and to reduce injuries to the receivers. It did prove successful in cutting down on injuries.

Implementation of the new rules would soon be seen to place a great advantage on more fleet-of-foot ball carriers, as referees now were required to call a penalty if team members were caught pushing or pulling the runner at any time (especially prevalent under the old rules as he rushed through the line). This emphasis on speed would lead to much more dramatic, broken-field gains as coaches caught on to the advantage of recruiting speed over brawn. Dobie was one of the early advocates of this important upgrade to the game. This also would lead to the introduction of specialists as the rules for substitution were liberalized. It was now possible for a coach to insert a talented field goal kicker into the game who was not skilled in the high-contact positions. He could be removed after the play, sit out for the remainder of the quarter, and later reenter the game.

Unlike many coaches, Dobie received these new rules with a positive attitude. The prior winter when the National Football Committee announced the changes, he was quoted as saying, "I said that the game would be the best this season it had ever been, and I still think so." The coach admitted that when he was at Minnesota, there were rule changes made at that time that opened the game, and he prophesied disaster. Once the team adjusted to the new rules he soon saw that they greatly benefited play. He was widely perceived as rigid and intractable as we have shown, but here he's beginning to display a modicum of flexibility. Does it strain credulity to believe that this is an early sign of maturity?

The *University of Washington Daily* (renamed from the *Pacific Daily Wave* that year, 1910) noted in reporting on a Men's Club smoker, perhaps unwittingly, that there was another sign of the coach's improving social skills. "The Men's Club smoker last Friday evening will go down in history as the first gathering west of the Rockies to secure a real life-size speech from Coach Gilmour Dobie. For three-quarters of an hour the great pigskin pedagogue, with his intense face alight and with quick, characteristic gestures of his lean hands, held a crowd of students in absolute attention, while pipes and cigars went out as they listened to his revelations of the new rules." Never one to play up his chances for the upcoming season, Dobie right on cue was somber in announcing that Washington didn't have the team this year that it had last year. But for once he did exhibit the personality in public that close friends said he displayed in private with this remark: "Cheer up, neither will the other colleges."

### Preseason

The preparation leading up to the first preseason contest with Lincoln HS wasn't going as well as could be hoped. Practice was inhibited by unseasonably heavy fall rains. There were only four good days of practice in the first three weeks. Considering the significant rule changes that had to be learned, preseason practice was all the more important that year. The 1908 captain and halfback Melville Mucklestone was suffering from knee problems that forced him off the team. Wee Coyle was irregular at practice with a case of walking typhoid, and fullback Tracy Baker, who at first had an eligibility problem to straighten out, got that cleared up but then decided not to play because of his class schedule conflicting with practice. The loss of two experienced backfield men who definitely were the type of athletes whose running style was adaptable to the new rules was a serious blow to the team. When it appeared that Coyle's health was back up to par, he still wasn't making practice to the coach's satisfaction. As Dobie would often do to straighten out such a situation, he relegated Coyle to second string in practice to assure that he didn't get too full of himself. The coach hadn't gotten over his deep-seated fear of his star players believing their own press clippings.

The first game was played on a muddy field with light rain falling through-out. The game did accomplish just what a preseason game is supposed to do: provide an assessment of team preparation. The game showed that the team overall was doing better than anticipated considering that seven regulars from last year were lost to the team (Tracy Baker, fullback; Louis Diether, fullback; Bill Mattson, end; Charles May, guard; Melville Mucklestone, halfback nonpareil; Leonard Taylor, halfback; and Fred Tegtmeier, center extraordinaire). The miserable field conditions didn't provide an opportunity to gauge just how the new rules would affect play, as the passing and on side kicking attempts were severely compromised. One advantage of the new rule allowing liberal substitutions permitted twenty Washington players to see action. The brightest performance came from that "second stringer" Wee Coyle, who did his customarily outstanding job as field general. Third-year man Bill Cook at left halfback, starting for the first time, was described as a scintillating runner; Polly Grimm anchored the line in supreme fashion; and, despite poor footing, Max Eakins picked up where he left off the year before in the punting department. The scoring was all the Varsity's, with a touchdown by Bill Cook, a score by a pass reception by Warren Grimm, a dropkick for three points by Wee Coyle, and second-year man but first-time starter right halfback Roscoe Pike scoring a touchdown by way of the run. Coyle made two of his three kicks for the point after, bringing the final score to Washington over Lincoln 20-0.

The next game, set for October 15, had originally been scheduled with Whitworth College, but on October 3 the Presbyterians notified Manager Zednick they would have to cancel because there hadn't been enough men turning out to field a competitive team. A replacement game was scheduled with the University of Puget Sound (newly named the Loggers that year) to be played in Tacoma. The field at UPS was primitive to the extreme, with mud holes and not just gravel but large rocks and debris scattered about. When a player set his foot down, he could never be sure if he would be so fortunate as to remain upright or twist an ankle. Field obstacles posed as much of a hazard as did the opposition. While the game was played on a sea of mud holes, the storm had passed and by game day it was hot and sunny.

All told, the Varsity scored nine touchdowns and kicked six of their extra point tries in this lopsided game. Fred Sparger, as a second-year letterman, scored twice in the first quarter to get the game off on a strong note. At the outset the ball carriers were cautious due to the constant guessing game of what was underfoot, but after staking out the worst areas to avoid were able to adjust and put on an impressive showing. The game, being so one-sided, allowed Dobie to assess how well his backs could do on line plunges under the new rules prohibiting assisting the runner by pushing and pulling. He came away convinced that his team had adjusted to the new restraints. The final score: Washington 51, University of Puget Sound 0.

## Whitman College

Dobie's attitude towards the year's first conference game depended on who you were talking to. To one reporter he was sure his boys would put up a strong fight but couldn't predict the outcome. To another he was unmistakably clear that Washington was in for one good drubbing. Whitman, while never posing too great a threat, did bring a more experienced team to Seattle that year. Washington, returning only four regular starters due to graduation and fallout, added to the uncertainty. Going back the previous ten years, Washington held the edge with six wins, three losses, and one tie. Coach McCaa of Whitman, as if following Dobie's lead, said he couldn't predict the outcome but his men had a fighting chance.

This marked the seventeenth game for Dobie at Washington and by all appearances was the toughest one his teams had faced. A pair of fumbles, one each coming at the expense of Polly Grimm and Max Eakins in the first quarter, resulted in a dropkick and a touchdown to put Whitman in an early lead, 8-0. Washington coughed up the ball on its very first possession. Fans, unaccustomed to such stress, got into the game, sensing the threat that Dobie's streak could very well come to an end. Allen M. Lacey, sitting in the stands, reported that the coach famous for total focus on the field during his games turned to the crowd, gestured, and said, "Never mind boys, Washington hasn't lost yet!" Summing up the crowd's mind-set, Lacey observed, "The loyal Washingtonians were not frightened, they were only scared to death."

In the second quarter Washington's defense tightened up, and the offense put an end to gifting field position to Whitman via the fumble. The Varsity's first score came off a slickly executed pass play from Coyle to Warren Grimm that was judged by the referees to be inches over the line. With the successful point-after kick, this brought the score to Whitman 8, Washington 6, which held until halftime.

There are two consistent accounts of how, at halftime, Coach Dobie handled the dire situation in which the team found itself. Allen Lacey, writing in the *Washington Alumnus* in 1910, and Wee Coyle, writing forty years later in the *Seattle Times*, had remarkably similar takes on how the team mentor reacted. From Lacey's account of what he observed in the locker room: "Coach Dobie was that day as one transformed; he spoke to us encouragingly; he met his men between the halves calmly, without the torrent of words that marks a coach's railing. He said, 'Boys, I think you can go out and lick them so do it!' The effect was electric." From Wee Coyle's recollection in 1949 of Dobie's demeanor: "Dobie was more nervous than any of us and between halves showed for the first time his true spirit as a man. He appreciated our position, and instead of going after us in his old rough-and-ready style, he was very considerate of every man. I'll always remember that of old Dobie. He was truly afraid of the outcome of the game and didn't want to make it appear that he would jump on us when we were down."

In the third quarter. Eakins missed a 37-yard field goal attempt that would have placed his struggling team up by one point. Whitman singled out Warren Grimm to shadow when Washington had the ball, and other than his one whisker-thin score, he was effectively taken out of the game. It took a play that Dobie pulled out of his bag of tricks with Warren's big brother, Captain Polly Grimm, running a 50-yard tackle around play to put Washington in position at the 4-yard line for the go-ahead touchdown. It was Whitman's left halfback and Warren's shadow that pulled Polly down. On the third and final down, Roscoe Pike, right halfback, managed to force the ball over, again by mere inches. Coach McCaa took exception to the call, even to the extent of going onto the field to lodge his objection. The call held, but he may have gotten some comfort in another close call a little later that took off the scoreboard what Washington thought was a touchdown. Coyle, in running the ball in from midfield along the sideline, appeared to the partisan crowd to have made a touchdown. Referee George Varnell noted a cleated imprint on the chalk line, deduced that this was made by the scampering quarterback, and called the run back. It should be noted that Varnell was a very experienced and highly respected referee, so the benefit of the doubt most definitely weighs in his favor.

Going into the final minute of this nerve-racker, the score stood at Washington 12, Whitman 8. The game was in doubt right down to this point, and it was only because of the most fortunate circumstance of the final bounce of a punted ball going to Washington that it was able to squeak out the win. It was a cruel twist of fortune for Whitman, and many could say a gigantic lucky break for Washington. The ball was fumbled inside of Washington's goal, and with two Whitman men in excellent position to pounce on it for the go-ahead touchdown, the Varsity's Bill Cook was swifter afoot and fell on the ball for a touchback. If Washington ever pulled victory from the jaws of defeat, the hometown crowd for the Whitman game of 1910 could not deny—this was it.

### University of Idaho

Coach "Pink" Griffiths scouted the Whitman game, witnessing Washington's nail-biter. Idaho was buoyed by their win over a heavier Washington State team, 9-5, and quarterback E. Perkins was praised as a wonder. This and other cracks in the Dobie machine must have led to an understandable hubris emanating from the Idaho camp. Word had circulated that the Varsity would be playing without Captain Polly Grimm, who had been suffering with water on the knee but, to make matters worse, it was now discovered that his brother Warren was out with a left-hand thumb fracture. Dobie's team had already shown they sorely missed the several stars from last year's squad, and this disastrous news meant they were now down to only two marquee players, Eakins and Coyle. With the line weakened to such an extent, the coach felt this could be a close game decided by a field goal, since that was one of the scores Whitman had made. He put the line through extra drills just focusing on defending against the kick.

Idaho had seven of last year's veterans making the trip. Griffiths also publicly admitted that the 50-0 drubbing from last year still rankled dedicated Idahoans, giving them added incentive to balance the books. Such an embarrassment called for his team to take advantage of this great opportunity destiny had bestowed. Manager Zednick, when in Moscow making game arrangements, was given an offer of 2-to-1 odds on the contest by an exuberant fan. He, of course, as a university official, was reported to have ever-so-politely declined.

Tom Griffiths, switching from his usual guard position, took Polly Grimm's place, and freshman Wayne Sutton, playing his first game, filled in for Warren Grimm, both turning in excellent jobs. Griffiths was described as a moose on defense and, just as his great predecessor did, made 5 to 10 yards every time the tackle-around play was called. Last year's stellar backfield of left halfback Leonard Taylor, fullback Tracy Baker, and right half Melville Mucklestone was replaced by what appeared to be the less-talented trio Rex Hosley, William Cahill, and Walter Wand. On a day rich in animal metaphors, Wand was depicted as a bear at line smashing. To the surprise of many and as a testament to Dobie's ability to get the most out of the hand he was dealt, all performed superbly as new starters. Together with quarterback and acting-Captain Wee Coyle, they delivered the strongest performances of the game.

As it turned out, the Moscow eleven had been over touted, along with the fact that Seattle having to play shorthanded was underrated. Taking advantage of the new rule liberalizing substitution, Idaho used fourteen players and Washington fifteen. It's interesting to note that Dobie substituted for both halfbacks and the fullback late in the game. This strategic move allowed him to use fresher legs in these skill positions in the later going when he brought in right half Roscoe Pike, fullback Fred Sparger, and left half William "Deacon" Cook. The Dobie machine was portrayed as being demoralizing to the "panting Moscow gladiators." This was yet another payoff of Dobie's emphasis on physical conditioning. Now being able to more easily rotate players, this gave him an even greater edge. There was much consternation over frequent interruptions to play from the "putrid work" of Umpire H.M. Hockenberry's officiating, but then, as now, the calls over the course of a game balanced out. Hockenberry was accused of "calling attention to every little infringement of gridiron etiquette."

Idaho failed to make a first down in the game. The Varsity outplayed the visitors in every department, be it offense or defense. It seemed that Washington had assembled an entirely new squad since the painful struggle just two weeks before against Whitman. The extra week's practice seemed to pay huge dividends, as the ragged play displayed in that game had vanished.

The first UW score came via a fumble of an attempted punt by Idaho's visibly excited Changnon that was pounced on by rookie Wayne Sutton, who at that point had only five total minutes of varsity experience. Coyle's extra-point kick was good. The second touchdown was set up by a 20-yard run by Coyle, a 30-yard run from Hosely, and the remaining 20 yards coming by way of Cahill for the touchdown, with Eakins blocking to clear his path. He crossed the goal line very near the corner of the field. In that day the game was played with no hash marks to establish the placement of the ball as are used today. Modern rules dictate that a ball being downed outside the hash marks be placed on the hash marks, which, in college ball, are sixty feet in from the sideline. A touchdown scored in the Dobie era near the sideline meant that the extra point try was placed where the ball went over the goal line, requiring that the kick be attempted from a severe angle. Here a variation of the on side rule came into play, allowing a punt to be kicked to a teammate who could receive the ball farther into the field of play, allowing for a straighter shot at the extra point. This was done, in this case, with Eakins punting out to Wand. Coyle then kicked the extra point.

Washington was not without mistakes, as Walter Wand fumbled after a long run and Sutton did likewise after receiving a pass from Eakins, turning the ball over after picking up 24 yards. The third touchdown was placed into reach with Coyle recovering the ball via the on side rule on a Washington punt. He then faked a pass, pulling the defense in one direction to follow the receivers while Coyle dashed the other direction for the touchdown. With another Eakins' kick-out to better align Coyle's extra-point attempt, the quarterback was again successful. The fourth score for the home team saw an exchange of intercepted passes, first by Idaho getting the ball and then Washington turning the trick. The third pass from Eakins to Sutton ended this game of giveaway. Coyle, sensing a weakness in the Idaho line between left end Hillman and left tackle Favre, called for two runs through this soft spot, placing the ball on the 4-inch line. He next gave the ball to fullback Bill Cahill, who forced the oval through left guard and tackle for the score, with Coyle adding the extra point. The final score was a gift from Captain Thornton, Idaho's punter and left halfback. He scuffed the kick into his own linemen, with Coyle recovering the ball and racing around left end for 15 yards. He was tackled in the corner of the field just one yard short of the goal. Wand took the ball over for the short run for the fifth touchdown. Coyle's only missed extra-point kick came on this final try, bringing this surprisingly one-sided game to a close with a score of Washington 29, Idaho 0.

### Washington State at Spokane

The prior year's game against Washington State never happened due to Washington's claims that Pullman was playing ringers and wasn't enforcing conference student-athlete eligibility rules. Dobie must have been making a concerted effort to put the issue to rest with this olive branch he gave at a huge rally just three days before the 1910 game: "I want to give Pullman credit this year for putting a clean team into the field." He wasn't foretelling any terribly dire outcomes for his boys but also wasn't looking ahead to any kind of win. WSU made it real tough for him to be all that gloomy, as he grasped at straws to justify any faint chance that the Purple and Gold might lose. Since the easterners had lost to both Oregon State and Idaho, he was hardly able to mount an argument that disaster lay ahead. But since he was ever vigilant in planting even a faint strain of doubt in his player's minds, he rationalized those losses as luck not falling State's way.

Well before technology had caught up with fans' desire for instantaneous sports coverage straight from the playing field, the *Daily* sent a reporter to the game in an early attempt to satisfy this craving. The paper hooked up a telephone connection in the grandstand for its sports editor, Archie M. Major, to a telegraph office where, via United Press, it was sent directly to the *Daily* in Seattle. There presses had been set up to publish a special edition giving a full play-by-play account as soon as possible after the game. The student paper succeeded famously and scooped the major Seattle dailies by having its full issue covering the game on the street within twenty-two minutes of the final whistle. The front page featured a dramatic oversized image of Maxwell Eakins in full punting mode with a banner headline in two-inch, heavy bold type. On this day Dobie mania had reached its zenith. Looking back, one can only reflect on how this state-of-the-art communication link, despite all of the complex logistics, would have fallen flat had the team not delivered a win.

Both teams and their fans were away from their home bases because the game was played in Spokane. With two visiting clubs in town, the pregame revelry was notched up considerably as both schools held parades and rallies around town. Because of the natural rivalry of these cross-state teams, pre-game interest was electric. The contest was played on a beautiful, crisp, fall day with Washington State fans clinging to muted hopes their team could be the one to knock off the mighty Dobie squad. Three reasons for this wishful thinking (however restrained) were Coach Osthoff's remarkable success in utilizing the forward pass, the weight advantage his players had over the Purple and Gold, and the expected absence of the Grimm brothers. The pass was executed very well by Washington State, but through the air they were never able to put the ball downfield far enough to reach scoring range. Rules did not permit scoring via a pass when the ball was caught beyond the goal line. Further diminishing State's chances, Polly Grimm was able to suit up and play. As was his oft-used strategy, Dobie didn't give any advance notice of his lineup so no one was aware of this prior to game time. Dobie, in rarely exposing his hand, did everything he could to avoid giving the opposition any advantage. While it never rained during the game, a storm from earlier in the week left the field soggy, and playing conditions grew muddy and slippery as the game progressed.

The game turned out to be the most savagely fought contest of the season for both teams. In the first few minutes of play, time had to be called because of injuries. The officials weren't going to let the game turn into a brawl and didn't hold back on flagging both squads for unnecessary roughness. At one point Coyle shouted out to yell king Jack Todd for three "rahs" for dirty play. Washington took it to the men of the Palouse from the get-go. Right after the first exchange of punts, a pass from quarterback Coyle to right end Peter Husby struck pay dirt, and with the QB's extra-point kick, the Varsity had six points at the seven-minute mark. Very shortly after that, fullback Bill Cahill intercepted a pass from WSU's right halfback, Foran, and made a brilliant 65-yard run, racking up the second TD of the quarter. With the ball at a sharp angle, Washington tried a kickout that was missed, foiling the chance for the extra point. This turnabout couldn't have come at a worse time for Washington State, because they had recovered quickly from the first scoring drive and were now moving the ball well. The second score coming as it did, with Cahill's backbreaking run happening so quickly, seemed to strike right at the heart of State's resolve.

The third touchdown was set up by a strategic mistake by State in the second quarter, allowing great field position for Coyle to begin the drive. On third down there was only a yard and a half for the Crimson and Gray's first down with the ball on their own 32, but this was over a muddy patch left over from the prior day's rain. Their attempt of a straight line buck on this treacherous footing failed, giving Dobie's men a short field to launch their assault. Sports reporter Archie M. Major, in his detailed game account, described Washington's play as "a succession of brilliant passes, alternated with terrific centripetal smashes which pierced Pullman's long line and doubled up her secondary defense and jammed the ball over the last mark again." With two well-directed passes, one of 11 yards and the other netting 19 yards, the second placed the ball on the 2-yard line. Cahill took the ball on the first down, running up the middle, and was stopped on the 6-inch line. On the second try Walter Wand shot through for the touchdown. The extra-point goal was missed, bringing the score to UW 16, WSU 0.

Rough play continued throughout the first half, with several men from both teams being carried off the field. Play was interrupted in the second quarter with what was described as a "slugging bee." Realizing how arduous game conditions were, Dobie's halftime pep talk was totally supportive and instructional. Allen Lacey reported this account in 1910 of the locker-room scene, writing in the *Washington Alumnus*: "Coach Dobie was not lashing his charges with stinging words but was quietly sizing up Pullman's offense and defense, telling them what to do and what not to do, rather than offering severe criticism for what they had done."

Just as with the start of the game, the second half began with Washington threatening to score in the first few minutes. With the ball on WSU's 8-yard line, the drive was dead-ended with an interception. Washington assumed a strategy of protecting their lead and went into a conservative mode with punts on the first or second down to preserve field position. With only three downs to work with, the punt on first and second down was widely used in such situations. Hoping to pick up yardage with their own kick with a recovered fumble, Washington State wisely matched Eakins' kicks with their own from Foran. For them this was excellent football, for if they were able to pick up a loose ball, they could get back to midfield and have a better shot at the goal line. The third quarter was a kicking duel, with each team resorting to the punt five times. After this kicking extravaganza, the total outcome for Washington's efforts was to move the ball back 2 yards farther from WSU's goal line from the 8- to the 10-yard line.

The fourth quarter was much the same kicking game, but Eakins did have a decided edge over Foran. With seven minutes to go and the ball on the 20, Coyle tried a dropkick that missed by inches. In the waning moments the ball ended up just about where matters started, back on the 10-yard line with the Varsity threatening to score. At the final whistle, with WSU showing their frustration at the inevitable loss, Galbraith, their standout right end, cajoled Coyle to pass the ball into his territory. In a weak moment, Coyle took the bait and Galbraith promptly intercepted the ball. This positive note at game's end provided some satisfaction for the easterners, as this prevented a likely Washington TD. The scoreless second half gave Washington another win in this hard fought game 16-0.

The loss wasn't received well in the WSU camp. This was the first year of the more open passing game and in the opinion of the *Evergreen*, Pullman's student newspaper, luck played a large part in the outcome. State had greatly improved in this department, and since Washington's first score came by an interception they wrote this off as a fluke. This overlooked the role of defense. Opposing coaches didn't neglect defense, but, like everything else that he did, Dobie stressed defense with his players as if nothing else mattered, just as with offensive drills. The end result was to get his players better able to play the total game. That made the difference in this crucial contest. Pullman, coming into the matchup with a vaunted passing attack, was up against a coach that always prepared his players to match strength with strength. Where he excelled was in the total level of commitment to every detail on both sides of the ball.

### Oregon State, Thanksgiving Game

This would be the last game for two of Dobie's all-time standouts at tackle, Polly Grimm and Maxwell Eakins. Both were picks on many All-Northwest teams, and Grimm was the first Washington player ever selected on the WCF All-American team, being selected that year as third-team tackle. Eakins was universally picked as the best punter in the Northwest for all three years he played. His controversial eligibility question had by now finally been resolved. Since he had played at North Dakota Agricultural College for one year under

Dobie, he and Melville Mucklestone were ruled as eligible for only three years at Washington.

Coach Dobie was enjoying a run of positive press since his rocky start in Seattle. From being publicly blasted his first year, the undefeated streak, together with civilized behavior, finally brought Seattle sportswriters to his side. Nothing like a winner to turn attitudes around. The *Post-Intelligencer,* going into the game, couldn't seem to reach high enough in its praise: "Coach Gilmour Dobie is the football genius who has turned out championships at the Varsity. Dobie has been whipping teams into shape for eight years now, and during that long period his teams have not once been defeated. Few football mentors can show such a brilliant record." As if such platitudes weren't enough, it seemed of late that local writers had taken a moratorium on the unceasing reportage of Dobie as the prophet of doom and gloom. Either they weren't able to milk such downcast predictions from the very quotable coach or Dobie was taking a sabbatical in light of his undeniable success. He even predicted a win, which must have set off gasps of disbelief around town. "Dobie and Schildmiller [OSU Coach] are close-mouthed when it comes to talking of the result, but both feel confident that their teams will be returned the winner." Making sure to not be accused of happy talk, Dobie earlier had said that if UW were somehow to win the Thanksgiving game, it would be psychologically impossible for them to win next year. He concluded that to get the fighting edge, the team, faculty, and fans had to "get up against it," and they definitely didn't have it now as they took winning for granted.

Both teams had developed highly effective passing attacks, and the weight comparison was pretty much equal. The weather would prove to be clear and dry, with just enough chill in the air for ideal football conditions, particularly for an aerial game. Washington had more highly regarded athletes and had home field advantage, which counted for a lot in these days of train travel. But with the championship target on their back, Washington knew every team in the Northwest was itching to be the one to finally knock them off. As recently as 1906, Oregon State was the pride of Northwest football. Both the team and fans were well aware that their return to prominence ran through Denny Field.

Despite the seeming prospects for a competitive game, this was not to be. Pregame predictions on the effectiveness of Dobie's passing game would be proven out, as this component of the Varsity's arsenal was overpowering. The *P-I's* lead-in to coverage of the passing attack was headed, "Forward Pass Is a Wonder." The article illustrated just how varied and creatively it was employed under what was termed Coyle's Napoleon-like generalship. "Dobie has developed this play with all possible variations, in all its intricacies. Sometimes the tackle throws the ball, sometimes a punter, Max Eakins sometimes, the quarterback, end or tackle [sic; most likely the reporter meant halfback.] But always they know where to toss it and who is to receive it. For three years this has been the best thing in the Coyle repertoire. College scouts have watched it work, have gone home, told how dangerous it was and defense built to break it up. Yet Dobie's men have always got away with it. The forward pass works because it is used at the psychological moment."

Analyzing the games of 1910, it was clear that under the new rules revolutionizing the game via the pass, Dobie had made a much better adjustment to its usage than his competitors. More teams were making use of the pass, but Dobie's brand of coaching by micromanagement and a fervent emphasis on preparation, clearly enabled him to better prepare his players for this new brand of football.

The leather helmets of the early 1900s opened up an opportunity for creative play calling which Dobie instituted that year and which, next year, would bring national attention to the team. Early in the first quarter, with the team advancing to the goal through a mix of passing and running, Coyle tucked his helmet under his arm and headed for the right end, drawing Oregon State after him. The ball actually was in the hands of Polly Grimm, who picked up a first down on a 4-yard run, placing the ball 6 yards short of the goal. Fullback Bill Cahill picked up 3 yards, and from there right halfback Walter Wand carried the ball over for the initial touchdown. With Coyle's kick, this put Washington up, 6-0.

The visitors must have sensed that with Polly Grimm's recent injury, they could wear him down as they repeatedly ran the ball at him and Eakins. This proved futile. However, Washington's running game showed much more imagination and was just as effective as the passing attack. Right halfback Rex Hosely, together with Walter Wand, Cahill, and Coyle, were virtually unstoppable. The crowd was dazzled with a series of seven running plays by the backfield, including five consecutive first downs placing the ball on the 4-yard line. Reversing the ball carrier sequence for this scoring attempt, Wand took the first call, with Cahill picking up the second touchdown with a hard-fought plunge fighting for the last yard to get the ball across the goal line. Coyle missed the kick, bringing the score to 11-0 for Washington.

The Coyle headgear fake worked so well the first time, he called it again early in the second half, with Polly Grimm plunging up the middle for 15 yards. After an exchange of downs Oregon State's defense stiffened, forcing a punt by Eakins. The ball was fumbled by the receiver, with Captain Polly Grimm picking up his second fumble recovery for the day. With the team in excellent scoring position on the 5, Coyle dropped a quick pass into Husby's arms for the third touchdown. With the ball out of alignment for a point-after attempt Eakins punted out to the middle of the field. Coyle was successful, bringing the score to 17-0.

Though on the short end of a three-touchdown margin, Oregon State did have some fight left in the fourth quarter. The Black and Orange were putting up a strong defense but still weren't able to mount a consistent offense. With neither team moving the ball effectively, the game by now had deteriorated into a punting duel. Since Warren Grimm had missed game time with his injured hand, he was short five minutes of playing time to qualify for his letter. Towards the end of the game, with a three-touchdown lead, it looked like it was safe to put him in for this short span. However, we have one of the tough-as-nails Grimm brothers here. Not one of the three (there's also young brother Bill in line for the team for 1915) ever slacked off on any play. The cheers greeting him as he entered the field had hardly died down when, favoring his injured hand, instead of tackling Captain Hastings with his arms on a punt reception he plunged into him, dislodging the ball. Pete Husby jumped on the pigskin for the recovery, but Grimm couldn't get back on his feet and had to be assisted off the field. Freshman Warren Harvey replaced him.

Considering Harvey's fresh legs, Coyle shot the young recruit a quick pass that he caught and then fumbled, but Washington recovered on the 2-yard line. Walter Wand drove up the middle for the final touchdown, with Coyle missing the point after. The final score for their third consecutive championship was another shutout: Washington 22, Oregon State 0.

With the playing field flooded with joyful fans looking to foist Dobie on their shoulders, all he had on his mind was to look after his soldier wounded in battle, Warren Grimm. The doctor diagnosed this second injury as a badly wrenched hip. After the game it was also discovered that at some point during the action, brother Polly had broken his nose in this last game of his great career. The Grimm brothers' reputation for all-out play was well deserved, as so abundantly evidenced this last time the two of them suited up together.

Illustrating just how important punting was in the three-down era, Eakins had 14 boots for 542 yards to OSU's Keck, who also kicked 14 times, totaling 473 yards. Washington thoroughly dominated every category of play: first downs, UW 18, OSU 4; total yardage running, UW 348, OSU 102; passing, UW 4 for 10, OSU 2 for 5.

Fans of every stripe who followed Washington football were solidly behind extending Dobie's contract in this, his third winning year. There was a clear effort under way to build up Dobie's standing in hopes of putting aside the bad blood growing out of his first year's immature antics. His pattern of behavior had shown improvement through his second year. He now seemed to be on the way to redemption, since much of the press now advanced a more positive image of this complex man. It certainly was true that he presented challenges to the cause. His bull-headed determination to do things his way would never change. The love affair localized in Seattle was often drowned out with a constant drumbeat of negative press from the competition's camp and distributed on national wire services. Nothing wrong with this process, but it attracts vastly more readership to report misbehavior than good behavior. After all, tribalism drives fan behavior.

One area in which Dobie was consistent throughout his distinguished career was placing scholarship above athletics. Because of his dust-ups with faculty from time-to-time, some have taken these battles as evidence that he dismissed the students' position in the classroom. The record reflects that this is not the case. Victor Zednick in 1910, in reflecting on Dobie, had this to say: "Dobie exerts an influence for good on every student in the university. His example is an inspiration. He tells his players scholarship is more important than football, and the year around he watches them and encourages them to study harder. Every student can learn a lesson from his attention to the most minute detail and his constant application. No matter how apparently weak his opponents, he worries that he has overlooked something and when the teams meet, you can wager Dobie has forgotten nothing."

In only three years Dobie had turned attitudes around, even in the sports writing community, which was doubtful of his longevity when he first arrived. As we have seen, this is what saved his career, considering the coach's self-inflicted troubles. Now that the lanky mentor had gone a year on his best behavior, those closest to him were feeling a bit smug. Witness the *Washington Alumnus'* take on the turn-around of the formerly dreaded downtown sports editors. "He set about to right conditions. In doing this he trampled on toes and as a result he made enemies. It was amusing to hear the sporting editors downtown vie with each other now in an effort to be 'the original Dobie man.' "

All that remained was to settle the contract issue for next season. On December 9, it took a total of four minutes' debate at the Student Board of Control to make the decision to retain Dobie on a unanimous vote. The Faculty Committee had one dissenter; Professor David Thompson voted no on the grounds that he didn't feel any educational institution should pay that amount for its football coach. The new contract was for a term of three years and boosted the head coach's salary $500 per year to $3,000 and authorized payment of a salary of $500 per year for his assistant coach. Joe Cutting had served as Dobie's assistant since 1908 and now decided to go back east. Max Eakins was tapped to take his place. In summing up the justification for giving Dobie a whopping 20 percent pay raise, the attitude was not unlike how these matters are justified today. In sport, a winner pays, and a loser has no standing. The board acted largely on this truism.

# CHAPTER FIVE

## *The Mysterious Fake Play—1911*

"The Washington quarterback used one of the most mystifying plays that has been used on Portland gridirons for many seasons, when he sent Sutton down the field for a touchdown on a fake pass, since called the "bunk" play. The play stupified the spectators and few were able to fathom the workings of the fake. The touchdown came after a delayed pass, Coyle drawing the Oregon defense after him, while Sutton carried the ball down the field with no tacklers in sight."

*Ralph Casey, Class of 1913*

A tradition born in 1911 was inspired by the three undefeated seasons Dobie had at the time. Yell King Bill Horsley had a giant ten-foot hook carved out of solid oak to symbolize the team's football supremacy. The idea evolved out of the vaudevillian practice of the time to "get the hook" out to unceremoniously pull ham actors off stage who had overstayed their welcome. There was no mistaking Horsley's intent in bringing this symbol into his rallies and marches to demonstrate what the pep squad thought would soon befall Washington's ill-fated opponent. Contrarily, the Varsity's rivals made no secret of their hostility toward the despised chunk of wood. It was particularly loathed when paraded in huge serpentines around the field at halftime.

There was only so much that opposing fans would put up with in these kinds of in-your-face gestures. Some sort of sabotage was brewing in just about every big game as Dobie's record grew to seeming invincibility. That year for the Oregon game, the hook was taken to Portland and, though flaunted through the streets before and after the game, it was returned safely to Seattle. However, this was not without a furious effort by Oregon to kidnap the patronizing symbol for use as fire wood at their next campus rally. The following year, when the team traveled to Portland, the hook was left safely back at home, but a phalanx of Varsity loyalists did capture a fake cloth hook meant to parody the real thing. This trophy and others were cremated at a pep-rally bonfire on campus to stir up passion for the Thanksgiving game with Washington State.

Since Dobie never lost, the hook never lost its effectiveness as a symbol of power until after he left Washington. The tradition was maintained as a badge of honor for several years, and for the 1919 season the "Knights of the Hook" were formed to be its official guards and custodians. The *Daily* came to describe the wooden icon as "perhaps the most sacred of Washington's emblems and the oldest of them all." At the close of each season, the scores for the year were ceremoniously notched on the hook to forever venerate each team's accomplishment. As Washington's football fortunes ebbed and flowed following Dobie's reign, the use of such a dominating symbol proved not to be as meaningful in the off years of the program. Without the consistency of a Gilmour Dobie, the hook itself eventually faded into history. However, the Knights of the Hook evolved into the Intercollegiate Knights and existed over many decades as a national service organization with chapters on many campuses across the country. Washington, as the leading charter member, identified itself, quite naturally, as "The Hook" chapter. In what may have shocked the senses of impassioned Dobieites of the time, the first national convention was held in 1924 under the sponsorship of Washington State's "The Cougar Guard" chapter. Some would deem this payback for the misery of sitting on the losing side of the field as the very inspiration for the organization was paraded/flaunted before their eyes.

### Preseason

The best personnel news coming out of the Washington camp was the return of Melville Mucklestone from his knee injury suffered in the '09 season. He slipped right back into his all-star groove, immediately displaying his strong running game. This would help bolster the backfield as Wee Coyle and Fred Sparger also returned. Boding well for the season, the line was also well stocked with returning vets. Tom Griffiths, Warren Grimm, Pete Husby, BeVan Presley, Royal "Pink" Pullen, and Wayne "Pete" Sutton had all committed. Missing stars that year were Max Eakins, universally acclaimed as the best kicker ever to boot the ball in the Northwest, and the past year's Captain Polly Grimm. The lesser notables who would not be back would be missed, as all of these players were lettermen and served valuable roles on the team. Bill Cahill, who only played one year; speedy halfback Rex Hosely, who also played only one year; quarterback reliever William "Deacon" Cook; halfback Roscoe Pike; and journeyman lineman George "Guy" Swarva completed a total of seven lettermen that would be sorely missed.

The first practice game was played against Lincoln High. The game offered Dobie the chance to get every one of his players on the field, allowing him the luxury to assess his overall talent pool. It appeared rich and deep as the Varsity coasted to an easy 42-0 win. One touchdown each was scored by right halfback Fred Sparger; quarterback Wee Coyle, left halfback Charles Smith, left tackle Tom Griffiths, and three by right halfback Melville Mucklestone. In all, twenty-seven men got into the game for the winners. The most eventful TD of the game couldn't have been recognized as such by the crowd out to see an otherwise routine game. This final touchdown was made by a future mayor of Seattle named Charles Smith, who was so far down on the depth chart that it was only a game like this in which the obscure freshman had even a faint hope of seeing action. It would be two years later that this unlikeliest of athletes would make an indelible mark on Washington football. Upon his shoulders alone would rest the preservation of Dobie's unbeaten record in what the coach would describe as the greatest challenge of his career.

The next warm-up game was scheduled with a highly touted team of soldiers from the military base at Fort Worden. Their advance press as posing a viable threat was quite plausible since they were defending Pacific Coast Army/Navy champions and their solid record against a stellar field of semipro teams. The publicity (not surprisingly) was emanating from the press, since Dobie was rather mum on the subject. He seemed to be content with letting the press conduct all the pregame hype. But, as always, there was the ever-present threat of overconfidence that his watchful eye could detect, even if no one else saw any signs of this menace.

Dobie was busy shaking up his first team in practice by relegating the big guns to the second team. This being an annual occurrence done more in his effort to trim the stars' egos than anything else, it might seem that by now it wouldn't be treated as news. But without him building up the other team and trashing his own, hungry reporters had to find other angles to pursue. So with no apologies and without much backup, they gleefully plunged into the game of singing Worden's praises. Excerpts of some of their gems tell the tale: "Worden Soldiers Have Fast Team," "Dobie will whip his huskies into shape for the first lap of the hard schedule which faces him," "Close Gridiron Battle Expected," "Prospects that the contest will be closer than anticipated," "protégés of the Grand Old U.S.A. are confident as ever of trimming Washington" and finally "Nothing Known of Team Which Tackles Dobie's Machine." None of these headlines and opinions came from any hard evidence—they were all trumped-up fillers designed only to hype interest in a game wholly undeserving of such attention. Many sports reporters of the day worked under the principle that if there was no news, manufacture some.

The only ink that had any relevance to the real world that week was that portion dedicated to next day's *Post-Intelligencer* headline, "VARSITY SWAMPS WORDEN, 99 TO 0." Supporting your author's take on journalistic ethics of the day, there were no opinions proffered as to why just yesterday, these Army/Navy defending champions looked so tough but turned out to be such patsies today. At least Dobie proved prescient in not ballyhooing the game.

Wee Coyle was the star in a game that didn't help much to presage just how strong this year's assemblage would be when the league opened for business. In just the first minute Coyle made a brilliant run to set up the first touchdown brought home by Mucklestone. Coyle soon followed this with a 70-yard touchdown run of his own. This week there were twenty-eight men that Dobie rotated into the game. The halftime score was an effortless 47-0. The 42 points of the second half were made when Dobie reached deep into the second and third string. More distance running than football, this marked the one and only time that Fort Worden would hazard to arrange a game with Washington. When time ran out, the scorer had tallied seventeen touchdowns for the afternoon.

As the final pre-conference game with the University of Puget Sound Loggers approached, Dobie was still heavy into his banishment of the starters to the ranks of the junior achievers. The latest swelled heads to be shipped to the bush league squad were Melville Mucklestone and Royal Pullen. Dobie explained that they were "swollen with pride over the Fort Worden score." A coach less judgmental and obsessive than Dobie might excuse Mucklestone for a little chest pumping. Admittedly it was against lesser competition, but over the last twelve days, in two games, he had scored five touchdowns. It seems that Dobie saw some terrible flaws in their game that had come on all of a sudden. Former Captain Mucklestone had forgotten signals, and all-around athlete Pink Pullen was not in form. Perhaps Dobie hadn't been paying attention to the ever-reliable pregame reporting that had conflicting takes on UPS: "Reports say the University of Puget Sound has the best team in its history." To compound the dilemma as to which team Dobie should place on the field (if one is to put any stock in newspaper analysis) there were "reports from Tacoma, which make light of the Methodist organization."

The conscientious reader could take his or her pick as to the outcome. Dobie for two weeks in a row was only putting out carefully guarded remarks. While not losing his senses altogether and predicting victory, he had gone so far as to state that he wasn't cocksure of capturing the game easily but, along with Wee Coyle, he did expect to win. Such a disclosure by Dobie was tantamount to him predicting a six-touchdown blowout. Sticking his neck out with an announcement of confidence in his team was not a matter he took lightly.

Somehow, between Thursday and Saturday, the terrible flaws detected by Dobie in the game of Mucklestone and Pullen had sufficiently been rectified to permit them to start. There is no report of a state-wide sigh of relief from Washington fans over the threat of losing these two great players to an onset of incompetence. It appeared that Dobie may have (surprise) been just trying to teach them a lesson for strutting a tad too much after the blowout wins of the prior two games.

In this game Dobie again freely substituted and took advantage of the chance to put twenty-three players on the field against the sixteen that UPS used. It was another convincing shutout with a final score in favor of Washington, 35-0. The Varsity put the ball over the goal line for a touchdown six times. For those two or three people in the Northwest who may have taken Dobie seriously that Mucklestone "had forgotten signals," they would be comforted with the discovery that he scored two of the touchdowns.

## University of Idaho at Spokane

The observant football fan would have had a difficult time getting a take on the first league game of the season. Reading the reports on Idaho's plucky performance against Washington State, one could only conclude that a rough game was ahead for the Varsity. Accounts of the matchup centered on how hard they fought and how well this challenge put them in good stead to blister Washington when the teams met in Spokane. There was little mention of Dobie having "abandoned" the team to teach them a lesson over Mucklestone's impudence. Dobie's very predictable behavior of cracking down on the stars served to narrow the margin of victory and returned the team to the control of their "supreme commander" (as Wee Coyle put it).

On cue, Dobie stated that the team was up against the stiffest proposition in years. He may have been facing the "stiffest proposition," but as far as facing a stiff game, reality didn't seem to bear this out. He played fast and loose with the facts, saying that he feared the strength, weight, and power of the Idaho eleven. With his team having a weight advantage of nearly fourteen pounds per man, this argument didn't hold water. The next day, after catching his misstatement, he felt no qualms in recalibrating his story to fit the updated state of affairs. He was now stricken by concern over a revision of reality where he feared nothing so much as the speed of his lighter opponents.

Dobie could never relax before a game. Call it an anxiety complex, nervous energy, or fear of the unknown; this was inevitable behavior on Dobie's part. He was always obsessive in his pregame ritual. His compulsiveness extended to involvement in every detail of practice; fear that the team was never game-ready, concern that his players were perpetually self-obsessed and worried over competitive bogeymen. Any coach goes through such concerns at some level. Dobie just ramped up the volume beyond the norm, thus for him this was routine. The great weight of evidence is clear in one regard—the coach *was* consistent. His fans grew to accept such behavior because it brought the end result they wanted. His detractors found his behavior an easy target for criticism and hyped-up reportage. Gossip was as popular then as now.

Before the Idaho game, Dobie deemed conditions to be so dire that he must reach into his psychological tool kit for something to right the sinking ship. He wasn't satisfied with the performance of his first string in practice, and matters of this order called for remedial action. Given his skills in teaching fundamentals and game preparation, this situation, coming as it did three days before game day, necessitated an attitude adjustment. He had several means to accomplish the task: we've seen him ceremonially demote one or more of his stars to the second team, double down on the intensity of practice, call for additional laps, declare the team's chances for Saturday more ominous than usual, ascribe a powerful new attribute to the other team that had suddenly emerged, and there was always his old faithful, the ever-reliable anti-pep talk.

Dobie was an advocate of the managerial theory that drastic events call for drastic measures. He had made great progress in cleaning up his public manners, but he remained an advocate of boot camp techniques for game preparation. Let's consider the terrible situation facing the coach on the eve of the Idaho game. His Washington teams hadn't lost a game in over three years. For a string of twenty-three games, almost 80 percent of those games were shutouts. In the preseason they had scored 176 points, while the opposition had never crossed their goal line. No matter how hard the press would try to pump up interest in this game, the fact remained that Idaho had just been blanked the week before by Washington State, seventeen-zip. Dobie knew full well his players were impressed with themselves and could see they were convinced of their divinity. When David meets Goliath, he rationalized, here indeed was a case calling for drastic action. And to do the job the anti-pep talk would bring his prima donnas back down to earth. The lecture from the pigskin professor was described as a regular rampage on the part of the coach. It was said that he had never before chastised his men like he did that night.

After this verbal roughing up, Dobie still felt that the extreme case of over-confidence running rampant on the team called for even more intervention. Pete Husby, right end, was called out for loafing, and the coach announced to the press that for such an unpardonable sin he was to be relegated to the second team. Maybe it was just the threat of demotion that turned him around, but Husby hunkered down and proved his worth (having only two light practices to accomplish the feat) and was back on the starting roster. Richard Devine was publicly called on the carpet for showing little class for the past week. Not being a very good football classifier, it wasn't clear if this infraction merited his demotion. However, Dobie saw fit to start him despite the player lacking class. Ben Koehler was another matter. He was also singled out for underachievement in practice and was replaced in the game by fullback Fred Sparger. For the problems he faced, which can only be described as a crisis of riches, the coach had this parting shot: "Washington is going to have the hardest rub she has had in a long time. My team has loafed too long, and now they can't come back. We go to Spokane tonight with the weakest team we have sent to that city since I have been at this institution." Serious, serious trouble.

The Idaho game, in the earliest moments of play, hardly lived up to its pregame billing that this would be a tightly contested pairing. Nor did it evidence any resemblance to the game Dobie had foretold. On the initial kickoff, Idaho's Gilder fumbled as he was tackled by Warren Grimm, with Tom Griffiths falling on the loose ball. In six plays from the 20-yard line, Mucklestone carried the ball over for the touchdown. With Wee Coyle's extra-point kick, the first score was chalked up in less than two minutes. With the game still in the first quarter,

Coyle passing to Grimm from the 50-yard line netted 15 yards. With Mucklestone advancing the ball on running plays up the middle to the 15-yard line Coyle again lofted a pass to Grimm for the second score. Coyle missed on the kick, but Washington led 11-0 almost before the crowd settled into their seats.

The second and third quarters told a different story. Idaho now had figured out how to run against the visitors and repeatedly marched the ball deep into Washington territory. Even though they were able to steadily move the ball between the 20-yard lines, they called a very conservative game when they were in scoring range. This timidity proved their undoing. In the third period, the Coyle-Grimm-Mucklestone trio went to work again. At midfield Coyle sent Grimm, his favorite receiver this day, on a passing route that picked up 20 yards. Sticking with what worked, Mucklestone again put his shoulder into a series of off-tackle line bucks for a total of 30 yards and the final touchdown, compiling yet another shutout. Coyle's kick was good.

In the last quarter Tom Wand (Walter's brother) came in at quarterback to replace Coyle, who suffered a severe muscle bruise to the leg. This switch is historically important in the annals of Washington football for two reasons. It has been widely reported that Coyle played in every minute of every game during his Washington career. This was not the case. Tom Wand, now a junior, had faithfully played on the team for the prior two years but had never earned a letter. Coyle's injury appeared to be serious enough to rule him out for next week's Oregon State game. If Wand could get into that game for both halves, he would finally have enough minutes for his **W**. Events that did play out prevented this, and the exceedingly talented Tom Wand never received an official letter despite his proven ability.

Washington's showing was far from impressive. This opinion was universal, as it was shared by fans, sportswriters, the team, and Coach Dobie. The coach, never one to hide his views, called this a miserable showing. Were it not for Idaho seemingly getting cold feet and playing it too cautious when they were in striking distance, they could have broken the streak right here. Even though the score shows the game was a 17-0 shutout, it hardly reflects the very real threat the Varsity had faced at the hands of a well-coached Idaho team.

### Oregon State

Gamesmanship in the constant struggle to downplay the home team's chances and build up the opposition was in full swing this week. Dobie did have credibility with Oregon State coming into town, having been proven somewhat correct in his call on the Idaho game. While not broadcasting outright defeat, he had correctly predicted a tight struggle. And for this he took full advantage. In his interview with the *Daily*, he elevated his concern to new heights with this revelation: "I am sincere when I say that Washington is suffering from intoxication of overconfidence…I have never lied about my team. I have never told that which I did not think was true when I said it…I am here to tell you that we have no championship team. I have reiterated again and again that I have mediocre material and no world beaters." This mediocre material included seven players who would be included in any knowledgeable judge's list of the greatest players of the entire Dobie era: Herman Anderson (right tackle), Wee Coyle (quarterback), Tom Griffiths (right guard), Warren Grimm (left end), Melville Mucklestone (left halfback), BeVan Presley (center), and Wayne Sutton (right end). Dobie's declaration that "we have no championship team" could only have relevance if he were able to somehow contort his mind into actually believing "I have mediocre material." In chapter 10 you will be interested to compare this mediocre material with Dobie's picks for his all-time Washington team.

Why all this fuss? Why, despite incontrovertible facts to the contrary, would someone reach so hard in an attempt to make this point? The way Dobie was constructed, he had no other way to accomplish his sole objective during football season—to win that week's game. He was not skilled as a rah-rah motivational speaker. He was a teacher of fundamentals. He demanded discipline and could only get this from his players by deploying his brand of management: (1) a highly disciplined system, and (2) command and control. While the system demanded much more attention to detail than most people bring to the table, Dobie possessed this ability. In achieving his command and control, he brought his skills into managing his players by setting the strictest of standards coupled with his powers of persuasion. Being a master of the manipulative arts through psychology, this rare gift allowed him wide latitude in up-close interactions with his players. It can be fairly concluded that he often was overbearing. But since it was profoundly clear to his men that he knew what he was talking about in matters of football, they accepted his leadership. As a teacher whose methods worked where his players learned their roles to such an exceeding degree, he was always able to deliver the goods to both his teams and fans.

Had he been given the ability to fire up his charges in coach like fashion with great oratory, that could have helped in his efforts to keep his players' egos in check. This not being the case, he chose the route of reverse psychology that we see him execute so masterfully throughout his career. We have a highly intelligent man under review here; he most assuredly did not look over his 1911 team, weigh their relative strengths and weaknesses, and conclude they were mediocre. But he did know that he had a flock of testosterone-induced young men fully capable of inflating their own self-image. He chose a way to deal with this problem that got the job done. His coaching record and the demonstrated excellence of his players confirm that.

Whirling around the athletic offices of both teams was another controversial matter commanding a great deal of interest among Northwest sportswriters. Victor Zednick had received notice from Oregon State that players Christman and Jessup were under investigation for eligibility. The OSU Athletic Office had not properly responded to a league requirement in registering all athletes entering college. Carrying over from an eligibility question from last year, Captain May was also in question. They insisted on playing these men, but without resolving the issue, Washington naturally resisted the effort until the matter was resolved. Dobie didn't want to let a widely reported issue like this go to waste, so he could only conclude that if they all three were bumped, his chances were 50/50, but if they played he was afraid his team would learn what it was like to be on the short end of a 10-0 score. For his part, according to the *Argus,* Coach Sam Dolan and his team were confident of winning.

This was hardly enough of an issue to whet the fans' appetite for pros and cons on the game's outlook, so an oft-debated standard of the day was introduced into the equation: which team is heaviest? Dobie swore it was Oregon State. The *Times* cast its vote for Oregon State. The *Post-Intelligencer* gave the weight advantage to Washington. I bring this up only to illustrate the futility that a concerned fan of the day would go through in trying to evaluate his team. This wouldn't be the first or the last football game in which an earnest fan might want to lay down a ten-spot on his pick. If his wager was large enough, he might want to look into a key indicator, such as comparative weights of the teams, before placing his bet. Such stats are provided for dopesters to do their work. In these simpler times, a player's published weight was at best a moving target. At worst it was a deliberate deception. For this game, the published weight comparisons were absolutely comical. None of the weights for any of the players on the two published lists agreed, nary a one. An inaccuracy rating of 100%.

Washington hadn't been scored on for exactly a year now, so there were opinions expressed in many quarters that the Oregon State game was not as foreboding as was the official line drifting out of the Varsity camp. Dobie's response to such heresy was to close the week's practice sessions to the press. This was a very common practice of the time. Fans have complained about the likes of Harvard, Yale, Michigan, and Ohio State in modern times over the same issue. Since Dobie's public pronouncements were made for the sole purpose of downplaying the team's strengths, it would only conflict with his slant should a reporter advance a theory that things didn't look so bad. What news did leak to the outside world showed that Dobie's practices for what should be considered a less demanding challenge were just as rigid as if he were playing for the league title against an unbeaten team. This was a purposeful tactic on his part meant to signal to the team that what he said was the real skinny (never mind those outside dopesters that don't know what they're talking about.) He was conducting detailed chalk talks on every sort of defensive and offensive strategy, the team was being put through running drills in what was described as a human race track, and the coach was setting up one-on-one conferences with each of his starters.

Such compulsiveness paid off for the coach. Game-day preparation may have been Coach Dobie's single greatest contributor to the streak. Luck played a part; teaching fundamentals was a key; his skill at matching players to their natural roles was important; psychology was an asset; an emphasis on athletic conditioning cannot be overlooked; his attention to detail was a factor; his rather militaristic demand for obedience was vital; and his contrarian motivational style added something. But the approach he took to getting ready for that week's adversary was the characteristic that elevated him to greatness in the national coaching ranks. Had he and his Washington teams been a couple of thousand miles closer to the likes of the Walter Camp Foundation or the eastern press, he would have gained even greater acclaim than he has received.

Dobie's remarkable game preparation can best be illustrated by considering that in all of his games at Washington, his teams were very rarely in threat of losing. Not only did they never lose, they were never behind in a cliff-hanger requiring drastic measures. There was never a need to make major revisions to the game plan to offset some strategy thrown at them that put them in trouble. Dobie would adjust his tactics to exploit weaknesses that were exposed during the course of a game or to adjust for problems his team was having, but these were more midcourse corrections than acts of desperation.

The Oregon State game serves to demonstrate this point. There was no time where Washington was threatened. It only took three minutes of play for Dobie's men to show that they had the upper hand. Coach Dolan's men could never mount any consistent offensive that posed a risk to the home team.

By game day, the skirmish over Oregon State's ineligible players was put to rest as all three men started, but Dobie's worry that they would bring a shutout with them never materialized. Captain Coyle, right up until the day before the game, was expected not to play, but he too started. This was reported as a surprise, but any student of Dobie's pregame maneuvering would hardly raise an eyebrow. It was only four days before the game that Dobie locked the press out of the practice field. As has so often been demonstrated, he loved to use the press to do his bidding. If they had been on the field that week, however, they would be looking to get the scoop on whether Wee Coyle was in or out. This clearly would not serve Dobie's purposes, so block the gates and announce that the "true facts concerning the team had not been told." Yes, a true fact such as Wee Coyle, arguably the best player on the field, had recovered and was fit to play.

The opening of the game was played out as a risk-averse punt-a-thon as both coaches were content with a game of footsie so they could size up the situation. Washington was first to ramp up play and, in so doing, was able to move the ball on the ground at will. They seemed to be making up for the mediocre showing against Idaho. The initial scoring drive started inside the OSU 40 and, on a succession of straight running plays, placed the ball in range for Mucklestone to carry it over for the first score at the nine-minute mark. The second drive was much like the first as Washington stuck with what worked, eschewing the forward pass. Right halfback Melville Mucklestone and fullback Fred Sparger equally shared in driving the ball straight up the middle. Tackles Bernard "Jack" Bliss and John "Jack" Patten opened up the gaps to spring the backs loose. Left halfback Walter Wand got the last call of the drive and delivered by taking the ball across the goal for the second touchdown.

The defense was not to be outdone (of course, back then they were the same players), racking up the third touchdown via a fumbled punt that Reynolds, the Oregon State QB, just touched as it bounced by him. Alertly seeing that the ball was up for grabs, Jack Bliss scooped it up just as it was inches from the goal line. While still in the first half of play, Coyle decided to mix it up and called for a series of passes on consecutive plays, first Mucklestone to Warren Grimm for 20 yards, and next Coyle to Wayne Sutton, who caught the ball just as he stepped over the goal for the fourth and final touchdown of the first half.

In the third quarter Dobie began freely substituting by rotating in a total of eight men off the bench. Tom Wand was one of these men, but he only got credit for one quarter, which would not be enough to earn this beacon of constancy his letter for the year. But the substitutes did make big contributions. Calvin Hazelet, in at left halfback for Walter Wand, and left tackle Grover Winn, in for Jack Patten, both scored touchdowns. Hazelet's was on a 10-yard run off right tackle, and Winn scored his on a tackle-around play. Coyle kicked two of the six extra points, missing two, and Andy Devine, substituting at left guard, kicked the other two, placing the score at a convincing 34-0.

In today's game the officials are prohibited from offering any opinion on the quality of play, since this is fraught with conflict of interest risks. There was no such prohibition in 1911, so referee Roscoe Fawcett (also sports editor of the Portland *Oregonian*) answered reporters' questions about the game. He had also officiated the Idaho contest, putting him in the ideal position to judge what took place on the field. He concluded that Washington had shown great improvement in a week. He was in full agreement with Dobie that in Spokane, UW had made frequent, inexcusable fumbles. In one short week, a team emerged that cured every flaw in execution that plagued them against Idaho. The credit for the remarkable turnaround was given to Dobie. The doctor correctly diagnosed the patient and administered the cure.

### University of Oregon at Multnomah Stadium, Portland

The most acrimonious rivalry with any team on Dobie's schedule was with Oregon. The bad karma between the teams came about quite naturally. Being adjoining state rivals tucked up in the farthest corner of the Northwest created a territorial enmity that was easily aroused, but the most important dynamic can be easily explained based on head-to-head competition. Prior to Dobie's arrival, Oregon dominated the series that dated back to 1900. The very first game between the two teams resulted in a 43-0 shellacking of Washington. Between this first game and 1907, things didn't get better for Washington. In those years Oregon dominated with four wins, one tie, and one loss. Oregon's one loss was a 6-5 squeaker. There was no disputing that the Northwest belonged to the state of Oregon. Washington's fortunes against Oregon State were only marginally better. In a series dating to 1897, State led over Washington with three wins, two losses, and one tie. A winning percentage against their two southern rivals of .333 for the eleven years prior to Dobie's arrival and one of .933 for the nine years of his stay at Washington dramatically illustrates his impact.

When Dobie arrived in town, Oregon's dominance came to a screeching halt. The turnaround of fortunes was so sudden and so dramatic, there is little wonder that the bitter feud mushroomed into the grudge match that has lasted for over a century. Gil Dobie taking over the reins is the one factor in the equation that changed everything. For eight years Oregon won, and for nine years Washington won. Such is how rivalries are born. In 1911 the pregame hype definitely took on even greater proportions. While the athletic hostility has been waged for over 110 years, it should be noted that the game of 1911 is still talked and written about to this day. It would be more accurate to state that one play is still talked and written about.

Preparation for the Oregon showdown began three weeks before the game itself. There was a bye week after the Oregon State game that allowed a luxury of time to prepare for what was universally regarded to be the biggest struggle of the year. No game between the two teams had been played the prior year, and both sides were screaming chicken, accusing the other of running for cover. With opposing fans blaming the other side of ducking that game, there was talk of evil curses being cast from both banks of the Columbia. Adding to the drama, the game was to be played in Portland at Multnomah Field, which was a much better site for drawing fans for both teams because it was right on the state border. For this game, predicted by Victor Zednick as an Appomattox battle royal, eight thousand fans turned out, the largest crowd to date for either team. A special train ran out of Seattle filled with students, the band and pep squad, dignitaries, and assorted fans.

With so much speculation being bandied about that Dobie's string indeed could be broken, both coaches clamped a veil of secrecy over their practices. This would only serve to churn up the gossip mills, giving Dobie a lot of welcome company in advancing the theory of his team's collapse. Washington had a much better passing game, and with wet weather threatening, this advantage could be neutralized. Also, Washington was just settling into this winning business after so many losing seasons, and there was talk that students were overconfident and trending to apathy. With Oregon being reported as so much stronger this year, they were growing cocky. This didn't escape the attention of Dobie's players, who openly admitted they felt the pressure. Through their good fortune of playing their game at Washington State in the same week

Washington was in Spokane playing Idaho, every member of Oregon's team was able to scout Washington. Coming into the contest that week, Oregon was also undefeated. It seemed that from all fronts the championship trophy that had found a three-year home in Seattle was about to be shipped south.

For this game Dobie placed even a higher level of secrecy around the practices, not even letting the second team in on a new play he planned to introduce. He took the first team aside and, with great ceremony, appealed to them as men of honor that they were to take a sacred pledge to keep everything they would learn about his plan in strictest confidence. No one outside the coaching staff and the starting eleven were to know anything about the play they would learn over their three weeks of preparation. At the end of practice, when the second team had been directed to the locker rooms, the starters practiced nothing but this one play for thirty minutes every night.

"Try it," was Dobie's instruction to Wee Coyle on the Tuesday before the game. The second team was lined up on defense, and the play that had been meticulously drilled into the very fiber of each of the first stringers was given its first test. Owing to the team's typical machinelike efficiency, the play was executed to perfection, with Wayne Sutton crossing the goal line on the very first attempt. The habitually stoic coach had a remarkable reaction to the perfect workings of his grand design; he broke out into riotous laughter. The players gathered around him were witness to a rare event—their coach letting his guard down. Coyle tells the story that this was the only time in his four years under the dour Scot that he had ever seen such a thing.

It didn't take Dobie long before he resorted to form, calling together all of the players who were now privy to his masterwork. The squad was placed on notice that any break with secrecy was, *ipso facto*, treason. Even thinking about the play around others rose to the level of mortal sin. The law was put down: keep quiet or suffer the consequences of the grand team inquisitor himself.

With all the cloak-and-dagger drama, tensions were mounting as game day finally arrived. Dobie called Coyle to his room at the Multnomah Hotel to once more go over the game plan before they would leave for the stadium. With a paternal pat on the shoulder, he reached out to his quarterback as if to prepare him for a loss, "Kid, they may get us today, but don't ever let them say a Washington team got licked without putting up a fight."

He had also called to his room sports reporter and game referee George Varnell, who arrived shortly thereafter. Dobie was obviously setting the stage for something big in the verbal assault he soon delivered to the very person who would be calling the shots for or against Dobie. He and Varnell over the years had become very close friends, so this offered the chance for Dobie to put his theatrical act on full display. He went through his melodrama for the obvious purpose of giving Coyle more confidence in the role he was soon to perform in the super-secret play the crafty Scotsman had invented just for today. There is no other reason that Varnell, in his capacity as a football referee, would put up with such seemingly condescending treatment. Especially from one of the contestants in the game he would soon be officiating.

"Varnell, I never did trust you. You're a rotten referee! If you don't watch for a certain play today, I'll do something I might later regret." Cover all your bases—that was a fixture in Dobie's preparation for everything he did in life. He then proceeded to explain step-by-step the detailed play specially devised for this most important of games. The coach and ref shook hands to seal the pact, Varnell agreeing that he would be on the lookout for the trick play. The stage was now set with the team and referee fully synchronized. Dobie's fixation for detail had run its course, and he was now satisfied that he had done everything in his power to assure victory. The general had painstakingly set the battle plan; the outcome would now be decided by the troops on the front line.

November 18, 1911, was a day blessed with clear skies and ideal conditions for football. Multnomah Field's wood shavings covered the turf. The field being dry would favor Washington with their stronger passing game, as would the reported injured kicking toe of quarterback Latourette, who punted for the Webfooters. At kickoff this would be about all that anyone in the stands could foretell as an edge either team would have over the other. The importance of the game was weighing on the Washington players who, in the words of Wee Coyle, were nervous and shaky in anticipation of the difficult struggle ahead.

Jack Patten kicked off to Oregon, and for the opening minutes of play the game was all about conservative football, with nothing more exciting than who would gain field position on an uneventful exchange of punts. The Purple and Gold settled down midway through the first quarter, with the backfield trio of Mucklestone, Walter Wand, and Sparger picking up good yardage on a series of off-tackle plunges. A beautiful triple pass that changed hands from Coyle to Wand, Wand to Mucklestone, who lofted a perfect 20-yard strike to left end Warren Grimm, set up the first score. At the eight-minute mark, after two line plunges, Mucklestone, running off tackle, carried the ball over from the 5-yard line. A near miss of the point after left the initial score at 5-0.

The second quarter opened with a punt by Coyle to Oregon's 45-yard line, but Oregon failed to move the ball and punted away to Mucklestone. He ran the leather back to Oregon's 40. Coyle was quick to line up his players and called for the play that his team had been practicing for the past three weeks. No one except Washington's starting eleven and Gil Dobie were able to follow the play. The Oregon team, sportswriters, every fan in the stadium, and the officials (even after Dobie's pregame disclosure) were thoroughly confused. Newspaper articles on the play-by-play were not totally sure of how the trick play worked and were not too proud to admit they were baffled.

The best official guesstimate was offered by the *Seattle Times* datelined game day:

> "The mysterious fake play that sent Sutton from the center of the field across the goal line electrified the great throng. A football crowd was never so completely dazzled as when in the second quarter the new and unexpected trick play was pulled. Out of the mass of players suddenly shot Sutton dashing down one side of the field, while all of the Oregon players were on the other side, desperately combating their opponents to get at some other player whom they thought was carrying the ball. There wasn't anyone within yards of Sutton, and he romped down the gridiron easily. He had crossed the chalk mark before the spectators could get their breath and before even the officials, as Umpire Forbes afterward admitted, knew what had happened."

The play worked so well that this professional observer was only able to report the decoy on the play as "some other player" rather than winning journalism points by identifying him as Wee Coyle. Touchdowns are usually received with a loud outburst and every sort of shouting and cheering by the recipient fans—but such was not the case since no one was clear if or how the football had crossed the goal line. When the officials finally solved the mystery to their own satisfaction and belatedly raised their arms to signal that the ball was across the goal line and indeed Sutton had placed it there, pandemonium ensued. The one thousand Washington fans went from a state of confusion to wild frenzy as it became clear that this play of remarkable deception had worked with such stunning efficiency. The seven thousand Oregonians sat in bewilderment and confused silence. With Coyle's anticlimactic extra-point kick and everyone still shaking their heads, the Portland invaders advanced their lead to 11-0.

Washington took full advantage of their shell-shocked opponent and controlled the ball for the rest of the half. Mucklestone and Walter Wand had their way running the ball, but the key that placed Washington into advantageous field position was a Wand-to-Grimm forward pass for 25 yards, placing the ball an inch from the goal. Latourette attempted to punt out of trouble, but the attempt was blocked. Sutton fell on the ball beyond the goal line for the TD. Coyle succeeded on the point after.

Oregon's best chance to get back into the game came on a fumble recovery by right end Bradshaw, who scooped up the pigskin for a 20-yard run before being tackled on Washington's 30-yard line. With time running out, Captain Main kicked a field goal to finally break the ice for Oregon. The score at the halftime break showed Washington ahead 17-3.

This wasn't Oregon's day. Even though they were in their home state before a decidedly partisan crowd, the Portland *Oregonian* disparaged not only the football team but their rooters. "One if its writers could not see anything but the Washington rooters and he spread words over nearly a column of space telling about it. He explained that the Oregon rooters suffered a serious attack of bronchial trouble and at times were unable to speak above a whisper. He declared Washington's Bill Horsley as the 'Captain of All-American Yell Kings' and was beyond profuse in his praise of "a hula-hula dance and the gigantic on-field serpentine line, marching to the band's 'Alexander's Ragtime Band.' "

The third quarter was all Oregon, but despite long drives that netted them impressive yardage, none of their efforts put any points on the board. On the kickoff, Latourette ran the ball back for a 50-yard gain. He followed this in the next series with a 30-yard punt return, and left halfback Walker picked up 20 yards on a play from scrimmage. But none of these potential game breakers created any sustained momentum. As the third period was drawing to a close, a real back-breaker befell Coach William J. Warner's squad. Main tried a field goal from the 30-yard line that was blocked and recovered by Warren Grimm.

This only served to portend worse things to come. As the fourth quarter opened, Washington soon found themselves in possession of the oval on the 50-yard line. The off-tackle play continued to click as Washington brought the ball downfield to the 25 with no running play more fancy than this. Coyle did so well calling the Walter Wand to Grimm forward pass in the second quarter that he went back to it for 20 more yards this time. It took four bucks up the middle to reach paydirt, with Wand bringing home the touchdown on a gimme. Coyle again booted the extra point.

Even Mother Nature was in Washington's favor. Not that they needed it, but when Coyle switched to a conservative game to coast to victory, he even had the wind at his back when punting. On one of his wind-aided punts, the multitalented Latourette badly and uncharacteristically misjudged the ball. Wayne Sutton beat him to it, falling on the prize on the Oregon 15-yard line. Mucklestone, on two off-tackle plays, pushed the ball across the line. Coyle did his job on the kick. This settled the matter of Northwest supremacy, the final score: Washington 29, Oregon 3.

With no instant replay or slow-mo cams to analyze just what happened in the mystifying play, speculation was rife as to just how Dobie pulled this one off. Newspaper accounts left wide gaps in the ball-handling exchanges and exactly when and how the critical moves were made. Wee Coyle was a firsthand participant and kept written records and published many articles over the years. In 1923 in the *Seattle Star* and again in 1949 in the *Seattle Times*, he gave the authoritative report of what has become known as the Bunk Play.

Lineups for 1911 Oregon vs. Washington:

| Washington | Position | Oregon |
|---|---|---|
| Grimm | Left End | Chandler, Fenton |
| Bliss, Anderson | Left Tackle | Hall |
| Pullen | Left Guard | Noland |
| Presley | Center | Kellogg |
| Tom Griffiths, Devine | Right Guard | Faris |
| Patten, Winn | Right Tackle | Bailey |
| Sutton, Husby | Right End | Bradshaw |
| Coyle | Quarterback | Latourette |
| Walter Wand | Left Halfback | Walker |
| Mucklestone | Right Halfback | Main |
| Sparger | Fullback | Johns, Kiser |

Wee Coyle's account of the Bunk Play as reported by him in 1923 and 1949:

"The play had no signal of its own, but followed a given signal when a point midway between the goal posts and sidelines had been reached. Wayne Sutton, the right end, slipped in between the left tackle and left end, instead of returning to his regular position. The backfield was in its regular position, the quarterback directly behind the center.

"On the word 'hike,' Presley, the center, passed the ball back into his own stomach and started to count silently, '1-2-3.' Sutton also started counting silently, '1-2-3.' The two guards fell in front of the center to protect him from attack.

"As quarterback, I made an obvious show of taking the ball from center, at the same time pulling my headgear from my head and tucking it under my right arm so as to make it look like a football (the color of our headgear was the same as that of a football). The three backs made a pocket for me and we all beat it for the [right] sidelines, not trying to make any distance.

"The whole Oregon team lit out in our direction, yelling 'Get Coyle.' Six of them hit me as I ran out of bounds, throwing my headgear in the air as they ganged on me.

"Meanwhile Presley and Sutton had finished their count; Presley turned on his right knee, keeping very low; Sutton came out of the line. Sweeping close to the forwards, and under the cover of Presley, (Sutton) took the ball and ran around our right end for a touchdown without being touched or even seen by an opposing player.

"Varnell, although primed to be on the lookout for the play, followed the headgear. Forbes, the umpire, was fooled so badly he helped pull off the Oregon players to get what he thought was the ball. In all my experience as a player and fan, I never have seen or heard of a play that was timed or executed more perfectly."

The "mysterious fake play" wasn't critical to the outcome of the game, as was apparent considering Washington's dominance throughout the afternoon. This could not have been known to Dobie or the team since, at the point the play was executed, the second half had just begun and the Varsity only led by a thin 5-0 margin. It can be argued that it so bedraggled the Oregonians that they were out of step for the rest of the game. But the play was run and executed to perfection. The follow-up press on the play far overshadowed the game itself. Since the play involved Wee Coyle as a stalking horse by the trickery of using his helmet as a faux football, the howls of protest came in from far and wide. There was no rule against such a play when it ran, but in a few years it was declared illegal.

Since the bar had been raised so high with expectations that the contest would be a nail biter, postgame analysis was decidedly unkind to Oregon. Some of the offerings of Oregon loyalists:

Foscoe Fawcett, Sports Editor, the *Oregonian*: "Well known as a football referee, throws the throttle wide open in telling how much better Washington was than Oregon. Among other things he says: 'Oregon's team was outclassed in strength, strategy, knowledge of the new game and execution. Aside from that it is presumed the Oregon team was all right.' "

Bill Hayward, University of Oregon Trainer, Football: "It is the best team I ever saw. Dobie has beaten us every year since he has been on the

Coast but this is the best team he has ever sprung on us. I expected a strong team but Coyle's crew is 100% better than I looked for."

Moullen, former Oregon placekicker: "The teamwork of Washington was little short of wonderful. I never saw a team where every man fitted into his place like this one does. There is nothing flashy about it, but when it comes down to smooth running three-cushion billiards play, Coyle's team is the best I have ever seen. My hat is off to Dobie, he is the best I have ever seen—he's a wonder."

Bob Forbes, former Oregon coach, umpire of the game: "I did not expect to see Washington so completely outclass Oregon. There was no comparison in the work of the two teams. The Washington team played like one of the well-drilled machines of a big Eastern university. The work of Grimm particularly impressed me. That big fellow is a fine end man. Yet Dobie, the man who built the machine, tightened the coils until it works without the slightest friction and at a speed that amazes the onlookers, was not a bit swelled over the victory. He was pleased, of course, but not puffed up. The Oregon team was weaker than I had been led to believe."

Looking at the Bunk Play in a longer historical context, it is worth noting that deception per se still was not illegal in college football and would remain so for another fifty-four years. Ironically it would be a game where Washington was on the receiving end of a similar ruse, with UCLA pulling off a legal play that many considered to be ethically challenged. The game was played on November 6, 1965, at the Los Angeles Coliseum, with Jim Owens coaching for the Huskies and Tommy Prothro in his first year for the Bruins. The Rose Bowl game was up for grabs and both teams were in contention. Washington's league record coming into the game was two wins and two losses, while UCLA's was one win and no losses. Washington played all seven conference opponents for the season, while UCLA played only four, filling out their schedule with tough nonconference games.

The deceptive play that set off similar howls of complaint as had the Bunk Play a half-century before involved a ruse with UCLA on offense. Just before the ball was passed from center, a back began excitedly running for the sideline as if he was an illegal twelfth man trying to avoid a penalty. In running as if hurrying off the field and then zigzagging downfield for the deciding touchdown, the play has become known as the "Z Streak." It worked perfectly, as the Washington defense sent no one out to cover him. He was wide open as the pass was lofted and had nothing but a clear field ahead. The touchdown made the difference in a tight game, ending with a win for UCLA, 28-24. The play caused such a national stir at the time that it too was soon declared illegal. UCLA went on to beat Michigan State in the Rose Bowl, 14-12.

Coach Dobie stepped completely out of character in summing up his reaction to the game against Oregon. He was downright effusive in his summation of the contest and his players. His concerns expressed to Wee Coyle of possibly "getting licked" would appear to be genuine. The extraordinary effort he put into getting prepared for the game must have been due to real concerns he harbored of the possibility of coming up a loser on the trip to Portland. "The Washington team played phenomenal football, almost throughout the entire game. The precision and accuracy with which they executed their plays was fully 50 percent better than any other past performances. The Washington team fully realized the honor and responsibility at stake, and played accordingly. Personally I am highly pleased and greatly surprised that the team performed so admirably throughout the game. Every man did his best, and his best was good. Coyle proved that he is still a great general and made his near-rival, Latourette, look insignificant in every particular save carrying back punts. Warren Grimm also came back to his own, and his performance here today fixes him as the great end in the northwest."

## Washington State

Oscar Osthoff, in his second year at the helm of Washington State, was one of five coaches for that school during Dobie's reign at Washington. On paper he had even better football credentials than Dobie. He was an All-American from the powerful Wisconsin team, and, from the experience of the 1910 squad with the Varsity having a reasonably tough 16-0 matchup, an argument could be made that this year's Thanksgiving game could go either way. Both coaches were predicting that their opponent had the edge. There was reason for concern from Washington because of a finding that Wayne Sutton was ineligible because of academic deficiencies. The ruling was found to be a paperwork mixup, but the faculty decided after all the hubbub to keep him out of the game so as not to attract charges of record tampering. With the unprecedented four-year streak still alive, the team was under microscopic scrutiny. The faculty felt that playing shorthanded was better than drawing a charge of foul play. Osthoff was hoping that he could keep Washington down to two or three touchdowns, but he was saying privately that he expected them to rack up more. A win would mean a complete generation of Washington students who had never lost a football game.

The weather for the game on Denny Field turned ideal, with clear skies and a dry, fast field. Washington State's Leo Coulter executed the kickoff at one o'clock on the button to Fred Sparger, who gained 10 yards on the runback. For the first ten minutes it appeared the game would live up to its advance billing. The visitors put a big scare into the locals with their touted passing game that got the best of Washington's defense for two long and threatening downfield assaults. The only thing missing in the visitor's game plan, unfortunately, was the ability to get the ball over the goal line.

With the contest still up for grabs and neither team able to take charge, the hometown fans were witnessing what looked like the unthinkable; they just might lose this one. With their boys backed up to their own 5-yard line and a hit-or-miss offense, no one could blame them for the sense of dread settling in around the field. Neither team seemed to be in a mood to take chances risking a fumble, so conventional wisdom called for a punt. The crafty Coyle would have none of this and took the game into his own hands. Risking disaster, the pass from center was perfect, and before the defense had figured out that the quarterback was running the ball rather than kicking, he was well on his way to the line of scrimmage. He had to fight and squirm his way through a legion of tacklers but battled out of danger for 25 yards. This was the play that calmed the nerves of both the team and their ever-so-anxious supporters. There was a distinct sense that the game was finally turning the corner in the Varsity's favor.

With their newfound confidence, Mucklestone and Sparger were able to take the game right to the strength of State's interior line on a series of plays for another 18 yards. At this point the crowd was witness to just how carefully and brilliantly Dobie set out his game plans. The play that followed was referred to in those days as a "trick," but today it would be standard fare in every team's repertoire. It was considered a trick not because it was particularly deceptive, but because it was a style of play not often seen at the time. Dobie was not unusually exotic in his choice of plays, but he would frequently have a special play in reserve for just this type of situation.

The game was only about eleven minutes old, but the offense was sputtering, and since they were just now coming to life it was time to make a statement. Dobie could not signal a play or send a man in with a play, but he had laid out a detailed game plan. As Wee Coyle himself explained, he felt his pregame strategy sessions were the toughest meetings he ever sat through in his life. Dobie's plans included contingencies for desperate situations such as confronted them here. With the championship on the line and the team in need of momentum, Coyle would know that it was up to him to call the play created for just this eventuality. The series of runs was the strategic move that set up Dobie's special play. Intended to lull the defense to sleep, a spectacular play could break the game wide open.

Coyle dropped back as if to punt and then faked a pass to a decoy receiver, drawing defenders covering him. He then threw to his right end Pete Husby, an obvious receiver who would be expected to catch the ball and head for the open field. With these successive moves confusing the defense, Husby, to the opposition's surprise, reared back and threw a perfect strike to left end Warren Grimm, who by now was deep into Washington State territory. He wasn't brought down until the 2-yard line, having picked up 50 yards. Mucklestone took the ball in for the first score, with Coyle adding the extra point. The more knowledgeable observers in the stands would have been impressed with Dobie's execution of this play that turned the game around. Everyone else on

Washington's side could finally breathe a sigh of relief that somehow the team had found their legs.

Bliss was fleeting as Washington State showed that one game breaker deserves another. Quarterback Gaddis picked up 25 yards on the next play from scrimmage. The play was so well executed that it was only thanks to the last man, Walter Wand, that Washington was able to make the tackle. Mixing up their plays well, "Tubby" Laird (weighing in at 210 pounds) then picked up 15 yards on a tackle-around play. A potential game changer of their own from left halfback Eddie Kienholtz to right end Tom Tyrer, a Seattle boy, placed the leather on the 3-yard line. Right halfback Leo Coulter got the call to push the ball over for the chip shot attempt, but as Coyle tackled him he fumbled just as he crossed the line. But right tackle Laird was on top of the play and fell on the ball for the score. Kienholtz added the extra point to tie the game.

With the game back to square one as the second quarter opened, it was time for Washington to see if lightning could strike twice. The Bunk Play had worked with such flawless precision in Portland; why not dust it off for another try? There was only one obstacle to such a bold move, and that had to do with how well Coach Osthoff had prepared his team for the matchup. It was widely reported that he had spent "many weary hours in the style of plays that he had seen Washington use." He was confident that he was ready for most everything that Dobie could throw at him. As for the Bunk Play, he was absolutely right—the play was stopped dead in its tracks. This would be the last time Washington would ever attempt the play. Since it developed slowly and there were many tip-offs exposing it as the Bunk Play, it could be easily defended and was not an offensive weapon that had a long shelf life.

WSU took over the ball and immediately cast another dark cloud over the hopes of the Washington faithful. Left half Coulter ran through a blockade of Dobie's strongest, picking up 20 yards before Coyle could bring him down. This early seesaw battle seemed destined to end with the last one holding the ball coming out on top. But for all the strength the easterners had shown up until now, this would soon change. With the ball on their own 30, Mucklestone recovered a fumble and, in five plays, he drove the ball over for his and the team's second TD. Coyle's kick brought the score to a tenuous 12-6 for Washington.

The Purple and Gold, realizing their big game breakers weren't effective in throwing their talented rivals off kilter, finally settled down to play fundamental football. State was held deep in their own territory on the kickoff and was forced to punt away from deep behind their goal. Taking advantage of this gift Washington gave themselves through strong defense, they immediately went back to work. A Mucklestone-to-Husby pass netted 20 yards. Wand and Sparger muscled and smashed their way up the gut to the 3-yard line, where Sparger brought the pigskin home for the third score. The worried home crowd could again relax; with two successful drives in a row, this was the kind of football they had come to expect. With the ball spotted where the touchdown was made, the point after try was at a sharp angle, but Coyle made it look easy. The score was now a more comfortable 18-6.

Late in the second quarter, Wee Coyle, who had already put in a flawless performance, uncorked the play of the game. On a quarterback keeper that looked as if two tacklers had him nailed in his tracks as he crossed the line, he squirmed loose for a spectacular 45-yard touchdown. Joe Harter, left guard, who was both fast and big managed to grab the 151-pound Coyle by one foot short of the goal as he crossed the line with his other foot for the score. The ball was again at a challenging angle for the extra point try, so the captain punted out to Mucklestone and then kicked the extra point from there, bringing the score to 24-6. From its rocky start the Varsity now found themselves comfortably in control.

Judging from the play of the third quarter, it seemed as if both coaches must have given their players the same halftime talk. There was more passing in the game on both sides, but most of the attempts fell incomplete. Osthoff's squad battled hard even though odds were against them as time was running short. They would show spurts of strength in moving the ball, but the major problem was lack of a sustained effort. Their chances to score would inevitably be cut short by a fundamental error, be it a missed block, fumble, or a poorly executed pass play. Coming up against Dobie's machine that, through such rigorous practicing, minimized these correctable mistakes, the competition was at a decided disadvantage. To illustrate this point, Wee Coyle, who played all sixty minutes of the game, made only one mistake as quarterback. This was a pass that he threw over the head of Pete Husby, who could have scored had the pass not been too high.

The final touchdown came at fourteen minutes into the third period. The on side rule allowing the punting team to recover possession even if the ball wasn't first touched by the receiving team, set up the score. Grimm was first to the ball on a low-flying punt that QB Gaddis couldn't get to. Mucklestone then made an 18-yard run, placing the ball at what was described as "in the shadow of the W.S.C. goalposts." The visitors fought hard in a valiant effort to prevent Washington from benefiting from this mistake, but with waning strength couldn't stop the determined Mucklestone. Coyle, still in his zone, put the ball through the uprights to close the scoring for the day at 30-6.

Gaddis still had a lot of fight left in him and soon would pull off the best showing of power and athleticism of the day. Getting a poor start on a quarterback run, he ran into a wall of five defenders but, purely through his own strength and agility, was able to fight clear. His blockers must have seen him being trapped by this swarm of tacklers and gave up. As he broke out of the five-on-one struggle, he managed to gain 25 yards without benefit of interference clearing his path.

This play energized Osthoff's men for the fourth quarter. Several times they knocked on the door of Washington's goal but failed to score by loss of downs. They moved the ball on the ground and in the air even better than their improved showing in the third quarter. But in the end they had nothing to show for the effort but improved statistics. It should be said that the players in exhibiting this will to fight to the end did leave the field with their heads held high, proving they were not quitters.

Detailed statistics on games in the early twentieth century were not always available, and when they were, could often reflect wide ranging inconsistencies. The playing field itself was not as well marked, and except for the primitive filming done on some games, there was no visual record to double check. Many times two reporters writing for the same paper and both having attended the game would publish conflicting stats. This year's Thanksgiving game by the cross-state rivals did give a summary of statistics that present an interesting profile of the teams' efforts. The breakdown illustrates just why Washington won.

The game stats as reported in the *Seattle Post-Intelligencer*, December 1, 1911:

|  | Washington | Washington State |
|---|---|---|
| Pass Completions | 3 for 7 – 42.9% | 4 for 13 – 30.8% |
| Punting | 22, 41 yds avg | 16, 36 yds avg |
| Total yards Run | 576 | 227 |
| Fumbles | 4 | 7 |

As the season ended, close followers of the program were lamenting that this year would mark the end of Washington football dominance. How could it be otherwise with Dobie losing seven seniors from the squad? Grover Winn, Peter Husby, Walter Wand, Melville Mucklestone, Captain Wee Coyle, Royal Pullen, and Warren Grimm would all be missing next season. While all made important contributions, the superstar trio of Mucklestone, Coyle, and Grimm, who had been with Dobie since the beginning, were virtually irreplaceable. The great coach was known for working wonders in maximizing his athletes' skills, but replacing three players of such demonstrated talent would put him to the ultimate test. However, there was an upside to the challenge: Dobie's preseason tales of woe would be believed this time.

# CHAPTER SIX

## *Under the Bleachers—1912*

"Football is a strenuous game. It is by no means a parlor pastime. I have never yet seen a player by the name of Harold Cholmondelay. Generally a star player is known as 'Flash' or 'Slam' or 'Buck' or 'Mike.' Names like that seem to fit better some way. By that, understand, I do not mean that football is a brutal game, but the game is the thing, and a man to play the game must have a cool head, quick brain, and plenty of good old American nerve, the very things that are necessary for him if he is to be a success in life. And if he hasn't got them and if they can't be developed, then the prospective player might just as well turn in his suit and go sit in the bleachers. When I was a boy they used to call me 'Gillie.' Just fancy! It was the hardest thing I had to overcome when I started to play the great college game."

*Gilmour Dobie*

As the practice season opened, the bad news for Coach Dobie refused to go away. As if matters weren't challenging enough with the departure of seven seniors from last year's squad, he now received the news that three-year letterman and Captain-elect Fred Sparger was not returning to the university. This completed the total destruction of the Purple and Gold backfield. At fullback Sparger could be depended on for pulling down the tough yards up the middle, and he was a rock on defense. He was replaced as captain by Tom Griffiths, a right guard who himself was an extremely tough competitor. Griffiths had received only one vote less than Sparger in the team's polling so he was the natural choice. In his four years on the interior line during these most rugged of times, he played every minute of every game. His teammates knew him as someone they could always count on. With this brand of leadership he was the perfect pick to step into the captaincy. Having so many new faces on the team, now more than ever, a steady hand on the tiller was crucial. It couldn't be known to anyone, but there was a freshman from Spokane named Walter Shiel waiting in the wings who would go on to football prowess at fullback beyond even the most rabid fan's dreams. He was Student Body president for 1916 (after his last year of football eligibility). Among his many athletic plaudits, he was singled out by Gil Dobie as his greatest fullback at Washington.

There was another player that fall who unceremoniously walked into Dobie's life and, from what would appear to be a happenstance meeting, a great friendship was born that would last throughout Gil Dobie's life. The bond of mutual respect led to a business partnership eighteen years later, with the player joining Dobie at Cornell as his assistant coach. Their friendship ran so deep that in 1948, the family honored the player by selecting him to be a pallbearer at the coach's funeral in Ithaca. The young man who Dobie came to love was singled out by him as the favorite player he ever coached. This singular appellation can be traced to both the endearing personality of Raymond Hunt and the universal respect he garnered with his tireless work ethic. His nickname was "Mike," but in a show of how his personality and work ethic were regarded by his team, Dobie and the players soon paid him the highest compliment by variously referring to him as "Mother."

The account given in the *Washingtonian* by Clark Squire, "Gilmour Dobie, Wizard Coach," provides a charming snapshot of their earliest encounter. This 1912 version of bringing a player onto the team is in sharp contrast with today's process of flying candidates into town for elaborate dog-and-pony shows and offering full scholarships but with slim chances of landing the star out of high school:

> "One late October afternoon, three years ago, alone and unconsoled, the great directing genius of Northwest football destinies sat on the dressing room steps, nervously spitting an imaginary particle from the tip of his tongue, his most noticeable characteristic. Powerful conference teams were seeking revenge and a massacre was momentarily expected.

> "The squad was on the field and Dobie was about to follow, when a clumsy 'frosh,' with a green cap set jauntily on his head, aimlessly wandered around the corner. At sight of the tall mentor, the youth stopped, reddened, stammered and walked away in confusion.

> "' What d' you want, kid?' volunteered the figure on the steps.

> "The 'kid' cautiously returned, approaching in doubt.

> " 'I want to see Mr. Gilmour Dobie,' he said meekly

> " 'I'm Dobie. (Ptew.) What d' you want.' The coach answered, spitting characteristically.

"The 'kid' struggled for air.

"' My name is Hunt. I'm from North Yakima. I would like, sir, to play football. I think—'

"'You play ball?' Dobie interrupted with a laugh. (Ptew.) 'Well, if you want to, you can come around tomorrow and see if you can find a suit that will fit you,' he compromised, leaving the 'kid.'

"Hunt was so deeply impressed with Dobie that he could not help working his hardest. It is related how the coach would have men running down the field for Hunt to tackle, hours at a time. And 'Mike' tackled them all."

Mother Hunt, who almost walked out of Dobie's life out of shyness and insecurity, would become an anchor on the team, holding down the left end slot and, in his senior season was voted captain by his teammates.

This year saw more sweeping changes in the rules of the game that would vastly improve the sport. Football traditionalists saw the rapid development from a game of brute force to one of athleticism as a harmful movement. Two legends of the game are included in these ranks, Walter Camp and Amos Alonzo Stagg. The most vocal even predicted that the "basketball passing threat" would soon grow tiresome and rules makers would reverse course back to the manly sport of off-tackle football. This, of course, was never to be. The rules changes of the early teens were actually the revolutionary turning point that broadened the game's fan appeal. This launched the era allowing football to develop into the most popular spectator sport in the country. Because of technological advances in travel and communications, the 1920s are popularly considered the advent of the modern age of college football. But the actual foundation of the modern game came about as a direct result of the far-reaching rules changes introduced in 1912. These are the rules that brought the modern era of college football into being:

1. The length of the official field of play was reduced from 110 to 100 yards.
2. A 10-yard-deep zone measured from the goal line was added to each end of the field of play.
3. Rules now called for four downs to gain 10 yards for a first down.
4. Scoring of a touchdown was increased to six points.
5. Previously on a punt, once the football hit the ground it was live and either team could gain possession and advance the ball. This rule was revised, requiring that the receiving team must first touch the ball before it becomes live.

6. The 20-yard limit on a forward pass was eliminated, allowing for a gain through the air of any length.
7. If the ball happened to be touched by a player on offense who was not an eligible receiver, the pass was ruled illegal and possession was awarded to the opponent, with the ball placed at the line of scrimmage.
8. With the addition of the 10-yard zone, a forward pass could be utilized to score a touchdown when the ball was caught beyond the goal line and within the zone (later to become the "end zone.") Catching a pass beyond the zone was ruled incomplete. The goal posts remained on the goal line and were not moved to the end line until 1927.
9. If the opposing team intercepted a pass in the zone, this was ruled as a touchback, and the ball was brought back to the 20-yard line.
10. Kickoffs were moved back from the 50-yard line to the 40.
11. The break between quarters was reduced from three minutes to one minute. The fifteen-minute halftime break was retained.
12. The clock was to be stopped when the ball went out of bounds and when a penalty was called to allow time for the referees to invoke the penalty for the infraction.
13. Rules were adjusted allowing for a reduction in penalties, and because of this the field judge position was eliminated, bringing the required number of officials to three.
14. The size, weight, shape, and a requirement for full inflation of the football was standardized. An elongated shape was chosen to make it easier to grip the ball. The new shape aided in throwing a spiral. This greatly enhanced the passing game and facilitated the passer in gaining length and accuracy.

### Preseason

The first preseason contest with Everett High was held on October 28 with Washington winning the practice game 55-0, does not show up on the official records of Dobie's games. Preseason games were credited towards the overall win/loss record but had no bearing on league standings. But the official accounting of it is not shown in his overall tally of victories despite irrefutable evidence that the game was played. The game was fully written up in three reporters' press box accounts in the *Seattle Times*, the *Post-Intelligencer* and the *UW Daily*. This means that Dobie's official record of games in his national undefeated streak must be increased from its prior total of 58-0-3 to 59-0-3.

Everett was one of the area's perennial contenders for state championship honors. The team was coached by Enoch Bradshaw, who played halfback and quarterback for Washington from 1904-07 and captained the '07 team. He also distinguished himself in UW football lore as the Huskies head coach for 1921-29 with a record of 63-22-6. This would be the first opportunity to play under the new rules, with an expectation that Dobie would call for more passing since the aerial game was now greatly liberalized and ball possession was increased to four downs to make 10 yards. There were only three passes attempted, however, as it was apparent that Dobie was still trying to figure out his lineup after losing eight lettermen from last year. That year Dobie had the biggest manpower challenge to face him since assuming the near-impossible task of creating a team out of thin air at South High School back in 1903. He could only look upon this great chance with a soft opponent as a gift to see if there was any hope at all to get through the league undefeated. On the surface no one was so bold as to venture a guess on his chances. After the game, Dobie, in a weak moment when asked about the prospects for this year, was caught smiling despite the many holes in the lineup.

Word from the University of Puget Sound this year fell right in line with the sniping remarks offered up by everyone else in the football world: Washington was "notoriously weak this season." With all the talk on the street that Dobie was beatable, Coach Pitchford clamped a tight veil of secrecy on his practices. With nothing of great consequence to back it up, bluster abounded to the effect that the Methodist's had the strongest team in its history. Dobie was muted in his response. He didn't have to say much since the bulletin board clippings from Tacoma did his work for him. And since there had been such gnashing of teeth over the loss of so many headliners from the team, anything he could add would be redundant.

The game itself was decidedly anticlimactic, but there was a bigger story afoot. While the game was in full progress, a grand plot of sideline skullduggery was unearthed. The comic opera began with a Faustian bargain between Coach Pitchford of the Missionaries, (possibly) Coach "Pink" Griffith of Idaho, and an accused spy named Paul Savage, an ex-player from Idaho. Savage, a co-worker in a city job together with Pitchford, had offered his name to referee the UPS contest. Dobie exercised his veto of this choice without knowing of his personal connection to the rival coach.

While at the game, Wee Coyle spotted Savage on the sidelines studiously taking notes in a rule book. Knowing him to be a former Idaho player, he tipped off Dobie as to the suspicious behavior. Smelling a rat, the tall Scot collected a goon squad of five of his second stringers and Assistant Coach Max Eakins to do some detective work. When confronted, Savage claimed to be an assistant coach of the visiting Missionaries, but Coach Pitchford disclaimed this. Dobie and his men, not so politely, dispossessed the ersatz assistant coach of his copious notes on Washington's plays and banished him to the grandstands.

Scouting games was commonplace in the league, but the professional courtesy expected of those conducting such research was to do it openly but from the paid seats. It was not unheard of for an opposing coach or scout to view the game from the sidelines or the press box, but it was standard behavior to do this with approval from the opposing team. Dobie was not one to take such unethical behavior lightly. To him football was serious business to be conducted in the full spirit of gentlemanly competition, albeit with all the force and might one could muster. To do otherwise meant swift and sure retribution. As he stated to the Seattle *Times*, "Back in Minnesota they would tie a can around a spy's neck and drop him in the river." It was not proven, but speculation was rife that Coach Pink Griffith had sent the "spy" on this mission of espionage since their game was coming up in two weeks.

A new freshman quarterback named Allan "Bud" Young was given a tryout that day. Knowledgeable observers had their eye on senior Tom Wand, who looked to be the logical heir apparent to Wee Coyle. Wand was still short of enough playing time to earn a letter, but he showed great promise in the first preseason game. Unfortunately a serious injury to his finger in practice the week of the game with Bremerton Navy Yard took him out of action for some time. Wand, being Walter's brother, did come from good football stock and won the Flaherty medal last year for his conscientious service. Wand was one of the three players who was given what today would be considered a "lifetime achievement award" for his four years of conscientious service without compiling enough playing time to earn a **W**. Dobie was trying out four men to start at QB, including Wand, but he was overthrowing his receivers and putting too much mustard on the ball. Charley Smith started the Everett game but was moved back to his halfback position. This opened the door to the untested Young, who didn't exhibit the cool head so evident from Wand. Now was the time for him to step up if the team had any chance of defending their championship. The next quarterback on the depth chart (a term not used back then) was another freshman, Deming "Dick" Bronson, of whom much would be accomplished in later life. We will review more of this great man to follow.

Neither team would do much today to instill confidence in the hearts of their faithful. The passing game was downright comical, as fans from both sides laughed the few times it was attempted. It was evident that the teams hadn't adjusted this early in the season to the new rules that provided a wide array of options when attempting a pass. There were only ten total passes for the game, with each side completing just one of its five. The Purple and Gold made it into the newly installed end zone eight times for the new six-point touchdown. There was one field goal, but the winners could only muster two successful extra-point kicks out of their eight tries. The scouting report from UPS that Washington was notoriously weak turned out to be just as weak as Idaho's bungled plot at getting some up-close inside dope from its spy. The game ended as a humbling experience for the University of Puget Sound, with Washington blanking the Missionaries, 53-0.

Aside from the mocking attempt by the *UW Daily* in predicting a 60-0 shutout of the Varsity that made light of Dobie's woeful outlook against most of his opponents, no one felt there was much of a threat posed by next Saturday's game with the Bremerton Naval team. A dedicated contingent of sailors was on hand and the navy band made the trip to add color to what otherwise was pretty much a routine preseason game.

University of Washington Libraries, Special Collections, Neg. No. UW21965          1912 Starting Lineup

Backfield: (L to R) Fred Jacquot-RH, Walter Shiel-FB, Cedric "Hap" Miller-LH, Allan "Bud" Young-QB
Line (L to R): Wayne Sutton-RE, Jack Patten-RT, Herman Anderson-LG, BeVan Presley-C, Tom Griffiths (Captain)-RG, Bernard Bliss-LT, Raymond "Mike" Hunt-LE

The coaching staff, having had two games to assess their talent, was drawing closer to knowing just which players would be placed where in the lineup. Dobie had begun to single out freshmen such as Walt Shiel (fullback), Raymond "Mike" Hunt (left end), Allan "Bud" Young (quarterback), twin brothers Elmer Leader (left tackle), and Edward Leader (right end) as potential starters. Not a single person following Northwest football, in his wildest imaginings, could foresee the impact that these five would make on football in this far corner of the sporting world.

As events would unfold, the team, rather than losing ground compared to the 1911 squad, would soon put eleven men on the gridiron that surpassed last year's pool of talent. Dobie was the one responsible for this. He took very good athletes and elevated their skills well beyond what most coaches could achieve. This is largely attributable to his single-minded dedication to teaching fundamentals. Each man selected by the coach must first master every aspect of his own position—only then would Dobie place him into the overall mix. Then began the ever-so-detailed choreography of fitting the eleven parts into a perfectly coordinated whole. It was for good reason that throughout his long career his teams came to be described as a "machine."

The navy men gave the Purple and Gold everything they could handle until the team was able to settle down and figure out how to offset the weight advantage of the heavier sailors. Washington put an underwhelming total of seven points on the board in the first quarter and only led by 20-0 at halftime for a practice game that shouldn't have been this tough. The sailors' defense put up a much stronger fight than expected, but were unable to gain traction on offense.

After embarrassing themselves the week before with the complete break-down of their passing game, such a performance couldn't stand if the team had even faint hope of defending their title. Dobie, as we've seen, was a firm believer in taking full advantage of new rules, and he saw this year's more open passing game as the key to the future. The much wider offensive strate-gies now offered by the expanded passing rules came just in the nick of time to save Washington's scalp in this game. Not that there was a threat of losing, but the sailors were described as fighting like wild men every time Washington was in sight of their goal. With the newly designed innovation of an end zone, the answer to this problem was to loft the ball over the battlement. Right end and nonletterman Abbott was the one who got the call and started the game in front of regular starter Wayne "Pete" Sutton, who was hobbled with a sprained ankle. He caught two passes for scores deep down field. No record is made as to whether either or both of these were caught in the end zone, but under the old rules a pass was not allowed to be caught beyond the goal line, and it could not be thrown beyond 20 yards. The job for the defense was now much more difficult as they had to be more wary of the forward pass as teams threatened the goal.

Ray Hunt, the shy freshman, wasn't yet playing up to his potential, but taking over the position vacated by graduating senior Warren Grimm meant big shoes to fill. For a player who would later set the hearts of his fans on fire, he turned in a mediocre performance. The green recruit fell down badly in the pass department. Freshman quarterback Bud Young, who also would com-mand much attention in subsequent seasons, was decidedly unimpressive. The question at the time was whether Dobie would replace them or work his magic in transforming these inconsistent newbies into contributing team mem-bers. The outstanding run of the day was turned in by Hugh "Pitt" Schively, at 130 pounds the lightest man on the team. Substituting at left halfback, he scored on a spectacular 40-yard run around left end. Even though Washington won the game 55-0, there were big questions as to whether the backfield was up to the task against a highly touted Idaho team coming to town next week. With the luxury of putting nineteen men into the game, Dobie did get another chance to review all of his potential starters at a time when several positions were still fluid.

## University of Idaho

There was near unanimity concerning who would win the game against Coach Pink Griffith's much more experienced team. He had nine starters back that year, compared with Dobie's five, which left most everyone believing Idaho was the strongest team in the league. This opinion was shared by a multitude of sportswriters, Washington fans by the score, Victor Zednick, and Assistant Coach Max Eakins, just back from scouting the Idaho win over Washington State. Coach Griffith felt his team would win even though being somewhat tepid in saying, "We do not underestimate the strength of the four-time champs, but we feel we can take Washington's measure. This is Idaho's year in the Northwest Conference. We are confident that at least Coach Dobie's crew will not trim us." There was a notable holdout among all of the prognosticators considered to have an informed opinion on the subject—one University of Washington Coach Gilmour Dobie. He didn't see this game as every other dopester did in being a surefire loss for his team. Going into the first league game of the year there was no gloomy forecast, no exalted praise for the Idaho squad, and even the inevitable weaknesses he spotted on his own team didn't foretell imminent doom.

For most observers of the day, such un-Dobie-like behavior was downright shocking. Here the week before the first league game, with a team mostly made up of new recruits, he isn't predicting a drubbing? To add further to any beliefs that there was a new and improved Dobie this year, he approved the opening of practices to the public. The Washington mentor surprised everyone with what he had to say about the upcoming contest. If we view Griffith's opinion as lukewarm, Dobie, the straight-talker, was downright wishy-washy, "As to the outcome of tomorrow's first real test for the green Washington eleven, I cannot say. I have spent a great deal of time training two players for each position on account of the preponderance of new men. Injuries have made me change the lineup of my first string repeatedly. Hunt at end, and the entire backfield quartet, Shiel, Jacquot, Dorman, and Young, have never played a single conference exam. In case of rainy weather, this lack of experience and the fact that the Idaho players are heavier than my pupils will handicap Washington. The result? I cannot prophecy." With so many facts on his side entitling him to take the defeatist's way out, it seemed strange indeed for him not to see his cause as hopeless.

Or did it? We have seen there was a widespread belief shared by his players, friends, and sports journalists that he was a master of psychological manipulation. He didn't employ this mastery just in one-on-one coach/player encounters but also knew how to take advantage of just such situations as were now on the table. The easy way out for him would be to play to form. All evidence was clear that his team would be killed. But Dobie was too clever for such sophistry, as doing so would not distinguish him from the crowd. If he joined the chorus of naysayers, he had everything to lose and nothing to gain. Had he predicted a big loss and this came about, he could later be criticized as giving up and failing to prepare his team when the chips were down. The captain doesn't abandon his ship when it's taking on water, and this is exactly the assessment that Dobie took in this rare instance where his team was the legitimate underdog. By assuming the contrarian's role and playing his cards so cleverly, no matter the outcome his reputation could only be enhanced. Of course, predicting a win would be so ridiculous as to be absurd. This fell right into Dobie's long-set pattern of behavior: predict a loss if all odds favor a big win, but lay low if the odds favor a loss. He was not universally gloomy!

In time those closely following his professional demeanor would better understand this complex manipulator of men, even attributing aspects of genius to how he dispatched his duties. Certainly the title must be used advisedly, but it has been widely expressed in regards to Coach Dobie. Considering the evidence before us, the designation does fit when we connect Dobie's Washington hiring to the current game just two days away. Then we can better understand why he chose to soften the rhetoric in the Idaho pregame cacophony. From where he had been just three years ago, he survived the near disaster of public ridicule brought on by the puerile behavior in his first year. He endured countless critics, who could easily find a newspaper to expose his actual or construed shortcomings. His personality was easily caricatured, much like that of a tough drill sergeant or pampered prima donna. By 1912 he had a near-perfect platform with which to exercise his exploitation of the media to his advantage.

As his reputation grew he found himself in the role of the dominant force in Northwest football. In modern marketing parlance, Dobie had to protect his brand. He was not the creation of a PR machine but was an original; oftentimes quirky, but still the real deal. We can see that with the passage of time, his sharp tongue and demanding behavior slowly came to be understood. A greatly appreciated talent he possessed (meticulous attention to detail) came to be held as essential to his success. This can be seen in his insistence on physical fitness, maintaining a healthy diet, a rigorous practice regimen, sizing up players' skills to best fit specific roles, play sequencing, team unison, player compliance, game strategy, and religious adherence to fundamentals. He was an early advocate of the modern-day foundation underlying success in athletics as requiring honor, unity, and brotherhood. His bouts into harsh language and overbearing behavior commanded the headlines, but these core beliefs were the root of his success.

The same effort he expended in his single-minded focus on game day preparation, he also applied to the cat-and-mouse posturing that took place leading up to game day. Every disparate element had a voice, be it students, alumni, faculty, the business community, sportswriters, outside fans, his team, the opposing team, and the league at large. In that day it was not considered a conflict of interest for even game officials to weigh in. By now he had figured things out and understood that he also had a voice—a voice that framed the discussion. Having control of the stage, he could use his manipulative skills to fully serve his purpose. This was on display leading up to what everyone saw as the inevitable conclusion to the Idaho game, his team would be walking the plank. Everyone except Dobie, that is.

On Wednesday of game week, Dobie was still trying to build a fire under his linemen. They were the one glaring deficiency this late in getting ready for Idaho. With four new faces in the lineup, there was little wonder that they weren't yet up to Dobie's phobic standards. But regardless of how well a segment of the team was doing, the great coach needed someone or some group to call out. This time it was his interior line's turn. He announced that the team's slump was caused by center BeVan Presley, right guard Richard Devine, and none less than captain and left guard Tom Griffiths. What looked like an unsolvable problem on Wednesday suddenly in just one day's time now had resolved itself. This was a classic of the coach's tactics. Disparage the supposed slackers; put the players through a tough practice on the last day of hard contact; and the next day announce to the world that the players were now fit to compete. The clear message to the team: listen to me when I spot a problem, work hard in practice to correct the weakness, and receive a pat on the back just before game time when I see you are finally back on track. Since use of such an exercise was rare for Dobie (after all, it involved public praise), those times he dared to be so bold, it worked to great benefit.

This week's open-practice policy helped advance the widespread angst over the Varsity's newfound underdog status. Fans could see the team in action, and their opinion wasn't positive. One unflattering depiction had them performing as "rottener" than past years. The *Times* described a campus rally that turned into more of a prayer meeting than a chorus of support. Rooters were looking more to miraculous intervention than football prowess to pull their boys through. The fans could be excused for their anxiety because they hadn't found themselves in such a fix since Dobie hit town. As for his take, this was the best of worlds. He had seen the Washington loyalists as drawing more complacent with each win. Now in his fifth year the fans had forgotten the bitter taste of defeat and winning had become a birthright. The coach's obsessive fear of overconfidence wasn't a malady only befalling his players—it could just as easily afflict his followers.

Wayne Sutton is held in high esteem in Washington football lore for scoring the touchdown in the famous Bunk Play against Oregon, and he racked up another honor against Idaho. The first touchdown in the school's history coming by way of a pass into the end zone came with Captain Griffiths throwing a perfect strike from the 30-yard line to Sutton as he was tackled just as he stepped on the goal line. The play was described by the *Post-Intelligencer*: "A Moscow player nailed Sutton at the goal line but the Varsity right end crushed himself over into the zone where points are counted." The dramatic score came only five minutes into the game. Rain had seriously hampered practice all week, but by Saturday with the skies still threatening there was not a drop during the game. This proved to be greatly in Washington's favor, considering their miserable passing exhibition against UPS.

Idaho began the game with a case of stage fright that Washington's steady teamwork quickly turned to its own advantage. The team having been described as rottener than those of the recent past now was being hailed as a "machine rolling along like a steam roller." In other words, nothing different than most other teams that Dobie fielded. The nervousness over starting five freshmen and having lost seven lettermen was immediately laid to rest. It is not an overstatement to say that the Northwest football world was stunned by the performance of Washington. A reporter described the spectators as being astonished by the backfield's hammer-and-tong onslaught in the first quarter.

Tom Wand's painful injury that completely ripped off a fingernail kept him out of the lineup again for the week. The sketchy freshman Bud Young had previously exhibited talent, but past erratic play put serious doubt in the minds of those who had seen him in action. He did get the call to start, which meant he would now have to prove himself under the rigors of Dobie's boot camp game prep, variously described by eyewitnesses as intense, repetitive, demanding, painstaking, and brilliant. This game was his trial. Virtually everything written about Young up to this point centered on his being a work in progress that would make a contribution, but only at some time in the future.

Underscoring the pregame attitude of Northwest football observers, the headline for the *Post-Intelligencer,* "YOUNG REAL DISCOVERY," speaks to their surprise. This astonishing turnaround came as the fortuitous marriage of two talents: Young's innate athleticism that was still raw around the edges and Dobie's skill at fast-tracking latent talent. With the hit-and-miss performances of the green first-year recruit, it was perfectly understandable for sideline observers to peg him to come into his own after more time on the battlefield. The fact that he went from a questionable starter one week to instant stardom the next did not happen by accident. Dobie knew how to make the most of the hand he was dealt, and Bud Young is a prime example of this much-desired coaching skill.

With the game still in the first quarter, freshmen right halfback Frank Jacquot and fullback Walt Shiel moved the ball into scoring position with impressive gains both in the air and on the ground. Dobie had given Jacquot added incentive with a side bet of a new hat that he wouldn't gain 20 yards in the game. The Scotsman happily lost the wager, with Jacquot picking up 30 yards in just his third carry of the day. Tackles Bernard "Jack" Bliss and John "Jack" Patten opened up holes in the line with seeming ease to clear the path. With the ball on the 6-yard line, Young faked a pass to Jaquot, drawing the defense out of position, and marched across the line for the second score.

The one-man wrecking crew of Bud Young was also instrumental in setting up the third touchdown. In the second quarter, Young, with a 25-yard run, brought the ball to Idaho's 4-yard line. Walt Shiel did the honors on the first play from scrimmage straight up the middle for the score.

The play of the game that everyone was talking about long after the last whistle came late in the second quarter. Young, standing on the 40-yard line, was well back of the line for the pass from center that came in on a bounce from BeVan Presley, giving the Idaho linemen time to rush Young en masse. Having to stoop for the ball and momentarily juggling it as he positioned himself for a 50-yard dropkick, he managed to put the ball through the uprights for three points. Not only was he passing with great skill, running the ball with alacrity, and leading the offense like a seasoned vet—with this boot he proved his ability to deliver under immense pressure.

Coach Pink Griffith's plan was to open up his game with an assortment of passes and trick plays, hoping to catch Washington's defense off guard. For the entire first half there was nothing that his team could call that fooled the defense. Washington's interior line stopped everything up the middle, and the team read the development of the trick plays and pinched them off for little or no gain. It wasn't until very late in the second quarter that the visitors were able to gain their only first down of the half. The sports reporter for the *Times* assigned to the game "confessed" that he had been duped by the dopesters as to Idaho's strength. He got right to the point in his analysis of how Washington did so well: "The Washington boys beat Idaho doing everything." He concluded that Washington played far better than the most optimistic rooter had any right to expect. At the half Washington led 22-0. The only weakness shown was Patten making just one of his three tries for extra point.

For the second half Washington had to fight off a determined Idaho team that hadn't given up, but the Moscowites' efforts proved fruitless. The Varsity was content to sit on their lead and played a conservative game for the next thirty minutes. Idaho threw caution to the wind as quarterback Lockhard attempted a double pass to his left halfback Burns. But before Burns could get off his throw, Patten burst across the line and dropped him in the end zone for a safety.

In the fourth quarter, Dobie brought in eight substitutes: Hap Miller (left halfback), Richard Devine (right guard), James Bruce (right tackle), Charley Smith (quarterback), Earle Clark (left end), Ed Leader (right end), George Gallagher Jr. (fullback), and Burke Griffiths (center). Idaho made only one substitute, Shipky at right end. The lopsided game that surprised everyone, or more probably was a result of everyone underestimating Gilmour Dobie, ended with only the two-point safety being recorded in the second half. The final score with Washington blanking Idaho: 24-0.

In one of his rare moments of postgame openness Dobie acted as surprised as everyone else with the total dominance of his team. "I can't say that I am disappointed with my team. I know what they can do now. They played good football today—better than I expected." He smiled as he muttered, "Well, we got one game anyway." This for Dobie was a ringing endorsement of the events of the afternoon.

### Oregon State at Multnomah Stadium, Portland

The win over Idaho coming as it did, with everyone counting Washington out that year, brought out a rash of notable football experts offering praise for Dobie's work. The *Times* called the increased confidence in the coach "the talk of the town." There were seven prominent football experts who had knowledge of both the Northwest and the national football scene who, after four years, were now convinced that Washington's coach was no fluke. The general feeling held that with the abundance of talent on last year's squad the coach's job was made easier. The final decision as to whether Dobie was merely a good coach or a genuine innovator had now been settled. Being able to fill as many vacancies as he faced and not just compete, but excel, was the clincher. Breezing through the practice games and then starting the season as strongly as last year ended was attributed to inspired coaching.

Even with two weeks to prepare for the game in Portland, rain had seriously affected practice. Coming off the successful passing game against Idaho and sizing up his best strategy for the Oregon State game, Dobie had hoped to do a lot of passing. Because of the heavy rainstorm, the team hadn't been able to work on their aerial game, plus Wayne Sutton, the team's best receiver, was limping from an ankle injury and projected out of the game. Mike Hunt, at the other end, hadn't yet developed into a reliable pass receiver. The game plan that Dobie hoped to put in play was scrapped, and the focus was shifted to the run. Dobie was quick to point out that he made this key decision and passed it along to the press. Releasing breaking news as to his team's actual weaknesses was not typical of the tight-lipped mentor. When the season was under way, he lived only to win football games. This announcement was clear and simple a setup. The sly Scot had a motive behind telescoping such a juicy tidbit to the opposition.

In the interview that Dobie gave to Clark Squire for a 1915 *Washingtonian* article, Dobie made reference to the need for a coach to turn this type of situation to his advantage. Broadcasting his team's obviously weak passing game, while not something he would ever let out under normal circumstances, made perfectly good sense with a critical league matchup just two days away. In Squire's interview, Dobie stated, "Personality and practical judgment make a football coach." No great revelation here, but he followed this up with an illuminating insight that explains why Dobie would go out of character in bluntly disclosing the fact that "Washington will make a poor showing, both at Portland and for the rest of the season at handling forward passes." Dobie revealed to Squire in the interview how it was that he turned such situations as he faced against Oregon State back against the opponent. "He attributes his success to his ability to adapt himself to the surrounding conditions."

This adaptability can be seen time and time again as we witness Dobie extracting himself from his self-induced employment scrapes, the backlash to his harsh personal traits, and, most revealingly, to his facility for molding a loose collection of players into a tightly run machine. In the issue at hand—the triple whammy of bad weather, injury to the team's best receiver, and an inexperienced receiver not ready for prime time—adaptability would be tested to the limit. For Dobie, being noted for closed practices, his players' absolute discretion, and an iron tight veil of secrecy cast around every week's game plan, to come out and flatly reveal that he would not—indeed could not—pass was odd indeed. Sam Dolan, the Oregon State coach for 1911-12, only had two seasons to observe Dobie and, like every other follower of Northwest football, would have known of Dobie's insistence on secrecy, but this didn't stop Dobie from trying to catch him off guard. It is not known whether or not Dolan caught on to Dobie's sudden generosity of spirit in letting it out that his team's passing game was so utterly hopeless. By this charitable gesture, all Dolan needed to do was prepare his defense for Washington's running game.

Coach Dobie complained that the game played that day was more water polo than football. Greeting the teams was a sea of ankle-deep mud mixed with sawdust. There was as much slipping and sliding in place as ground gaining. Fumbles were frequent and costly for both sides. Later in the afternoon a thunder and lightning storm intervened but calmed down to a mere steady downpour that lasted throughout the second half. The game deteriorated into a punting duel because the terrible conditions had raised such a risk of fumbles that both sides were satisfied to play for field position. Washington came out on top of the kick fest, with both teams often booting the ball on second down. Young, punting for Washington on seven attempts, averaged 35 yards and beat out Oregon State's left halfback, Blackwell, who kicked thirteen times for an average of 22 yards.

The contest's early moments seemed to pick up where the previous week left off, with the Varsity having their way. Oregon State kicked off with Jacquot receiving the ball on his 30 and advancing it a few yards in the swamp masquerading for a football field. Jacquot and Young traded off showing strength up the middle and made the first down, but Young was forced to punt on the next series. Right end Ed Leader downed quarterback Reynolds before he could take a step. On the very first play from scrimmage, with the ball on the 12-yard line, the Orange and Black committed their first of many fumbles in a mistake-prone afternoon. On the next play, Dobie's concerns on using the forward pass were confirmed as the first attempt failed. It should be emphasized, however, that the pass attempt, coming as it did on this horrible stormy day and less than four minutes into the game, could lead one to believe that his self-proclaimed horrible passing game may just have been less than accurate. Close followers of Dobie's skills of manipulation would see this as proof that all of his chatter about passing was deliberate but fair subterfuge. No matter how they did it, the ball was on the 12-yard line right between the sidelines. This was a perfect place for a dropkick, and on the next play Young put his foot behind the ball that split the uprights for three points.

Washington fans were feeling pretty smug, but they soon discovered that Oregon State wasn't going to sit idly by and let the visitors take over the game. For every good series of downs that Washington was able to muster, the next would soon end in a fumble or a good defensive stop by the southerners. Young made a brilliant 20-yard run around end on a fake punt, but this was soon to be outdone by Blackwell. Just as the first quarter ended, he dodged and weaved for a 30-yard run of his own.

With the rain now approaching major storm levels, every spectator out in the open headed for cover. After a few short advances to start the second half, Blackwell tried a risky 42-yard dropkick that fell short. When Oregon State next got the ball, they had to punt away from midfield and buried the Varsity on their 15-yard line. Conditions were only made worse in the accelerating storm as Washington could not make an inch and fumbled the ball away in the ever-worsening quagmire. Blackwell seemed not to notice that he was playing in near-monsoon conditions and, from the 20, calmly booted a placekick to tie the score at 3-3. Thunder and lightning now added to the drama, but there was no movement to call for a delay in the interest of safety. Not just the teams but the officials and fans of those days were tough. The rainstorm soon turned into a fierce, pounding downpour, forcing both sides to fall back to a conservative punting duel. But while both teams continually lost the grip on the ball the entire game, there were no more catastrophic fumbles this quarter such as opened the half.

Hail was next on the weatherman's agenda, but short of an earthquake splitting the field in half, there seemed nothing that would deter either team in this battle against the elements. Both Young and Blackwell tried dropkicks for scores in the third quarter, but neither succeeded. These were obviously intended as surprise plays, since the dropkick requires great timing and precision, both of which were totally negated by the worst storm of the season. On one of Young's dropkicks, he slipped and fell just in the act of attempting the kick and turned the ball over to Oregon. This miscue was only one of a plethora of misfires that were the standard for this fifteen minutes of play. As the quarter ended, it seemed that the storm was destined to take the game away from both teams. A tie ball game was the likeliest outcome, based on the poor footing, poor visibility, monstrous winds, rain by the bucket, lightning, thunder, hail, and biting cold.

There was no let-up in the storm as the fourth quarter got under way. A few runs worked for both sides, but the pass had long been taken away from both teams just as Dobie had predicted. Who would be foolish enough to try a pass, given that every factor necessary for a completion, such as timing, footing, a dry football, and decent visibility, was absent and was never to return this afternoon? What few hardy fans still holding on were getting weary of a game that had deteriorated into punt/fumble, run/fumble, make a fair gain on a run, stall out—and repeat the sequence. It was bad enough to be soaked and freezing sitting in the stands but the tie game was doing nothing to help those still hanging in there take their minds off their personal misery. Some fun, this game.

The clock was mercifully ticking down below five minutes when there appeared to be a break from the monotony. Young, who had been playing a close second fiddle to Blackwell, got off a whopper of a 50 yard punt. On the next play Oregon State decided to put it all on the line with a pass, but the newly invigorated Young intercepted. Washington then, for another time that afternoon, made good on Dobie's prediction that they couldn't pass and flubbed again. Giving up on this risky business of going for broke, both teams resorted to their afternoon staple, punting on second down. Washington found themselves on Oregon State's 32-yard line, and time had now taken over for the weather as the critical factor weighing on the outcome. With the game on the line, the team that couldn't hit the side of a barn from the inside threw caution to the wind with a pass from left halfback Hap Miller to left end Earle "Click" Clark, placing the ball on the 5-yard line. Fullback Walt Shiel couldn't get the ball over, so with three minutes left, Miller got the nod for the next play and slogged through across the line into pay mud. Kicking in ankle-deep slop, the point-after failed. Under even worsening skies the final gun brought an end to the misery with Washington at 9-3 over Oregon State.

The real credit must be given to Gil Dobie, to the extent that his sob story of Washington's terrible passing game was bought by OSU. In analyzing what took place, we must remember that there was once again the fortuitous break of an extra week to prepare under stormy conditions which allowed Dobie to practice passing in the rain. It was here that his unprecedented disclosure was released of how lousy the Varsity was at passing. Suspicious? What couldn't have been known to anyone else since Miller was a freshman was that he exhibited great promise as a passer. In fact, as his reputation grew he would become recognized as the most talented passer in the league. With UW's best receiver out of the game, Wee Coyle the team's best passer just having graduated, and given the horrible weather with time running out, there was no way that a pass would be called for. Since conditions dictated game strategy, the Black and Orange were most likely to give credence to what Dobie had so earnestly broadcast—his team most assuredly would not pass.

But the result speaks for itself. The unknown quantity Miller threw a perfect strike to another under-the-radar freshman, Click Clark, for 20 yards, setting up the touchdown. In all, nine freshmen were on the field when the go-ahead points were put on the board. At crunch time it was a pass during a fierce storm, with untested players that placed the ball at the goal, making it possible for a short run to seal the victory. The final blow was the direct result of the game strategy cooked up by Dobie fourteen days earlier. With wins such as this, it is easy to see why witnesses to his magic came to use words such as "genius" and "wizard" in describing him. Oregon State was rallying late in the game but fell short.

For such a tight duel, the fact that Dobie used seventeen men as opposed to Oregon State only deploying eleven was surprising. Even more surprising was the fact that Dobie played ten freshmen in this most difficult of games under the most challenging circumstances. Dobie substituted so freely knowing the debilitating effects of the fifty-year storm the players had to deal with. His fresher men, while battling the same horrible conditions, had an edge. Since Dobie had a skill for assessing talent and drawing it out, he knew the risks of playing so many freshmen. He had already sized up their ability—another factor as to why his team walked off the field with a win on that most wretched of days.

### University of Oregon

In the week between games the storm had moved on and pass-friendly conditions were restored. But Washington fans were more worried about invaders from back east than either Oregon or the weather. Front-page news that week announced that the University of Pennsylvania now planned to switch from their long-held graduate coaching system to the hiring of a professional coach. It was widely reported that Dobie, not having lost a game for eight years going back to his high school days had received an attractive proposal. There was an announced salary of $10,000 per year behind the deal. Dobie's contract with Washington lasted another year, and since he was now comfortably situated in his job at Washington, the forays being made by Pennsylvania alums never progressed beyond scaring the collective pants off Dobie's devoted followers.

In summing up the Oregon game on Denny Field, Sidney Brunn of the *Post-Intelligencer* reported this was a game "that offered no spectacular runs, no goal line heroics, no story book finish," and for the most part didn't rile up the fans of either camp. However, it was a textbook Dobie game, his team described, as was so often the case, as being a machine. Washington fans liked everything they saw for the first three quarters, but the last fifteen minutes were a horror story in the making. It was certainly no secret that three-fourths of Dobie's games were shutouts, and with their bone-crushing efficiency, this had all the appearances of being one more goose egg added to the list. But when you learn that the official Dobie cigar count had reached six by the fourth period and he was reported to be "eating" the seventh in a nervous fit, something must have happened to get him even more hyped than usual. If Dobie was worried, the packed house needed resuscitation. Brunn described the "stunning surprise as leaving Washington rooters gasping for breath."

The first quarter of the game, to the contrary, could have lulled even the most loyal of Dobieites to sleep. With robotic efficiency the locals had their way just about every time they got the ball. The only score of the period came at the seven-minute mark off the toe of Bud Young, who sent a dropkick 28 yards through the standards. But early in the second quarter, if any of the crowd had dozed off, they would have missed the strangest touchdown ever to be recorded in the one-hundred-plus-year history of Washington football. This one even topped the previous year's Bunk Play, and once again it was Wayne Sutton bringing home the bacon.

A fumble by Oregon's Captain Walker set in motion the turnover that led to this touchdown for the ages. He couldn't handle a punt just beyond his own 10-yard line. It was never a good idea to provide such a gift to a Dobie-led team, but the way Washington was playing that day, it was most definitely a prescription for disaster. On fourth down, after three attempts up the middle, right halfback Frank Jacquot got the call but could only advance the pigskin to the agonizingly close 1-foot line. For the moment it looked as if Oregon had miraculously dodged this bullet. Left guard Fenton, from deep behind his goal, stepped back to punt as interior linemen Jack Bliss, Tom Griffiths, and BeVan Presley powered across the line and batted the ball that bounded backwards across the end line. For the day's large crowd temporary bleachers had been set up just behind Oregon's end of the field. As the ball bounded towards the stands with Wayne Sutton in hot pursuit, it bounced under the lower row of seats. Sutton leaped over the fence, dove under the seat and downed the ball for what Brunn described as "probably the only touchdown ever scored in a grandstand." Under the possession rules of the day, this comic spectacle counted for six hard earned points. The Oregon players who had been duped last year by the Bunk Play could only feel history had repeated itself. As they saw it, here two years in a row they ended up on the short end of a fluke play. Coming as it did at the hands of haughty Washington was doubly galling. Patten added the point after bringing the score to 10-0.

There were two Varsity touchdowns scored in the third quarter, as Dobie's men again were able to move the ball at will just as they did to start the game. Only this time rather than fizzling out as they neared the goal they were able to keep rolling. Both scores came after long downfield possessions with Jacquot each time powering the ball over the line from short distance. The final touchdown came shortly after the fourth quarter opened, made possible by a fumbled punt recovery by Patten at Oregon's 15-yard line. From there, a pass Shiel caught at the 5-yard line was muscled into scoring territory. Patten kicked two of his last three extra-point tries, giving Washington a comfortable margin of 30-0 with most of the final period still left to play.

But for the fourth quarter there was a complete role reversal. The first three quarters Washington put on a running clinic that Oregon had no response for. The fourth quarter Oregon suddenly discovered the pass, and Washington's defense looked as if they had never seen such a thing. The big question from all sides was, why did Oregon wait so long? In a remarkable passing exhibition by the smallest man on the field at 125 pounds, Anson Cornell made several athletic receptions paired with slippery maneuvers that totally outfoxed his hapless defenders. Within a span of five minutes, due to this one-man show, Oregon recorded an achievement for the history books. Their fourteen points gained by the pass make up the largest score ever achieved by a team playing against Dobie in his nine years at Washington. Remarkably, this also was the only time a team scored in double figures against him. His teams accomplished the feat fifty-six times plus one triple figure score.

Even though the final score ended up with a 30-14 margin of victory for Washington, the game exposed the glaring weakness of pass defense by the Varsity. The team always seemed to be a step too late and incapable of adjusting to Oregon's aerial assault. The visitors completed 252 yards on six passes against only 40 yards on three passes for Washington. They completed a total of 43 percent of their fourteen attempts, while Washington could only manage 38 percent on eight tries. It was only due to the dominance of Washington's running game that they salvaged this one. In both pass offense and defense they were caught flat-footed. With this game serving as the perfect blueprint as how to get to Washington, it was for certain that WSU Coach Johnny Bender had his offense working overtime on passing drills.

### Washington State

The *Post-Intelligencer* headline for November 27, 1912, read, "Specimens of Husky Players of W.S.C. Eleven Which Tackles Varsity Tomorrow on Denny Field." No, this was not a base scheme by crystal ball seers from Pullman co-opting the future Washington mascot. Had they been able to foretell the future, however, this certainly could cause the blood to boil for the loyal Purple and Gold. On closer inspection, the "husky" description was intended to feature the photographic proof of four intimidating men coming over from the Palouse hell-bent on doing some serious damage on Thanksgiving Day.

The uninitiated student of Coach Dobie would feel that going into the last game of the season there was every reason for pessimism to rule the day. After all, his team had demonstrated how not to defend against the pass and allowed Oregon, with seeming ease, to post their score for the ages. Washington State was coming to Denny Field with both a more experienced and heavier lineup. Coach Johnny Bender made no secret of his take on the opportunity before him. He personally scouted the Oregon game, as described in the *Daily*: "When the visitors made their series of forward passes completely dazzling the champ's defense, the stocky little football teacher was tickled to death. 'We're going to give Washington a fight for their lives when we come over here Thanksgiving. Do you know that we cancelled our game with Montana so that our injured men might get in fine shape for the game over here?' "

But what the uninitiated student would not know and what experience tells us of Dobie's reaction to this type of circumstance are two different matters. We have seen his behavior was tediously predictable, and here is a textbook case of how he would respond when the chips were (apparently) down. We must recognize that he worked best when there was a clearly defined challenge ahead. If this challenge was in the form of an obvious strength of the opponent or a flaw of his team, he had a standardized response. That week the pass defense flaw was delivered to him on a silver platter. His response called for unending and disciplined drills until his men were able to defend against every conceivable airborne attack. They could defend against the run, they could make yardage by the run, they could block, they could tackle, they could kick, but the previous week they totally fell apart defending against the pass.

So this week, after Dobie's men stood around in a trance for the fourth quarter against the "Webfooters," as sportswriters referred to them, it only stood to reason that he would attract banner headlines across the Northwest of looming disaster. But with no reports of laryngitis, the Washington mentor had suddenly lost his voice. His statement of being noncommittal contrasts sharply with that of Bender as being beamingly hopeful. The reason, of course: Dobie did not have to come out with a doleful take on his prospects—the team did this for him with their inexplicable breakdown on pass defense.

University of Washington Libraries, Special Collections, Neg. No. UW 2850

Dobie often crouched on the sidelines and his game day dress was always an overcoat, suit, tie and most often his trademark derby. Here he is focused on the action at the UW vs. WSU game of Nov. 28, 1912.

His Caspar Milquetoast behavior this week was unlike that of his calculated understatement before the Idaho game. Back then his team was widely predicted to lose because of the unanimity of the dopesters that Idaho was just flat-out superior. This week he was seen to be a surefire loser because of the team's glaring weakness. Logically, how could even the Wizard correct a problem of such proportions with only a week to work his magic? Besides, it made much greater play in the papers to stir up controversy rather than side with a team coming into the weekend with a 32-0-1 record. Bad news sells newspapers, and with the overly anxious attitudes of fans spoiled by a team that never lost, they sought out anything in print that differed from their conviction of invincibility. And, as if the newspapers didn't already have enough going for them in this citywide crisis of confidence, Dobie locked the gates again. This was after allowing open access to practices all year long. He even had the likes of Wee Coyle, Walter Wand, and yell king Bill Horsley escorted off the premises.

There was hardly a person in the Northwest out of diapers who wasn't aware of Dobie's inclination for covering all bases. Teach the team the elements of pass coverage and win, or leave them to their own devices and lose. If there was ever a time for Dobie's multifaceted approach to game-day readiness, this was it. Being the Thanksgiving Day game, the twelve days to prepare would serve them well as there was no shortcut to the pursuit of perfection. The task ahead meant taking huge blocks of time out of each preparation ritual and doing what the players hated the most of the perfectionist's practices—devoting hour after mind-numbing hour going over what they could do in their sleep. After all, this was the last game of the season, and with the new rules that encouraged use of the pass, the coaching staff had already devoted endless hours to pass defense.

Dobie didn't win his games by leaving matters to chance or paying heed to player complaints. In his prescription for winning, pass defense being indispensible, was broken down into its constituent parts, such as timing, speed, footwork, shadowing receivers, defending a territory, rushing the passer, reading offensive deception, tackling after the reception, pass blocking, pass interception, and running interference on an interception. The way Dobie taught football, any one of these fundamentals justified hours of drilling. That's why his players described his practices as living hell but were quick to credit them for never losing. Maxwell Eakins summed up the players' attitude: "Drill (practice) those days was the toughest part. At least while we were playing the game on Saturday, we had some fun. Dobie drove us hard but there was great satisfaction in the end. We always won."

As we've seen, Dobie taught each player his narrowly defined assignment and then, most importantly, was able to impart just how each role fit into the overall scheme. The system worked so famously because every player came to learn that success meant total obedience to the program. Cliché or not, Dobie constantly preached the fundamental tenet that a chain is only as strong as its weakest link.

When the game was under way, it wasn't long before there was quick confirmation that Dobie had gotten the team back on track. Verified by Ralph Casey writing in the *Post-Intelligencer,* the game was everything that was expected. "After three minutes of play Miller crashed through the W.S.C. line giving the Varsity its first points, following a *march of mathematical unfeeling precision* (emphasis added) from midfield where the university received Kleinholtz' punt." Dobie had returned the machine to good working order. Yet to be determined was whether his charges had learned to defend against the passing attack Bender surely had up his sleeve.

After several exchanges of possession, Casey crystallized what it was that set Dobie apart from the other coaches he came up against. "Bender's eleven fought with sterling vigor but could not sustain its attack and Rock's gallop of 30 yards on a quarterback run was the only feature of the advance." Comparing Dobie's "march of mathematical unfeeling precision" versus Bender's "could not sustain its attack" is the ideal juxtaposition of circumstances that explains the perfectionist's success. Here, in stark contrast, we see an intense, methodical tactician facing off against an excellent football mentor fighting back with only a pedestrian line of attack. Dobie excelled while Bender, knowing full well his opponent's weakness, could only get by. With both coaches drawing their players from similar talent pools, competing in the same game and on the same playing field, with one enjoying a vastly more successful outcome, there must be an explanation. With the benefit of one hundred years to look back, we see that Dobie was indeed ahead of his time. He brought a management style to what he did, portions of which are open to justifiable criticism, but his proficiency at getting the last ounce of skill from his players cannot be denied. He inspired their desire to follow his leadership, motivated them to follow his instruction, encouraged them to play as a team, and promoted a hunger to win. This is all that can be asked of a coach. He had the same ratio of average players to stars, and yet his teams always won. Modern-day coaches can study Dobie's methods and benefit. None can copy what he did, but there is a profound opportunity to learn and benefit from the system he employed.

Washington State's backfield plunges couldn't gain any traction, but Bender's extra efforts in teaching his men did earn them substantial yardage. The only problem with the yardage they racked up was that none of it was across Washington's goal line. The Varsity's pass defense had improved to the extent that they now would pull off the occasional big stop. Against Oregon this didn't happen in the short time Oregon attacked head-on with the pass. Washington's juggernaut defense, as it was described by Casey, could not be stopped for most of the afternoon with one great exception—when they were in close proximity of the goal. Had this been earlier in the season with the team developing fumbleitis, it might have spelled disaster. But in the last game of the season, the exacting work ethic that Dobie lived by did produce a win. He recognized his team's weakness and coached them beyond this exposure.

As the game proceeded, both teams showed an extraordinary aversion to risk. At one point after neither team was able to move the ball with any constancy. There were three consecutive possessions where the teams traded punts on first down. This had been Dobie's strategy going into the game. He felt that giving up possession for a possible field position advantage on a fumbled punt was a risk in his favor. Early into the second quarter, Washington intercepted a pass, demonstrating some progress in their weakest department. Miller, Jacquot, and Shiel took the ball on a succession of line bucks up the middle from the 45 to State's 30. From there Bender's men held, and Young, on a dropkick, placed the ball dead between the sticks, bringing the score to 9-0.

The Crimson and Gray's quarterback, Rock, peeled off the best run of the afternoon with the game still in the second quarter but soon gave up the ball on a broken-up pass play. After Kleinholtz' punt, the Varsity got a 15-yard break on a roughing-the-receiver call as Young was attempting to receive the punt. They patiently advanced the ball; a touchdown seemed in the offing. Two forward passes, Young to Sutton and Miller to Hunt, failed. More evidence of Bender's good coaching. From the 20-yard line, Young put his foot into another dropkick that split the uprights. Halftime score: 12-0.

The second half saw Washington State coming up short on their predictable strategy of directly attacking Dobie's supposedly pass-challenged defense. This served as further proof that the long, depressing hours of drilling on the ABCs of pass defense had paid off. The passes that were completed didn't provide much yardage, so the effort served only to discourage the easterners. It was late and it seemed that nothing could help. Here Washington's plan of punting the ball early as a play-it-safe strategy was working to their benefit. Young hadn't had a punt blocked all year, so the game plan fell right into place.

A dispute broke out as the fourth quarter was drawing to a close, with WSU's Captain Joe Harter up against it due to a protest lodged by Coach Dobie. The kerfuffle took several minutes to straighten out after a review of the play between the coaches and game officials. The play seemed simple enough, with Harter making a critical reception of a pass from fullback Foster. There was one crucial issue to iron out—that of Harter being a guard, therefore an ineligible receiver. Dobie's objection ruled the day and the ball was turned over to Washington.

As if this wasn't bad enough, State was soon flagged for placing quarterback Rock into the game twice within the same quarter. This clear-cut violation of the new substitution rule also was not a judgment call. But yet the visitors argued with the referees, who slapped them with a delay-of-game penalty on top of the initial infraction. This cascade of events buried the visitors on their 1-yard line, where they punted out to Washington.

Dobie's strategy of forsaking possession for field position was still in place. On first down Young booted the ball across the goal line for a touchback. It was here that the Washington Wizard's game plan finally paid off. State's right guard Goff stepped back to kick from his 20 as Captain Griffiths plunged across the line, blocking the punt. Right tackle Jack Bliss fell on the ball on the 4-yard line, essentially back where it was a few plays earlier, only then in the visitor's possession. Within a few short plays, their rash of penalties, together with Dobie doggedly sticking to his punting game plan, meant disaster for Washington State. Freshman fullback Walt Shiel carried the oval into pay dirt from there with Pink Pullen adding the extra point. This would ice the game for Washington, ending all scoring with their twenty-fifth shutout out of thirty-four games. At the final whistle the scoreboard showed Washington winning 19-0.

This marked another perfect season for Dobie and his men, with four shutouts and only seventeen points scored against them. Talk around the league by now was decidedly anti-Dobie, as could well be imagined. Every sort of complaint was thrown his way. His personality only served to escalate the dialogue as his demeanor left plenty of room for criticism. His off-the-cuff verbal gems made for juicy headlines that could heat up an opposing fan's passions to a red-hot frenzy. But such a reaction goes with the territory. It's only human nature to support your own, win or lose, but the real sports fan takes it personally when he or she gets beat up repeatedly by the outsiders. Five years of total domination on the short end of the scoreboard makes for bad blood.

# CHAPTER SEVEN

## *The Dreaded Specter—1913*

> "Under proper chaperones, there is no sane reason why all the co-eds who want to should not go to Portland next Saturday. The chaperones are now perfecting plans for the trip and will register their fair charges at the Multnomah hotel. Such a trip for the co-eds is something of an innovation, but when one stops to think of it the wonder is that the girls have not made up parties long before this and accompanied the team on its trips to different parts of the Pacific Northwest."
>
> *Portus Baxter, P-I Sporting Editor*

This was to be the year that stands out above all others in Coach Dobie's nine-year reign at Washington. It was in 1913 that opposing teams scored the greatest number of points against his team. The Oregon game, with only a three-point margin of victory, was the closest a Dobie-coached team came to losing. For that year his opponents put a total of 21 points on the board against the Purple and Gold's 267. This being the coach's worst year is the greatest expression of how his teams totally dominated Northwest football for his nine years in Seattle.

Coach Dobie was not one to offer up insights on the team's preseason readiness. After five straight years of championships, the hunger was insatiable for any insider tidbits he might drop. Alas, his avid followers could not look to the coach for anything outside of "I don't know." To do so could send the wrong signal to his players. The coach saw his duty as inducing the players to constantly strive towards bettering themselves. Part of his program was to let it slip to the rest of the world that he didn't expect much out of the material he was dealt. In surveying competition in the league for 1913, he saw powerhouses everywhere except Seattle. "Beyond a doubt this will be the hardest, most closely contested season in the last five years," was his take. He professed that he knew nothing about his chances of winning. Being the obsessive stickler for details that he was, his veracity on these issues just might be called into question. When asked by *Daily* Sports Editor James "Jimmie" Street to sum up the strengths of the twenty new men trying out for the first time, he pleaded ignorance, insisting that this question would have to be raised with his assistant coach, Thomas Wand. This must have raised eyebrows, as Wand was brand new to the coaching staff and, while he had played for four years on the team, winning the Flaherty Medal twice, he never won his letter. For certain Dobie knew the skill level of every man on the roster better than anyone else in the state.

That year Ralph Horr took over the reins as graduate manager from Victor Zednick. He had been in communications with the University of Michigan to arrange a game to be played in Seattle. Football enthusiasts in the Northwest were anxious for such a game to settle the issue of how well Dobie's machine would match up with the highly regarded "Hurry Up" Yost team. West Coast football could not get proper acceptance by the East Coast and Midwest colleges because the distance factor made scheduling games so very difficult. It was true that many fans who saw both Dobie's team and their easterly cousins play felt that the Varsity would most assuredly be competitive, if not superior. Word of Dobie's success was reaching the East Coast, as a Yale graduate advised his team to "go west and get that man Dobie and Harvard never would win any more games." Unfortunately, even with Washington favoring a matchup, word had come from Michigan's faculty that the game had been squelched. They felt the team would be away from their studies too long at the close of the first semester.

After five years and no defeats, talk started to mount that the team and fans would actually benefit from a loss. It's certainly true that the players oftentimes felt that Dobie's magic would take up the slack if anyone on the team let down. Never losing played a big role in Dobie's obsessiveness in his ceaseless struggle to harness inflated egos. As for the fans, game attendance was continually rising, and loyalty to the coach and team was well demonstrated, but they too were getting a bit blasé towards winning. The string became an entitlement. The attitude was now being expressed in many quarters that this excess of success could lead to their downfall.

Dobie was credited with raising the level of competition throughout the league, and while paying him his due, the other coaches were not shy in letting it be known that he could be beaten. Leading into preseason play, there was widespread talk that Washington could be knocked off. As was the case most every preseason, the Varsity appeared ragged. The coaching staff shuffled a large variety of players into positions trying to find the right mix. Even Jimmie Street seemed to be jumping off the long-standing bandwagon as the season drew near. He didn't hold back his feelings with this headline: "Dobie's Men Make One Sad Showing." He went so far as to state that it would take a miracle for Washington to defeat Oregon State and that "Oregon will beat us sure." Hardly a ringing endorsement coming from a source usually expected to temper such judgments, even if they were accurate. The editor didn't give up all hope; however, he did conclude that if the team were to blast a few tons of dynamite under the men each time they charge, Washington would be able to gain some ground. There is no record of Dobie's response to Street's negativity. Why would he when this perfectly sums up what he would say if asked?

## Preseason

The preseason schedule included games with Everett High, the All-Navy team stationed at Bremerton, and Whitworth College. So far it was impossible to get a handle on just how well the team would do. What with every coach in the league gunning for Dobie, the malaise setting in with constant winning, and the reported weaknesses of this year's squad, it appeared to many that once again this could very well be that year the team would taste defeat. Putting aside Dobie's funereal outlook, there were legitimate signs of concern. Captain Tom Griffiths had graduated, stellar right tackle Jack Patten didn't come out for football that year, and right halfback Frank Jacquot had not returned to the team as of the opening game. Louis Seagrave and Elmer "Cy" Noble were two freshmen new to the team who were showing promise, but their range was unknown at this point. This question would soon be answered, as they both earned letters all four years and rank at the top echelon of men who took up football at Washington.

Cy Noble and the celebrated Grimm brothers (Huber, Warren, and Bill) all came out of Centralia, a small town in western Washington just south of Seattle. All were four-year lettermen in football. Huber was on the Washington baseball team that toured Japan in 1908. Tragedy would strike two of these players shortly after their graduation. As an army first lieutenant in World War I, Cy Noble would be killed in battle in 1918 on the Argonne-Meuse front in France. Warren Grimm, after serving in World War I, came home and was shockingly murdered in the Centralia Massacre, a bloody labor riot erupting at a parade ironically celebrating the first anniversary of Armistice Day on November 11, 1919.

The first half of the Everett game bore out Dobie's downbeat prognostications. Fumbling, erratic line play and an inconsistent backfield best describe the team. It was only thanks to an interception that Bud Young took in for a touchdown that put Washington up 7-0 at halftime. Dobie shook up the team with several substitutions to start the second half; Warren "Mike" Hardy went in at guard for Louis Seagrave; Ed Leader took over Raymond "Mike" Hunt's end position; a nonletterman, Murphy, assumed Cy Noble's place at right halfback; and Calvin Hazelet moved into nonletterman Davidson's slot at left halfback. The game ended with an unimpressive score in favor of Washington, 26-0.

The All-Navy team from Bremerton brought everything the Varsity could handle on their October 11 game through the opening half, drawing first blood and forcing Washington to play catch-up to tie the score at 7-7. The consensus among sportswriters centered on Washington's perceived weakness in their line as leading to this season's inevitable downfall. Fans were described as nervous with a foreboding outlook for the year's schedule. The way UW was being pushed around the first thirty minutes, this was justified. Perhaps owing to a touch of dramatic license, but the rooters in the grandstands were described as having "made a heroic effort to appear composed." Play on the field, however, was far short of heroic.

After their sluggish start, Washington managed to ramp up their blocking and tackling in the second half. The sailors were rough, played rough, and even talked rough when given the chance. QB Allan Young, who had the unenviable job of replacing all-everything Wee Coyle, turned out in many analysts' minds to have a greater set of skills. He could pass, run, punt, and turned into a highly respected field general. He was described as "phenomenal" by the Seattle *Times*, and his play supported such acclaim. One illustration of All-Navy's rough (but clean) play: on a run around right end, Young was tackled and suffered a terrible knee injury, threatening to keep him on the bench for four to six weeks. As to the sailors' rough talk, there was an eight-minute break in the action while the referees sorted out a ruling on a downed punt where they seized the opportunity to dump on Dobie. The coach smiled at the effort but didn't appear nervous at their razzing. Assuming a bit of Damon Runyonesque speech, their jabs went along these lines. "Say Dobie, wait until Pullman gets at youse guys. Da'll wallop you shore. No chanct for you to clean 'em. Dere da class."

What walloping was left to be done in this preseason game didn't come from All-Navy. In the second half, Young scored a field goal to go with two more touchdowns, for a final margin favoring Washington 23, All-Navy 7. Dopesters were now sidling up alongside Dobie and his gloomy forecasts for the future. With two suspect ordeals behind them and their only quarterback out with an injury, it did seem there was no rational argument for Washington to defend its title this year.

Dobie had many sleepless nights over his concerns for replacing Wee Coyle, who had been the rock of his backfield for the first four years he was at Washington. He told Bobby Boyce of the *Argus* one evening in 1915 while the two were having dinner at Boyce's ranch just how nerve-racking the sudden turn of events was for him, describing his elation over Young only now to lose him so suddenly to a knee injury. "And then out of the clouds of gloom that surrounded the campus, who should flash forth but little 'Bud' Young, a man who was born a quarterback, and during the first weeks of the season we didn't have any more trouble than a corpse. He could kick and run and pick a weak spot as well as any man who ever wore the moleskins and it seemed all over except for arranging of a schedule for the next year. Then, of course, it happened. He was too good to be true, that's all, and we carried him off the field one night and into the dressing room, and there, when I took one look at his twisted knee I knew we had about as much chance to win the championship as Greece would have to lick the German army."

Dobie readily admitted that this crisis was the most difficult coaching situation he ever faced in his career at Washington. He took stock of his men and initially didn't see any potential in Charles Smith. Smith was short, stocky, and bowlegged. The coach rated him as too even tempered and gentlemanly to take on the rough job of quarterbacking. He had already been passed over for halfback, but in desperation Smith was tapped for the position. Oregon State was a week away and there was no time for indecision. Under any other circumstances, Smith would not have made the cut, but time pressures forced Dobie to act.

Even after the choice was made, Smith did not take charge and exhibited no leadership skills as required of a team general. Dobie was beside himself. The hard-driving coach took his reluctant charge aside in practice and took him home at night for one-on-one counseling. This bore only fleeting results. Dobie would see hopeful strains of his stiffening up, but the next day in practice Smith would resort to his old puppy dog ways. With less than a week until game day, Dobie described what he had to do.

"And then I played my last card. It was right in the midst of a stiff scrimmage practice. Running out from the side lines, I stopped the work and then, with his college mates all around him, I lit into the boy and talked to him as I have never talked to a human being before or since. I told him he had a streak of yellow up his back as broad as the Mississippi River and that he didn't have enough nerve to pick up a knife at the table for fear of wounding himself. And I ripped him up first one side and down the other until he grew white in the face and that was all that was necessary. I got him fighting mad, see? And his work the next Saturday against O.A.C. was a dream—wonderful. Oh, yes, we're good friends—always have been, I guess. The boy developed into a great placekicker, a heady general, a gritty player, and all told was one of the most dependable men I had."

Boyce was personally acquainted with Smith's father, Lou Smith, sheriff of Auburn, Washington. The father revealed that young Smith had very much the same reaction to Dobie's public rebuke as had those before him who had undergone the same fate. Boyce passed this on directly to Dobie, knowing the thought had never occurred to him: "My dear coach, what a struggle that same little chap had to keep from walloping you a clip on the jaw." Boyce went on offering his opinion that the ends did indeed justify the means. Speaking of the father, he said, " 'But I guess he was glad you talked to him just the way you did because the lad had it in him all right, and sure you brought it out.' 'Oh, well,' said Dobie, sinking down on his back and cocking his heels up in the air, 'he was a great little quarterback, wasn't he?' "

Dobie, of course, orchestrated the entire episode of bringing the reluctant Smith up to speed. He was not a "born quarterback," as the coach so accurately described Young. Smith never applied for the job. He was not blessed with the natural all-around talents of Coyle or Young. There are other proven coaching techniques to prepare a player for his role on the team, but the way Dobie handled the challenge of turning Smith into a quarterback was *his* management style. It is not an approach that many leaders can pull off, and it does come at great risk. As often shown, Dobie had the strength of personality to bring his players right to the brink of their ability to maintain self-control, then back off. Time and again the players singled out for Dobie's evil eye treatment would swallow their pride and raise their game to even higher levels. This had previously been seen with Wee Coyle, Melville Mucklestone, Penny Westover, Pete Tegtmeier, now with Charley Smith, and there would be more to follow in Dobie's long career.

Concern going into the weekend still lingered over how well Dobie's men would do in their Whitworth warm-up. As game day approached, no one had any idea as to what was ahead. Bud Young's shoes were filled by Charley Smith in the first half, and substitute Fred Madigan played out the second half. This gave Dobie the chance to assess both players. It was Smith who registered the best showing. The best summation of the visitor's performance came from the *Daily* in its description of Whitworth as being "overtouted and press agented to death." It was hard to argue that something went terribly wrong in the prognosticators' camps, as no one saw what was soon to be played out on Denny Field with Washington's total domination in every aspect of the game. In fact there were even a few brave souls who dared speculate a victory for Whitworth.

Washington scored fifteen total touchdowns with these men: Hap Miller (two), Walt Shiel (one), Captain Herman "Andy" Anderson (one), freshman Elmer "Cy" Noble (six), Charles Smith (two), Ed Leader (two), and Calvin Hazelet (one). Everything they tried worked, whether it was passing, line bucks, wide sweeps, and tackle-arounds. There can be no claim of running up the score, as Dobie used twenty-one players. This was the second largest number of players ever to get into a Dobie-coached game while he was at Washington. Sportswriter Ted Cook's headline in the *Times* for the game, "Washington Scores Century in Game with Whitworth," was decidedly kinder than the *Daily*, "Dobie's Machine Makes Fricassee of Whitworth." The story of the game was domination from every vantage point one cared to consider. The final score speaks for itself: Washington 100, Whitworth 0. This marked the last time the two teams would play.

### Oregon State

Coming off the overwhelming win against Whitworth, now that the league schedule was about to begin, Washington's prospects had sunk to crisis proportions. But to the rescue there was the one bedrock principle of Coach Dobie's behavior that could always be called up in an emergency—concoct a scenario of doom and make sure it is aired in public. Putting a century's worth of points on the board would seem to strain even Dobie's great skills at the task of going negative, but despite the challenge, he wouldn't disappoint. Some of the gems he dispersed for the team's consumption: "If O.A.C. were properly coached, they could whip the best team in the world, Yale, Harvard and Princeton included." "Certainly we can't hope to win the game Saturday." "We haven't a kicker, and what can a team do without a man to kick?" "Those fellows have played football ever since they have been able to walk. I won't predict the score because that is impossible." The cataclysmic defeat ahead for Dobie's team had to have some basis in fact, as he well knew. The crux of his argument for the crushing defeat this time was due to the weight advantage enjoyed by Oregon State. He quoted the disparity as more than twelve to fifteen pounds per man, which to his credit was correct. The coach wasn't concerned that his reasoning lacked substance; just getting out an outrageous claim suited his purposes. His doleful strategy was an adaptation of "You can fool some of the people some of the time."

A Seattle *Times* writer in 1913 was given to rhyme in casting doubt on Dobie's forecasts:

## CHEERFUL—CHEERLESS
## GIL DOBIE, COACH

---

By HANK
Where is the team of yesterday; the
limelight's ruddy glare
Shines not upon a football squad the
coach said "wasn't there."
Where is that bunch of cripples from
the campus in this town
Whom Dobie swore would sure get
licked; would scarcely make a down?

Where is that bunch of raw recruits;
that ivory-headed crew
That couldn't work a forward pass nor
bust a line in two?
Oh Dobie, Gilmour Dobie, coach of all
our football hopes,
They knocked your "info"—cheerless
stuff—clear against the ropes.

They say you're pessimistic Coach, but
somehow I believe
That all the time you firmly knew
you'd something up your sleeve.
You gave us chills and shivers for a
fortnight more or less
And made some loyal rooters feel
disconsolate, I guess.

---

> Gone are the wrecks of yesterday, the
> spavined, battered team;
> Gone is the nightmare "Cold defeat,"
> that sleep-disturbing dream,
> Never again will Little Me take heed
> of that sad talk
> When Dobie says the other team will
> romp home in a walk.

---

It mattered not to Dobie that many writers would mock (some respectfully, others derisively) his incessant low-balling of his team's chances despite obvious evidence to the contrary. He was focused only on winning. In his view the only way to win was through a team effort, and the most destructive force working against the team was for players to stray from his control. He was never satisfied since he had to have his fingers into every detail. He was the conductor and, as any maestro would demand, every player must be in perfect tune with all others. There was no margin for error, thus the painful attention to the most elemental facets of the game. In making his audacious predictions for upcoming games, his audience wasn't the fans or sportswriters but the contestants on both sides of the ball. He put out his message unconcerned that the "Little Me's" like Hank saw through him, but to embed his marker in the minds of the players on both teams.

Another more serious problem than the team weight disparity was brewing, and it threatened the cancellation of the match as late as two days before kick-off. This problem stemmed from a charge that Oregon State had ineligible players on its squad. Not just Washington, but Idaho, Whitman, and Washington State also claimed that OSU was in violation of the "Ringer Rule." This conference regulation prohibited incoming players who had previously participated in college-level sports from claiming freshman status at their new institution. President Kane, Graduate Manager Ralph Horr and Coach Dobie were all up in arms over their claim that Oregon State was in violation. Not one to turn down a golden opportunity dropped in his lap, Dobie was outraged. With characteristic hyperbole he fired this shot off Oregon State's bow: "We are playing the biggest gang of ringers ever assembled under any flag." The matter was still unsettled the day before the game, and rather than calling it off, Ralph Horr threatened to lodge an official protest with the league. The soap opera came to an abrupt conclusion at the eleventh hour when OSU's Coach Dr. E. J. Stewart agreed to pull the three players under dispute.

Sports Reporter Ted Cook of the *Times* described Washington's play against Oregon State as "Dobistic" in summing up the game where Washington "fairly slaughtered the Oregon Aggies." So much for Dobie's pregame concerns of his team being the one about to be slaughtered at the hands of the southern powerhouse. The one legitimate point that Dobie did make was that in losing his star QB, Bud Young, he was playing with a replacement that had no experience in conference play. This proved to be a nonissue, as Charley Smith more than answered the call with his excellent generalship. There was also a benefit to the publicity given to Dobie's mournful predictions and all the pregame wrangling: it filled the house and the crowd spilled onto the field, standing several rows deep to get a close-up vantage point on the action. Many of these fans, dressed in purple and gold, were tagged to go onto the field at halftime for a gigantic serpentine ending at a large **W** fireworks display.

Dobie was not known for jovial outbursts, but he was known to break into smiles on big occasions. This was one of those moments. He must have convinced himself that what he was predicting was true, but when all was said and done, with the game behind him, his face lit up into a broad smile of satisfaction. Many sports historians have reported that because of his dour countenance, he never smiled. This is another of those anecdotes meant more to shock than to accurately report. Dobie, being a strict disciplinarian, was sparing in letting his guard down, lest he be exposed as having a softer side. He saw the public role of the leader as weighted more towards the iron fist. His velvet glove was reserved for his off-the-field private life. Those instances where he did exhibit a softer side in public, while rare, were repeated throughout his career.

The Oregon State game played out like so many others of Dobie's tenure at Washington, with pregame dopesters and opposing fans expecting a competitive game that never materialized. That year there were many who felt that OSU was the team to take the title away from the Purple and Gold. With as much hype as preceded the game and with it being played out with such a huge turnout of fans, a tighter struggle would be expected. Anyone hoping for a nail biter was sorely disappointed, with the Varsity turning in a commanding effort.

There was not much to be learned from this game other than a continuation of the hard-core Washington fan's belief that another conference championship was in the bag. This was definitely a stretch considering this year's stronger competition, the team's injuries, and the trials ahead in getting inexperienced players up to speed. With five years of no-loss teams under their belt, Dobie's fans were even more of a mind that winning was their birthright. Such complacency was precisely what the coach obsessed against, but his message wasn't always well received. In the past the press attacked and editorially jousted with Dobie and would show little respect. He would return the favor. It came down to not understanding each other. Now growing into his job, and with the press gaining insight into this idiosyncratic character, the marriage of coach and press was approaching normalcy.

Not many coaches, fans, teams, and sports reporters have experience with constant winning. Losing is the equalizer that helps to center one's mind-set. Win after win, now running into a sixth year, brought out a lot of huffing and puffing. Human nature being what it is, there needs to be challenge ahead to improve. This is the very reason that, in this circumstance, Dobie felt he needed to manufacture challenge. He played the lead part in the process, depending on what happened on the football field last week and what could be anticipated next week. In this Dobie was a newspaper reporter's dream, as he could be counted on to take a controversial stance. To him big wins caused just as much concern as small wins. Strong teams ahead are just as much a concern as weak teams ahead.

We've seen he often took a contrarian stance. This was not just to be ornery or pessimistic. It was calculated. Depending on where he was in the weekly cycle as to big/small win or strong/weak team, his behavior was predictable—contrarian, but predictable. He sought to broadcast a message both to his team and the competition. In this he partnered with the fans and sportswriters. In the scenario of big and strong, he doesn't have to do much, as the fans and sportswriters, as we have seen so often, do his work for him. Everyone else does all the moaning and groaning and Dobie lays in with a noncommittal take or just clams up since his water is being carried by his partners. In the case of small and weak, he takes on the full load. This plays out with his pronouncements that Nero is coming to town and he's going to burn down the stadium. In the end, what Dobie is looking for is to instill uncertainty into the mix and motivate a cocky player to practice harder. For the other team, this firestorm in the press makes life doubly difficult. While this distraction is playing out, back at his office the one guy in the middle of everything is working harder than everyone else as he grinds out that week's game plan.

Washington's performance excelled on the field in every regard except for fumbling, the worst vice a player could commit. For the first half of the game, regardless of perfect field conditions, the team couldn't seem to get a handle on the ball. Dobie was known to repeat a play in practice dozens of times if there had been a fumble on its use in the prior game. While his blowups at the players were so much hot air for effect, he reserved his most heightened animus for a player committing a fumble in a critical game situation. Despite knowing full well that the team would pay the price for this crime of crimes, the boys were just not able to maintain their grip in the first half.

At halftime Dobie delivered one of his stock lectures on the sin of fumbling, sent in straight from central scripting. Returning players had all heard it before and newcomers to the squad certainly had heard about Dobie's passion on the subject, not to mention his predictable rants unmistakably directed at the offenders.

Oregon State, seeing that Washington dominated in everything they tried on offense, resolved to play for field position and punted repeatedly on first and second down to force Washington back. Dobie's response was to pull out all stops. With everything going for them, he approved use of the trick triple pass from Jacquot to Miller to the ends. Hap Miller, coming off his All-Northwest selection as a freshman, proved in this game he was for real. He did virtually everything that could be asked of a halfback. In the first quarter he passed for the first touchdown to Pete Sutton and kicked the extra point for the only score in this session. Throughout the game he gained yardage, no matter if it was running up the middle or on an end sweep. The next touchdown came in the second quarter on a run by Miller, who kicked the extra point to complete the scoring for the first half.

Miller continued his spectacular play with a touchdown in the third quarter, set up by a 35-yard run by Walt Shiel. As Mr. Everything in this game, he again booted the point after. Miller returned the favor to Shiel along with Jacquot setting him up for the Varsity's fourth touchdown with terrific broken-field runs of 21 and 18 yards, respectively. With Miller's kick, this brought the score showing Washington up 28-0 at the close of the third period.

The one stellar aspect of the visitor's game was quarterback Ira Blackwell's punting, but with Miller doing the punting for the home team, his great toe served to nullify any advantage OSU had hoped for. Miller wasn't through with his dominance of the game, scoring the first TD of the last quarter after (not surprisingly) what was described by the *Times* as, "a spectacular thirty-five yard run through a broken field." He finally proved a human side with his first miss out of five extra-point efforts. Since the game was now out of hand, both teams began wholesale substitutions. Doc Stewart did it in a vain attempt to build a fire under his team, and Dobie put in his subs to balance the skill level on both sides of the ball. Dobie used nineteen players in total and Stewart fifteen.

Miller left the game with a badly wrenched ankle, and with him out as the contest was winding down, fans must have thought the afternoon's excitement was behind them. Oregon State could be expected to make a showing now, but this was not to be. Cy Noble picked up where Miller left off with some excellent footwork in the open field and racked up two touchdowns. Nonletterman Benjamin Gill, who came in for Shiel, was given the kicking duties, making one of his two attempts. A game expected to be a tight battle ended up anything but, with a final score of Washington 47, Oregon State 0.

## Whitman College

In the last seven games between these two schools, the Varsity had won all seven and enjoyed a 167-27 advantage. With this preponderance of evidence, could Dobie muster a credible argument that this game would end the streak? Of course, but, odd as it seems, his wasn't the only voice holding fast to this opinion. There was a lot of noise coming out of tiny Whitman that they had the horses to take it to Washington this year. They did have Royal "Tubby" Niles, a unanimous choice for All-Northwest fullback the previous year, and Clark Slover at end, said to be the fastest man on any conference eleven. The game was variously called the battle of the season, Dobie's fight of his life, the real thing, a good fight, a big game, and Whitman's opportunity of a lifetime.

In a determined effort to stir up interest in a game that looked like a walkover, Jimmie Stewart of the *Daily* declared that the downtown men spoke as one in agreement with the coach. As self-appointed team ticket barker, he jumped on the chance to pit the doubting businessmen against the ever-loyal students. They weren't buying the Dobie line, but after six years of wins they had good reason. Stewart reported, "Not a student in the university will believe that Dobie means a word he is saying about Whitman." Even though it came through a sly reporter's manufacturing of the conflict, his tactic worked. Attendance was well above expectations.

With Hap Miller out with his bad ankle and Bud Young still recovering from his injured knee, there was reason to worry, but elevating concern to being in "really bad shape," as Dobie viewed matters, overstated the obvious. This came out just one day before the matchup, and we find Stewart still sowing the seeds of doubt. In fact, he went out of his way to line up behind the coach. Showing no pretense of unbiased reporting, his statement left no room to doubt where he stood: "Ludicrous as it may seem, what Dobie says is the truth." Stewart's theory rested on a rather thin premise that at some point in the season, a team simply goes flat. Whether the team becomes just stale or lazy isn't clear, but on this the reporter lays his claim that a loss could be in the offing.

Stewart having worked so hard to spike up a bit of pregame drama, the *Daily* rewarded the talented freshman with the lead assignment of reporting on the game. There did seem to be a good bit of hubris in his staunch backing of the Great Gloomer's prophesies, but early on it appeared that the cub reporter had the sports story of the year before him. What a scoop was unfolding, and he called it! In the opening minutes of the game, Washington, after taking the ball on the kickoff to midfield, marched it downfield to Whitman's 3-yard line. There halfback Frank Jacquot fumbled the ball, where it bounced for what was described as an interminable length of time before rolling to a stop. Emory Hoover, the Whitman QB, on the run scooped the ball up with both hands and sprinted down the field 97 yards for the first touchdown. Ted Cook, sports reporter for the *Seattle Times,* called this "perhaps the most spectacular touchdown ever registered on Denny Field." Niles kicked the point after as the partisan crowd hooted and hollered their lungs out. And just like that, it seemed for all the world that maybe-just-maybe Dobie, the downtown businessmen, and Jimmie Stewart were on to something.

This energized the Missionaries and, in the next series, the Varsity was forced to punt. Niles wasn't able to make yardage and then punted to Charley Smith, who made an excellent return of 25 yards. Not showing any consistency, Washington coughed up the ball again by halfback Calvin Hazelet fumbling to Niles. It seemed everyone wanted to get into the act on fumbling, with Hoover, on their next possession, committing the flub with center BeVan Presley recovering. Washington hadn't yet put their game together and after three line plunges couldn't make a first down. On fourth down, a pass from Hazelet to

Wayne Sutton finally put Washington on the board. With Charley Smith's kick, the score for this tight game evened up at 7-7 at the half.

The hometown crowd now had a game on their hands, and the stands buzzed with excitement. As has been seen, constantly winning has its downside of lulling the audience to sleep, but today was unexpectedly different. Fans respond when their team needs them, and this was one of those days. In the locker room Dobie likewise had all the material he needed to get the players focused, what with their fumbling and a tie game on their hands.

The traditional serpentine stringing out of the grandstand seemed longer and more energetic as the crowd cheered them on. The Whitman corpse led the march, and as the band played the "Devil's Ball," a red-caped Satan complete with horns and pitchfork claimed the unfortunate soul for his own. As a blaze of fire and smoke erupted, he carted the deceased Missionary off the field to his dreadful fate. While the halftime show was rather blatant as to how yell king George Mathieu and the student fans stood concerning the game, this belied the actual events taking place on the field of battle. But a game like this was just what the doctor ordered. It served to support Dobie's unabashedly gloomy predictions and provided that much-needed shot in the arm to rev up the crowd.

As the second half unfolded, Whitman hadn't lost a step in their relentless campaign. Washington's passing game was working well and it looked now as if Washington could get back into the mix. Charley Smith was growing in confidence and proved to be an able replacement for the injured Bud Young. Johnny Bender, the WSU coach, was scouting the game and, from the press box, rendered the opinion that Oregon's highly touted quarterback, Anson Cornell, didn't have a thing on Smith. High praise considering that Cornell and Young were regarded as the best in the league.

Whitman in the third quarter was moving the ball well, completing a 15-yard pass followed by a pass-interference call tacking on another gift of 15 yards. The next play, a 50-yard dropkick by Niles that failed, proved to turn the game around. On the play, right halfback Bishop of Whitman suffered a broken shoulder that put him out for the season. With the oval in their possession, Washington seemed to find their legs. They placed the ball into scoring position in large chunks with a pass from Hazelet to Jacquot, a sensational open-field run by Smith, and a long run coming on a tackle eligible from Captain Anderson. Hazelet punched the ball over, but the try for the extra point failed on the kickout attempt to put the ball into position.

The Purple and Gold closed out the third quarter in grand fashion with touchdowns from Sutton, picking up a blocked kick by left tackle Elmer Leader, and two touchdowns by fullback Walt Shiel. In the last quarter Dobie brought in subs Benjamin Gill, Tony Savage, Ed Leader, Warren Hardy, who would earn his letter after four years, and nonletterman Carnahan. Cy Noble brought home the final score to complete a convincing win for Dobie's squad, 41-7.

Being that it was painfully slow in developing, the bandwagon of naysayers daring to prophesy a Varsity loss did deserve a modicum of respect. But on this first day of November, 1913, there was no question as to which was the superior team.

### University of Oregon at Multnomah Stadium, Portland

Mostly hype but with some basis in fact, this game was widely anticipated to be tightly contested. With Washington's undefeated record, Oregon's loss to Willamette University, and their 10-10 tie game with Oregon State, win/loss comparisons wouldn't seem to cast doubt on the outcome. Bud Young was finally back for light practice but reinjured his knee, keeping him out of the game, and Hap Miller, having returned to the lineup, wasn't strong enough to assume his kicking duties. There were four other starters who were suffering from injuries, but by game day Cy Noble of this group was the only one not able to play. With half of their starters limping, this would cause some doubt in the minds of the Washington faithful, but for this game there was an extra week of preparation, which greatly helped to work out the kinks.

Dobie took advantage of the open date Saturday and scouted the Oregon State/Oregon game himself. The account of what he saw in this game gives us a window into understanding just why he was so consistently negative in sizing up his own team's chances when facing a team playing below Washington's level. The evidence is abundantly clear that he fielded strong, well-coached teams who dominated the opposition. Away from the football field, those who knew him personally found him to be intelligent, a good conversationalist, friendly, and upbeat. Anything having to do with his on-field endeavors was famously the opposite, revealing a meticulous, controlling, demanding, and sharp-tongued nature. Just what may have been behind this Dr. Jekyll and Mr. Hyde behavior was put on full display when he gave his scouting report on the deadlocked Oregon/Oregon State game.

It was only thanks to a late-fourth-quarter surge with Oregon down 10-0 that they managed another touchdown and a field goal to tie the game. Squeezing out a tie against a team that Washington had beaten 47-0 three weeks before didn't seem to cut any ice with Dobie. In a Jimmie Street interview, he somehow saw a team that, based on their recent on-field accomplishments, didn't seem to stack up to the coach's assessment. "Bezdek's men played magnificent football. The Oregon team is better than I ever imagined they could be. Their backfield is far better than I thought they could possibly be. The men are fast and heavy. The Oregon line is exceptionally good. I did not think that they had a team down there like they have. I had heard a lot about them and knew, of course, that they must be good, but I never thought for a moment they could be so good as they are. They are heavier and faster than ever before in their history." Dobie showed no concern for such an obvious inconsistency in that it was just three weeks earlier he told the world his boys' chances were completely hopeless against Oregon State.

University of Washington Libraries, Special Collections Neg. No. UW 29085    Students marching with bagpipes and The Hook.

The Hook was devised by yell king Bill Horsley in 1911 as the symbol of Washington football domination. Here students are marching to the game in Portland against Oregon on Nov. 15, 1913 at Multnomah Stadium.

He saw his team as behind the eight ball but, despite undeniable evidence to the contrary, Oregon was a surefire winner. Now with six years to observe Dobie, a pattern of behavior was coming into focus. He had well demonstrated his skills of psychological manipulation and his fear of the win streak going to his players' heads. He didn't have the backing of the press in sizing up Oregon as the underdog, so he had to invent it. How could his players back home, the sportswriters, and Varsity fans refute this? There were only newspaper reports and Dobie's eyewitness account to go by. He carried much more weight than the reports—after all, he had never lost a game. The coach was signaling his team, pure and simple. The message? He saw something that scared him; the players better hunker down, because there's a battle royal ahead. By going to the effort to personally scout the team, this proved his suspicions. He saw in the press that everyone else predicted an easy road ahead, so by checking out matters for himself, he had firsthand evidence to argue the contrary. So goes his masterful campaign to convince his players that they couldn't slack off in practice that week.

On Wednesday before game day, a combined rally and love-in for Coach Dobie was held. The rally was to feature the predictable Scot, who didn't disappoint, coming out with his bold prediction that Washington's reign as champs was to last but two more days. With this opener as backdrop, Professor of Journalism Frank G. Kane took charge of the love-in. His gushing praise of the five-time champion coach was the perfect counter to Dobie's crystal ball reading that the Varsity was soon to join the ranks of league also-rans. Dobie: "I can give you any number of examples where a team supposed to be invincible has gone down to defeat before a team nobody thought had a chance." Kane: "There isn't a better coach in the United States than Dobie. The team he has coached is the only team that ever played without suffering a defeat." And so it went as if the two had concocted a script designed to best exploit the young students' emotions. It wasn't in Dobie's nature to take part in such a face-off, but he obviously enjoyed the afternoon. He broke out in broad smiles when Captain Herman Anderson revealed some inside dope on the team, when he saw the huge reaction of the students to Professor Kane's praise, and when the professor sanctioned the coach's constant efforts to tamp down the team's overconfidence. He showed a vulnerable human side after all; he smiled.

Another momentous event in the annals of Washington football occurred at this game. This groundbreaker can best be described as it was written up in the *Seattle Times* the day before the game: "For the first time in the history of the institution, a party of coeds and sorority girls from the University of Washington will make a trip away from home to witness a football game, the Oregon-Washington contest at Portland on Saturday bringing about this innovation. Why these trips should not have always been undertaken and the girls afforded the pleasure to which their station and position in the scheme of varsity life entitled them, is not clear, but anyhow, they are going to the Portland game." This "innovative" move could be called into question as being a bit behind the times, considering football had been played at the university since 1889 and women's suffrage was enacted in the state in 1910. In what can only be judged as beyond prudish by today's standards, women's freedom of movement was still highly restricted. Described as being "marooned," they were assigned their own two private cars, but "the smiling lassies," showing an independent streak, were also seen to frequent the smoking car. To assure proper behavior, strong assurances were given that the women were under the vigilant eye of three chaperones; Mrs. Thomas Kane, wife of the university president; Miss Isabella Austin, dean of women students; and Mrs. Loren Grinstead, wife of the former graduate manager and currently a state representative for King County.

Yell king George Mathieu led a major on-campus drive, complete with ramped-up rallies, name badges to wear, and a special travel package for everyone signing on. The goal of one thousand fell a few hundred short, but seventy-five coeds were pulled in thanks to the stunning new admittance policy. This would prove to be the largest outpouring of fans for an away game in the school's history. With such bargaining power, Graduate Manager Ralph Horr reserved a special train with upgraded steel railroad cars at a round fare of $7.50, a special rate of fifty cents per room at the new Multnomah Hotel, and student seats for the game of seventy-five cents. The newly liberated women finally overcame entrenched custom and actually attended an away game.

This newfound liberation, however, still didn't qualify them to participate in the parade from the hotel to Multnomah Stadium. Eliminating any risk that the young male and female students might resort to mingling, the women were whisked to the field in private cars while the men marched to the game. The men's parade featured "The Hook," which was escorted into the stadium with proper ceremony. There had been rumblings from Oregon that the Webfoot fans had seen just about enough of such a public display of arrogance, so several plans were afoot to capture this worthless chunk of wood. On hearing of these acts of war, the northerners redoubled their defenses and introduced, with no great concern for disguising its intent, "The Big Stick." Described as a huge, seven-foot-long, spiked war club, it was assigned to ten "huskies" of the Big **W** Club to do battle in guarding the exalted Hook. However, through some mix-up, the intimidating new weapon never made the trip. Its unveiling would have to wait another week until Washington State came to town. Perhaps it was just the mere threat of the Big Stick that scared off any interlopers, as despite the dire threats from the Oregon camp the Hook did make its way safely back across the Columbia.

Dobie's alma mater, Minnesota, and Coach Hugo Bezdek's Chicago team just happened to be playing head-to-head at the same time as the game at Multnomah Stadium. The two games showcased the premier teams of each league. While play was under way locally, updates of the game in Chicago came in over the wire and were announced to the crowd. The opposing coaches also listened in for updates. The early going of the two games closely paralleled each other. Both games were tied at 7-7 at one point, but the eastern game came out in Bezdek's favor. When he won he smiled broadly, but Dobie didn't show any emotion as he walked away down the sidelines. This was the only time Washington football fans would see their coach come out on the short end of a score.

Back on the western front Washington drew first blood early on, with Hap Miller accounting for most of the yardage up the middle, but Oregon stiffened at the goal. It took two passes, Miller to Pete Sutton, to set up the score, with Miller completing the drive on a 2-yard line buck over left tackle. The extra point put Washington in the lead, 7-0, which would hold as the only score in the first quarter.

There were many players performing at the top of their game. Left halfback Lee Marlarky, diminutive quarterback Anson Cornell, right guard Carl Fenton, and right halfback John Parsons were standouts for Oregon. On the Washington side, left halfback Hap Miller, right end Pete Sutton, fullback Walt Shiel, right halfback Frank Jacquot, and quarterback Charley Smith turned in career performances. It was a hard-fought game with Washington having a stronger finish that enabled them to land this one in the winner's column.

The game proved to be a study of predictability. No matter the side and for a good bit of the game, the team on offense would make good yardage, sputter out, and be forced to punt. With this back-and-forth routine, it seemed that neither team wanted to take charge until amazingly, history would repeat itself. Just as had happened two weeks before when Frank Jacquot fumbled, allowing a 95-yard run back, he this time fumbled on Washington's 40 to Parsons, who, breaking out of Smith's grasp, took the gift straight through the right side of the line for a 60-yard romp for a score. The successful point after evened the slate at 7-7.

The tied game coming in such dramatic fashion showed Coach Bezdek that they could go head-to-head against Washington, so he decided to roll the dice with some more aggressive tactics. Finding themselves backed up against their own goal line, Oregon tried a fake punt that backfired almost costing them a safety. Carl Fenton then booted from behind his own goal line out to the Oregon 45. The Varsity then marched the ball down within striking distance but came up short when a Smith pass was intercepted by left tackle Sam Cook at the 15. Cornell called his team together for a conference to continue their go-for-it strategy. After the break he tried to pull off the same two forward passes that were used in scoring against Washington last year. These both failed, forcing Oregon to punt, again reaching their own 45. Washington did move the ball well but ran out of time after reaching the 25-yard line. At the half the score was tied, but a glaring weakness showed up in the imbalance of punts between the teams. Washington played a much too conservative game, kicking the ball eight times to only four for Oregon.

Another example of Bezdek's riskier game plan was his use of the onside kick on the kickoff. Dobie had never tried one, nor had Washington ever seen one attempted against them. It was such a little-used practice that in the game account of the *Times* it was called "a kickoff formation new to the Purple and Gold team." The first try went wide, and on upcoming tries Washington was prepared and the risky maneuver failed every time.

The third quarter continued the seesaw affair where the teams had left off. Washington eventually stepped up the tempo, moving the ball to Oregon's 15-yard line. This threat fizzled with the ruling of those times calling for a touchback on an incomplete pass in the end zone. Oregon took the ball on the 20-yard line but couldn't do anything and punted to safety. Neither team crossed the goal line, and the period ended with Washington in possession on Oregon's 30. The home team outpunted the visitors three to one in the third quarter, so by this dubious measure Oregon, to their detriment, was gaining on Washington.

By game's end Washington had punted ten times to Oregon's eight. Fenton's kicking for Oregon was decidedly superior to Sutton's; however, Washington did the best job of coverage on punts by getting downfield consistently and dropping the receiver in his tracks.

The fourth quarter began with Washington only 30 yards short of the goal line, but Oregon put up a furious defense, stopping them on their 23-yard line. Field goal kicking for Washington was spotty at best, and the last thing Dobie wanted to do was be forced to have to use this option, but this is where he found himself. This early in the quarter there was plenty of time for Oregon to come back with a touchdown for the win. Charley Smith was designated for the job should it be necessary, and remarkably, he had never before even attempted a field goal in varsity competition. At this critical juncture, with the game on the line, he called his number and, just as well as he performed in all other aspects of the game, approached the ball and gave it a boot that evenly split the crossbars. This broke the tie and put UW in front 10-7. The nervous Washington fans could only breathe a momentary sigh of relief, for this cliff hanger had one more big test to follow.

On Oregon's next possession they were able to beat back a stiff Washington defense with a drive that ended up with them in a kicking situation on the Varsity's 35-yard line for a chance to tie. It was not lost on the partisan crowd that Dobie's teams had a 34-game winning streak going back to the game against Oregon in 1908. Win or tie, they wanted this five years of misery to stop here and now. The packed stadium rose to their feet in silence except for the hopeful chant coming from the Washington side, "Break that up, break that up," as Fenton approached the ball. The pass from center Wallace Canfield to Cornell holding was a bit wide, throwing off the timing for Fenton's kick as Sutton and Shiel rushed in to block. With the play slow to develop, Fenton, because of the poor snap, was forced to adjust his kick to avoid having it blocked. He overcorrected, aiming the ball a bit high and wide forcing the ball to sail outside the left goalpost. For the time being the streak was intact.

This proved to be the critical point of the game. Washington, from Oregon's 20-yard line played it safe, not taking any risks of a fumble and punted to safety on fourth down. It was do or die for Cornell, who made a valiant attempt to find a working formula. This year he was again the smallest player on the field, even called a midget by sportswriters, but what he lacked in size he made up for in guile. He called for a series of "split bucks," faking to the first back through and handing off to the next. These only went for short yardage as Washington now stiffened their defense. The wily QB also threw in a mix of forward passes, with one to Parsons who fought his way for 15 yards into Washington territory, where he was brought down by Jacquot and Smith. With one minute on the clock, a pass from Fenton intended for Captain Bradshaw was intercepted by workhorse center BeVan Presley, squelching Oregon's last chance for victory.

This was another of those critical plays essential to extending the streak as the ball was turned over on the 30-yard line, well within field goal range.

Time ran out in this tightest of battles that easily could have ended in defeat, but by the slimmest of margins in Dobie's nine years at Washington; he went home with another win. The strongest evidence that both coaches felt the pressure of the struggle was evidenced by them using only twenty-three players for the entire afternoon. Dobie's eleven played the entire game, and Bezdek only had one lineup change, bringing Cornell in for Bigbee after the first few plays.

Dobie summoned up that infrequently visited reservoir of outreach he held so tightly within and termed this a wonderful game. He gave high praise to John Parsons for his dazzling touchdown run, noting that virtually every man on defense had a shot at him but the great runner's skill allowed him to elude them all. In this he was being entirely consistent, as he had also singled out the talented Oregon halfback in his pregame rundown. The coach proved to be pitifully sparing in praising his own team, but this game was decidedly different. He admitted as to how his team "made an excellent showing." He even relaxed his fear of pumping up the players' egos by not qualifying his tribute to the team. Admittedly most pats on the back from Dobie were delivered in his understated manner, but this only served to make the rare nods from the coach all the more meaningful. "Everything in connection with the game was well handled." Hardly a ringing endorsement, but he did call up the word "everything," which takes in considerably more territory than Dobie usually covers. This would prove to be the most difficult battle and the closest margin of victory for Dobie during his remarkable nine-year run. As the final whistle sounded, the scoreboard showed only three points to spare in extending the run, with the Varsity out in front 10-7.

### Washington State

John Bender, Washington State's coach was in his second year on the job and, because of this, discounted his team's 19-0 whitewashing of last season. As any good coach would do, he had a positive outlook for the upcoming contest with his cross-state rival, remarking, "Wait until next year." Next year had arrived, but advance word from the Bender camp was anything but boastful. It seemed he was bringing a squad of cripples to an anticipated slaughter on Denny Field. In the verbal war of signaling his team's imminent defeat, Bender overlooked the fact that in coming up against Gil Dobie, he was doing battle against the undisputed world champion of marginalizing a team's chances. Dobie would have nothing to do with such talk. The *Seattle Times* clarified the coach's position should there be any doubt as to where he stood: "Dobie expects the Pullman boys to be in shape to buck their way through a concrete wall tomorrow, despite the stories sent out by Bender, and he gives Washington only an even chance to win." The easterners were heavier and the team boasted veterans with as much experience as the western eleven, but they hadn't done well in their two previous games.

Despite last week's wake-up call against Oregon, there was still much chatter around Seattle that the Thanksgiving game would be another 30-point blowout. With the streak long since having become an anticipated walkover to the hardened fan, any evidence to the contrary bordered on heresy. But this played right into Dobie's hands. He had a good "I told you so" story coming out of the close call of last week. Dobie no doubt appreciated the support his fans provided. Bender saw that his lambs were being led to the slaughter, and this was backed up by the Washington faithful. It only followed that it was Dobie's job to predict defeat. Not having done so would signal to his boys that they could slack off because the game was a pushover.

Buoyed by the enthusiastic turnout of women on their first away game last week, special plans were made to generate attendance for the big Thanksgiving wrap-up to the season. Yell king George Mathieu arranged for a rooters' section on the East end of the north grandstand, with the women occupying the west end and separated by the press box. To assure that none of the coeds would have to unduly suffer the company of male rooters, strict conditions were set out, of course. It was emphasized that the coed grandstand was for coeds only and that the Washington men were to occupy the rooters' section. There still was societal resistance to any thought that women should or indeed would want to engage in the spectator sport of rooting on one's team. The day before the game in the *Daily*, Mathieu, showing no interest in doubling his vocal output from the stands, drove this point home with no fear of condescension. "His place is in the rooters' section. Most of the girls haven't much use for a fellow who will fuss at a game anyway. They had much rather see him exercising his lungs in some of the peppery yells we have provided for the Thanksgiving contest. So take warning fellows, and come where you belong."

It rained just about all of Wednesday night before the game, and it was raining when the game started. This cut down on the crowd, but the sun did break through the clouds during the contest. Field conditions were predictably miserable and would alter the tactics of both coaches. The outstanding senior end, Wayne Sutton, would be the exception, as the unsteady footing and slippery ball didn't seem to matter; he was able to complete several spectacular catches in tight coverage.

The sloppy field stifled both teams' running game in the first half, with neither side gaining much traction. In the opening period, caught deep in their own territory, State punted to Frank Jacquot, who signaled for a fair catch, downing the ball on the 35. Rather than take a chance on a miscue and give up the ball, Washington went for a field goal from there. From a Jacquot hold, Charley Smith put the first three points on the board.

In the second quarter Washington moved the leather to State's 20-yard line and, failing a pass on third down, decided to go for another field goal. With the

Washington crowd shouting an Oskey wow-wow chant in support, Smith put his second boot through the standards. This made it three-for-three for this remarkable athlete, who never signed on as a kicker but displayed tremendous resolve under intense pressure in both games he was called on to kick. If Dobie needed a man for a special assignment, his coaching technique of breaking the skill down into its constituent parts served him well in bringing an athlete up to par. He would teach players every movement required to learn the skill through daily repetitions in practice, and by game day execution was a matter of going on auto-pilot.

The halftime show, with the official christening of the Big Stick and a pyrotechnic display burning Dobie's name in a fiery salute at midfield, energized the crowd. With the game in question and the dreary weather, the hometown fans needed a pick-me-up. The Washington State crowd was content to still be in the game, having entered the contest with that nagging doubt Northwest teams held when coming up against the rarely scored-upon Gil Dobie. His teams held their opposition scoreless two-thirds of the time. With only a six-point advantage, the State crowd could still hope for a win, but the unalterable reality of a zero on the board was not a good omen. When the teams came back on the field there was another sign deemed to be a bad omen by the visitors: Dobie felt relaxed enough to light up a cigar. In actuality, Dobie would light up a cigar whether worried or not. His team was also better prepared for the terrible field conditions, as all of the players now sported clean and dry uniforms for the second half. Bender's team came out and was described as looking like chickens left out in the rain. The mud-soaked uniforms put on a good ten pounds of weight to further burden their already troubled outlook.

Dobie was a superb halftime strategist. With his single-minded focus in analyzing everything going on during the game, he could synthesize this into a second-half game plan for the players. He was a master of the X's and O's chalk talk. His mind-numbing obsession with detail served him well in this all-important aspect of the game. Dobie had the ability to zone in on just what adjustments were necessary to exploit the other team's weaknesses and to augment what his team was doing well. Certainly all coaches go into the locker room with the objective of fine-tuning the team for the second half of play, and with a staff of assistants each aspect of the game can be reviewed. In this early day of football, however, the vast weight of just how to critique and how to adapt largely fell on the head coach. Some coaches do not have the attention to detail, the powers of analysis, or the ability to impart this found knowledge to their players. Dobie came to the game with these skills in abundance. In large measure this is why he rose to the rank of becoming one of the greatest coaches of the game.

His skill for midcourse correction came to the fore in this contest. For the second half, the team was moving the ball with authority and effectively blending their running and passing games. The plan was to get into position for a touchdown, which would allow Dobie to better enjoy his cigar. But after moving downfield in close range of the goal, their determined effort fell short. Washington State let it be known they were still in this game. Smith, with his perfect record in the field goal department, was called on to make another try, but this time his kick from the twenty was blocked. Dobie spent a lot of time on blocked kick recovery drills, and it paid off on this critical play with three players swarming over the ball to maintain coverage.

The Varsity offense was now up against a somewhat tighter defense and continued to make steady yardage, but this time by inches and feet. After a completed pass that placed them in excellent shape for a touchdown, it was called back for offsides. Smith again attempted a field goal but missed once more. On Washington State's possession, they couldn't get out of the shadow of their own goal posts and were forced to punt. On Washington's third drive of the half, they again made steady yardage, driving to the 10-yard line. From there Hap Miller used every ounce of leg drive he could muster in fighting off State's determined counterpunch but finally pushed the ball over for the long-awaited six points. Smith regained his kicking touch and added the extra point; score: 13-0.

In the fourth quarter Washington was again on the move, with a brilliant 35-yard run by Smith. He was built like a fire plug and being close to the ground, was hard to tackle in the open field. Shooting over the left side of the line he shook off five defenders, including "Shorty" Harter, said to have stood seven feet tall. He took a swipe with his long reach but couldn't pull him down. This slowed his progress just enough that the sixth and last line of defense between the stocky, bowlegged QB and another touchdown forced him out of bounds at the 15. The Pullman eleven stiffened once again, forcing another try for a field goal by Smith that bounced off the goal post.

Considering the score and the limited time remaining, State seemed to make a strategic error in punting the ball away from the 20 on first down. With this gift Washington pounded the ball downfield using halfbacks Miller and Jacquot for most of the yardage. On his last run Miller deposited the ball on the 1-foot line. From there Walt Shiel hammered the it over for the touchdown, with Smith kicking the extra point: score 20-0.

Running short of time and in a deep hole, Coach Bender began wholesale substitutions, putting in seven men off the bench to see if he could get something started. Dobie only replaced Mike Hardy for Burke Griffiths (Tom's brother) and Cy Noble for Frank Jacquot, just to allow them enough playing time to earn their letter. With the game pretty much decided and mostly fresh players on the field, Bender decided to pull out all stops. He set up a formation with only Captain Coulter in the backfield, his three backs crowding the line, essentially creating a ten-man pass formation. With his halfback captain in what could be considered an early shotgun formation, Coulter took the center pass from Shorty Harter and heaved what came to be known as a Hail Mary. The razzle-dazzle worked. Remarkably this same play was run for seven successive times and worked every time, with State picking up 70 yards total. Setting up in the same formation, Washington was fooled on a trick play, thinking Coulter was attempting another pass, when a lineman suddenly popped up with the ball. The slow-of-foot lineman was described as "lumbering down the field" when Smith finally stopped him at the 10-yard line. The game ended there with Washington State fans asking, "Why didn't we play this kind of game from the beginning?"

With everything on the line and Washington tired out and playing to protect their lead, this was the perfect opportunity for Bender to open up the game. How successful he would have been had he brought out this strategy earlier can't be answered. But since the passing game with this novel alignment worked so spectacularly well, it does appear that some more moderate passing scheme implemented early in the half could have reaped benefits. When the half opened, the locals only had a six-point lead, so one good drive could have turned the game around. However, this was not to be, and with his muddied warriors defending their goal line, Dobie's most challenging year came to an end. In giving up twenty-one points for 1913 this closed out Washington's weakest year, but they did bring the sixth championship trophy to their fans. This hardest-fought game of the season was fortunately their last. With injuries sustained by Miller, Shiel, Jacquot, Presley, Seagrave, Smith, Sutton, and Hunt, another game on the schedule would not be welcome.

Bobby Boyce, the *Argus* sports editor who back in 1908 did his best to get Dobie fired with his open letter to President Thomas F. Kane calling Dobie out for his immature public behavior, was by now good friends with the coach. Boyce continued to be fascinated with the peculiarities of Dobie's personality, but he grew to understand probably better than any other writer of the times, just what made him tick. He wrote of Dobie's pessimism and linked it to his "premonition of disaster." This premonition was described in another pointed description Boyle penned as "the dreaded specter" of losing. Showing no trepidation for literary overkill, he likened this premonition to what Napoleon faced on the eve of Waterloo, what Pickett feared going into his fatal charge at Gettysburg, and what Jefferson must have felt in framing his thoughts for his writings of 1776. Even given this colossal overstatement, he made his point. Dobie's obsessive pursuit of perfection led to his all-consuming fear of losing.

This year Boyce had been given the opportunity to sit on the bench with the subs to get an up-close look at the team. He got to know the players and the coach intimately, and after the Thanksgiving game with Washington State was even having Dobie over to his house to celebrate the holiday. He was invited into the locker room after the big victory and gave an illuminating account of just how the enigmatic Scot interacted with his men. There was great respect felt by both sides, but the newspaperman gave an account illustrating that while Dobie was not demonstrative in showing affection, the team did know and learned to appreciate Dobie's unspoken manner of expressing his appreciation for their play.

Here is how Boyce described the postgame locker-room scene:

> "As he came toward me I couldn't help but think of the fact that he had just won his sixth straight conference championship, hence it didn't surprise me when he said: 'Let's go over to the gym before we go. I want to see the boys a minute.' Of course he wanted to see the boys—his boys. He wanted to make a little speech to them and congratulate them, and pat them on the back, and sort of mother them and thank them for their faithfulness. And you bet I was just as proud of them as Dobie was.

> "And so we enter the gym. And there was the sweaty, dirty muddy team—the champions—in all sorts of undressed uniform. Some of them stood naked under the shower. Some were pulling steaming sweaters over sore and muddy shoulders. Others were singing and some were kidding each other. The season was over. The long hard grind was done. But nobody paid any attention to Dobie.
> 'How's the shoulder, Sut?'

> "And then he glared at a youth who, before undressing, had stopped long enough to roll a cigarette. But the season was over; the culprit was without the pale of Dobie's jurisdiction. And then suddenly he yelled, 'Who put the sweater over the radiator?'

> "And as the guilty player rescued the aforementioned sweater, Dobie took one more look around the room and then, turning to me said: 'Come on Bob, let's go.'

> "And so we passed out of the gym. No words of praise. No thanks. No nice little motherly talk. You see I hadn't stopped to think that there wasn't anything motherly about Dobie.

> "But as we were passing out of the door, a husky substitute, who had been my bench mate during the season, whispered: 'We played a swell game today.' Why? I whispered back. 'Because Dobie didn't say anything."

As a newspaperman, Boyce, had he known of Dobie having lost both his parents and being shipped off to an orphanage by the age of eight, would have undoubtedly used this knowledge to help explain why Dobie could never let his emotions show at times like this. The coach's role model for conducting himself in a superior-subordinate relationship came from what he learned in a cold institutional setting. The "little motherly talk" that Boyce so wanted to hear had never been experienced by Dobie in these settings, so he was only behaving as he had been taught.

While Dobie had an aversion to personal demonstrations of his feelings, he would express his thoughts in writing of how he valued his players' athletic talents. That year he gave glowing accounts of all of his stars in summarizing his picks for the all conference team. This year was the first time he caved in and named a team. The dreaded specter of losing was only exceeded by his career-long fear of overhyping his players' egos. Even selecting a player for an all-star team, to his thinking, could trigger this inflated self-image. His turn-around was based on a concern he saw building that since all other coaches were making selections, his holding out would penalize his players. While this may not be seen as much of a concession, in Dobie's very compartmentalized life, it really was progress.

Dobie's contract was set to expire on December 1, 1913. With national attention mounting, there were many overtures from other colleges directed his way, so the university wasted no time in buttoning down his renewal for three more years. His salary was bumped up to $3,100 per year, with an added clause that he would get a voice in the selection of game officials. Ralph Horr was elated. "The best news I've been able to give since I came to this office." Victor Zednick, his immediate predecessor, was even more effusive in his praise. "Gilmour Dobie is one of the most remarkable football men that the country has ever seen." The signing took place on December 3 in an exercise that was a foregone conclusion. The university family and the influential downtown business community all had their issues with Dobie in the past, but many of these problems were now resolved. The coach's rough edges were wearing smooth, and six years without a loss put smiles on the faces of many detractors.

# CHAPTER EIGHT

## *Perfect Deception—1914*

"Most of the credit given me as coach belongs to the mothers of the boys. A football player should be kept normal. Give him the good home cooking he is accustomed to, his home bed, and home surroundings. The one thing I bar is intoxicants. I never have small men on my teams. The small man does not belong in football. A good player needs to be big from the waist down. He gets his drive, the thing that counts, from his legs. Players should be kept in good mental condition. I send my boys into a game thinking they have a good chance of being whipped and only a small chance of winning. That makes them fight."

*Gilmour Dobie*

By now most fans and sportswriters had caught on to Dobie's real purposes in emitting a cloud of doom before many games. He was often characterized in cartoons with an ominous, dark cloud over his head, much as cartoonist Al Capp did many years later in popularizing the hapless Joe Btfsplk. In just such a cartoon before this season started, the *Daily* depicted the coach seated on his throne, with black smoke from his cigar wafting upwards in clouds of doom as a heavy sword marked "defeat" hung precariously over his head. The visual would have been easily interpreted by even the most casual observer because most everyone knew of Dobie's penchant for self-created gloom. But the cartoon's caption thoroughly drove the message home: "When tired of reading the bombastic reports of European ministers of war turn to the advance notices cut by that master strategist, Gilmour Dobie, for the express purpose of luring the enemy on."

Preseason sportswriters, after the summer doldrums, were hungry for material. Unwittingly they played right into Dobie's hands. The coach knew full well that publicity was the grease that makes the wheels of sports run. Before radio, the Web and twenty-four-hour sports channels, newspaper reporters were the go-to guys to get your message out. They never tired of straight or manufactured reportage of the predictable mentor's downbeat outlook. When Dobie hadn't offered up bilious quotes from his own lips, creative reporters weren't above a bit of puffing, knowing full well their readership loved anything that would stir the pot. If there wasn't an on-the-record slam of the home team or flattering praise of the next opponent available, why not do a perspective piece on his past behavior? This always worked.

Such was the case as Dobie's seventh season opened. "One beauty of Dobie's methods is that he places the capabilities of his opponents at the maximum, and estimates his own team's power at the minimum." Nothing new here but the fascinating dichotomy of always winning, but reporting on a coach that is so often negative was a surefire formula for attracting readership. If you're writing what your readers want to read, don't risk change. Another perspective that was offered since Dobie hadn't favored the public with an outrageous take of his own: "He thinks that most of his men are too green to be of any great value to him. Then he gets his Scotch up, tears into the practice, scolds here, corrects there, taunts, but seldom praises, and in a short while he has worked wonders." There was no good reason for Dobie to hire a publicity agent when independent reporters served his purposes so well.

College football was steadily evolving into the modern game, with each new set of rules coming down. Together with the rules upgrade of 1912, the decrees of 1914 changed the majority of what was left of the old game. One rule that would forever alter Dobie's style was a new prohibition against anyone walking up and down the sidelines. Rules were more clearly defined as to what constituted roughing the kicker, and an important rule was put in place charging a 10-yard penalty for a passer intentionally grounding a forward pass. The injury-prone practice of hitting the passer just after he passes was also disallowed. A rule was enacted allowing for a pass that went out of bounds on the fly or was touched but fell incomplete by either side to go to the opponent. This served to diminish use of the forward pass and, because of this, it was later reversed. Such a pass then was ruled merely to be incomplete with no loss of possession. Also that year, the rule was put into effect requiring that a receiver of a forward pass must have both feet within the end line or side line for there to be a completion. Linemen coming up to the line when shifting into a formation could no longer encroach upon the neutral zone. If either team crossed the neutral zone after lining up for the play, a 5-yard offsides penalty would now be charged. To put an end to the sneaky practice of "hiding" a man on the sidelines, this was now categorized as unsportsmanlike conduct. As another safety measure, tripping by hand was added as a penalty to go along with the existing prohibition of tripping by foot and leg.

Collection of Gilmour Dobie's granddaughter, Eva Zayha, 1911

Dobie's future wife, Eva Margaret Butler. They were married in Detroit on January 2, 1918.

## Preseason

Bobby Boyce of the *Argus* again that year had the opportunity to closely observe Dobie on and off the field. He offered a discerning account that shed some light on the question which he termed, "What manner of man is Gilmour Dobie?" The coach's intractable behavior was widely reported across the country and gave rise to much speculation. Was he just an odd duck, a genuine pessimist, or worse, the victim of some unexplainable mental disorder? Boyce felt that in having known the man for so long, and now with unhindered access to the coach, he was in the best position to render an opinion.

Boyce was accurate in his assessment that after six years of Dobie consistently crying wolf, nobody believed him any longer, adding, "even if he went to church." But it is here that the reporter posits a rather profound observation that in actuality the coach is telling the truth—the truth as interpreted by Robert Gilmour Dobie. He states, "I don't believe the man ever sent a team into battle yet with the belief in ultimate victory. I don't believe he ever had a player who was as exhausted mentally or physically at the end of a contest as Dobie himself...Put him in the middle of the Great Sahara Desert and he would return to America with an Arabian football team that could kick Harvard into the sea."

Boyce supported his case with the example of Dobie's mental state as the preseason game with Aberdeen approached. "When Dobie looked over his football team in the rough, he had never thought of the game that would take place in Seattle with Pullman next Thanksgiving Day. His whole energy—heart, soul and brains—was centered on the contest with Aberdeen High that took place last Saturday afternoon." Boyce went on to explain how the team had trained the entire month of August, how much everyone fixated on "licking Dobie," and there was always the possible horror of a team "slipping one over." For an objective observer to come anywhere near an expectation of loss and to actually believe that it could happen was shown to be all the more outlandish with even the most casual review of history. In the prior six years Dobie's teams outscored the opponents in preseason games 721-16. Given this record and knowing that the tall Scot was intelligent, he obviously didn't come to his gloomy predictions logically. In Boyce's notion, Dobie was not so afraid of getting beaten itself as he was afraid of the *fear* of getting beaten.

This obsessor of detail was incapable of planning out a strategy for the whole season. When the final play of a Saturday afternoon was in the books he immediately was consumed with thoughts of how his team would approach next week's game. During the football season Dobie lived, breathed and thought nothing but football. His single-minded nature did not permit him the luxury of long-range planning; there were vastly too many contingencies he had to track in any given contest. He had the ability to shut out extraneous distractions and totally focus on the game ahead.

I believe Boyce was onto something with his theory that Dobie really did feel, in his own mind, that he was telling the truth with his pessimistic forecasts. This is supported in Boyce's conclusion that Dobie was always striving for unattainable perfection. As we have seen, there are many others who proffered this same opinion. A perfectionist streak ran through virtually every aspect of his life, and this was doubly applicable to his approach to coaching. Depending on such a standard breaks down due to the not-so-insignificant detail that football is a game requiring human machinery. The coach being more engineer than artist, this was wholly lost on him, or at least he wouldn't allow himself to believe it. This allowed him to blithely advance game by game, unconcerned that his fans, sportswriters, and players were pooh-poohing his views as to how the football world really worked. Boyce wrapped up his synopsis of just where Dobie's team fits into the picture as relates the rest of the league: "Out here in the Northwest, every college in the conference would kill the prodigal and wayward calf and burn incense to the God of Joy if they could take a victorious swat at poor, little skinny Gillie Dobie."

The Aberdeen game featured second-year man Cy Noble scoring two of his three touchdowns in the opening quarter, one coming on a 45-yard run. If this game against a nonconference opponent was any indicator, the season ahead would have to be judged as thorny indeed. Other than Noble's play, there wasn't much to be said for the Varsity. While the outcome was never in doubt, the primary accomplishment of the afternoon was to reward Dobie for calling this one when he said before the game, "My men haven't even got in physical shape, let alone team work." Their play most assuredly confirmed his observation. In the second half, Washington put only one more touchdown on the board, and the visitors also managed to score a touchdown on an 18-yard run. Dobie did take his starters out of the game for the fourth quarter. Final score: Washington was on top, 33-6.

The second preseason game against Washington Park Athletic Club brought out a rebuke for the ages from the coach. On paper WPAC appeared competitive, being a solid collection of former college and high school stars. However, neither team would play well. Even considering Dobie's past accomplishments for finding fault, this established a new standard of reproach and was reported to be one of only a few mild and repeatable things he had to say. "It was the most putrid football game that I've seen a Washington team play since I came here, more than six years ago." Mike Hunt and Hap Miller both turned in their usual stellar games, but they were about the only players who stood above the pack. The giant right guard "Shorty" Harter, who played for Whitman last year, was now on this all-star team and was responsible for much of Washington's troubles on offense. Center Lester Gellatly, who had the unenviable duty of anchoring the middle of the line, was singled out for poor play by Dobie. Harter's play and that of a much smaller Abe Feingold continually stifled the Purple and Gold, forcing them out of their game plan. Feingold was everyone's pick for the most outstanding player of the game. From his end position, time after time he weaved his way into Washington's backfield, stopping plays before they made it to the line of scrimmage.

Washington's final score of 45-0 may not seem to fit the coach's description of "putrid," coming as it did against two teams just starting their season, but from all accounts it wasn't far off. The team did not display the noted discipline and consistency of a Dobie-coached squad. This was undoubtedly what was behind his singling out this game for the bottom of the barrel of the forty-three Dobie had coached to date. He held closer games that were hard-fought athletic contests in high regard, but he was unwavering in his criticism of sloppily played matchups such as this. But deep down inside, Dobie must have appreciated the game. Going into the contest, he brought up the ugly prospect that overconfidence was showing up more with this team than any time in the past. How wonderful for this master manipulator. Before the game he says their egos are out of control, then they turn in a bad performance, thus proving his point. He couldn't have scripted it any better.

Spirits were lifted in the final warm-up game with Rainier Valley Athletic Club, as the Varsity's performance now seemed to show the teamwork and dependable play Seattle fans had grown to expect of a Dobie-led lineup. RVAC was not able to complete a pass, and for Washington Tony Savage put on a receiver's clinic with fingertip catches while being very well defended. He was also able to break away for long gains on two of his catches. Ernest "Tramp" Murphy, playing at the right halfback slot, picked holes in the line all afternoon and got the yardage needed when called on. Hap Miller at left halfback found his running game too and also passed for long yardage on three plays. The prior week Charley Smith had played poorly, but the added practice since then seemed to work wonders. He ran the team just like the previous year, and he too found his running legs when carrying the ball. Captain Walt Shiel at fullback turned in his typical bulldog performance and made only one miscue, kicking off with only ten men on the field. The line didn't have the services of Herman Anderson but, unlike the week prior, they seemed to perform with a newfound strength from end to end.

The buzz around town in one short week turned from doubt to boundless optimism. The ragged play of two weeks prior was now a distant memory as General Dobie was able to once again marshal his forces for battle. Confidence was particularly uplifted due to the fact that Rainier Valley AC was stocked with ex-college and prep stars and was expected to put up quite a battle. Their thrashing at the hands of Washington, 81-0, was evidence enough that Dobie's troops would again bring home the championship. There was only one small matter to deal with—the entire league schedule had yet to be played.

### Whitman College

Comparing the injury list of the two teams going into the final week before kickoff, Whitman came out the better. Three of their starters who had to sit out the Oregon game were now back, but Washington had five men whose chances of not being able to play ranged from doubtful to definite. The most serious injury was to right end Ed Leader, who would fail to earn his letter this year as he was out for the season with a broken wrist.

The Varsity had a relatively new team this season, considering there were nine men who had either graduated or didn't return to the team. There were ten new men on the squad who would earn their letter either this or in subsequent years. But there was one amazing measure of strength that this team possessed that surely would have to place them at the pantheon of any Washington team ever assembled by Dobie. There were seven players on the team who earned letters for all four years of eligibility: Arthur "Andy" Anderson, Ray "Mike" or "Mother" Hunt, Elmer Leader, Cedric "Hap" Miller, Elmer "Cy" Noble, Louis "Louie" Seagrave, and Walter "Walt" Shiel. Allan "Bud"

Young, who many consider to be Dobie's greatest quarterback, would be on this list except for his foot injury that kept him off the field that season. The players garnered five captaincies and were honored with four Flaherty Awards. Surprisingly, Hap Miller was the only player to win neither but was a unanimous pick on the 1913-14-15 All-Northwest teams. If superior teams are to be judged on outstanding performance over their years of eligibility, this group of bluebloods must be included.

With his team now coming together and with the obvious factor of so much experience within his ranks, Dobie wasn't predicting apocalyptic defeat for the Whitman game. He only came out with mild references to the Missionaries having given Washington some scares in the past. Twice Whitman led against Washington during Dobie's time—a feat no other opposing team accomplished. He complimented Coach Archie Hahn for being able to compensate for his smaller team with cleverness and speed. They had lost to Oregon already, but this was on a wet and sloppy field that went against a team built around speed and footwork. The game-day forecast for Seattle showed there would be a dry field for Saturday, and Dobie declared that under such conditions, "there isn't a team in the conference that could afford to slough for a minute."

The "cleverness" that Dobie was looking out for was soon put on display. It was just last year that Emory Hoover had embarrassed Washington with his spectacular 97-yard TD run on this same field. Dobie singled him out for the watch list. He was to get special attention from the local defenders. His performance proved that he stood head and shoulders above any other man on the team and most assuredly would have starred on a Dobie-coached squad. He completely buffaloed Washington with running plays when they expected him to kick and kicking plays when they expected him to run. The *UW Daily*'s account reported, "He made the Washington ends look like they had lead in their shoes, and on wide runs that would mean a loss to most any back in the conference, he would get fifteen-yards ahead of the scrimmage line before he would be dragged down." Right halfback McDonald also accounted for major yardage and almost duplicated Hoover's run of last year by breaking through the left side of Washington's line for an 80-yard touchdown sprint accounting for the visitor's only score.

University of Washington Libraries, Special Collections Neg. No. UW 21827

Serpentines comprised exclusively of male fans were a fixture of Washington home games throughout Dobie's term as head coach. Here the parade concludes with a fight song as the hook formation spreads from goal line to goal line. In this day, it was not proper for women to participate with men in the parades.

Dobie's scouting report was on the money in predicting that exceptional team speed posed the greatest threat to his team's skilled but slower squad. Being quicker of foot, whether it was on offense or defense, Whitman would continually squirm, twist, bounce, or dodge their way past their stronger adversaries. On defense, even when Washington put up a solid line of blockers, the smaller and quicker Missionaries could slip through and nail the ball carrier. The outcome of the game came down to the imbalance of muscle, with the heavier men able to overpower their lighter but swifter rivals as the game wore on. With muscle making the difference, left tackle Elmer Leader was the standout of the game. He was described as a "bulwark" holding up his side of the line, discouraging any efforts of Whitman to try to pierce the territory that he controlled. He also delivered critical yardage when dubbed to carry the ball on tackle-eligible plays. These were popular plays in the early 1900s that added an exciting dimension to the game back then, since the resistance didn't as easily know as they do today who would be challenging the line for yardage.

Given the ideal playing conditions, Washington's passing game was the biggest disappointment of the afternoon. Yet on defense considering Whitman's superior speed, the Purple and Gold was able to shut down every single pass attempted against them. Due largely to a near breakdown of Washington's efforts to pass, the first half looked to be anyone's game. In the second quarter the defending champions, sporting their lineup of seven all-stars, featured a display of foolish penalties, runners that couldn't run, and passers that couldn't pass. The halftime score with Washington up 14-7 hardly gave team, fans, or coach much to crow about.

Dobie, as could be expected, drew a penalty for the new rule against marching along the sidelines, but his halftime adjustments more than offset what damage the infraction cost the team. As was so often the case, the tweaks he employed to right the sinking ship did the trick. Tony Savage was now able to get in position for passes, and this sparked a turnaround. George Smith, in his first year, coming in for Savage at left end proved to be an exceptionally gifted athlete. With the passing game having been in such disarray, Dobie also tried first year man Don Abel, who replaced Mike Hunt. All this second-half fine tuning altered the game as Washington managed fourteen more points after the break and was able to keep the quick-footed visitors out of the end zone.

As clear evidence that Dobie saw a need for desperate measures, he played seven substitutes. With this tight a score, he usually would never substitute so freely. He saw that he needed to shake up the squad to find a winning formula. The player changes did click, as Washington finally gained the upper hand over the scrappy visitors, who just as easily could have won this one. A coach does make the difference for better or worse, and in this game both coaches did a superb job. Hahn's bench wasn't as deep as Dobie's and, in the end, this tipped the scales for Washington. But Coach Hahn put Dobie to the supreme test. To pull this one out, the Washington mentor had to call on every resource he had available, be it scouting, halftime adjustments, play selection, or shuffling the lineup. Against this athletic and very well-coached team, the Varsity scored two more touchdowns in the second half to win by 28 to 7.

### Oregon State at Albany

Yell leader Herb Finck made it known that word was leaking from the Oregon State camp that an assault was under way to kidnap the Washington Hook. Laying a guilt trip on any undecided fence sitters not committed to going to the game, he vowed, "The varsity men can scarcely hope to return with the hook of Washington unless more fellows decide to go and guard that emblem of rooting spirit." Rooters were warned that every man will have to put up the scrap of his life. Team loyalists, sensing a tough struggle afoot, were pulling out all stops to ramp up support.

Pregame interest peaked through a variety of circumstances. Oregon State had been recruiting for some time with the primary aim of beating Washington. The Purple and Gold had dominated the "Aggies" since their glory years of 1904-05, and Doc Stewart, now coaching at Oregon State, was determined to balance the books for the former indignities suffered. The stage was set for what many observers viewed as the hardest struggle facing Dobie since he took the reins in 1908. But it does seem that the hardest game in history came up about every year. This is the first year that I observed in print that Oregon State's team mascot was named "Beavers." Many mistakenly say the naming was not until 1916.

The Friday night before the game, a *Seattle Times* reporter found Coach Dobie in a somewhat conciliatory mood. He couldn't bring himself to tell the press what they wanted to hear: that Washington faced looming peril. He was well aware of the widespread belief that this was his biggest challenge since coming to Seattle. Totally consistent with his contrarian stance, the team's fate, by his account, seemed to be a toss-up. "I expect one of the hardest games we have ever experienced. The score will be low. Oh no, I'm not predicting defeat, and I'm not overconfident of winning, but we're not quitting, and the Oregonians will know they had a football game when they get through with us."

This was the day for left halfbacks, as Hap Miller of Washington and William Lutz of Oregon State turned in the best games on an afternoon when miscues and underwhelming play were the rule of the day. Heavy rains produced one hundred yards of mud and gooey slime, which accounted for much of the fumbling and bumbling that took place. The Northwest hadn't had much rain thus far in the season, so the teams hadn't practiced under these conditions. This was one of those rare occasions that the ever-vigilant master of detail missed in his pregame planning. There hadn't been a weather prediction showing the strong possibility of rain, which caught him off guard. Balmy fall weather that suddenly turns to rain being so probable, Dobie and his staff can also be criticized for not having adequate shoes for the sloppy conditions. Their shoes were designed for dry footing, while Oregon State's players enjoyed drier feet thanks to added shoe caulking. The coach who never missed on the little things was tripped up this time.

One matter is certain: other than on the scoreboard this day, Washington was beaten. The Beavers showed better team speed than the Varsity, their line was stronger, and their offensive backfield proved the better in moving the ball. Were it not for disastrous fumbles that cost them dearly, Oregon State very well may have racked up a victory on this most miserable of playing fields. The surface of the field was sloped, causing deep pools of water and mud to collect and wreaked havoc for the punting and running games of both teams. With the slippery football, Oregon State's passing game could not get on track; they completed only one pass for the entire afternoon. Stewart had introduced the direct pass offense to OSU, but, regardless of past skills in deploying this weapon, it wasn't working today. Hap Miller on two punts stood in ankle-deep water and muck, causing him to give up valuable yardage on both exchanges of possession.

For the opening quarter it appeared to be business as usual, with Hap Miller making good yardage on the ground until he seemed to show strains from the heavy field conditions. When Dobie's men finally turned the ball over, Oregon State was unable to mount a threat and had to punt. Washington blocked Lutz' punt, limiting it to a puny 20 yards. For the rest of the first quarter, the Beavers decided to play ultraconservative and punted on first down for every play. Steady but short ground gainers up the middle on a Washington possession advanced the ball to the Beavers' 20-yard line. Miller then completed a 5-yard pass, and the small band of rain-soaked and shivering Washington fans must have thought Dobie's magic had finally made all this misery worthwhile. The vaunted machine did what it was supposed to do, as Miller picked up another yard and big 201-pound Mike Chapman picked up two more. On third down the ball was again given to Miller, who, seeing the goal marker in sight, made a desperate lunge forward, depositing the ball emphatically over the line. The jubilant Hap had scored again just as he'd done so often in the past when muscle was needed in sight of the goal. Alas, as the referees assessed the situation, the fluid field conditions had introduced a circumstance that no amount of coaching or athleticism could overcome. It turned out that there were now two lines marking the goal only inches apart, and instead of putting six points on the board, the ball was ruled to be six inches short of a score.

On fourth down there was no question as to who was the best man on the team to entrust with the ball to bring home a cinch touchdown—Captain Walt Shiel. At the end of his stay at Washington, Dobie in assessing all of the players of his many teams, ranked Shiel as the very best of all his fullbacks. But on this play and on this day, Oregon State had the final say; Shiel failed to move the ball over the second white line adjudged as marking the goal. On the next play, with his heels precariously near the two-point safety line, William Lutz kicked the ball out of danger. This dire shift of fortune seemed to rip the heart out of Washington. Up until now they had their own way in moving the ball, but the tables had turned and an energized OSU eleven seized the opportunity. They took charge and for the rest of the half, it was Washington who did the scrambling.

With the seven men on the squad who would earn a football letter for all four years of eligibility, it would seem there was no shortage of talent. But digging a little deeper into the picture, there is evidence to support a theory advanced in some quarters that Washington actually had the weakest team in the past six years. They had lost eight lettermen to either graduation or men not turning out for the team, and for this game six nonlettermen were playing their first important game. These were right end and substitute Don Abel, right end and substitute Tony Savage, left end and starter George Smith, center and starter Lester Gellatly, left guard and starter Andrew McPherson, and right halfback and starter Mike Chapman. Since only fourteen men competed for Washington, over 40 percent of the team were rookies. With Dobie's intensive training techniques, he had a national reputation for turning newcomers into stellar performers, but his magic didn't work this quickly.

The lack of experience seemed to make the difference, with the heavier Oregon State squad having their way with the Varsity defensive line as the second quarter lurched forward. Halfback William Lutz found his stride, and every time he got the ball he was able to tear off 5 to 20 yards at a clip. He both kicked punts and was the receiver when Washington's Miller punted. On his returns he far outpaced what the northerners were able to do. Another weakness showed on Washington's kicks, as Miller was rushed and, on a couple of boots, barely got much leg into the effort, making only short yardage. Field conditions worked against Miller because of the deep water he found himself in as he launched his punts. On every exchange this placed the Beavers closer to the goal.

It was an Oregon State punt that dealt the biggest blow to Washington when Mike Hunt was thrown out of the game for roughing the kicker. As he jumped to make his attempt, he lost his footing in the mud and slid into Lutz, who wasn't knocked off his feet. It seemed the sliding motion caught referee George Varnell's eye, causing him to eject Hunt rather than assess a penalty. Since Lutz didn't lose his footing, the impact wasn't that great. A Washington sympathizer would naturally conclude that the ejection was overkill, but a Beaver fan would see unnecessarily rough play. There is some justification for the ruling no matter what side you were on. This was a game, even for this era, of brutally rough play. The Seattle *Post-Intelligencer* called it "the fiercest fighting ever seen in a conference contest." On six different occasions, a time-out was called for men who had to have additional time to gain their composure after exceptionally hard hits. A good referee cannot be criticized for making an example of kicking a man off the field to send a message to both teams, as was done in Hunt's case. The fact that the player happened to have been one of Dobie's greatest linemen of all time was an unfortunate circumstance, but where player safety is at issue, this is a small price to pay. As an illustration of just how serious the issue was, Mike Hunt had been knocked cold twice in his short playing time, and Charley Smith at halftime, in his confusion, was asking how many times the "Aggies" had scored. The concussion showed no long-term effects, as Smith (sometimes referred to as "Chunky") became Seattle mayor exactly thirty years later.

If wins and losses were based on comparative performance rather than the scoreboard, the game belonged to Oregon State. It wasn't a commanding win, but by a thin margin they did outplay Washington. Dobie's men as was usually the case, had a far superior passing game on this wet and slippery day, completing four passes to only one for Stewart's men, and that for barely 5 yards. It was in running the ball, mostly by star performer of the day left halfback William Lutz that Oregon State excelled. Quarterback Brewer Billie did a much better job of team generalship for the home team than did Washington's Charley Smith, who had an uncharacteristic off day. Washington's inexperienced line couldn't get any traction in holding back the unremitting assault of Oregon State's backs.

Much of this un-Dobie-like performance can actually be blamed on Dobie for leaving the proper footwear back in Seattle.

Oregon State fans were treated to several sustained drives, but just when it appeared their boys had the momentum to score, someone would cough up the football with Lutz being the chief offender. The costliest fumble of all was just short of the goal line, and had the Beavers' held on to the ball, this would have ended the Varsity's reign. The wet football and bad footing had to have their effect, but what a disappointment for their loyal followers, who could feel a win in their grasp only to have it blow up in their face. Another play in particular brought both teams' fans to their feet on what looked like a sure score for Oregon State, only to have the ruling go in Washington's favor. It's understandable that the orange-and-black-bedecked fans, on a day of such poor visibility, would be grumbling over this seeming touchdown, but the referees did make the right call in not allowing a score. However, there remained room for dispute as to where the ball was to be spotted.

The crucial play involved a punt by Lutz to Smith, standing near his own goal as the receiver. Smith badly misjudged the ball, with the first OSU man downfield attempting to recover what he thought to be a fumble as he dove for the water-soaked leather. It slipped from under him and started rolling towards the sideline when another Oregon State man, taking a running jump, was able to grasp the ball fully in his control as he slid over the goal line. In all this confusion, hopeful Beaver fans with good enough eyes to pick out their man crossing the goal with the ball saw this as a touchdown. But, as was the case earlier with Washington fans putting a phantom six points on the board, the OSU fans suffered the same fate here. The referee responsible for the call ruled no score. The ball was declared dead when it was touched by the first defender, according to the account of the game, since Smith, in losing sight of the ball, had never touched it. This was the referee's judgment on the call that prevailed. But there was a legitimate gripe that loyal Oregonians could make in that the ball was placed on the 20-yard line as the play was ruled a touchback. In reality it had been downed on the 3-yard line, and Washington should have taken possession with their backs up against their own goal line.

In the closing moments of the game, with the Varsity in possession, it looked as if they just might pull this one out of the fire. In a remarkable turn of good fortune, Herman Anderson recovered a blocked punt on the Oregon State 30-yard line. A brilliant 17-yard run by Miller and a couple of line bucks put the ball on the 10-yard line, where the Beaver defense tightened the screws. Perhaps it was the muddy conditions that caused Washington not to risk a field goal, but on most days this would have been a gimme. The Beavers had tried from the 42 and missed by a long shot, so the poor footing or bad angle may have discouraged Washington. Rather than try for the chip-shot field goal on fourth down, they gambled on a pass that failed. The scoreless deadlock ended with Lutz getting behind a booming punt, placing the ball well out of danger on Washington's 40-yard line.

With this, Washington's thirty-nine-game unbeaten, untied streak, dating back to the November 14, 1908 game at Oregon came to an end. The Oregon State fans were jubilant, paying no mind to wading through the swamp and carrying Doc Stewart off the field on their shoulders. They could rightly celebrate in what was termed a "virtual victory" since they were able to hold a Washington team scoreless. They accomplished what no other team had done in the six years of Dobie's total domination of Pacific Northwest football. A celebration was definitely in order, considering that in the team's prior five matchups in the Dobie era; they had been shut out five times and had been outscored 147-0. For his part, Coach Dobie showed his appreciation for a great performance when he ran onto the field and slapped William Lutz on the back and shouted for everyone to hear, "Lutz, you're there a million ways."

## Oregon

The following week Dobie faced a strong competitor in the negative-outlook department. Besides the drama of the never-ending undefeated streak bringing out loyal fans' anxiety—could this one break the string?—with Oregon in town fans could also enjoy raucous pregame verbal fisticuffs between the two coaches. On balance Dobie gained a lot from newspapers' constant drumbeat of headlining his quirky nature. But when Hugo Bezdek came to town, sportswriters worked overtime in turning out the latest update as to just which team would have the most dreadful showing. The visiting coach was just as skilled as the tall Scot at seeing nothing but catastrophe ahead. But he was handicapped in attracting national headlines by not launching his career with thirteen straight undefeated seasons.

"Coach Hugo Bezdek A Gloomy Mentor," "Varsity Not Up To Form For Battle With Oregon," "Oregonian's Sporting Editor Says Dobie In For A Hard Rub," "Oregon Football Squad On Way To Lick Dobie," "University Of Oregon Eleven Faces Hardest Schedule In Its History," and "Weak Line Is Oregon's Fear" read the headlines, intended to incite fans' passions. It had been seven seasons that reports of Dobie's pessimism dominated the sports pages. The times when Dobie would be noncommittal or even deign to venture a positive opinion were soon forgotten. This year the feeble movement turned the corner ever so cautiously in bringing some balance into published accounts of pregame cynicism. "Both Contenders For Championship Weakened By Injuries In Lineup" and "Both Coaches Are Dubious" sought to declare a standoff over just which team took the lead in the Northwest misery index. As events unfolded, this outlandish attempt to dethrone Dobie as the anti-optimist would fail to succeed. The upcoming Oregon game brought out a campaign of reverse psychology taken on by Dobie that far exceeded any of Bezdek's efforts at manipulation of the masses.

Melville Mucklestone was on campus to help rally the troops for the big game, and even though he thought neither team would put points on the board, he sung Dobie's praises as a great coach. This and all of the other chatter around town seemed to drive Dobie to reach even deeper into his verbal assault weapons in an attempt to shock his team out of what he saw as chronic overconfidence. Coming off the historic tie the previous week, he hardly had any other choice than to ramp up the dialogue. On the eve of the game, he came out with this zinger: "One or two of the overtouted stars have done more to retard progress than all the new men put together. They are slow and are weakest right where they ought to have the most strength. I've said time and again that this game will prove our Waterloo, and I believe it absolutely."

In sizing up Oregon, he told a *Post-Intelligencer* reporter, "They are heavier and faster than ever, while we are right in the middle of the worst kind of a slump. Bezdek has no license to do anything but whip us tomorrow." Bezdek did put up a fair to middling rejoinder with his counter: "We've been doped to lose everywhere from seven points to thirty-five. None of our friends give us any chance to win, and Doc Stewart says that our chances are about one in a thousand." From the sound of things, with two such inept teams on hand it would be logical to call the game off altogether. At the least spectators should get in free, as by the coaches own admission the game obviously wasn't worth the cost of a ticket.

Dobie's practices, as with any good coach, were skill development sessions with the focus on getting his men fully game ready. But the Washington mentor was not one to let an opportunity dropped in his lap slip away. Football practice where he held supreme command was the perfect venue to apply his skills of mind control. He has been seen many times over the years to demote star players to the second team, and this week's hapless victim was no less a personage than standout Hap Miller. The coach made no secret of his displeasure with players who he derisively termed "some of my All-American material." Getting inside his players' heads was guaranteed to garner results. These were eighteen-to twenty-two-year-old youngsters after all, pliable, volatile, malleable, and controllable. Whatever it took to gain the upper hand was the surefire route to bringing a star up to standard.

Miller was a supremely talented young player from Vancouver, Washington. It was for good reason that he had gained the reputation as the best passer in the league. This was his third year under Dobie, and in his first year he earned a letter as a freshman, and in only his second year he was selected as the All-Northwest left halfback. With this sterling record, the coach had this to say of arguably the best athlete on the squad: "I'm greatly tempted to pull Miller out of the game entirely because he has retarded the team more this year than all the new men put together. If Miller goes in in place of Murphy, it will be because I don't want him to be on the sidelines when there is a chance of our getting beat." Dobie was never one to be restrained by overstating his case, and those who knew his penchant for less than delicate phraseology would pick up on his reference to being "greatly tempted." He did leave himself some wiggle room just in case he had to resort to calling on that miserable wretch of a player to fill in for a few minutes in the losing cause.

In Dobie's defense it had been exactly 365 days ago in Portland that Washington barely escaped with their skin intact, squeaking by on a razor thin 10-7 score against Bezdek's men. With all of the quotes attributed to Dobie, it would appear he had a reporter dogging him around the clock. But in publishing every doubtful utterance he could muster, how else to drum up interest in a team that had not been beaten for forty-six straight games? Noticing all of this attention from the press, Dobie had one of his own quite predictable theories on this love affair by stating, "People are really beginning to believe me." There is no recorded counter posed by any member of the fourth estate that there are also a goodly number of people who really believe in Santa Claus.

As if the blizzard of words from the coaches wasn't enough to hype up matters swirling around Denny Field, Mother Nature added another bit of excitement to the mix. A real 64-mph wind blizzard whipped across the campus off Lake Washington just two days before the game. It wreaked havoc with the telephone and electrical system, the campus golf course, and the amphitheater; ripped off large stretches of fencing around the field; and tore off the top of the old north grandstand. There was some doubt as to whether the game would be played at all, but Arthur Younger was able to round up a construction crew who worked overtime to repair the destruction.

There hadn't been a game previous to that year's Oregon contest that garnered as much consternation as to which was the superior team. As everyone knew, Dobie most often was fully aware of the favorite, that being whoever he faced that week. But this game was different. There was more doubt than usual expressed by the sportswriters, and even diehard fans were not voicing quite the same level of optimism. Those who actually believed Dobie that Hap Miller, his star halfback, was so drastically undermining the team that he was sitting this one out must have had heart palpitations. This, coupled with the vendetta the visitors held over their painful loss the previous year, was cause for concern. Of course, everyone knew there was still lingering resentment by Oregon over the famous Bunk Play—even three years later.

Anxiety mounted as the scheduled kickoff moved past its deadline. Washington had taken the field and completed their warm-ups by the appointed time of 2:30, but the Oregon team was nowhere in sight. No word had come from the visitors' locker room that more time was needed, so all that could be done was for Washington to twiddle their thumbs and wait. Neither the players nor Dobie were any too happy, and anxious fans were grumbling over what was later described as a bush-league stunt on the part of Bezdek.

Once Oregon came onto the field fifteen minutes late and finished their pregame drills, it wasn't long before the big question of the day would be answered. Would Hap Miller ride the bench or would Dobie find a way to justify some playing time for his star that mysteriously had lost all ability to play the game? It would turn out that Miller not only started but played every minute of the contest. The other Dobie-described "All-Americans," Mike Hunt, Elmer Leader, Walt Shiel, and the great Louis Seagrave, who were giving him so much trouble, also played the entire game. In fact, there was only one substitution made by Dobie in this extremely hard-fought contest; left guard Harry Wirt spelled Andy McPherson. The logical question would be to ask, just what was this concern that Dobie had that his top players were all going soft? Students of Dobie and his behavior have no problem with the answer—this was just another display of his psychological gamesmanship. Not every coach would risk knocking a player's legs out from under him as a motivating ploy and expect to get away with it. But Dobie commanded such respect from his men that he could exercise these harsh measures and inevitably bring out a career performance from his men.

The game was hard fought from start to finish, but Washington maintained an edge throughout. During the first half Oregon failed to make even one first down. There was one standout play that evidences the lengths Dobie would go to set up a game-breaking play. All week leading up to the game, he went out of his way to disparage not just his chances to win but to openly bad-mouth Hap Miller. It merits noting that Miller just happened to be the best passer in the conference. The one standout play that decided the game also "just happened" to be a pass launched by Miller to Hunt that was executed to perfection. Coincidence? Two years later, Bobby Boyce, writing in the *Argus*, confirmed that this was indeed not just happenstance but a splendidly calculated plan engineered by Dobie. The coaching feud between Dobie and Bezdek was well known, and it was the Washington coach who placed the most effort into gaining the upper hand. For this game he did devote thirty minutes every night to working on this one pass play designed only for Oregon.

To resolve whether Dobie may have intended his public pillorying of Miller with no grander purpose in mind, one only needs to consider that a play such as this game breaker would have required several days of endless repetition before the coach would approve its use. When he taught a far less important play, he was known to devote an entire practice to its mastery. With the complex play Dobie was about to spring on Oregon, given his commitment to detail, he would need to have spent days in engineering every move of every player. With the play centering on Miller, the coach would have been glued to him in buttoning down every move he needed to make to assure success. Ironically, just as was the case in 1911 in preparing for the Bunk Play, he again enjoyed the luxury of an extra week of practice. While he publicly demeaned Miller, he privately set up a game breaker in practice that featured him. After the game,

Bezdek said to Dobie, "You beat us but only by a lucky, fluky forward pass." Dobie, ever composed (whether winning or losing, as we will later see), kept silent so as never to reveal his hand. Bobby Boyce, who attended many of the practices leading up to the game, confirmed that the pass play had been the centerpiece of every session, and Dobie's public derision of Hap Miller was all part of the elaborate scheme. Dobie won so consistently for many reasons, but his thoroughness in game preparation, so well exhibited here, is a primary cause. The only score in the opening half came by way of a Charley Smith 30-yard dropkick in the first quarter. Smith had done a masterful job in calling plays to keep the ball midway between the sidelines to set up the kick. Since he was playing on a bum ankle, Dobie had given him explicit instructions not to run with the ball. Some observers in the stands thought he was dogging it in never carrying the ball and calling for a fair catch receiving punts, but he was just following coach's orders.

At the halftime break the teams had just put in two of the all-time toughest quarters either had ever battled through. With only a slight edge going to Washington, the outcome was still up for grabs. The first half was played conservatively on both sides, with a lot of punting as was so often employed in that day to secure better field position. Neither team gained an inch as the kickers and receivers neutralized each other. It was apparent that one of these two masterful coaches would have to find a better plan in the second half for any chance at bringing home a victory. Up to now neither game plan was getting the job done. By halftime Dobie was convinced that he would have to employ the special pass play that he so meticulously built around Miller and Hunt. If they were to win, now was the time to put the game into the hands of two of his best men.

The third quarter started out much as the second had ended, with neither team able to make a serious scoring threat. In the early minutes Miller fumbled the ball, which was recovered by Oregon's fullback, Raymond Bryant. On their possession, a 30-yard pass from left tackle J. W. Beckett was intercepted by Charley Smith. Washington wasn't able to make any headway and punted the ball, but it was fumbled by quarterback Shy Huntington with center Les "Shoes" Gellatly recovering and picking up good yardage on an open field.

The big pass play came rather inauspiciously. Dobie had lulled Oregon to sleep up to now by instructing Smith to call only running plays. Washington tried only three passes for the entire game. All three were called on this possession, just after Gellatly's recovery. The first of these, a quick pass, Miller to Hunt, failed. The second attempt, with Miller again passing to Hunt, failed. The stage was now perfectly set for the play that followed. All eyes on and off the field could plainly see that the Purple and Gold's passing game wasn't working, so it was back to the running game. Miller received the ball from center and headed for the sidelines on a very well executed end sweep, drawing the entire defense in hot pursuit. But just short of the line of scrimmage, Miller suddenly stopped and, exhibiting the athleticism he was so well known for, threw the ball back cross-field 30 yards on a perfect strike to Mike Hunt. With a wide-open field, Hunt easily sprinted the 15 yards for the touchdown. Writing for the *Times*, Conrad Brevick described it as "perfect in its deception, in its perfect long throw and in Hunt's catch." The play ended, however, on a terrible note. Shy Huntington, a big freshman from The Dalles, Oregon, can possibly be excused due to inexperience, but the play definitely didn't look good. Hunt, not expecting to be hit after he was well across the goal line, was knocked out cold on a blindside tackle. Smith booted the extra point to put Washington up 10-0.

Even by the hard standards of the day, the game was a brutally fought contest. Bill Hayward, Oregon's trainer, was accused of stalling tactics in running out on the field with his medical bag to treat injuries, some of which seemed unnecessary to hometown loyalists. The game did take two-and-one-half hours to play, which was quite long for this commercial-break-free era. Soft-spoken but hard-hitting Mike Hunt took the roughest beating of the day. The fastest man on the field was Oregon's great right halfback and captain, John Parsons. On defense it was Hunt who drew the primary assignment of stopping the 160-pound Parsons. Hunt, at 181 pounds, had a weight advantage, but Parsons was both fast and powerful, so this increased the load endured by Hunt in this grueling slugfest. Adding to the beating taken by Hunt, right tackle Dave Philbin, at 205 pounds, was the heaviest man on the field, and Bezdek wisely placed him in front of Parsons to open up holes in the line. At his end position, Hunt would first have to fight off this giant if he had any hope of stopping the fleet-of-foot Parsons.

As the game was drawing to its dramatic climax, there were an unusually large number of penalties in the fourth quarter. Not to be outdone by Bezdek, who received a 5-yard penalty for going on the field in the first quarter, Dobie drew a penalty for the same reason in the fourth. It was after a pretty run by Parsons that Dobie went onto the field to make a personal appeal to pull the injured Hunt out of the game. Hunt was not one to quit a fight and was well known for playing through pain. In this game, everyone could see he had suffered too long and too hard, but he refused to accept Dobie's pleas to relieve him. For this Washington incurred a 15-yard penalty. For his part Mother Hunt was later to receive the highest praise ever granted a player from the lips of Coach Dobie.

The fourth quarter was Oregon's best in moving the ball, but it would prove too little, too late. In a hurry-up game the visitors put together an array of fake kicks, assorted trick plays, and passes, and effectively drove the ball to Washington's 5-yard line. A penalty for pushing the ball carrier from behind placed them back on the 10 at third down. Parsons tried a chip-shot field goal from there, but Washington's charging linemen caused holder John Beckett to rush the play, throwing off the timing of the kick and sending the ball wide of the cross bars. The ball went over to Washington with just seconds to play. They punted the ball to safety as darkness was falling and time ran out.

Assessing the overall game, both lines were closely matched, with only the slightest margin in favor of the home team. Washington did make more yardage than the score would indicate, with seven first downs to Oregon's three. Hap Miller bore the brunt of the demanding running game, being called on for three out of four running plays, and local sportswriters rated him the star of the game. It was quite obviously in Dobie's game plan to not attempt many passes to set up his signature play of the day, but only completing one out of three on perfect field conditions was well below standard. Oregon attempted ten passes, but their aerial game didn't help their cause since they completed only three for short yardage. Washington duplicated its ten-point scoring output of last year, but for 1914 Oregon didn't cross the Varsity's goal line.

In the dressing room, Dobie, by his standards at least, was in a buoyant mood. He announced to his boys that they had played a good game. He didn't dare go overboard and say too much, so with a pointed finger aimed in their direction he warned that next week's game with Washington State could surely be lost "if they didn't watch out." But it was here, in front of his players, sportswriters, and a swarm of well-wishers who were allowed into the inner sanctum, that Dobie handed down the greatest compliment he ever gave to one of his players. After the heroic game played by the popular Mother Hunt, and after his own determined efforts to pull the beaten and exhausted player from the field of battle, it was only fitting that this warrior should be singled out.

A sportswriter in the locker room at the time described the scene. "He went over to the big, bashful, uncomplaining fellow who so effectively smothered Parsons, and who refused to come out of the game, even after Dobie went onto the field in the last quarter to get him.

" 'Where'd they get you, boy?' he asked in a voice that seemed mighty tender to the fellows who have only heard him rasp and complain and fault-find during the trying season of training.

"Injured, limping, battered almost senseless by repeated hammerings of catapulting Oregon backs, 'Mother' Hunt tried to straighten up, and the cakes of dirt on his face began dropping off as he wrinkled his face up into one of those absolutely inimitable smiles. It wasn't much of a smile as smiles go, and it looked more like a grimace of a man in pain but it did service.

" *'If they broke both of your legs and arms, I wouldn't take you out. I've got that much confidence in you,'* said the tall Scotsman, patting the big fellow on the back. Which, coming from such a 'hard hearted' and 'emotionless' fellow as Gil Dobie is reputed to be, is some tribute."

### Washington State

Word from eastern Washington was boastful, borne more out of frustration than conviction. As with every other team in the league, the "Aggies" were sick and tired of losing to Dobie's teams every year. This fate was particularly galling for Washington State, being cross-state rivals and on the receiving end of so much punishment. Coach Johnny Bender was in an untenable position, being both graduate manager and head coach. There was just too much to criticize in placing such disparate jobs in the hands of one person. Being constantly compared to that evil force west of the Cascades made matters all the worse. It couldn't be known at the time of the big Thanksgiving Game, but this would be the last game coached by Bender at WSU. The heat that he was under may have accounted for the brash claims of finally bringing parity in football between the schools this year and a reported obsession to pull off the first win against Washington since Dobie's arrival. Ralph Benjamin, writing for the *Seattle Times*, was a close student of Northwest football and summed up State's supposed fixation this way: "They are laying awake nights down there talking about beating Washington. They eat it, sleep it, drink it and talk it from sun to sun. It will be a dangerous gang Dobie's men will have to face Thanksgiving Day."

It was late in 1914 that the looming events began to bubble over that next year would lead to the demise of the existing Big 6 League (Pacific Northwest Intercollegiate Conference). Even without Dobie's record, the financial reality of playing a game on Denny Field meant the visiting team was playing in the largest city at the largest university in the Northwest. Because of this, the other schools would look for higher guarantees playing at Washington and didn't offer reciprocal agreements. Needless to say, such hard-line negotiating didn't set well with the Scotsman. It was also at this time that California and Stanford were contemplating shifting from rugby back to American Rules Football. League President Victor Zednick was the strongest early advocate of expanding the league to include the California schools. Before the upcoming December 4, 1914, annual meeting in Spokane, he wrote a letter to all of the universities of the conference advocating opening the discussions to expand the league to include these schools. As events would unfold, Dobie's disenchantment with contract negotiations, primarily with Oregon and Washington State, Dobie's league dominance, and Zednick's favorable attitude towards league expansion set the stage leading to the formation of the Pac-10 (later Pac-12) Conference. In December 1914, in his capacity as president of the Northwest Intercollegiate Conference, Zednick wrote to both the University of California and Stanford inviting them to join a new league made up of "all the leading institutions of the Pacific Coast and not...confined to the Northwest alone." This was the earliest advocacy of such a move by an official in a position of authority to bring about such a move.

Thanksgiving would be a busy day for the league, as all six teams had a game on tap. Oregon was up against the Multnomah Club team, who had been an annual event on their schedule as far back as 1896. Oregon State, who tied Washington, also tied the score in their game against Oregon, 3-3. This put the Varsity in the driver's seat for a seventh straight championship if they were to prevail against their Pullman rival. Oregon State was predicted to win by two touchdowns in their first game ever against USC. Idaho was going up against Whitman on the Missionaries' home field in a game that looked to be a toss-up.

Yell king George Mathieu caught the sentiment of Varsity partisans anxious to extend Washington's championship string to seven straight. He organized a gigantic parade of twelve hundred nightie-clad and faux chorus "girls" through the streets of downtown Seattle, females still being relegated to the sidelines. The brass band, a fife and drum corps, clanging cow bells, tin pans, and as early as this in UW's football history what was referred to as the "famous siren" served as accompaniment to the howling rooters. Seven years later, the tradition of the siren had grown in stature and was now used to blast out to the world every time the Huskies scored in their new stadium. This was another of the many traditions that started as a result of Dobie's long reign of football supremacy. This brought out a boisterous but creative flock of followers whose exuberance gave birth to many long-lasting campus traditions. Another bit of excitement had been engendered at Brown and Hulen's Billiard Rooms, where the precious Washington Hook was on display for fans to ogle. Reports of several underhanded attempts to "threaten" the ancient hook were made by WSU students, but to no avail. Charles Hulen was on to the skullduggery and successfully fended off the cross-mountain invaders.

Dobie actually loosened up a touch in a pregame statement, admitting that his team was in excellent shape going into the weekend. Washington State had lost their games with both of the Oregon schools and despite this Dobie chose to take a cautious view of his team's chances for Saturday. He had to do a bit of reaching to come up with an angle and wasn't his usual creative self, only being able to muster a lackluster prediction of misfortune. Bender had focused on the showdown against Washington and personally scouted all of the Varsity's big games. Dobie had not seen any of State's games and used this shortcoming as the basis for his argument that he was destined to lose. It was most definitely a stretch to come to this conclusion, but Dobie was never constrained by the need to present a convincing case. His objective was to just get some uncertainty in print, knowing that there would be those doubting souls out there who bought into the line. Coach Bender left no question as to where he stood. "I firmly believe that I will be able to give Dobie the greatest battle that he has ever had. My boys are all on edge and they are going to make a great showing."

Dobie's pregame reservation compared to Bender's impassioned fervor would prove to be an odd counterpoint to the game itself. There is no way to soften the description of the outcome. No matter that the Washington State coach had a firm belief that he would give Dobie his greatest battle, the headline, "Pullman Buried by Dobie's Champions," told the tale. The *Post-Intelligencer* reported that this was the most crushing defeat ever administered against a Washington State team. And that it was.

Not only did the Purple and Gold execute a near-flawless offensive attack, their defense was even better. The visitors never made a first down until the fourth quarter. It wasn't for lack of creativity, as Bender had laid out an excellent mix of trick plays, passing attempts, and runs, but Washington's defense would consistently drop them in their tracks. Often, the defense held the line so well that after three downs State would find themselves closer to their own goal than when they started.

Hap Miller, showing no signs of Dobie's claim last week of being such a destructive force to the team, was in top form. He was the number one ground gainer, but Captain Walt Shiel and Mike Chapman also carried the ball for consistent gains, and all scored touchdowns. Charley Smith at quarterback played one of his best games ever in running the team and doing his part at carrying the ball. He kicked a field goal in the opening period for the first score and was a perfect six for six on extra points. Coach Bender, who had wide coaching experience in the Midwest, declared Smith to be the greatest kicker he had ever seen. On the line, both tackles, Andy Anderson and Elmer Leader, together with center Lester Gellatly, were standouts on offense and defense. The closest threat made by the outmanned Pullman squad came on separate long and catchable passes to ends Heg and Tom Tryer that fell into their hands but were dropped. If caught, both of these could have been touchdowns. Football being such a game of momentum swings, these two scores had the potential for reversing the entire disposition of the contest. The passes failed not because of brilliant defensive coverage but just lack of execution by the receivers.

The frustration for Coach Johnny Bender in his last game as coach for Washington State can best be exemplified by one series in the first quarter. One would hope that the team could shake off such inept play, but, rather than recovering from misfortune, the series only proved to be a harbinger of things to come. Following the kickoff after Charley Smith's field goal, State put the ball in play on their own 10-yard line. They proceeded to fumble on the first set of downs but fortunately recovered the ball. Having a reprieve, with the game still fresh and getting a break such as this, a shift in momentum would be in order. This was not to be on a day where everything was going in Washington's favor. On the next play, State would execute one of the most disastrous series to befall a team, back-to-back fumbles. Call it luck, bad play, or good defense by Dobie's men, the outcome is all the same. Playing in his last game, left tackle and 1914 Flaherty Medal winner Herman "Andy" Anderson scooped up the ball for the second of the six touchdowns that Washington would score. The game ended in another shutout, 45-0.

Native American Johnny Bender had coached at Washington State originally in 1906-07. It's rarely done, but he was called back to Pullman and again took up the head coaching reigns from 1912 to '14 after in-between stops, one of which was at St. Louis University. Bender had been compared to a popular charm doll called a Billiken, and his players became known as Bender's Billikens. Thus the coach who left St. Louis to return to the Palouse country left behind a lasting legacy, having created the inspiration for St. Louis University's team name, the Billikens. His overall five-year record at Washington State was 21-12 for a .636 winning percentage. In this, his last year, he posted his poorest performance of two wins, four losses.

# CHAPTER NINE

## *Pride of Washington—1915*

> "The restoration of intercollegiate football to the California curriculum was a financial and a popular success but Dr. Dobie's physicians unfortunately killed the Golden Bear during the operation. Not only did they make a corpse of Bruin, but they disemboweled the critter, reduced his flesh to mincemeat and departed with his shaggy hide, vowing to nail it to the front door of old Siwash College. There is nothing left of the Golden Bear save a grease spot. Never was there a more humiliating defeat administered to the University of California in its history than that 72 to 0 walloping which Washington handed the Blue and Gold on California yesterday."
>
> *Billy Fitz, Oakland Tribune, November 7, 1915*

This proved to be a pivotal year not just in Pacific Northwest football, but indeed football in the western United States. Since Dobie first sprang on the scene, his teams were 46-0-2. Washington had played their chief rivals every year with only two exceptions and had beaten them all seven years save for the ties with WSU in 1908 and OSU in 1914. The Varsity's league opponents were held scoreless 70 percent of the time. However, a look at Washington's schedule for 1915 surprisingly shows no games with any of these three teams. What happened? The answer leads us on a direct path to the founding of the league known today as the Pacific-12 conference. At the center of the controversy, we find the one man most responsible for elevating West Coast football to the preeminent national status it occupies today, the indomitable Gilmour Dobie.

Dobie arrived in the Northwest the year that Washington, Washington State, Oregon, Oregon State, Idaho, and Whitman (the Big 6) gathered to form the Pacific Northwest Intercollegiate Conference. Needless to say, once the conference was launched the other coaches in the league were not pleased with being on the short end of the score in virtually every contest undertaken against Washington. For the last one hundred years, much has been written of Dobie's penchant for speaking his mind and the demand for total control. The reasons for his success on the football field extend well beyond these traits but did serve him well in teaching his youngsters the finer points of the game. As he grew in reputation, he felt that success entitled him to dictate where and when games were to be played, another reason for resentment from the coaches. Dobie's ploy in attempting to gain the upper hand with WSU in scheduling the 1915 game was all too obvious when he remarked that playing them "was too much like kindergarten." This less-than-charitable characterization came from his assessment of the previous year's lopsided Thanksgiving game. Dobie was accused in WSU's campus paper, the *Evergreen*, of being "a dictator." Ironically, just as the traditional Thanksgiving cross-state rivalry came to its abrupt end, both teams went on to undefeated seasons in 1915. The debate still hasn't been settled as to just which was the superior team. Alas, comparative scores are of no help in settling the conflict since they both won against their two common opponents. Washington had the scoring edge with Gonzaga, and Washington State led in its margin over Whitman.

The conference held its meeting to set game schedules for 1915 in Spokane. However, in an effort to break Dobie's stranglehold over his competitors, they all gathered for a prior meeting with a plan to bring down the dynasty. Graduate Manager Art Younger attended the meeting. The *Evergreen's* dictator charge not being too far off the mark, Younger had direction from Dobie as to how the 1915 schedule for Washington was to be set out. It's the case today, as it was back then, that any coach prefers to spread out his major competition over the full season. Dobie, playing every angle, certainly wanted the sequence of games in his favor. Younger proposed Dobie's preferences to the other GMs as to WSU, Oregon, and OSU. This was stonewalled by these three, who stood pat on a demand to not do anything until Washington had first scheduled weaker Idaho. It seemed fishy to Younger that such a united front would be so adamant, and he called Dobie with his suspicions. Dobie saw they were putting him in a squeeze play and instructed Younger to likewise stand pat. The end result of all the poker playing was for Washington to end up with only one conference game with Whitman on its schedule. This clash of football egos left the Northwest Conference in a shambles. Its marquee team, not competing against the best in the league, was left to look beyond the Pacific Northwest to complete its dance card.

Much to the chagrin of many fans, the University of California and Stanford had opted to play English rugby rather than American Rules Football in 1906. They decided against the game played in America because it was getting too dangerous, with terrible numbers of deaths and injuries in this anything-goes era. Fortunately, in December 1905, representatives from sixty-two colleges met and made a number of revisions to eliminate brutality from the game. It was too late for Cal and Stanford. California did not return to American Rules Football until 1915, and it wasn't until 1919 that Stanford returned to the game. USC did have a developing program that mostly played local athletic clubs and small colleges in these early days (later it also switched to rugby for 1911-12-13), and UCLA wouldn't play its first game until 1919, losing to Manual Arts High School, 74-0.

For its revamped schedule, Washington enjoyed a wide choice of teams eager to get a shot at the seven-time Northwest Conference champions. Washington filled in its schedule with preseason games against the Ballard Meteors and Washington Athletic Club and its regular season against Gonzaga, Whitman, California (twice), and Colorado. Now that California had returned to football and with Stanford still playing rugby, the famous matchup for the "Big Game" traditionally between Stanford and California was played between Washington and California.

The team that Dobie assembled for the 1915 campaign was a powerhouse, with nine players having earned Varsity letters in prior years: Captain Ray "Mike" Hunt, left end; Elmer Leader, left tackle; Cedric "Hap" Miller, left halfback; Ernest "Tramp" Murphy, right end; Elmer "Cy" Noble, right halfback; Louis "Louie" Seagrave, right guard; Walter "Walt" Shiel, fullback; George "Snake" Smith, right end; and Allan "Bud" Young, quarterback. Three players had experience as substitutes from earlier years: John "Mark" Markham, right tackle; Ross "Mac" MacKechnie, left end; and Harry Wirt, left guard. Rounding out the team were only three newcomers: Thomas "Tom" Cushman, center; William "Bill" Grimm, tackle and left guard; and David Logg, center. With a team so rich in returning players, it is little wonder that opposing coaches in the league would consort to knock Dobie off his pedestal.

Dobie had always run the team with only one assistant coach under him. The job had been held by former star and right end Wayne Sutton since 1914, but in 1915 he added Jack Fancher as a second assistant coach to focus on developing the third string for future work. Fancher had experience playing on the second string himself the prior year and was captain and player/coach of that year's basketball team. This would allow more time for Dobie to focus on what he did best—drill his players on fundamentals and spend more time with his ball carriers. He studied each man's personal strengths so that, by constant drilling, he could fine-tune his particular set of abilities to best advantage. This enhanced the primary fundamental of Dobie's system, assuring that the entire team worked in unison. It was often said that Dobie's quarterback could have called his plays out loud, but with every man working with such precision it wouldn't have made a difference.

University of Washington Libraries, Special Collections, Neg. No. UW 29125

Captain Raymond "Mike" Hunt, 1915 Dobie's favorite among all of his players.

## Preseason

With all the hope and promise that would seem to follow with the heavy concentration of experience, practice once again started out decidedly ragged. Players of the day worked in the off season more often than not in hard physical labor and were not in playing condition as they first showed up. This was certainly the case for the 1915 team. While Dobie assembled a top-flight team of experienced men, they straggled into camp on their own time, with the coaching staff never fully assure of commitments. Cy Noble, right halfback in Dobie's invincible backfield quartet, suffered a fractured nose in practice and was definitely out for the first game. As game day approached, however, the team began to fill in. The team they were to play wasn't known to them until the week before game day. The earlier team dropped out, with the Ballard Meteors jumping at a chance to play the mighty Varsity of Washington. Ballard was a club team composed of area players who were former high school stars. The *Post-Intelligencer* described them as "men who had they continued to a collegiate course would very probably be wearing the purple and gold jerseys of the Varsity."

Some of the "old stars," as they were described in the *Daily*, played so poorly that they were pulled out of the game and replaced with second stringers for the final quarter. They only managed fifteen points for the first three quarters. As an embarrassing exclamation as to the Varsity's poor performance, the second string put sixteen points on the board in their one quarter of action. In the second period with Captain Mike Hunt played so poorly he was replaced by Don Abel, and quarterback Bud Young by Roy "Rat" Wood, both second stringers. Such a move on Dobie's part sent the time-honored signal to the team as to his dissatisfaction. Walt Shiel did the best job of the linemen, and second stringer Ray Gardner got the strongest praise of players in the backfield. Hunt seemed to perform in streaks, but at least Hap Miller didn't join the ranks of early-season misfits.

At halftime, in another move meant to broadcast his displeasure, Coach Dobie appointed Miller as field general for the rest of the season. This is the position that traditionally goes to the quarterback, but Dobie obviously was not satisfied with the play of Bud Young, who many had considered to be the best field general in the league in 1912. Dobie expressed disappointment with Young's selection of plays and his manner of running the team. The game ended with the club team of former high school stars playing the entire game without substitution, while Dobie played two entire teams. The final score: Washington 31-0 over the Ballard Meteors.

When Washington withdrew from most conference games over the stand-off with league coaches, word traveled fast among unaffiliated former football stars in the Northwest. Club teams then had many more prospects to pick from, with these players itching for a chance to knock off Washington. Next week's opponent, Washington Park Athletic Club, had a highly touted backfield, and with players having resumes as stars in college and high school to their credit, the game looked to be quite competitive.

Dobie was now ramping up his workouts, focusing on his basic requirement of maximizing team speed. He was not satisfied with what he saw, and this week more intense drills were run. After the hard scrimmage, assistant coach Wayne

Sutton arranged the team's own track meet, with every player competing in 50- and 100-yard dashes topped off with seven laps on the 440-yard track.

Unfortunately, as game day neared, quarterback Bud Young wrenched his shoulder in practice, and his backup, Rat Wood, suffered a severely bruised ribcage, taking him out of action. This meant that quarterback duties fell on journeyman Dick Bronson for the upcoming game. Bronson was a player who came out for four years, always kept in shape, was a stalwart in practice, but in four years never got enough playing time to receive a letter. This year was no different, but in recognition of his faithful service and contributions to the team he was awarded an honorary *W* at the team banquet. This remarkable young man went on to national prominence in World War I, the recipient of the Medal of Honor for distinguished service in battle. Dobie himself always felt the rules for determining playing time to qualify for a letter at Washington were too strict. Looking back, he was right in this opinion considering how arduous the game was in those days, with players going three ways on offense, defense, and special teams. This was especially true considering the primitive nature of protective equipment. Injuries in practice kept numerous deserving players missing the game time necessary under the rigid rules of the day. In Dobie's nine years at Washington there were only seventy men who earned letters and three who earned honorary letters of the several hundred who served.

The year 1915 was Dr. Henry Suzzallo's first as university president. The week of the Washington Park AC game, he conducted a lecture for freshmen men on "college citizenship." It's interesting to juxtapose this message with the red-hot debates going on in society at the time over women's suffrage. It was just three weeks later that an amendment to the state constitution was on the ballot allowing women the right to vote (it passed on November 2, 1915.) President Suzzallo seemed to be a bit out of step with the changing times in his promotion of college traditions to this gathering of young men. His advice to this all-male audience, as reported in the *Daily*, was for freshmen to be on the lookout for seniors taking their dates to football games. "The senior who takes a lady to the game and sits apart from the rooters in the bleachers deserves to have a freshman sent after him to bring him down. The good college student will root for the team at the right time." The plot thickens because it was just the week before that President Suzzallo addressed five hundred campus women on co-ed independence! Here he told them that he was "happy to see the day pass when women could have fun without the benign company of men." He clearly drew the line on women's independence extending to sitting with their dates in the rooting section at a football game.

Despite the injuries to key players and the stronger club team assembled that week, play was much more of what Dobie's fans had grown to expect. An above-average twenty-three Washington men got into the game. The contest saw UW airing out the ball, with seven of fourteen completions. In passing, the substitutes put some pressure on the first string, showing much better speed and aggressiveness. Standouts for the game were David Logg at center, John Markham at right tackle, Ross MacKechnie at left halfback, Ted Faulk at left end, and Walt Shiel at fullback. Captain Mike Hunt finally got back into a groove that week. Third-stringer Dick Bronson gave the team a huge boost in taking over the reins at quarterback. The game ended in spectacular fashion with a pass from MacKechnie at midfield to Don Abel, who, just short of the goal line, lost the handle on the ball. As it bounded towards the sideline with substitute Charles Newton outpacing everyone on the field, he scooped up the pigskin and ran it in for the final TD. Considering the doubts going into the game, the final score was a surprising Washington shutout, 64-0.

### Gonzaga University at Spokane

With Dobie's emphasis on team speed, his game preparation and the games themselves were always a laboratory for his maneuvering the players into the positions most suited to their running ability. Thus far in the 1915 season he had not been satisfied with what he saw; in fact, "disgusted" would be the best description of his sentiments. As with any of his public remarks, however, there was always what Dobie said for public consumption and his real intent. Dobie was meticulously feeding a steady diet of calculated remarks to the press before the Gonzaga game. "They had four full weeks of stiff workouts, and one or two of the first-team men are so slow that it is hard to realize that they have practiced more than a week." "The slowest bunch I've ever seen. I can't lay it on too thick." "They're the slowest backfield on any good college team in the country." "They're so slow they look like their feet are dragging in the mud." To further drive the point home that his players should be looking over their shoulders, he added, "Unless a few of those men now holding their jobs on the Varsity get some pep into their systems, they are going to find someone else in their places when the hard games start."

Remembering that the 1915 squad had nine returning lettermen, is there a serious problem or might this be the master coach getting under his players' skin? If we take his words at face value, this would be an indictment of his own coaching ability. Dobie was never known to blow his own horn, but he certainly didn't heap criticism on himself either. Dobie always stressed speed, and to get full effort from his players, he felt that negative reinforcement was the best way to get any fight out of competitive young athletes. Job security on a football team is no different than anywhere else; when there's a threat, the obvious response is to pull out all stops. In his public remarks, the coach wasn't calling out individuals, but warning that "a few" were at risk of being replaced has some teeth in it. Whether he followed up on it or not, Dobie's sermon always hammered home that diligence in practice was a prerequisite to holding your position. In this Dobie was consistent, and he made it his mantra on every team he coached in his historic career.

But warnings in the press had to be followed up with tangible signals that Dobie meant business. As the days grew shorter in the fall and with no lighting on the field, the ghost ball was an annual event at his practices. Two brightly whitewashed balls had been brought out and were conspicuously placed on the field but not used until after a week of just sitting with other field equipment for everyone to see, as Dobie was stressing that something had to give—the boys had to either work harder and improve speed, or be replaced. The ominous visage of the ghost balls on the sideline was a not-too-subtle warning. It wouldn't do for the coach to just announce one day that the team was holding over and working into the evening with poor light. For maximum effectiveness he needed to create some drama. This stage prop brought the message home loud and clear as to the best route for job security.

The Gonzaga game matched up teacher against former pupil. William "Wee" Coyle was practicing law in Spokane after graduating and moonlighted for just this year as Gonzaga's coach. Whenever Dobie looked back in later years, reflecting on players he coached, Wee Coyle was always mentioned. Since he won two national championships at Cornell in 1922-23 (alumni would also claim 1921) and went undefeated in 1921-22-23, Dobie was obviously a good judge for comparing West Coast players with the East Coast. He rated Wee Coyle as one of the best quarterbacks he ever coached. The combination of intelligence, athleticism and on-field generalship placed him at the top. With Dobie's methods of coaching and game strategy proven to be keys to success, there wasn't much doubt that Coyle's game would be fashioned after what he learned from his great mentor.

The trip across the state was originally envisioned as a contest with Washington State after a five-year absence of the rivals last meeting in Spokane. Such an event would have drawn a huge crowd. As it turned out, interest was feeble for the Gonzaga contest, which drew the smallest crowd of the year. With the Northwest Conference's seven-time champion only pulling one thousand people to a game, the longevity of the league didn't look any too promising. While the game against Gonzaga was drawing hardly a ripple of notice, the upcoming game with California, still three weeks away, was being touted across the country. Plans were already under way to reserve a block of cabins on the largest passenger steamer plying the Pacific Coast, the SS *Congress* to carry the Washington band and a shipload of fans south to Berkeley.

The game with the Catholic college did make history in one respect. Dobie's teams were considered invincible in defending against scoring by the forward pass. No team playing against his elevens had ever completed a pass for a touchdown. That is, until they tangled with the scrappy team of Wee Coyle's. It was in the fourth quarter that Captain Tom Berry eluded his coverage, snagged the historic pass, and ran 40 yards for the touchdown. Washington actually was successful overall in its passing game, completing five out of ten attempts, and their passing defense was also stellar in holding the opponents to only two for ten. Hap Miller accounted for all three of the Varsity's touchdowns. Fumbles were a problem, with Ross MacKechnie coughing up three that were recovered by Gonzaga. Cy Noble, recovering from his broken nose, was able to take over his position temporarily occupied by MacKechnie.

Dobie's constant whaling over the slowness of his team turned out to be warranted. He was able to keep beating this drum using unimpeachable stats from the Gonzaga game as proof. "They allowed a couple of ordinarily fast ends to come around and break up plays before they had gotten under way. What's more, they kept right on doing it and our men weren't able to put a stop to it. Just how slow we were is evidenced by the fact that we allowed them to score on a forward pass, something that has not been accomplished on a Washington team in seven years. When they get so slow that you can't even attempt an open game for fear that the opposition will grab all the passes and convert them into touchdowns, then you have something to worry about." You must think that deep down inside, Dobie couldn't be too terribly upset. One passing score in seven years in most quarters would hardly be a "worry." He came out a winner in the game and still was able to keep the pressure on his players to improve on speed and reaction time. The coach had been running a high fever on the trip over and was feeling ill for several days. The illness was attributed to a passing bug and not to the poor performance of his team.

Washington's scores came through touchdowns in the first, third, and fourth quarters, and a Bud Young dropkick for goal in the second quarter. Wee Coyle's boys only scored one time in the last quarter, rocking Washington to its core with Captain Berry's worrisome pass completion. The final score showed Washington on top, 21-7.

### Whitman College

Washington over the years had many yells and songs for the rooting section, but they didn't yet have a rousing fight song. It was a challenge by way of a California fight song, written by a Cal student that really got the UW students riled up. A direct challenge was laid down by Cal's song, with these combative words as its intro:

> Down from the North comes the Purple and Gold
> To skin our Golden Bear,
> Washington's eleven will never hold
> The charge of our mighty Bear.

The Senior Council, together with the *UW Daily*, took up the cause and sponsored a contest to create an original song to counter the challenge lodged from the upstarts down south. A $25 prize for the winning entry was offered by donations from alumni. Any student or alumnus from Washington was eligible to enter. The contest was won by Lester J. Wilson of the class of '13, with "Bow Down To Washington" winning out of the fourteen entries submitted. Two others received honorable mention: "The Death of the Golden Bear," music by Martin Easton and words by Emil Hurja, and "The Good Ship Washington," music by Donald Wilson and words by Harold Allen. The upcoming California game on November 6 was the catalyst in getting the movement started. One important requirement was that the song had to include a reference to Washington's superiority over California. The release of the winning song, complete with band accompaniment, was to have its premiere at the Big Game at California. A trial run was scheduled for the Whitman game with songwriter Lester Wilson accompanying on the piano. Since this song has gained in prominence far beyond its humble origins, coming at a price of $25, it's appropriate that its formal introduction was at the home where it was born. As evidence (if it was really necessary) of Dobie's high station in the minds of loyal fans, his name was featured in the chorus of the original version:

Dobie, Dobie, pride of Washington;
Leather lungs together with a Rah! Rah! Rah!

With train travel to Berkeley coming up, the team could only work in four practices for the two games with Whitman and the Bears. Considering the efforts still being advanced to bring team speed up to par and to correct some of the ball-handling miscues, Dobie was sending out strong signals of probable doom. This being not an atypical mind-set as game day approached, there wouldn't be too much cause for alarm, but his logic seemed to actually be more than just his usual pregame posturing. This time his analysis of the situation *was* downright believable. "I've had to use men who really have no business even turning out for football," he announced. He was explaining for everyone who would listen that today there was a newer, more open style of game, and that slower players of the past who were beefier and consequently slower than these modern players didn't have a chance. He made a lot of sense in pointing out that California had an advantage since it was coming off eight years of playing the open-style rugby game, with its dependence on speed. These rugby players now formed the core of the popular California Coach Jimmie Schaeffer's team. He won over Cal fans by beating Stanford the year before after several years of dominance by their rival.

Before the season began, Jimmie Schaeffer recognized that the game of football had changed dramatically since he had played the game as a freshman at Berkeley. He approached Gil Dobie unannounced and requested that he give him a total immersion lesson to bring him up to date on the vast changes in the game during California's sabbatical. Dobie spent three full days as his instructor, and who better to teach the intricacies of the game than the indisputable master of West Coast football?

Whitman was bringing an experienced team to Seattle, including McDonald of the year before, who had reeled off an 80-yard touchdown run against the Purple and Gold. Quarterback Emory Hoover, another veteran known for giving Dobie's teams fits, was able to gain yardage through the line with seeming ease. On the eve of the game, we have a Washington team not playing up to expectations and a Whitman team with experience that just might be able to do something no other team has accomplished for seven years, but the wild card, as usual, centers on what it is that Gil Dobie has up his sleeve. He sees opportunity for Whitman in his remarks to the press: "If Whitman ever had a chance to not only score on us, but actually beat us, they have it this coming Saturday."

In Dobie's player selection, careful observers might have gotten a hint that something was up. Dobie had listed Captain Mike Hunt as a starter, and it was just a couple of nights before that he was practicing with the third string. If this was done just to motivate, these scare tactics, as history demonstrates just about always worked for Dobie. He put his players out on the window ledge, and before they jumped he pulled them back in and they performed better than ever. Even with all the doubt swirling around the team, it seemed that the outcome would decidedly be in Washington's favor.

Once the game was under way, no one ventured that the Varsity would immediately put the game away, but in their command of every football basic they were expected to systematically dictate the tempo. Quick passes coupled with off-tackle line plunges were working to perfection. On defense the home team's line, while slow, successfully broke into Whitman's backfield as plays developed and halted progress dead in its tracks. In the second quarter, UW got on the scoreboard with three consecutive plunges by Bud Young, who had been either injured or not performing up to ability prior to this game. Hoover, as anticipated, turned in a superior job for Whitman as field general. Final score: Washington 27, Whitman 0. Even though Dobie had reason to doubt the game's outcome and wasn't shy about sharing his thoughts, the end result was the same as always.

Hap Miller was the all-around standout for Washington, with his smart play and consistent passes scoring two touchdowns. His attitude, however, promptly placed him in the doghouse, the coach singling him out for a bad case of swelled-headitis. Everyone west of the Rockies knew this was a show to teach an object lesson, but Dobie threatened to sit Miller down for the California game. Self-importance had its price.

## University of California, at Berkeley

Dobie did have valuable insights into the makeup of the California team and their coach's progress. His credibility couldn't really be called into question this time when he cried wolf. Or could it? There weren't many coaches who were as good as Dobie at judging athletic ability and at being able to assess the strengths and weaknesses of his players and then put a training regimen into place to capitalize. This was one of the key factors that set him above other coaches. He could take the players he was dealt—some average, some good, a couple superior—and meld this collection as one and turn out greatness.

The game of the year was just ahead. Dobie still complained nonstop as to his team's lead feet. The California game pitted speed against a team clearly unable to keep up with the Bay Area gazelles. He was asking for speed, but by all accounts the case was hopeless.

California got back into football in a big way after their long absence since opting for rugby back in 1906. Coach Jimmie Schaffer had played football, so he had experience with the game, and his tutorial session with Dobie served to bring him up to date on rules and modern strategy. Prior to the November 6 contest with Washington, California went 4-1 against club teams, had won against the Sherman Indian School, split 1-1 with St. Marys, and lost one game to USC. The hands-down answer to any "West Coach Championship" clearly ran through Seattle with Dobie's long reign of dominance. California sent out signals that they played well enough to beat USC, but coming out on the short end of a 28-10 score, this amounted to a whole lot of puffing. The Golden Bears took the position that a double win against Washington would be the deciding factor of who could claim the West Coach championship. The home-and-home schedule of games with Washington for the 1915 and 1916 seasons were the recognized "Big Game" for each season.

The start of the long-awaited West Coast Championship series was the most widely watched and highly promoted athletic event ever held on the West Coast. With as much as this game meant in expanding intercollegiate football beyond its home base of the Pacific Northwest, enthusiasm at both campuses was epidemic. At California, Graduate Manager John Stroud announced that one thousand reservations with deposits were made on the first day tickets were placed on sale. Seeing that the game would be a major event, Arthur Younger, as early as two months prior, chartered passage on the SS *Congress*, at a special round trip fare of $16.

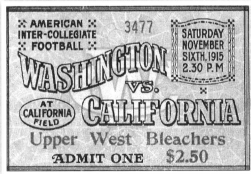

Puget Sound Maritime Historical Society                    SS Congress

Passenger steamer that transported Washington fans from Seattle to San Francisco for the historic game that led to the formation of the Pac-10 Conference. There were 326 fans plus 20 members of the marching band on board the giant 7980 ton liner.

University of Washington, Special Collections, Neg. No. UW 21828

25,000 fans at California Field witnessed the game that was responsible for elevating the quality of west coast college football up to the level played across the country.

Initially one hundred fans was the goal, but final turnout exceeded all expectations with over three hundred fans plus twenty band members making the trip. A "Send the Band" fundraiser met with great success in financing their travel from donations. As a historical note, it was one year later, in September 1916, that the 7,980-ton, 442-foot *Congress* caught on fire off the Oregon coast, with all passengers safely evacuated. The beautiful ocean liner was rebuilt, served for a time as the *Nanking* on a Hong Kong route, and then was recommissioned as the *Emma Alexander* in 1923 and returned to the Northwest, where it served for another twenty years, plying its main route between Portland and San Francisco.

That year's Varsity built its invincible reputation as a team more comfortable with strength up the middle than open-field play. Dobie, knowing that covering on defense took more out of a player than offense, used off-tackle line bucks to wear the opposition down in the early part of the game. His success came from the relentless efforts he made to button down every player's assignments to the most minute detail. The master was well aware that it was mentally debilitating to the defense to have the same play run at you for six or eight repeats, picking up 3 yards minimum every time. Varying this basic play only as to the right or left, with skilled athletes who execute to an exacting degree, Dobie knew he could always dominate the interior line. As the other team tired both physically and mentally, the game would then be opened up to passing and more sophisticated backfield maneuvers.

It was this aspect of Washington's greatest strength that most concerned Coach Schaffer. He expressed his doubts in a special to the *Daily*. "Since I began to study the game I have had a great number of plays shown me for offense, but not one man has come forward to show me any for defense. It is this handicap which California must face when she meets Washington." He wisely placed an emphasis on defense when he considered the experienced backfield he was facing of QB Bud Young, left half Hap Miller, right half Cy Noble and fullback Walt Shiel. It had long since become common knowledge that Dobie's training methods produced a backfield that was exceptional in every aspect of the game. The not-so-secret secret was solely one of near-perfect execution of the basics, strength up the middle, speed around end, a strong kicking game, precision passing, and relentless defense.

Because of the distance factor, Dobie wouldn't have been able to scout the Bears except for a fortuitous circumstance. Three weeks prior to game day, Dean Milnor Roberts, who also chaired the faculty Athletic Committee, was in San Francisco attending a professional gathering of engineers. The 302-foot campus landmark campanile was just beginning its initial runs to the viewing deck by elevator when the dean arrived. He was able to observe the full Bear's practices and gave a scouting report to Dobie when he returned home. As a Stanford graduate, Dean Roberts must have taken particular delight in being able to scout his cross-bay rival.

Anticipation for the upcoming contest was boiling hot in the Bay Area. "Washington Pilot is Pessimistic Despot," screamed a headline in the *Oakland Tribune*. Editors of the day were never shy in running such provocative headlines. Given the level of interest in this game, the more anti-Washington, the better. The writer, on balance, actually looked on Gil Dobie and the team very favorably despite his teaser headline designed to draw you in. "Dobie is undoubtedly the greatest coach in the west." "The academic standards of athletes at Washington are more stringent than here." Of course, no self-respecting reporter of the time can pass on calling up the mandatory claims that Dobie is near-maniacal in the treatment of his players. "He spends all of his time during the season of preparation in driving home to the players the fact that they are 'rotten' that they do not know the first principles of football and predicts that they will be disgracefully beaten in every contest." It should be noted that the author of these statements gave no sources showing that he fell into that all-too-common reporting school of recycling sensationalist copy over digging out the more-difficult-to-secure interviews and first-hand observations.

In never losing a game, the coach had a bull's-eye on his back. Dobie, as so often demonstrated, was not one to mince words when addressing his men with authority on the practice field. Being near-paranoid over the fear of his players getting too full of themselves, here, in his eighth year, he still wouldn't hesitate to verbally chop them down a notch or two. As to being "disgracefully beaten in every contest," he must not have checked out any of the numerous reports revealing, by this time, that Dobie had become increasingly contrarian in his predictions. The reservoir of Dobieisms was never short of juicy tidbits that the press could call up, place out of context, and feed to the locals, who never tired of reading about the Northwest tyrant hell-bent on performing human sacrifice at high noon on the 50-yard line.

Monday, November 1, two thousand rooters not making the trip gathered on Pier D and gave a rousing send off to the 326 fans (264 men and sixty-two women) plus twenty members of the marching band lucky enough to make the trip south on the SS *Congress*. The ship had five hundred passengers on board, so the Washington contingent clearly dominated shipboard activities. The *Daily* described the event as "perhaps the greatest spontaneous expression of enthusiasm that has ever been witnessed in the history of the university, as the big steamer, flying the university colors, swung out into the stream headed for San Francisco and the lair of the Golden Bear." The sight must have been spectacular, with the band performing for those on the crowded deck with the two thousand fans on the dock cheering the sendoff. Thousands of streamers were tied between the dock and ship, creating a colorful break between fans onboard and rooters ashore as the ship pulled out to sea. After the casting-off signal, the ship's cornettist played "Don't You Remember California In September?" The alma mater was almost continually sung by those on shipboard and dockside. With only 116 accommodations in steerage, over half the southbound fans happily discovered they were bumped up to salon class at no increase in price.

The team of twenty players plus staff traveled south, leaving the following morning at 9:30 on the Shasta Limited. President and Mrs. Suzzallo also were on the train. The team held the last scrimmage in preparation for the Big Game that afternoon in a moderate workout. The main objective was to get all twenty men familiar with the plays Dobie had worked out. As was his custom Dobie did not give out his starting lineup this far in advance. Even if he had announced a lineup, he would often change it just before game time. He never wanted the other team to try to see a pattern in his game prep.

Upon leaving, Dobie didn't have anything strong to say about the game considering its magnitude. He may have been keen to the fact that with so much national media attention focused on the contest, his words would carry extra weight in the press. This would especially be the concern with the press's penchant under normal circumstances for four-column banner headlines of his every utterance. He was quite tepid in outlook: "From what we hear California has a heavy team and is endowed with a world of speed. We look for a hard game and will be thankful to win by a small margin." Dobie, of course, covered all bases and was concerned with the alkali water and the "steamed brew" famous in San Francisco possibly making his players sick. He had enough hometown water, reported to be "bottled at the base of Mount Rainier," shipped on the train to last the team the entire trip.

The trip itself raised quite a stir as it progressed southward. John Markham, Cy Noble, and Bill Grimm were the latest of a long list of outstanding players that came out of Centralia. As the train passed through the small town, a large contingent of cheering rooters gathered on the platform at its brief stop. They also passed a train on a sidetrack in Oregon, with the entire Oregon team onboard on the way to their game with Southern California (won by Oregon, 34-0). This caused an outburst of mutual encouragement from both teams, with these two rivals shouting support to each other. Dobie kept the team busy en route with chalk talks and quizzes on football rules they needed to follow. A large delegation of California students, led by John Stroud, was on hand at the Oakland train station to greet the team for their 4:10 afternoon arrival on Thursday. The team was transported by car caravan to the Hotel Carlton in Berkeley. The attention paid to every last ceremonial detail was taking on state-visit proportions. That's how important this game was in the minds of both great universities.

Further adding to the air of celebration leading up to the Big Game, a World's Fair, the Panama-Pacific International Exposition, was under way. On board the SS *Congress*, the city skyline framed in the backdrop of San Francisco Bay and the fair pavilions built right on the shoreline were a magnificent site, made all the more enjoyable by the pleasant fall weather the evening of arrival. Fans crowded the deck along with the band, and under purple and gold streamers, suspended everywhere from the ship's rigging, held a boisterous rally right up to the dock. The *Congress*, nosing its way through the many ferry boats and other small craft, arrived at 7:45 on Thursday at Pier 18 as the band blared out their liveliest "Bow Down To Washington," with every fan crowded on the foredeck singing at the top of his or her lungs. The shipboard travelers didn't have much time to rest, as Friday was declared University of Washington Day at the fair. The fans were treated to a gala daylong reception, including dancing and entertainment, at the Washington State Pavilion. Dr. Suzzallo and his wife were on hand for the official proceedings, where he gave an address to the crowd and was presented with a bronze plaque to commemorate the event.

The afternoon of the game, bandleader Bruce McDougall led the band and a contingent of some three hundred fans on a march from the Carlton the short distance to the football stadium. The song of choice was again "Bow Down To Washington" as the marchers sang and serpentined their way through the huge crowds gathering for the game. A student guard was along protecting The Hook, raised above their heads to declare that Washington would indeed be hooking California today as it had every Pacific Northwest team for the past eight years. The protection of the hook was provided by chaining and padlocking it to a guard's body lest it be stolen as it was by Oregon a few years back.

"Vast Assemblage Sees Game," reported the *Oakland Tribune*. Vast it was, as a crowd of twenty-five thousand fans were on hand, including the presidents of both universities and a multitude of dignitaries. This was the place to be on that crisp Saturday afternoon, November 6, 1915. Conditions couldn't have been more perfect as game time drew near. Except for the first few minutes the game was played under overcast skies. The rest of the game was much like Puget Sound weather for this time of year. President Suzzallo, showing his team support, chose to seat his party of ten right behind the Washington Marching Band. A large group of Bay Area fans and nonstudents who travelled to the game also sat in the Purple and Gold rooters' section, creating a strong showing, but the crowd of twenty-five thousand was obviously heavily weighted to California.

It seems that the University of California of these times was no more progressive than Washington in the matter of women's attendance at games. It was reported in the *Daily*, "The Blue and Gold co-eds have a section reserved for them, following a vote this week that the co-eds should not attend the game in company with a man." Attitudes on the Berkeley campus indeed have changed since those days.

The *Oakland Tribune* reported that even though their numbers were much smaller, Washington made a good showing: "U.C. Licked In Bleachers As Well As On Grandstand." For its main rooters' attraction, Cal performed a very clever card stunt with a large Golden "C" on a background of shimmering blue that, on signal, turned into the Stars and Stripes as the band played the "Star-Spangled Banner." UW sent to the center of the field what was described as a "Washingtonian dressed in a large bear skin." Peck Davis, as the bear, danced for several minutes, and as suspense mounted an Indian impersonated by Frank Landsburg appeared and, surprise of surprises, a struggle ensued. It only took a short while for Washington to overcome the bear and bring him into camp. A large "W" with attached daylight fireworks was set off, creating quite a spectacular effect for the crowd as the furry battle trophy was marched across the field.

In 1922, in no less an authority than the *Tyee*, it was reported that the "Golden Bear, California's prized trophy," which was then on display at Washington, was "one of the prizes of intercollegiate trophy conquest." The bear in actuality was a Washington-supplied prop with a Washington-supplied student, inside so any trophy conquest was hardly such. Thus a storied legend was born many years after the fact, never mind that it had no basis in fact.

## THE LINEUPS

| No. | California | | Position | No. | Washington | |
|---|---|---|---|---|---|---|
| 8 | R. D. "Frick" Gibbs | wt. 165 | R.E.L. | 7 | Ernest "Tramp" Murphy | wt. 183 |
| 32 | W. L. "Chief" Bender | wt. 195 | R.T.L. | 2 | Elmer Leader | wt. 165 |
| 15 | Bill Russell | wt. 175 | R.G.L | 3 | Harry Wirt | wt. 186 |
| 17 | Jack Smith | wt. 175 | Center | 4 | David Logg | wt. 175 |
| 10 | Ward "Buck" Saunders | wt. 188 | L.G.R. | 5 | Louis Seagrave | wt. 184 |
| 18 | Lockhart | wt. 198 | L.T.R | 20 | John "Mark" Markham* | |
| 27 | Mat Hazeltine | wt. 154 | L.E.R. | 1 | Captain Ray "Mike" Hunt | wt. 181 |
| 7 | Roy "Bassett" Sharpe | wt. 147 | QB | 8 | Allan "Bud" Young | wt. 162 |
| 5 | Willis "Brud" Montgomery | wt. 166 | L.H.R | 9 | Cedric "Hap" Miller | wt. 174 |
| 3 | Fred "Fritz" Brooks | wt. 171 | FB | 10 | Walt Shiel | wt. 180 |
| 1 | Captain Cliff Canfield | wt. 156 | R.H.L | 27 | Elmer "Cy" Noble | wt. 177 |

Positions as listed in both the *Oakland Tribune* and *UW Daily*. *Vic Morrison listed in *Seattle Times*

Numbers had been used before by UW in the 1909 game with Oregon, but, as we have shown, Dobie felt this took away from teamwork and encouraged player showboating. An article in the *New York Times* quoted Dobie: "Over-confidence has lost more battles than superior opposition." Hap Miller was still on the outs because of being puffed up about himself in the outstanding game against Whitman. It looked to all the world that Dobie would follow through with his threat to sit his star down for the California game. Leading into the Big Game, as was custom, the lineup had not been released. Miller was liberated from purgatory just before game time, which must not have come as a great surprise to those who now were learning the coach's tactics. He made his point and, as would be seen by his performance that day, Miller learned his lesson.

The California fans, the coaching staff, Bay Area newspapers, and assorted dopesters prior to the game did not see a win for California. The *Oakland Tribune*, writing in a pregame account, concluded, "The 'dope' on tomorrow's game points to an overwhelming victory for the northerners." The Bay Area overall was delighted to be playing football again, and they were especially glad to have this game on their home field with the undisputed champion of West Coast football. Because of concerns that the outcome heavily favored Washington, there was practically no betting on the game. The Blue and Gold faithful were only willing to bet that the visitors would not end the game scoring over twenty points. The most widely advanced sentiment was hope the game wouldn't become a runaway. California's many years of playing rugby, with the style of play favoring leaner-bodied runners, was accurately observed as being to the Bears' detriment. Seven of the eleven Washington starters outweighed their opponents, and as soon as the players took the field for warm-ups, this was quickly spotted.

There were some feeble attempts to play down Washington's prospects coming out of Seattle, and no one had his heart into making chest-thumping predictions. Coach Dobie himself was characteristically muted in his comments. The lack of even a passing prediction of doom may have been the best indicator regarding his feelings. Looking, back it should have been obvious to those following pregame events that the enigmatic coach knew that something was up. As was the case here when others are predicting loss, Dobie would either clam up or go neutral. In this bigger-than-life contest, everyone else was doing the heavy lifting of predicting a California loss. With this, the contrarian could lay low.

A final score of 72-0 doesn't require much analysis. As headlines north and south shouted out, "Total Domination," "Golden Bear Crushed," "Grind of Washington Machine Goalwards Shock to California," "Varsity Crushes California," and "California Is Asking For An Explanation." The obvious conclusion was self-evident. This was complete and total defeat. Washington showed superiority in every aspect of the game. It also showed just how unfounded the widespread belief of the southerners was that they had a shot at keeping the margin of victory under control. It proved to be too much to expect of a team to transition from rugby to football in just one year and play at the highest level. There were many obvious challenges facing the Bears' coaching staff in doing this. Even the least knowledgeable spectator in the stands that afternoon could see that California had considerable work to do in every basic of the game. It's readily apparent that losing by 72 points requires a top-to-bottom review. In the end it was conceded that despite the glorious buildup and grand gestures from both sides for this historic game, enthusiasm faded even for Washington due to "the general gloom that surrounded the overwhelming defeat of their rivals."

Here is how the eleven touchdowns were made:

First Quarter
1. On the kickoff UW marched 70 yards on nine plays. Hap Miller scored a TD up the middle and kicked the extra point. Score after three and one-half minutes: 7-0.
2. Bud Young on a run around end for 15 yards for the touchdown. Miller missed the extra point. Score: 13-0.
3. Walter Shiel scored on a line play for 2 yards as the quarter ended. Miller again missed on the point after. Score: 19-0.

Second Quarter
4. With Washington following a fundamental line play strategy of picking up just about 10 yards per carry, the drive ending with Cy Noble scoring. The extra point try by Miller was blocked by California. Score: 25-0.
5. Bud Young intercepted a California pass deep in Washington terrltory, setting up Washington's long march downfield with Young capping off the drive. Miller kicked the extra point. Score: 32-0.

Third Quarter
6. On the first possession, Washington continued its conventional football game plan. Noble scored his second touchdown on a line play. Miller again kicked the extra point. Score: 39-0.
7. With Washington on the Bears' 40-yard line Miller connected on a pass to Ernest Murphy at the 5-yard line. Noble scored on a line buck with Miller kicking the point after. Score: 46-0.
8. On its own 35-yard line, Washington began another long drive, mostly advanced with classic Dobie off-tackle slants. The score was made on a quarterback sneak by Young from the 1. Extra point was again scored on a kick by Miller. Score: 53-0.
9. As the quarter was ending that California would just as soon forget, Washington moved the ball downfield on pass plays this time. The score was made on a pass from Miller to Captain Mike Hunt. Miller kicked the extra point. Score: 60-0.

Fourth Quarter

10. The opening minutes of the quarter saw numerous substitutes coming in from both sides. The next touchdown was scored by halfback Ray Gardner (#14) and the extra point was missed as the kick hit the crossbars. Score: 66-0.

11. Late in the quarter play was stopped for a substitute on an injury to California's fullback, Fritz Brooks. When play resumed, Washington's substitutes, showing impressive speed, scored the last touchdown in the final minute on a play by halfback Ross MacKechnie (#11). No extra point was tried. Score: 72-0.

In assessing what had just happened and what California should get out of the experience, Captain Cliff Canfield best summed it up: "Today's game was not just a defeat; it was a lesson, and one by which California will profit." An obvious California weakness was in the passing game. Washington passed the ball low and quick and did not try to get it past the secondary defenders. California's passes were high, slow, and long, allowing the Varsity ample time to break up the play. They were successful in defending on all but one of the Golden Bears' passes.

University of Washington Libraries, Special Collections, Neg. No. UW 29126

Elmer "Cy" Noble scoring one of his two touchdowns, against California in game at California Field, Nov. 6, 1915. UW Players with faces showing, left to right: Allan Young (standing), Ernest Murphy (on ground), Walt Shiel (standing), David Logg (standing).

Washington also seemed to be able to run the ball through the middle of the line with ease. Among other more obvious criteria the game exemplified was Dobie's long-standing emphasis on physical conditioning—the northerners, with all their running, also won in this department. Not being familiar with Dobie's fixated nature, Bay Area reporters misread the postgame laps required of the victors. Judging this to be motivated by some darker motive rather than his perpetual quest to keep his players focused on conditioning, the brief workout was viewed as odd punishment. Close followers of Dobie knew this to be business as usual. This game was in the books, and regardless of the outcome it was time to signal to the players that preparation for next week had begun.

The following day the *Oakland Tribune* led with a headlined article, "California Is Asking For an Explanation," with the subhead, "Followers of the Bear Express Dissatisfaction With Showing of Coach." This is a coach who was greatly respected over the years that he coached rugby. In severe and accusatory language, the author placed the blame squarely on Coach Jimmie Schaffer's shoulders for lack of knowledge of the American game. These direct questions were asked in print: "Why did our team not have the interference that the Washington backs used? Why all those shift formations that utilized only one or two of the backfield in the plays? How was it that on every play our line fell back a couple of yards on the charge, for the California line was as heavy as the Washington one?" California did have athletes capable of a better game; that is for certain. With so many breakdowns as illustrated by these pointed questions, the only reasonable conclusion was that most of the fault did lie with the coaching staff.

Contrary to the criticism of Schaffer, Dobie was being lauded for his work. The *New York Times*, in a November 6, 1915, release, headlined an article, "Gilmour Dobie Is a Remarkable Coach." It went on in gushing praise, "Turn the spotlight this way please, so it may shine upon the most remarkable football coach in the history of the college game—upon Gilmour Dobie, the unassuming pilot of the football destiny of the University of Washington in Seattle." The *Cleveland Leader* delved into comparison scores, starting with Oregon, whom Dobie's teams dominated and who had soundly beaten a strong Michigan team at Michigan, 20-0. The writer went on tracing comparative scores up the ladder to the number-one-rated school in the east, Cornell. With his suggestion, "Just dope it out fans," his conclusion is that Washington should beat Cornell in head-to-head competition. This was a victory that would reverberate for years and would have far-reaching consequences for big-time football out west.

The steamship SS *Governor* transported the Washington rooters back from the Bay Area, but it was delayed with stormy weather that blew in on its first day at sea. They arrived back home on Tuesday, November 9, at 6:30 a.m., too late for the rousing reception given for the victorious Washington team who could lay claim to the greatest win in the history of West Coast football. The Varsity rooters had received almost as much attention as the football team in their southern sojourn. Their names, faces, and movements were published in the Bay Area press. The *Seattle Times* reported, "Two fair Washington coeds also got theirs in the paper too. The *Chronicle* 'mugged' Miss Edith Brawley and Miss Helen Bolster. The girls, of course, didn't pose for the cameraman, but they did happen to have a Washington pennant stretched out between them, daintily held with their fingertips."

Since the band on the ship was held up at sea, a group made up of spirited members who had been left behind jumped in to fill the breach. Fifteen hundred students greeted the team at the train station with a raucous welcome in keeping with the magnitude of the victory. The biggest roar was reserved for Coach Dobie as he entered the station near the end of the line. Not known for off-the-cuff speaking, the master rose to the occasion and, as the *Daily* termed it, gave "a reply from the old slave driver's heart to the enthusiasm of the crowd. It was so unexpected that it will never be forgotten by the students who heard it." Never one to hype accomplishment, he didn't disappoint. "I expected a much closer score but it was not to be expected that the Californians could master the game in three months that they had not tried in ten years." In looking towards the next week's game, he did his best to lower expectations. "That game will not be as one-sided and we will have trouble making one score where we made three." Dobie turned out to be quite a prophet in his wrap-up: "Next year or the year after that I expect to see California turn the tables and sweep the coast." He was not far off; in 1917 California would blank Washington, 27-0, ending their sixty-four-game unbeaten streak. In 1921 the Bears mopped up against Washington, 72-3. The students didn't want the night to end any time soon and formed a three-block-long serpentine to the downtown Alhambra Theater. Women still were not able to actively participate, but a two-hundred-strong female gathering did serve as spectators from the sidelines for the celebratory marching, cheering, singing male students.

# CHAPTER TEN

## *His Lasting Legacy—1915*

"The ideal that Dobie has pointed out to his charges has been for them to play under the conditions laid down. He has demanded that the players keep up their work in the classroom as an ideal of loyalty, not only to the university, but to the team as well. It may be said of Coach Dobie that he never went before a faculty committee whining and whimpering to have a man below the scholastic requirements made eligible for a game…We should appreciate not merely the victory of the elevens coached by Dobie, but the psychology and strategy behind the victory."

*President Henry Suzzallo, 1915*

Sensing the historic significance of the two 1915 games between Washington and California, both student bodies and tens of thousands of fans were revved up like never before. There being no shortage of pregame hype, West Coast sportswriters competed to see how many ways they could invent to microanalyze the contest. The newly minted fight songs directed at the opposing teams have endured over the decades to underscore the significance of the matchups. Two stanzas from "Bow Down to Washington" clearly evidence the rivalry: "Bring the Golden Bear from his mighty lair, For we're going to hang his carcass in the northland," and "See the Golden Bear, with the glassy stare, Well he'll be a dead one in the morning." California was not quite so graphic in "Fight 'Em," but nevertheless directed its animus right back at the invading northerners. "Down from the North comes the Purple and Gold, to skin our Golden Bear; Washington's 'leven can never hold, The charge of our Golden Bear. Our team on the field is a line of steel, and every man is game; When the strength of the Blue and Gold they feel, Those Northmen will be tame."

### University of California

Just two days before the rematch, embattled Coach Schaeffer resigned his position as head coach of the Golden Bears. He had coached both football and baseball for seven years. He also played on the California team himself while a student. Since he had coached rugby for six years and this was his first year of coaching American Rules Football, it was asking a lot of him to be able to immediately turn his former rugby players into highly competitive football players. The final straw for California fans was the tremendous whipping that they suffered at the hands of Washington. Schaeffer still had two years to run on his contract but announced that his resignation was effective immediately after the upcoming November 13 game. He had always been a popular figure at Berkeley, and he took the high road in his official statement upon quitting: "It may be that now someone else is better qualified to teach the American game. I want the executive committee to be free to choose whomever it wishes to carry out this work." After the season ended, a former football standout, Andy Smith, from the University of Pennsylvania, was hired. He had strong coaching experience as head coach at Pennsylvania for four years from 1909 to 1912 and three years at Purdue. His first year record at California was 6-4-1. He went on to great fame at California coaching the "Wonder Teams" of the 1920s. Unfortunately his life and coaching career were cut tragically short with his death due to pneumonia shortly after the end of the 1925 season.

Football program cover, Washington vs. California, played at University Field, Nov. 13, 1915.

University of Washington Libraries, Special Collections, Neg. No. 29127

University of Washington Libraries, Special Collections, Neg. No. UW 29084

Cy Noble breaking away from California. Other UW players, left to right: Allan Young (blocking defender), Raymond Hunt (no helmet on ground behind Noble), Ed Leader (with helmet behind Hunt), Louis Seagrave (on knee, to right, blocking defender).

Prior to the game, the athletic department came out with a photo spread of the players' numbers of both teams for the rematch. In that day prior to public address announcements and ninety years before gigantic replay monitors fans were very much in favor of this minor enhancement. It wasn't that Dobie didn't appreciate his fans, but again, his fear of ego-centered players' showboating trumped every other consideration. Numbers had gone over very well just five days earlier in Berkeley, but this cut no ice with Dobie. The idea was scrapped at his insistence.

That week, coming off a 72-0 win, it was nigh on impossible for Dobie to paint his team as the underdog. The *Seattle Times* reported: "Coach Dobie remained optimistic over the outcome." He announced that because the Bears showed great speed the week before but were unable to pierce Washington's stronger line, he expected an aerial assault. In the *Daily* he stated, "now that they have played us once we can look for a much closer game tomorrow. Washington should win, but not by a score as large as last week." In practice Dobie's response to Cal was a game plan also built around a passing attack. His theory was that with their lack of experience, it would be easier to pull off his time-tested ritual of hitting the opposition with a dose of their own medicine. When scouting reports exposed details of favorite plays, he many times would drill the Varsity on the exact same formations. In doing the other team one better, he would teach how to execute the plays from both sides of the ball. With his meticulous game preparation, the Varsity, in running the identical plays, could break the opposition's spirit when they found themselves being beaten at their own game—another psychological ploy only made possible with his demanding practice regimen. Matters were made only more difficult for Andy Smith as the *Post-Intelligencer* was reporting that a ground game could be expected from Washington.

"Southerners Swamped One Week Ago, Hold Washington Eleven to Score of 13 to 7" read the stunning postgame headline in the *Seattle Times*. To say that Washington fans were in a state of shock is an understatement. No one expected the quality of play brought forth by the Blue and Gold, who had been so completely annihilated just seven days before. The *Daily* stated, "Never before in the history of football in the Northwest has such an interesting game of football been seen." Similar reactions were expressed in many other reports of the game. However, the amazing turn of events did raise a few eyebrows, with the *Oakland Tribune* reporting that some Berkeley fans were suspicious that Dobie's game was a "good piece of stage work." They were leery that another devastating blow inflicted on the Bears would force them back to playing rugby. The paper reported that sportswriters from the Northwest conceded that this was a straight game, however, and California really did improve that much in just a week. It certainly seemed that the Berkeley team learned a lot since suffering on the short end of a 72-zip score. Coach Schaeffer had gone from goat to hero virtually overnight. The team came out in unanimous praise of the coach and declared that the turnaround was due to his coaching skills, and several players called for him to be reinstated.

Captain Cliff Canfield's postgame quote just after the beating his team took at the hands of Washington would serve them well as a lesson for the future. Little did he know that his opinion would prove out in such short order. While no one would dare publicly venture the suggestion that California would turn things around so quickly, there were many who shared in the belief that the November 6 game was essentially a real-time tutorial served up for the Bears' benefit. R. L. Peck, president of the California Alumni Association, went so far as to say that it was thanks to the "object lesson" provided by Coach Dobie in handing the defeat to Cal as he did that Cal was able to rebound so quickly. And while it's embarrassing to be victimized by an eleven-touchdown onslaught, Washington's clear advantage of never having taken up rugby and the seven consecutive championships helped to assuage bruised egos. Peck, in the *Seattle Times*, went on to conclude, "Before that game Schaeffer could only tell his men what to expect. Afterwards with the stinging defeat fresh in their minds and the power of the Dobie eleven to ponder, it was comparatively easy for Schaeffer to make a football team of his men."

Considering the prior week's lopsided score, one would think that both coaches would make changes in their lineups. This was not the case. It would seem a perfect opportunity for Dobie to put in replacement players he was trying to develop, but this was not to be. He started with exactly the same lineup from the Berkeley game. Jimmie Schaeffer made only minor personnel changes, shifting Bill Russell from his position of right guard to center and taking out of the game Jack Smith, who had been the starting center at Berkeley. He gave H. K. "Doc" White the starting assignment at right guard. Both men were sophomores, and the switch may have been done to place a larger man on the line. The game program lists Smith at 175 pounds and 5 feet 11 inches, with White at 178 pounds and 6 feet 3 inches. Washington was a heavier team, which goes a long way in explaining why they were so successful in blocking off the line the prior week.

Referee George Varnell, who officiated both games, attributed the Bears' turnaround to defense. "That Washington didn't score more than they did was not due to listless playing because they played valiantly but in the superior brand of defense put up by California." Coach Dobie didn't limit his praise to defense. "California clearly outclassed Washington. Her playing was better all around and it was chance more than anything else that gave us the victory." *The Tyee* weighed in with praise for California. "The fighting Californians put up a defense many times stronger than in their first game, so strong, in fact, that Washington made yardage only eight times during the entire game." Both coaches are to be congratulated for remarkable performances when taking both games into consideration. Coach Schaeffer had a mountain to climb in getting his men up for another game with the team that had just annihilated their ranks, and Coach Dobie had the equally tough assignment of bringing his players down to earth when they must have thought they were invincible. That they both succeeded is quite evident.

The first three quarters of the game were a defensive struggle for both teams, with neither being able to put up a score. The game itself was not spectacular in its fan appeal. Game stats bear this out. In forward passes, Washington completed only 2 out of 10 and California went 2 for 9. The game featured a large number of punts, with Washington's Bud Young completing 8 for 293 yards, averaging 36 yards, and California's Fritz Brooks kicking 13 for 423 yards to average 32 yards. Only Washington crossed the goal line in the first three quarters, with Hap Miller gaining 30 yards around right end only to have the score nullified by a 15-yard penalty for holding.

Looking up in the stands, there were a lot of empty seats as a testament to the fact that Washington fans thought this would be a cakewalk. With the large number that traveled to Berkeley and witnessed the rout on November 6, there was every expectation that another track meet was in store. But this is football, a game played by young men who are subject to the quirks of human nature. It was human nature for California to want revenge after their humiliating defeat, and it was perfectly understandable that Washington would feel they only needed to show up and go through the motions. Lackluster attendance on Washington's part showed local fans were of the same conviction. The outcome of the game being what it was, sportswriters reported that low fan turnout proved to be a grave mistake. The home team desperately needed that intangible advantage instilled in the players' minds when they see the stands packed with supportive fans.

The first three quarters only being a scoreless prelude to all the action of the last period, here is a play-by-play of the fourth quarter as reported in the *Seattle Sunday Times* of November 14, 1915.

"The third quarter ended with the ball on California's 49-yard line. End of third quarter score: Washington 0; California 0.

Two forward passes were attempted by California at the beginning of the fourth quarter, Sharp to Brooks which failed and another by Sharp which grounded. Brooks punted 30 yards to Young, who was downed in his tracks. On a line buck Noble made some yardage, but two successive attempts brought Washington nothing and a forward pass by Young was intercepted by Sharp.

When California regained the ball Sharp assayed a forward pass which was intercepted by Noble who made 15 yards before he was downed. Miller, Noble and Shiel advanced the ball making downs and a forward pass by Young was blocked by Lockhart.

### Drop Kick Tried

Young again tried a drop kick from the 30-yard line, the ball sailing under the bar. California on taking the ball was penalized five yards for offside play, and after Washington had held Brooks punted 36 yards. Miller gained through right tackle and Noble added more yardage. A forward pass was attempted by Miller, but there was no one to receive the ball and when the pass was tried again, Miller to Smith, it succeeded, Smith gaining 15 yards.

With the ball on California's 5-yard line, the Washington men gathered themselves for a mighty effort and Shiel went over for the first touchdown. Miller kicked goal.

Score, Washington 7; California 0.

Miller caught the ball on the kickoff and advanced it before he was downed and Washington by successive line bucks made steady gains until halted when Young punted to Sharp for thirty-seven yards. A rugby pass, Sharp to Canfield, brought a slight gain and on a forward pass, Sharp to Giancelli, the California man got away and ran thirty-five yards for a touchdown. Brooks kicked an easy goal.

Score, Washington 7; California 7.

On the kickoff Shiel caught the ball and brought it back twenty yards before he was downed. A forward pass from Young to Miller failed, Miller dropping the ball. Young punted thirty-five yards to

Sharp who was downed by Hunt as he grabbed the ball. California was unable to gain and Brooks punted for forty-five yards giving the ball to Washington.

Miller brought the crowd to its feet with a spectacular dash for fifty yards down the field and was overtaken by Sharp on California's five-yard line. Noble went over for Washington's second touchdown. Miller missed goal.

Score, Washington 13; California 7.

With but forty-five seconds left to play, the ball was again brought back to the center of the field but neither side was able to gain before time was called.

Final score, Washington 13; California 7."

Rebounding as they did from their low station of the week prior, California could claim the victory, all accounts of the game declared. They didn't win on the scoreboard, but considering they were supposed to suffer another thrashing, the Bears were happy to survive with a moral victory. The *Daily* headlined, "California All But Licks Unbeaten Dobie Eleven." It was certainly accurate to describe the game as a phenomenal comeback, and it didn't matter if your heart was with Washington or California, the greatest acclaim was showered on the achievement by the southerners. Roy Sharp, the 147-pound California quarterback, was the standout on both offense and defense. In praising him, an uncommon venue for such acclaim, the *Tyee*, stated, "Sharp was the whole California offense." To demonstrate their respect for the brilliant job that he did, Washington rooters carried him off the field on their shoulders. The *Post-Intelligencer*, recognizing the historical significance of the contest, best summed it up: "Captain Canfield and his plucky, heady fighters made a place for themselves in Pacific Coast football history that will live as long as the grand old game is played." President Henry Suzzallo addressed the California team in their locker room, praising both sides for exhibiting clean play and great sportsmanship. He called this "from every angle one of the best contests that I have ever witnessed." What a scene it must have been. Coach Jimmie Schaeffer made it a point to shake the hand of every member of the team and was reported to be visibly affected. In losing in such magnificent fashion, he was now vindicated.

On this same Saturday afternoon, Los Angeles High School was playing the Bears' freshman squad at Berkeley. Progress of the Big Game up north was updated on the scoreboard as results were fed through by telegraph from Seattle. The California fans, hoping against hope that a repeat of the prior week wouldn't transpire, were ecstatic with the reports that their boys were holding their own. Even though the Bears never posted a score until only three minutes were left in the game, this meant nothing to the California rooters. Coming as they were from the pit of doom on this very field last week, they also judged this as a win for their team. The crowd went wild as tracking reports showed

California had a chance to win. The news that Washington pulled the game out in the last forty seconds meant nothing as the fans broke from the stands and performed a serpentine around the field to celebrate this valiant effort. This was the first time in four years that a serpentine had been conducted, no matter that the scoreboard showed their team had lost. The enthusiasm wasn't to die here. When the team returned to Berkeley, a jubilant crowd of three thousand fans greeted them at the train station. The street and train platforms were packed with bodies, with some daredevils climbing to the roof of the station for a better view. The crowd hoisted players onto a baggage truck so all could see them and, with their serpentine skills newly rekindled, formed a huge line carrying the players bodily to the campus.

In the two games, Washington came out on top 86 to 7 and 13 touchdowns to 1. This by any measure reads total domination. However, California's comeback that day in playing such a competitive game would have profound consequences for the future of West Coast football. The center of strength still resided in the Northwest, but the game illustrated that California was on the ascendancy, and we now can see that the battle on Denny Field on that fateful afternoon in 1915 did have far-reaching significance. From that game we saw a great West Coast rivalry develop, and the American game of football had arrived in grand fashion. The *Seattle Times* reported that "a new game of football has been introduced to the West Coast." Coach Dobie's role in this process cannot be diminished. He established a standard of excellence that served as a challenge for his peers to emulate. His pursuit of perfection accelerated the process. This is his lasting legacy.

## University of Colorado

The Colorado contest was selected as the season's homecoming game. Complacency had set in with both fans and the team from the Berkeley blowout, as recent events had shown. So far that year the Varsity had dominated their opponents by a total score of 228 to 14, so it's understandable that fans' interest would begin to wane. However, yell king Jimmie Eagleson had a much easier time stirring up excitement for this game now that it looked like Washington wasn't invincible after all. Maybe the guys on the field did need some support from the stands. The pregame parade and pep rally was ramped up to include new stunts, a men's nightshirt parade, speeches from alums, speeches by both coaches, speeches by both captains, a speech by President Suzzallo, music from the cadet band, prizes for the best floats, attendance by the Colorado team, and a dance at the Downtown Hippodrome. In a move that young women then and now for different reasons would find hard to believe, the *Daily* reported that Dean of Women Coldwell had "given permission to the co-eds to make the trip downtown and they will view the parade from the sidewalks fortified with a wealth of pennants and banners." Naturally, transportation to the event was arranged so that co-eds would be traveling in separate cars from the men. Both state governors, Ernest Lister of Washington and his Colorado counterpart, George A. Carlson attended the game.

The surprising outcome of the California game played right into Dobie's hands to get his men refocused on executing the kind of game he knew was essential for winning. He was first a disciplinarian when it came to methodology, and the sole reason for his seemingly harsh training techniques allowed him to drill into his young men's heads the importance of teamwork—the central tenet of his philosophy of coaching. The tight game with the Golden Bears left the door wide open for Dobie to disparage those men he felt had fallen victim to believing their own press clippings. In his first Colorado chalk talk, he announced that some promising freshmen were going to get playing time. California had a rule against playing freshmen, so they hadn't seen action for the last two games. The threat of losing their starting positions was made abundantly clear to those singled out for poor play.

Washington's fortunes were further dealt a blow due to a season-ending knee injury to the league's best passer in halfback Hap Miller. Ross MacKechnie, who of late was showing improvement in his play, was tapped to replace him. But Miller being far and away the best passer on the West Coast, his were big shoes to fill. Colorado, known as a team that had an immovable interior line and a very strong pass defense was bad news for Washington. The Varsity's strength was to alternate the running and passing game to confuse opposing defenses. Roscoe Healey, Colorado's fast left tackle, at 207 pounds was the anchor of the line and had built up quite an intimidating reputation. He signaled the crowd that he was now "fighting mad" when he would ceremoniously tear off his helmet in the middle of the action and throw it to the sidelines. With all the press reports of Colorado's strengths, Dobie would have been expected to back off since everyone else was going negative. As history reflects, doubting his chances would not be surprising. But the crafty master may have just been onto something when considering last week's game, Miller's injury, and Colorado's reputation for shutting down the very offensive system used by Washington. In any event, it gave Dobie an open door to once again set up his oft-repeated gloomy calculation and actually get some traction with it this time.

The week of the game there was shocking news breaking that Coach Dobie was going to resign after this game. Whether this was just rumor or based in fact wasn't clear. It did add another element of drama to a week not short on excitement. What with the California roller coaster and great interleague competition just ahead, the players were on tension overload. Both the *Post-Intelligencer* and the *Seattle Times* broke the story. The University of Wisconsin was expressing strong interest in hiring Dobie, which offered a ring of legitimacy to the story. It was known that for some time Wisconsin alumni living in Seattle were actively lobbying for him. The great Pat O'Dea, a living football legend from Wisconsin who lived in Seattle and a friend of Dobie's, was at the forefront of the movement. Dobie didn't deny the possibility. His statement: "There is nothing more to say at present. The main thing now is the game tomorrow; we're liable to get beaten with matters as they stand. After the game I will be in a position to discuss these matters more fully." Yes, an announcement, but this wishy-washy stance only served to heighten overwrought fans' anxiety.

" 'I can't understand it,' said a Colorado man. 'We knew that Dobie's favorite play is a smash off tackle and our men were coached for it. In Healy and Spring we think we have two of the finest tackles in the country, yet the Washington backs ploughed right through and over them in a most disheartening manner,' " was the mournful plea of a Colorado supporter reported in the *Times*'s postgame wrap-up. Colorado Coach Fred Folsom (namesake of Colorado's football field) had a national reputation as a great player hailing from Dartmouth, and his coaching career was equally well regarded. The sentiment on the Boulder side held that Colorado had a strong team, a great coach, and definitely could put up a competitive game against Washington. Circumstances proved this to be wishful thinking. In past years Folsom's teams were brilliant but, despite their ambitions, had fallen on hard times this year.

The game began with Washington showing its powerful presence in all aspects of play. In just the first four minutes and thirty seconds with thirteen rushing plays, the Purple and Gold scored their first touchdown, followed with the successful point-after kick by Walt Shiel. The outcome looked certain in the earliest moments that UW had shaken off the disappointment of last week and were now back in championship form. This was another game of domination and precision football on offense, defense, and special teams by Washington.

With the ground game working at near perfection, Dobie saw no need for passing and spread the running game almost equally among his backs. Heavy rain earlier in the day thoroughly soaked the field, which also altered Coach Dobie's game plan, removing any thoughts of adding an aerial attack. Right halfback Cy Noble accounted for two of the seven touchdowns, left halfback Ross MacKechnie made two, fullback Walt Shiel added two, and quarterback Bud Young scored one. Shiel attempted all seven of the kicks for the point after and was successful on four. As announced, Hap Miller, the strongest runner and best passer on the team, was not able to play. Shiel easily made up for the missing star, turning in by far the best performance for either team on offense and defense. Accounts of the game were unanimous in praising his strong running right up the middle.

Colorado, while coming into Seattle with expectations of a closer game and even having distant thoughts of a win, had these hopes quickly dashed. At no time could Colorado mount a long drive on any possession and never posed a threat to score. They were equally frustrated on defense and were unable to find an answer to Washington's multiple-back offense. Washington thoroughly disproved the widespread dope that no team could run up the middle on Colorado. The *Times* summed up the afternoon: "There were no thrills in the game and the sight of the Washington machine grinding its way to score after score got rather monotonous." The final score showed Washington on top, 46-0.

UW placed three players—Louis Seagrave, Ray Hunt, and Hap Miller—on the All-Northwest first team for 1915, selected by George Varnell, sports editor of the *Spokane Chronicle* and league game official. Elmer Leader, Bud Young, and Walt Shiel were selected on the second team.

Dobie selected his all-time top two Washington teams at the end of this year:

| First Team | Position | Second Team |
|---|---|---|
| Raymond (Mike) Hunt | End | William (Bill) Mattson |
| Warren Grimm, Wayne (Pete) Sutton | End | Anthony (Tony) Savage |
| Max Eakins, Huber (Polly) Grimm | Tackle | Herman Anderson |
| Elmer Leader | Tackle | Bernard (Jack) Bliss, John (Jack) Patten |
| Tom Griffiths | Guard | Louis Seagrave |
| Charles May | Guard | Andrew (Andy) McPherson |
| BeVan Presley | Center | Fred (Pete)Tegtmeier |
| William (Wee) Coyle | Quarterback | Allan (Bud) Young, Charles Smith |
| Melville Mucklestone | Halfback | Cedric (Hap) Miller, Leonard Taylor |
| Myers (Mike) Chapman | Halfback | Elmer (Cy) Noble |
| Walt Shiel | Fullback | Ralph (Penny) Westover |

### Formation of the Pacific Coast Intercollegiate Athletic Conference

Since Victor Zednick, former graduate manager for Washington and currently the president of the Northwest Conference had previously advocated that the conference include Stanford and California into a new league, it was now time to act on the matter. Washington had met both schools in crew and track, and he felt that such a union would elevate football on the West Coast to greater national prominence.

Members of the Pacific Northwest Conference gathered for their annual meeting at the Oregon Hotel in Portland on December 2, 1915. Gil Dobie had come to the decision that it would be best for the game if freshmen were not eligible for varsity competition. It was through his urging that the Board of Control issued its ruling that Washington would only compete in athletic contests with schools that would eliminate freshmen in games against UW. The concept was controversial at the time and was one of the lynchpins causing the breakup of the PNC and creation of the new Pacific Coast Conference. Technically the new conference came into being on December 3, as it wasn't until 1:30 a.m. that night, after long hours of negotiations that the final agreement was hammered out. This act launched the league that is today the Pac-10 Conference. The PNC had been so seriously wounded with the previous year's coaching plot to undercut Dobie's dominance that a major shake-up was inevitable. As events unfolded with Washington proceeding to again go undefeated in 1915 in such spectacular fashion, change came more swiftly than anyone could have predicted. Washington State, Idaho, and Whitman, fearing that this would put them at a competitive disadvantage, would not accept the new eligibility rule. Delegates from Stanford and California were in attendance, with Stanford stubbornly holding out against playing American Rules Football. Being unwilling to adopt the freshman rule, they were not eligible to join the league in any event. California joined Washington, Oregon, and Oregon Agricultural College (Oregon State) as charter members of the new league. Stanford can be seen to be the big loser, as it lost Washington as an athletic rival with competition in track, baseball, basketball, and crew. Washington and California are the only two universities that hold uninterrupted Pac-10 membership over the conference's entire history.

In the annual conference meeting held in Seattle on December 12, 1916, Washington State was admitted as a member competing in all sports, and Stanford in all sports except football. Because of transitioning from rugby and with the interruption of World War I, Stanford didn't take up football within the PCC until 1919. USC and Idaho were admitted in 1922, Montana joined in 1924, and UCLA in 1928. A clear chain of events can be traced back to the coaches of the old PNC in their attempt to unseat Gil Dobie that lead to formation of the Pacific Coast Conference, which became the Pac-10. One man, Gilmour Dobie, more than any other individual is responsible for the structure of league play in West Coast football as it exists today.

For all his success in football, it's a good question as to just why a Dobie-led team never played in the Rose Bowl (the game would come to be called that in 1923.) In a meeting of the UW Board of Control held on November 15, 1915, the board voted that it was not in favor of postseason play, which ruled them out of the Pasadena game that year, opening the door for Washington State. William "Lone Star" Dietz, in his first year at WSU, coached them to an unbeaten season, making them the logical second-choice pick since UW pulled out of the running. This was even though Washington State was not a member of the newly founded PCC. Unfortunately, with the rebellion of 1914, the freshman rule, and the creation of the new league in 1915, these two great teams never met in head-to-head competition in 1915 and 1916 to resolve just who was superior. As would be expected, the issue has been settled to the satisfaction of fans in Seattle and Pullman, but nowhere else on the planet.

But back to Dobie's never having played in the Rose Bowl; he didn't have an opportunity! The first forerunner to what would become the Rose Bowl game was played in 1902 and was won by Michigan over Stanford, 49-0. Stanford was actually the second choice of the selection committee when 9-0-1 California, strongest team in the west, inexplicably chose not to play. This was the last of such games in Pasadena for the next fourteen years, as the city fathers decided to wage chariot races after that inaugural game. Football never returned until New Year's Day 1916, with Washington State defeating Brown 14-0. The deciding factor that turned the tide against Washington for the 1917 game was geography. The Tournament of Roses Committee picked Oregon based on the fact that train fare was less from Portland than from Seattle. In any event, had the committee made the obvious choice of selecting Washington (undisputed initial conference champion of the new Pacific Coast Conference), Dobie would already have departed for his next prospective coaching job at Detroit by that date. As events unfolded, he left Detroit before the season started and took the position as coach of the Naval Academy. At Navy we will see another set of events placing Gil Dobie within an eyelash of being selected for the Rose Bowl game, but bizarre circumstances would once again get in the way.

Dobie Quits the Team

Immediately after the Thanksgiving Day Colorado game, the big news of the possibility of Dobie quitting was quickly realized. The *Times* seized the opportunity to crow about being right all along: "Despite the fact that some folks ran around in a circle shouting loudly that it simply could not be true, Dobie quit right on schedule, within three and one-fifths seconds or maybe it was three and two-fifths seconds of the time the *Times* said he would." The article, dripping with sarcasm as it was, gave the newspaper's sportswriters a chance to pat themselves on the back for this one. The football news of the year, and the *Times* was way out in front on the story.

The Athletic Department being conducted under the auspices of the students, it was Student Body President Russell Callow who received the written resignation. Callow stated for the *Daily*, "The board probably will accept the resignation. It is apparent that the coach is sincere in his desire to quit football for good, and there doesn't seem to be any inclination to compel him to serve out his contract for that reason." Arthur Younger echoed these remarks and was more open in his interview with the *Times*: "Under the conditions named by Dobie, that he is a nervous wreck, tired of coaching and of football, it is probable that the only action the board will take will be to accept the resignation." The first reports of Dobie's intentions asserted that he was through with football for good and he was going to visit his sister in Berkeley. Ellen, his older sister, was married to Frank Cornish who was the current Berkeley City Attorney. One report stated that Dobie was going to join his brother-in-law's firm. Younger sister Jane was married to Charles Gall and they too had moved to Berkeley.

Quite naturally, a visit to the Bay Area also gave rise to speculation that he had his eye on coaching the California team, but this turned out to be nothing more than juicy rumors. No one connected with the university claimed to have any knowledge of the coach's future plans. Dobie cut off any discussion. He was said to have told his players, along with thanking them for their loyalty and for standing up to the training under him, "I am sick and tired of football, and I'm through with the game." Taken at face value, this seems like a mind-set that a coach could reach who, going back to his two-year stint as a high school coach, had never lost a game in twelve years.

It's understandable that someone with this record could start to feel the pressure. Dobie's professional personality and style wasn't outreaching, to say the least. He always felt that the academic side of the university unfairly encroached on his domain. They criticized him for rough language, and everyone, sportswriters, students, faculty, alumni, and even the players, were critical of those times he chose to close practices. He won year after year, and in the coaching world this is the gold standard. Win, you're a hero; lose, you're a goat. For his winning, Dobie was undeniably the most popular man on campus, but the top dog does attract a lot of heat.

Dobie's hero status meant that he was cut considerable slack for his my-way-or-the-highway manner, however, there were some who were understandably put off. The ultra-successful coach did open practices and was warm and personable up-close, but as leader of the winningest team in the country he attracted a large following who wanted to feel more connected. There was a strong and rabid fan base and great boosterism shown by the students, but constant winning often leads to being taken for granted. This was the case with Dobie and can be seen to have weighed on him. The natural letdown of fans after the big win in Berkeley is clear-cut evidence. Dobie did announce that he saw a harder game coming up, but his fixation for casting doubt finally caught up with him. So for a lot of reasons the coach flatly ran out of gas. He resigned not to grandstand, but being a person famous for not publicly displaying his feelings, he knew of no other response.

Washington gained from the national attention heaped on the university with Dobie's incredible record. In the press he was universally acclaimed, his name being regularly compared with the greatest coaches of his era. However, Dr. Henry Suzzallo took office in 1915, and the long shadow cast by Dobie's fame did steal much of the limelight from the new president. There was friction between the two, as could be expected. Dobie was vocal in his displeasure with what he observed as interference inflicted on athletics coming from the academics. He respected the classroom and insisted that his players maintain the highest standards of the institution but felt that it was unfair that Washington so often set upper limits on grading standards that were well above other schools his teams competed with. This was expressed in an early public statement of Dobie that he wrote for *The Washingtonian* in 1908 during his first football season: "Washington is laboring under one handicap which I feel that a little serious initiative on the part of the faculty would serve to remove. I am the last man to say that football players should not be in good standing; but I do believe that the standards set should be the same in all the colleges whose teams meet in regular contests. I understand that Oregon, Idaho and Pullman have lower standards than has Washington, and feel that this is an unfortunate state of affairs, and one that should not be allowed to go by default." President Suzzallo wasn't totally disturbed with the apparent prospect that he was going to lose the famous coach. A new coach and a new president could share the spotlight on more equal terms.

For December 1915, the major activity on campus was devoted to send-off celebrations to recognize the tall Scotsman's contributions to the school. At a student assembly where Dobie said, "I am through with football," a gold watch was presented with an engraved football with his initials on the back and inside the case on the front: "Presented to Gilmour Dobie in appreciation of his services as coach of the eight-time championship team, 1908-15, University of Washington, by the student body and alumni." A special luncheon at the Butler Hotel was given by the alumni association to honor the coach, attended by over three hundred guests, including students, current players, former players, faculty, business leaders, and alumni. Dobie and ex-yell king leader and president of the alumni association Dykeman addressed the crowd, and headlining the event was President Suzzallo. The University Marching Band was also brought out to ramp up the energy level.

In his speech, Suzzallo gave a ringing endorsement to the Washington Wizard. "The students have the power of quick appreciation of character. Dobie is a character. He is a character of positive qualities. The university is a large place to make men, and the process takes place both in and out of the classroom. Dobie has aided in this building of men. And his greatest work has been to make our playfield a gridiron of victory and to keep it a field of honor." He notched his praise up even higher in his declaration that in the future he would personally employ the coach's methods: "It would be my purpose to carry into the academic life of the institution the principles the invincible coach has used in his remarkable success on the gridiron." Dobie received a resounding ovation of appreciation from the packed house, who dug into their pockets for the fifty-cent cost of the luncheon served at the gala. History does not record whether this included tax and tip.

Dobie decided in his talk to preach once again on one of his foundational principles, overconfidence. A subject he had already well documented, he could never pass up one more chance to drive it home. He told of Washington State's Coach Lone Star Dietz putting out a mournful plea to the opposing coaches in games with Oregon State and Oregon to have mercy on his pitiful Pullman crew. "Stewart and Bezdek puffed out their chests before the games with WSU. Their spirit was reflected in the mind and marrow of the players. That had its effect. The confident teams lost. The crafty Dietz won." There certainly was no love lost between UW and WSU, so this was not so much to sing the praises of Dietz (no matter how well deserved) but to give Dobie an opening to once again teach his favorite lesson on how to succeed in leading men. Switch Dobie's name for Dietz's in his little sermon and we see who the real "crafty" one was.

Dobie professed that he was never going to coach again, but this didn't gain much traction. The focus was divided between who could possibly fill his shoes and where Dobie would finally end up. The early talk of Wisconsin interest went from rumor to supposed fact, with newspaper reports in the *Daily Northwestern* and *La Crosse Tribune* both reporting that he was the strong favorite. Pat O'Dea, being an icon of Wisconsin football, was still lobbying hard with a direct quote that "Gilmour Dobie is the greatest coach in the country." The *Daily Northwestern* hardly masked its feelings and couldn't seem to reach high enough in its tribute: "The preference of the majority of students and alumni for Gilmour Dobie, the miracle man of football, stands out prominently. There has just been ended the public presentation of letters received from prominent sporting editors of the coast. The lavishness of their praise, the unanimity of opinion regarding Dobie's ability as a coach have not failed to strengthen the belief that Dobie is the man needed at Wisconsin." And with this, the writers were just getting warmed up. They went on to express that it wasn't just Madison but points far and wide that were in favor of Dobie. They had vetted luminaries from Harvard, Johns Hopkins, and several other colleges, but Dobie was the standout. The *New York Times*, writing on December 17, 1915, reported, "Colleges everywhere are ready to bid for his services. His record of eight years as a coach without having had any of his teams suffer defeat appeals largely to those colleges like Yale which are in search of a capable coach. It is reported that a number of colleges have made offers to Dobie."

There were more than thirty applications for Dobie's job, representing a veritable who's who of top-flight coaches around the country. Locally, Elmer Henderson, coach at Broadway High School, was highly touted as a possibility, as was the famous Washington quarterback Wee Coyle; Wayne Sutton star end and Dobie assistant; and Enoch Bagshaw, team captain in 1907 and future Washington coach. Across the country there were such notables as Doc Sweetland of Kentucky, Joe Pipal of Occidental in Los Angeles, Lone Star Dietz, and All-American quarterback Johnny McGovern of Minnesota, among others.

While the national search was under way Coach Dobie was in Berkeley visiting his sisters and didn't return until January. He thought he was going to get in some golf in the winter sunshine of California, but in actuality he grew sick of torrential rains during his stay. He would have been even more troubled with the weather had he stayed in Seattle, as the entire West Coast for the 1915-16 winter suffered unseasonable precipitation. This translated into one of the worst snowstorms on record for Seattle. Transportation, business activity, university enrollment, and classroom attendance all suffered as a result of the major storm damage inflicted over the region.

Collection of Dobie's granddaughter, Eva Zayha.

Gilmour Dobie on his December 1915 trip to visit his sister in Berkeley California after announcing he was going to retire from coaching football. Pictured in front of a 1915 Buick Touring Car, the trio strikes a fashionable pose. He stands between Ellen (Dobie) Cornish on the left and his fiancée Eva Butler to the right.

The hiring campaign went forward despite the ravages of the weather. Mysteriously, Arthur Younger, just at the time that the hiring committee was to meet on the night of January 19 with their decision of a man to recommend to the Board of Control, decided to take a trip reported as "some point south." Hmm, the "point south" being California, where Dobie just happened to be, must have been mere coincidence. On his trip he interviewed highly regarded Occidental coach Joe Pipal and gave a statement that now there was a dark horse coach from the Middle West who was also on the short list. On his stop at Berkeley, he found time to pay a visit to Coach Dobie. As jam packed as his work schedule was, it was quite nice of him to find time to meet with his old friend. Reports in papers around the country were still announcing that Dobie was on the inside track to accept the job at Wisconsin, so obviously this was just a social call. Certainly they didn't have any business to discuss. Only a cynic would conclude that; after all, Dobie had quit the team.

When our traveling graduate manager returned from California, a few more details emerged on this new candidate, who seemed to be getting a lot of attention from the search committee. The *Daily*, with a straight face, reported, "He refused to give out the name this morning, but intimated that the man would probably come for a reasonable figure, and that his two lines of athletics are football and basketball." Comes from the Middle West, expertise in basketball and football, reasonable salary figure; all traits that fit Coach Dobie like a glove. But hold it, he's quit the team; this must be just another coincidence.

It was an interesting juxtaposition of events; as the snow storm of 1916 paralyzed Seattle, not to mention the university, with even the football grandstand on Denny Field being destroyed by the blizzard, Gil Dobie came back to life. After all the farewell celebrations, after the national replacement search, after the multitude of wishful candidates applying for the job, and after Dobie's protestations to the contrary, he was back. Many felt that the mysterious "Midwest candidate" was just a way to stall for time to finalize negotiations with Dobie. In any event, even if there was no new Middle West stalking horse, Dobie did fit this description, as he was born, educated, played football, and first coached in Minnesota and next North Dakota.

There were several acts to this drama. The search committee reached the conclusion that there was no one on their very large list who could compare with the great coach they just parted company with. Dobie had just returned from his California trip on Thursday, February 3, and by Friday he was already having lunch with Younger. Surprise! He was later joined by a respected businessman in the community, S. M. Hedges, who met with the two men that afternoon and added his powers of persuasion to the cause. On Saturday the committee was to announce the selection, but instead made a complete reversal, passing a motion to go back to Dobie with an offer. This reversal, of course, wasn't a reversal; Dobie was the man all along. This behind-the-scenes activity gave the appearance that a selection process of weighing candidates was still under way.

The offer was presented to the coach by Younger and Callow that very afternoon to lessen any risk of losing the deal. Dobie only wanted to meet directly with Dr. Suzzallo before coming to his decision. The president and

Dean Priest met with the eight-time champion on Monday morning, and in this meeting Dobie and Suzzallo were able to smooth over any differences they held for each other and came to an agreement. Suzzallo was especially complimentary of Dobie in getting the league rule passed to exclude freshmen from varsity eligibility. Dean Priest, reporting in the *Daily*, noted, "Dobie's return is due entirely to the efforts of the special committee, and that the coach himself made no move to get his former job back. He even was reluctant to accept the offer for fear of drawing adverse criticism."

It does seem correct that Dobie harbored thoughts of getting out of football. He perceived there had been lapses of support from student fans. Most would deem this an overreaction, as the fans were passionately behind the team the vast majority of the time. But, as was shown in the second California game, too much of a good thing can wear thin. Reasons behind his resignation can be written off to feeling underappreciated and partly to the immense pressure he put on himself. Setting an impossible standard of perfection can wear anyone out—and the burden finally caught up with Dobie. But now he was back. With the huge outpouring of support shown him in the never-ending going-away celebrations, he saw he was appreciated, and the next chapter in his life was ready to be written. His ninth year of coaching at Washington, with all its pressures and unknowns, was all that lay ahead.

Students were ecstatic with the news, as were alumni and boosters in the community, winners having such wide latitude. The press reports, while playing up the eccentric side of Dobie that made such interesting reading, also were not too proud to get behind the shocking turnabout. The *Post-Intelligencer*, in a gushing level of exalted flattery, editorialized, "Tune up the sackbut, psaltery, harp and lute and anything else that will make noise, and let us sound a paean of joy over the return of the mentor whom we mourned as officially dead." Hardly words of disdain despite the paper's penchant for playing up the banner headlines often used in describing his obsessive side. He always made news, always won, and that was all that mattered. The master was back, and everyone could breathe a sigh of relief.

In the midst of the hubbub created over Dobie's resignation, the team's business had to move forward, and did so despite 24/7 distractions. That year's football banquet was held on November 30, with the first order of business being to select the 1916 team captain. Candidate Cy Noble, was one of the most respected members of the team during his four years at Washington. His ever-dedicated work ethic and willingness to support the team no matter how personally demanding was evident throughout his career. A remarkable gesture he made at the banquet, given his sterling reputation, surprised even those who knew him well. Being a letter winner and star from his freshman year on, he, along with Louis Seagrave, was on the inside track to be picked as team leader. Both equally deserved the honor. Rather than put the team through the difficult process of choosing sides during these trying times it was Cy Noble, in a selfless act of placing team harmony over personal honor, who quickly offered Seagrave's name in nomination and called for a unanimous vote. The acceptance speech given by Seagrave correctly caught the heroic tenor of Noble's tribute: "I cannot but feel that in electing me captain, you have elected the lesser man." The thunderous applause following this remark was deservedly for the man who stepped aside and not the new captain.

# CHAPTER ELEVEN

## *I Can't Get Mad Anymore—1916*

> "I believe the University of Washington is losing one of the best and most thorough football coaches in the country. In my opinion, the team of 1916 and its successes are the greatest exemplifications of his ability as a football coach that he has shown during his entire time at Seattle. He's a disciplinarian and a general, and I believe the tall Scotsman has the ability to get more out of his material than the average coach. Dobie in past seasons, has made great teams out of great material, but when a coach makes a winning team out of ordinary material, he's some coach."
>
> *George Varnell, Referee and Sports Editor, Spokane Chronicle*

Sportswriters were still keeping a very close eye on Dobie's goings and comings, even going into his ninth year. With football season three months away, the Wizard was about to embark on the most challenging, quotable, and entertaining period of his term at Washington. The summer of 1916 was the year the infamous struggle with Pancho Villa's attacks against American citizens began. President Wilson called seventy-five thousand National Guardsmen into service over the "Carrizal Affair." This international crisis was caused by no less a military personage than Brigadier General John J. Pershing mistakenly going into battle against official Mexican troops thinking they were Pancho Villa's rebels. This led to explosive tensions between the United States and Mexico, disastrously bringing them to the edge of war. Dobie lamented that four of last year's starters and three substitutes he was counting on to step into higher positions that year had been called into National Guard Reserve duty. Time would show that this was only the start. In the *Oakland Tribune* of July 27, Dobie stated, "We are confronted with a difficult schedule at best, and in the present circumstances I have no high hopes." Hardly worthy of the article's headline, "Gilmour Dobie Is Out With Usual Hard Luck Wail," but on slow news days it's not unheard of to promote a story out of whole cloth. What better story to attract a wandering reader's eye than an article on Old Reliable crying the blues?

By September, more bad news hit. Bud Young, star quarterback, who had taken over the reins after the great Wee Coyle graduated in 1911, was offered a teaching and coaching position at Bellingham. This would actually have been Young's fifth year in school; because of his 1914 injury, he didn't earn a letter and was still eligible. The talented Ross MacKechnie, who was tagged as the fullback successor to superstar Walt Shiel, was juggling his class schedule, reserve duty, and football, but couldn't find a timetable that worked, so he also pulled out. Bill Hainsworth (fullback), Ben Mayfield (right guard), and Sandy Wick (center) all registered late for school, causing a great deal of consternation for the anxious coaching staff. Ted Faulk (center), who started the year suffering from a broken wrist sustained while cranking a car engine, further aggravated matters.

The National Guard training camp was located at a winter resort on American Lake, well south of Seattle (site of the present day Fort Lewis), making it difficult for reservists to get to practice on time. Dobie eventually was able to arrange car transportation for his players. No one could possibly have foretold the trials that were to follow, but this struggle to balance reserve duty with football would play into spectacular events as the season came to an end. The starters who were called up and would suffer time restraints balancing school, football, and reserve duty were Ernest Murphy, Bill Grimm, and David Logg. To further add to the coaching staff's stress level, the team lost four star players to graduation: Hap Miller (left halfback), Walt Shiel (fullback), and Ray Hunt (left end), who were all four-year lettermen, and senior Ed Leader (right end), who played four years but only lettered in two of those due to football injuries. Leader was an outstanding athlete who went on to glory as one of the greatest crew coaches in Yale history, taking the team to the 1925 Olympics, where they brought home a gold medal. There is no doubt that without the injuries he suffered, he would have won his "W" for the four years he played.

"Denny Field Passes Into Memory" reads the headline of October 6, 1916. The Board of Control decided that the new field would be renamed "University Field" until a new name was either chosen by the students or selected in honor of a donor. Denny Field was never an official name, and since there already was a permanent building on the campus named in honor of the Denny family for their contribution, it was decided to change the name. University Field was a placeholder, as Arthur Younger intended to find a donor who would wish to contribute to the university for the honor of having the field named after him. This money-generating tactic came long before its ubiquitous use that we see in modern times. A celebration and announcement were on the drawing boards for the Thanksgiving Big Game with California. As events played out, this naming plan never materialized. Soon the plans to create a modern football stadium on Union Bay would supersede the program to further upgrade University Field.

It could not have been foreseen at the time, but this year's game between the two largest universities in the Far West would set into motion the events that would bring western football up to that of the eastern game. Because of eight straight years of total dominance, there was no mistake about it; Dobie's reputation only accelerated with every team west of the Rockies all too eager to knock him off. California was the most motivated of all, dedicating the unheard-of sum of $12,000 per year in salaries to attract a coaching staff for the express purpose of building the team to accomplish the task. For this commitment, eventually the school would be richly rewarded. Out of it grew the indomitable Andy Smith-coached "Wonder Teams" of the 1920s. The competitive pressure brought to the western football scene by Gilmour Dobie cannot be overstated.

## Preseason

The first preseason game at University Field was a ragged performance, much of which could be attributed to the reservist problems. An injury to left end Ted Faulk, players late to register, and graduation took their toll, but this couldn't account for the all-around weakness in most every aspect of the game. Defense was the only department that was even close to a Dobie standard. Nonletterman Miles Cary showed potential in carrying the ball, but most of the load went to the outstanding Cy Noble, who was still rusty. The backfield had to settle for nominal yardage throughout the game and never got off anything resembling above-average play. Noble's anemic run of 17 yards in the first quarter turned out to be the largest ground gainer of the afternoon. The most worrisome aspect of the game was its inconsistency. The team never could settle into any kind of rhythm. Just as they would put a series of tough plays together and appear to be functioning as a unit, a fumble would follow right behind. The weaker opponent was held scoreless, but this was hardly something to crow about. Dobie was not pleased and let his players in on his take: "You don't know how to play fundamental football yet, and there's no use of my trying to teach you anything else until you do." This start was not unlike many of the inaugural games of earlier years. The final outcome had Washington ahead of the Ballard Meteors by an underwhelming 28-0.

A game with the South Tacoma Athletic Club was cancelled, so this gave Dobie's boys a much-needed additional week of practice. The added time also helped with the many injuries plaguing the team. To take advantage of the open date, Dobie and Hap Miller, coach of the freshmen squad, held a scrimmage between the frosh and the Varsity. The practice game showed great progress had been made since their first warm-up affair.

The practice field was once again opened to the public, but, given past complaints, turnout was unimpressive. Yell king Herrick did everything he could to muster support, even pushing for women to come out, but spirit was still lacking. There's not much drama in never losing a game for eight years running. In an odd sense, there's nothing like a loss to build support. It could be fun to reflect on Dobie's pessimistic assessments, but since he was always proven wrong, even the amusement of trying to second guess the coach was denied the loyal fan. The enjoyment of Monday-morning quarterbacking was reduced to just the second-guessing of what could have been done to stave off the two tie games. There's much more steam to vent in a loss than a win.

This week the school was rocked with three blockbuster news events that must have sent the students into catatonic shock. The easiest item to absorb was the astonishing fact delivered by a highly credible source that life exists on Mars. This was announced by distinguished astronomer Dr. Percival Lowell in a campus lecture, backing up his conclusion with pictures of the man-made canals clearly evident on the surface. Of even greater significance was the ground-breaking declaration coming from yell king Herrick that he was announcing the formation of a women's song staff. New seating arrangements were in the works, but, probably fearing too much information would conflict with the students' concentration on studies, no details were disclosed. Whether the women would actually be permitted to sit in the rooting section unescorted would have to wait for another day. In clarifying just how monumental Herrick viewed this life-altering advancement to be, he declared, "On these girls' shoulders rests much of the responsibility for the college spirit of future years."

But if finding absolute proof of life on Mars and allowing women to participate in college rallies wasn't big enough, the real clincher made these historic revelations pale by comparison. Banner headlines broke the monumental story: "Dobie Losing Form, He Says So Himself." At the Monday afternoon rally held at the team's practice, attended by three hundred men (zero women), he announced to the large group, "I can't get mad any more. It doesn't seem to bother me at all that the team is doing miserably, and anyone who watches them will admit that they are in bad shape for having been working a month. I can't seem to get at the root of the evil like I used to." Uh-oh, the crowd must have thought; looks like the team is going to get swamped this week. A disaster ahead and a horrible prediction of total embarrassment equates to weak competition. Dobie going soft means a tough game in the offing. But this? Dobie can't get mad must mean that not just the streak is history, but Washington is due for a slaughter.

Saturday's game with the Bremerton Naval squad, however, turned out the same way as the good old days when Dobie would concoct some cataclysmic end about to befall the team. The defense showed up this time and was described as "smothering" the navy team. Senior Cy Noble also showed up and demonstrated that his play had not diminished despite losing backfield mates Walt Shiel and Hap Miller. It was one of the marks of Dobie's teams that no matter how many stars were lost to graduation, nor how many early-season roadblocks were thrown in his path, he could always assemble eleven players who would play at the highest levels in the league. Sooner or later every team, whether filled with God-given talent or built from lesser mortals Dobie lifted up, all came to be known as machines.

Despite turning over a new leaf, Dobie was giving early signals that some of the old punch was still left. Coming into the Bremerton Naval Yard game, Dobie found it essential that he demote his outstanding star, Captain Louis Seagrave, to the second team. Now this sounds more like the Dobie of old! It just wouldn't be fair if, after all this time that fans had invested in learning how to read him, all the rules would now fall by the wayside. Loyalty should be rewarded, not punched in the face.

Perhaps the coach overlooked the fact that his inordinately predictable behavior was well documented. He may have forgotten, but everyone else was aware of such proclivities as picking a player for an object lesson to the team. He had long ago been quoted nationwide with this gem: "I always go to my captain at the start of the season and tell him that a football team is composed of eleven players, not of ten players and a captain. For some reason the captaincy is likely to bring with it too much honor, so that the recipient of it gets it into his head he either plays the game, or he takes the honor so seriously that he cannot play his game. The result in either case is an eleven made up of ten players and a captain. That sort of team is bound to lose... And I have watched this captaincy business so closely that I have been able to win some of the big games when at Washington by directing our attack against opposing captains, linemen who, though thought invulnerable, had really let down in their play and were unable to cope on equal terms with their fellow players against our attack. Their players, believing in their captain, were demoralized by our success in attacking this point on their line. After all, football is mostly psychology." How relieved anxious rooters must have felt when Dobie, rather than not being bothered "that the team is doing miserably," operated true to form and cut the team captain's legs out from under him.

Ray Gardner at right halfback, who had just missed his letter in the 1915 season because of injury, was back up to form and showed that he was deserving of a starting position when the regular season began. Quarterback Clark "Ching" Johnson turned in the most promising performance of all, scoring four of the nine touchdowns. The quarterback in Dobie's era often was called on to carry the ball as much as a fullback or halfback. Johnson made the vast majority of his yardage on off-tackle plays, being a strong runner for his size with a fullback's penchant for making his own holes up the middle. Ray Gardner led the interference and was responsible for most of Johnson's long gains. Knowledgeable fans of the modern game are surprised to hear that the quarterback did not always call the signals back in these early days of play. Dobie considered that the quarterback was the field general and ran the team, even more so than the captain, but he would give the job of calling signals to the most qualified player on the team. In this case that man was Ernest "Tramp" Murphy, who played both tackle and end. His outstanding play this year put him in position to earn the captaincy of the 1917 eleven, and he also would be honored as recipient of the Flaherty Medal as Most Inspirational Player.

University of Washington, Special Collections, Neg. No. 21852

Captain Louis Seagrave was a third string Walter Camp Foundation All-American selection at end for 1916. He, together with Ernest Murphy, were the co-leaders in urging the team to strike over the suspension of Bill Grimm from the team over the finals' cheating scandal of 1916.

Worried fans could now relax as matters were settling down going into league play against Whitman. Because of losing track of the missing game against Everett, this game has been incorrectly designated the one hundredth win for Washington. Final score: Washington 62-0 over Bremerton Navy.

## Whitman College

Coach Dobie may have announced that he "couldn't get mad anymore," but his prickly ways were still in evidence. Not satisfied that enough spirit was being shown in the open practices, he partially closed the gates to outsiders once again. This was in contradiction to a statement he had made less than ten days earlier that he was pleased. It seemed he wanted it both ways. He did allow three reporters on the field; thus he had gotten over his fear that news would get out on the team's inner workings. Here was another contradiction regarding his conduct. Quite often Dobie had a willingness to share special plays that he developed. Erroneous reports that he had a near phobia for secrecy are from latter-day writings that base their opinion solely on the super-secret shield set up to protect his Bunk Play plans. In actuality he often would deliberately let the competition gain knowledge of his plays, and then, with his incessant practice techniques, have his men execute with such precision that the other team was unable to defend against a preannounced set—this being especially deflating to have had foreknowledge of what was coming. Here was more evidence to support the long-held claim that his teams were "machines."

That week the team's main focus was on defense, with concentration on the forward pass and spread formations. Injuries were healing well as the extra week off paid dividends. Ray Gardner was suffering from a bout of cauliflower ear but was able to practice with a felt bandage for protection. For all appearances it looked as if the Varsity was finally whipping into shape. With as many years as we now have to observe the team's preseason sloppiness eventually morph into a finely tuned construct for league play, we can conclude the acclaim for this solely rests with Dobie. There was no particular advantage that Dobie had for attracting talent; it's just that he had the skills to better draw out the best in the players he was dealt.

Kirby Torrance, a reporter for the *Daily*, taking a page from Dobie's script in assessing the Varsity's chances, declared that Washington's prospects were near hopeless. "As a team it has the hardest work ahead, the poorest material and the most discouraging outlook of any squad Washington has had in years." As for Dobie, he must have seen something in the Whitman Missionary team that history doesn't seem to support with his observation: "If Whitman is as strong as she was last year, we will get licked." It does seem a stretch to reach this conclusion, considering that last year's team went down to Washington 27-0. But, Coach Vincent Borleske's team was fully intact for this year, just having won against Idaho, and was judged in top form. Dobie rightfully praised Captain Emory Hoover at quarterback who was their leading rusher in the 1915 game. But Dobie did seem to reach a bit high in acclaiming he is worth any two of his own backs. Hoover's normal position was fullback, but he had some aches and pains from the beating that fullbacks take in running up the middle. As Dobieisms go, it would logically follow that if Hoover was playing his normal position and if he wasn't nursing his minor injuries, the coach would have professed him to be worth the entire Purple and Gold backfield.

Ray Gardner at left halfback was a player that most everyone had tagged as destined for stardom. He was popular with the fans and greatly respected by Dobie and the coaching staff. Unfortunately he suffered a broken collarbone on a block against a Whitman player, landing him on the sidelines for the season. His talent was abundantly evident in the early season work, and the coaching staff had predicted him to be a major contributor for this year's backfield. This made two years in a row that injuries knocked him off the team. His replacement, Arthur Anderson, a promising player in his first year on the team, suffered a fractured left ankle early in the game that also took him out of action for the year. These injuries placed a huge strain on the team's resources. Juggling players was a constant necessity given the smaller teams of the era, but losing two men of such ability was an unusually harsh blow.

Captain Louis Seagrave at right guard, Ernest Murphy at right tackle, and Bill Grimm at left tackle formed an impenetrable barrier on defense and opened wide holes for Washington's running backs in the sizeable margin of victory for the Varsity. They would repeatedly throw the Missionary backs for 5, 10, and 15-yard losses. Whitman had an experienced team with a good record, and with UW's many legitimate question marks, the winning margin was wholly unexpected. But judging from the numerous times in past years when the task at hand seemed formidable, Dobie still found a way to deliver.

Cy Noble played his usual brilliant game in the backfield at right half. Ching Johnson at quarterback did have experience from the year before as a substitute, but that day his running wasn't in keeping with past performance. The big question coming up for the Oregon game was who would be filling in the gap left by the injury to Gardner. With his athletic skills, and since he was calling signals as a lineman, early speculation leaned towards moving Murphy into the backfield. This would mean that the inexperienced Julius Calkins would be called on to fill the giant void left in the line by Murphy's absence. The Whitman game came out better than expected, but dark clouds loomed ahead for the upcoming game with Oregon on Kincaid Field. Final score: Washington 37, Whitman 6.

## University of Oregon, at Eugene

A touch of controversy swirled around the Oregon and Washington teams prior to the game. Johnny Parsons, an Oregon star halfback, was possibly ineligible to play the game, according to an interpretation of conference rules. If he played and Oregon won with him being declared ineligible, the game would be forfeited. Dean Arthur Priest of Washington was the university's representative who served on the conference eligibility committee. The issue was whether Parsons had completed his course work for the 1915 spring semester as required by league rules. With Washington's amazing winning streak getting such national coverage, this debate was just what the press needed to stir the cauldron.

To Dobie the Parsons controversy was downright foolish, as Oregon, even without him, was vastly superior. To illustrate his national reach, this is a Dobie quote from the *Janesville* [Wisconsin] *Daily Gazette*: "Oregon is foolish if she plays Parsons; she doesn't need him. Will we win? Say if we can win this year with the material we have, football is no game for me. We aren't entitled to win a game against a team of veterans like Oregon has. In the first place it is a physical impossibility; I simply haven't got the men and can't get them. The freshmen rule took away all chances I had to fill up the holes left by the old men." Dobie had led the charge on eliminating the freshman rule and Oregon had to observe the same rule, but what difference does this make in setting up your storyline?

Practice on Wednesday night didn't sit well with the head coach. Either to send a message or, less likely, because he was actually disgusted with the team's performance, he ceremoniously walked off the field before practice ended. His complaint was over the team's fumbling, missed tackles, and mixed-up signals for formations. Dobie's expectations being well out of reach for mere mortals on every detail of execution, the team got the point.

By Friday at Oregon's Kincaid Field, Captain Seagrave was voicing optimism that the team had a fighting chance at victory, but the coaching staff didn't hold out any hope for a win. Coaches Dobie and Sutton were not just expecting to lose, they were convinced that victory was impossible. A casual observer might think with the game being so hopeless that perhaps a flu epidemic had befallen the team, or was it that half the players were declared ineligible? However, no such tragic circumstance had hit. Dobie was floating the theory that he would finally be vindicated and this game, at long last, would settle the issue— Washington's record was due to nothing but luck and not high-caliber football.

Every year when Bezdek and Dobie faced off, it was a contest as to who would outdo the other in going negative. Bezdek first coached at Oregon in 1906, left for Arkansas from 1908 to '12, and returned to coach the Ducks from 1913 to '18. Bezdek was hired at Oregon with the specific charge to end Dobie's conference stranglehold. In their first head-to-head contest under Bezdek in 1913, it was only a dropkick goal that made the difference in the 10-7 score. Bezdek learned football under the great Amos Alonzo Stagg at the University of Chicago, and, growing up on Chicago's South Side, brought that street-fighter attitude to his coaching. From Stagg he learned the craft of pessimism from an accomplished master of the art. Bezdek believed in hard practices and intimidation, often creating animosity from his own players. Nothing a player could do was good enough. He was never at a loss for words in describing the underhanded deceptions that the opposition always had in store for his innocent elevens. When it came to the prospects of his team against his next opponent, he was beyond Dobie-esque in sizing up just how badly Oregon was going to lose. Just prior to the game, the *Post-Intelligencer* reported, "Oregon's head coach enveloped himself in a cloud of gloom as the rain continued throughout the day." This could have been more credible except that his backfield this year had proven themselves to be excellent runners in wet and muddy conditions.

Not restrained by political correctness, the preparations going into the game by the rally committee were compared to that of the "German Army." The excitement of the 342 strong boarding the overnight rooters' special for Portland was contrasted with the air of gloom of the players' train that left a day earlier. A twenty-five-piece band was on board, and a special parlor car with a large, polished dance floor was provided exclusively for the party. To ramp the pace another notch, an indoor track meet with events between each dance was organized, complete with prizes to the winners. A group breakfast was scheduled at the Multnomah Hotel before departing on a local electric train for the final leg to Eugene. There Oregon rooters scheduled a 12:30 luncheon before the game. After the game, as if they hadn't packed in enough action, a dance was held at 8:30 in the cadet armory on campus. A surprising turnout of eighty women signed up, showing much greater interest than in the past. Of course, in this proper age, assurances were made that female chaperones would be along.

As further guarantee that all women would be fully aware of the requirements of polite conduct, Miss Ethel Hunley Coldwell, dean of women, called an "essential" meeting for all women the day prior to departure. As for allowing women to finally be allowed to participate in student parades, the dean was holding pat that such outlandish behavior not be allowed, "It is therefore requested that all plans for the parade of Wednesday night [Nov. 28, 1916] which include women be discontinued. I feel certain that the sentiment among the women students will uphold my desire that they not be subjected to such publicity as a public spectacle of this sort would entail."

It was certainly correct that Dobie's backfield lacked the experience and strength of teams from earlier years, and the injuries to Gardner and Anderson only added to the problem. The two areas where he could expect excellence were the interior line and the dropkicking threat posed by Ted Faulk. Oregon was a heavier team on average, which gave an edge to them in what was predicted to be a closely fought battle. Royal Brougham, writing in the *Post-Intelligencer*, considered Oregon to be well balanced: "Oregon unquestionably has an eleven which is strong in every department." In a prescient observation underscored by this writing, he summed up the importance of this contest held so long ago: "They'll be talking about this little session long after the pigskin is put away for the season and Washington has hung up another gridiron title."

For this game the coaches agreed to have numbers on the players as they did in the 1909 Thanksgiving game. Since rain was a certainty, this was a fan-friendly decision greeted with delight. The playing surface was anticipated to be another of the muddy quagmires as was often the case on Kinkaid Field. Identifying players was difficult enough without numbers on dry fields, but in the mud, identifying players was nearly impossible. The controversial Johnny Parsons at right halfback was suited up and played the entire game. In fact, the players of both teams distinguished themselves in that every man on both teams played every minute of the entire game. Parsons played the most outstanding game of any player on the field and, with any kind of break, could have made the difference in the game. The athletic Ernest Murphy was moved from tackle to left halfback to replace Ray Gardner, with his position being filled by the lighter and less experienced Ben Mayfield.

The major factor of the game did turn out to be the terrible field conditions brought on by heavy rain leading up to the game and continuing for most of the afternoon. The field was a sea of mud, removing all hope for scoring via the pass or field goal. Conditions were a repeat of the terrible 1912 mud bowl against Oregon State in Portland. It was the "scare of their sweet young lives this afternoon on a sloppy, slippery Eugene field," as Royal Brougham summed it up. "The fighting, dogged determination of a Dobie team staving off defeat saved the greatest record ever made by a college team and where and when Referee Varnell's dear old whistle ended that battle, the Washington rooters crowded onto the field and carried every member of the team, the scrubs and even staid old coach Dobie from the field. It was a tie game but it was as big a victory as a Washington team has had in years." It was no less than Student Body president and former team captain Walt Shiel that boosted a smiling Dobie on his shoulders and carried him from the field. The fans getting into the act left muddy handprints of admiration on the coach's back as he passed by. Before leaving the field, Dobie was quoted as saying to the ecstatic fans and players, "If you think I'm not tickled, you're crazy. Did you ever see such a bunch of cripples play like that against an all star crowd like Bezdek's? Pretty lucky. Pretty lucky."

There were two outstanding chances Oregon had to score, both coming in the third quarter. Captain Beckett took a punt well into his territory and, despite the terrible conditions, threaded his way through Washington's defense for 20 yards. Parsons took over, eventually moving the ball on long gainers deep into Washington territory and finally reaching the 12-yard line. Everyone in the stadium could see that this outstanding drive would conclude with an Oregon touchdown. On the fourth down the snap from center went directly to Parsons, who momentarily bobbled the ball and then plunged right up the gut. Led by Captain Louis Seagrave, the defensive line and backs piled up Parson's advance short of the first down. With this dramatic turn of good fortune the stoic and unemotional Dobie jumped up, shook the waterboy's hand, and actually joined in the roar from the crowd. Later in the quarter, with the ball in Washington territory, Vic Morrison punted to Parsons on his 20-yard line, where he was tackled in his tracks by six defenders.

The ankle deep mud having removed any hope of passing or field goals, punting became the game saver of last resort for both teams. However, neither team gained a decided advantage with Oregon totaling 527 yards on 17 punts and Washington 548 yards on 16 punts. Shockingly there were only three first downs earned by Oregon from scrimmage and only four by the Varsity. Rushing statistics showed only 75 for Oregon with a below average 78 on the Washington side. Given the obstacles posed by Mother Nature no game could have been more closely matched. Late in the third quarter Oregon mustered one last scoring threat that could have won the game in this hugely exciting third quarter. The account of the play-by-play as reported in the *UW Daily*:

"Washington punted out of danger and Oregon in a few minutes succeeded in getting the ball to the Washington 35-yard line. Then came the
sensational onside kick that so nearly resulted in an Oregon victory. "Shy"
Huntington dropped back to kick. Parsons dropped back to within a few feet

of the Oregon punter and the stands looked for a fake. Shy received the ball two steps forward ahead of Parsons, putting him onside, and kicked to the northwest corner of the field. The rule concerning the onside kick permits any player behind the ball at the time it was kicked to recover the ball. So Parsons, once onside, raced across the field to the sideline and continued full speed down under the kick. (Washington's) "Ching" Johnson, thinking that the kick was a punt, was playing the ball safe and allowed it to roll across the Washington goal line, not realizing that Parsons could recover the ball. While the Washington back was waiting to take it back to his own 20-yard line, Johnny Parsons shot through the mass of players and dived for the ball. He hit it too hard and it slipped from under him, to be recovered by Shy Huntington. Had Parsons held the ball Oregon would have won a 6-0 victory [assuming the extra point try failed.]"

Shy Huntington was not eligible to actually recover the ball, so Washington took possession of the ball on downs at the 20-yard line, successfully dodging another bullet. The ball was in Oregon territory for much longer than Washington's but the Varsity was not able to take advantage of this field position edge. The scoring threats of Oregon, while being more spectacular than the visitor's, were matched by Washington but came up equally short. Washington reached the Oregon 15-yard line in the first quarter but didn't put the ball into the end zone. They also posed a threat in the fourth quarter with a strong drive that was killed by Oregon on their 20-yard line. Ironically it was on a very muddy field in 1914 at Albany against Oregon State where Washington last had to settle for a tie. That muddy, rain-soaked game also ended with neither team scoring.

Oregon had the better team that day but fell short of a total game. They brought much more all-around experience, and while the stats on their kicking and running games didn't show it by the numbers, Oregon was a notch sharper in both departments. But Dobie and his men figured out a way to overcome the manpower imbalance, keep themselves in the game, overcome the adversity of the weather, and come out with a tie. Losing both Gardner and Anderson weakened Washington's chances, considering this was truly a rebuilding year for Washington. They had suffered the loss of a legion of stars to graduation and the decision of Bud Young, their three-year starter, not to return. The Varsity's only three certified veterans were Captain Louis Seagrave, Ernest Murphy, and Cy Noble. In Cy Noble's case, he had suffered a broken nose in practice in October 1915 and here, one year later, he again broke his nose but completed the game. A consistent performer throughout his four years, he earned the nickname given to him by his teammates as "Good Old Truck Horse." It's no mystery as to why he would be honored at the annual banquet by his teammates for that year's Guy Flaherty award.

As to the lingering question of whether Johnny Parsons was ineligible to play, the facts were in and they proved that Parsons was indeed in violation of league rules. The week following the game, with time to double-check the evidence, it showed conclusively that Parsons was ineligible. Just prior to the game it was known to the committee that there was reason to believe that Parsons had withdrawn from school on May 1, 1915, which cancelled his credits for that semester's course work. Dr. A. D. Brown of Oregon State, a member of the Pacific Coast Conference advisory committee, and Dean Priest notified University of Oregon President Dr. Prince Lucien Campbell of the information just as the teams were taking the field. Dr. Campbell chose not to have Parsons withdrawn from the game. Dean Priest and Dr. Brown decided that they would not officially declare him ineligible because, in the pregame rush of time, they wanted to make sure their facts and evidence were in order. Washington decided that they would not ask for a forfeiture of the game but would accept one if it were volunteered by Oregon. Seattle sportswriters went so far as to put it in writing that Oregon would choose on their own to forfeit this game and their win over California, but this was not the case. Oregon decided not to volunteer forfeiture, so the record reflects that the game ended in a scoreless tie. This brought an end to the question, and the tie game stands. After the hard-fought game and considering the high level of athletic competition exhibited that day, it was only appropriate that the outcome was settled on the field, however, subject to a footnote. Both teams had their opportunities to score but were turned back by valiant defense from the opposition. A standoff is befitting everything that took place that afternoon on Kincaid Field. Final score: 0-0.

## Oregon State

Joe Pipal, the highly regarded coach of Occidental College in Los Angeles, had been hired that year to lead the football program at Oregon State. This is noteworthy, as it was Coach Pipal who was considered as the frontrunner to replace Coach Dobie on his 1915 "retirement." When he coached in California he developed great skill in the passing game of necessity, as teams converting from rugby heavily depended on the pass. Coming into the game, Oregon State was on a roll with wins against Idaho, Washington State, and Whitman, and a loss to Nebraska. Since Dobie's arrival on the West Coast in 1908, games between Washington and Oregon State were one-sided affairs. In the seven prior meetings, Washington held a commanding edge in scoring, 165-3. The new freshman eligibility rule hit Oregon State harder than any other team in the league, so this weighed heavily on their chances to challenge Washington. This would be Pipal's only season with OSU, where he ended the year 4-5-0 overall and suffered losses in conference games with Oregon and Washington.

Passing by now was being hailed as a "brilliant" aspect of Dobie's offense, but against Oregon State the team had a total breakdown in getting the ball into the hands of willing receivers. Out of the five attempted passes, two were intercepted, two were incomplete, and the only reception netted a meager

5 yards. This wasn't due to inspired defense; the passes were poorly executed and just plain sloppy. The two interceptions were near disasters for Washington. Being a perfect fall day for football, weather can't be blamed. In this instance those watching the game witnessed that rarity of a Dobie coached team, seemingly weak preparation.

Injured Captain Louis Seagrave was out of a game for the first time in his four years and was relegated to carrying the yardstick on sideline duty. With his captain unable to answer the call, Dobie had good reason to have his doubts on his boys' chances for a win. Ernest Murphy, who was moved into the backfield, was tagged to step into the captaincy and call the game. Right tackle Clarence "Vic" Morrison, taking over punting duties after not lettering in his first two years on the team, was a standout. In an interview in 2010, Morrison's daughter, Patricia Morrison Moriarty, stated that her father always spoke very highly of Coach Dobie attributing the lessons he learned from the hard work ethic demanded by the coach to his success later in life. He singled out the master teacher's crucial life lesson of never giving up as the reason he overcame the ravages of the Great Depression.

Dobie, being a stickler for mechanics, turned this somewhat erratic kicker into a consistent powerhouse. Up until 1912, with only three downs to make 10 yards, the kicking game was huge. The four-down rule enacted for the 1912 season did take the importance of the kicking game down a notch. But it was still very important to game strategy as could be seen in the previous week's mud-wrestling match at Oregon with a total of 33 punts lodged. Being the master of detail that he was, the coach still emphasized punting just as much as before, and it paid dividends. When the visitors had to punt, Ching Johnson, who was switched to right halfback from his normal QB slot, was a sensation in returning the ball but did make several fumbles, two of which he recovered. With the Beavers turning in such a strong performance on both sides of the punting game, this served as the only offset to the Varsity's atypical output in passing stats.

Royal Brougham in the *P-I* said it best in summing up the afternoon: "The Oregon Agricultural College eleven fell an easy victim before Dobie's champions in a contest which opened like a championship affair and ended in a rout." On a dry field under blue skies, Pipal would have been expected to air out the ball but instead opted to punt repeatedly, often on first and second down. The visitors registered only one first down for the entire game. This came on a 35-yard pass play that brought the crowd to their feet but went no further. Their only scoring threats resulted from Washington's two near-disaster interceptions. One was by Captain Bissett, who brought the ball to the 8-yard line. From there the Beavers lost ground and were forced to attempt a dropkick from the 18, which fell short. The other interception was brought down by left halfback Lowe, who picked up 30 yards but was taken down an eyelash from the goal. The Varsity stiffened and held the Beavers, forcing a short dropkick attempt by left tackle

McNeil that went wide. For the first three quarters, such inconsistency was the rule on both sides of the line. Fumbling and interceptions plagued both teams, making the game less than exciting for the seven thousand fans in the stands.

Only one score was made in the first half, and this was a result of the lone sustained drive of the day. The converted end Ernest Murphy at quarterback scored the TD on a short line buck after a steady march from midfield, mostly by Ching Johnson and Cy Noble. The second and third periods were scoreless, and the game was still in reach for the Beavers at the opening of the fourth period. But here the roof caved in. It didn't help the cause that captain Bissett exited the game in the fourth quarter with an injury, he being the anchor of the OSU defense. The Beaver line was the reason the game had been in check all afternoon. The first of the four touchdowns in the last quarter were carryovers of two blocked punts before the first half ended, one by right guard Julius Calkins and the other by right end Don Abel. With only a yard for the TD, Murphy muscled the ball over for his third six-pointer.

With the score 18-0, Dobie brought in six substitutes. This didn't alter his team's facility for defense against the punt, as two more were blocked, leading to the final score. The first blocked kick was launched from Oregon State's 5-yard line. Noble took the ball in for the score from scrimmage. Late in the game another kick was blocked at the visitor's 25-yard line. David Logg, replacing Noble, brought the leather across the goal line for the fifth touchdown of the day. Ted Faulk (left end) completed four of the extra-point kicks, and Vic Morrison (right tackle) made one.

With the long trip in store to Berkeley for the next week's game, injuries to right end George Smith and David Logg, newly installed in the backfield, were worrisome. It wasn't the prettiest game ever executed by Washington, but despite much adversity they held Oregon State scoreless. Final score: Washington 35, Oregon State 0.

### University of California, at Berkeley

Yell king Herrick asked for the rooters to "talk football, think football, eat football. California exists only to defeat Washington. If we are not careful they will defeat us through loyalty and enthusiasm. We have won so often that we do not realize that today we are facing possible and imminent defeat." After the many years that California played rugby, the university decided this was the year to let the world know they were a force to be reckoned with. The route to prominence went through Seattle, and the school put up the shocking sum of $12,000 in salaries to hire the best coaches available. This got national attention and was played up in the press as a revenge move over the two defeats of last year. The 72-0 score, deemed scandalous in Berkeley, called for drastic action. California assembled a staff of experts to focus on every aspect of the game. Newly hired Head Coach Andy Smith came with seven years' experience at Pennsylvania and Purdue. Three-year All-American fullback and last year's captain Eddie Mahan was brought in from Harvard to coach the backfield and kicking game. A. B. "Gus" Ziegler, three-year All-American interior lineman who played at Pennsylvania and coached at Michigan, was placed in charge of the line. Charles R. Volz, trainer, had prior hospital experience and was termed the "best trainer on the coast." Washington loyalists would brand such a claim as outrageous, since Dr. David C. Hall's performance had long since laid to rest any other claim to this title.

The scouting reports noted that Mahan introduced a great many Harvard-type trick plays into the Bears' arsenal. A threatening omen was the Bears' improving passing game, coming as it did in a year when defense against the pass was a glaring weakness for the Purple and Gold. The southerners walloped St. Mary's, 48-6, and won over USC, 27-0. The northwest remained the stronghold for West Coast football, with Oregon beating California 39-14. But with the two losses for California from last year coming at the hands of Washington, there was no mistaking that this was the game of the year for both teams. Since Washington didn't have an official mascot, Bay Area sportswriters would alternately refer to the northwest team as the "Indians" or the "Siwash." There was some relevance to this tag, however unofficial, as the first genuine team yell composed by Asa Lee Willard prior to 1900 was inspired by "Chinook Indian jargon." No matter the name, pregame publicity had this one billed as the Big Game, with a crowd anticipated to be the largest crowd to view an athletic contest at the school.

At their Friday practice at the California field, Dobie's team was met with an army of reporters and press photographers lined up nearly half the length of the sidelines. They clamored for several poses of each player and coach. Dobie usually tried to limit such distractions but allowed this local showering of attention for the team before he got down to this light practice session.

Arthur Anderson, George Smith, and Ray Gardner were still injured and didn't make the trip south. However thin, this provided Dobie with an excuse for his dreadful chances. Dobie didn't expect his team to come close. While this got widespread coverage since he hadn't lost a game in twelve years, his take wasn't getting a whole lot of support. Andy Smith would have none of the ridiculous claims of hopelessness being spread by Dobie. His big concern was not just that he would get beaten, but how his team would ever manage to keep the score down to respectable levels. For this he saw little hope.

That year the faculty put a stop to transporting a steamer full of fans to the Bay Area. By their view this came too close to the Oregon game to again lose so much study time. But there remained very strong interest on and off the campus. A crowd of thirty-four hundred came to University Field to hear telegrammed updates of the play-by-play. A freshman game was held on the field at the same time to keep interest up during lulls in the announcer's updates. Technology wasn't totally up to the challenge, as the crowd was misled by an announcement that Washington had scored two early touchdowns in the first quarter. This initial indicator that the Varsity may be on another tear was soon corrected, as it was announced by megaphone that the early score was actually much closer at 6-3. To ease the anxiety, at least their team was in the lead.

The teams played a defensive struggle in the first half with long gainers by both sides, but these would be offset by sizable losses that had the net effect of keeping most of the action in the middle of the field. California's play was remarkable in their attempt to confuse Washington by never lining up twice in the same way. The announcer called out wide end runs going for 40 and 50 yards and treacherous forward passes that could have decided the game for the Bears. But Washington's defense was up to the task. Cal Assistant Eddie Mahan concluded that it was Washington's stone wall interior line, anchored by right guard and Captain Seagrave, that won the game for the visitors. Only Captain Willis "Brud" Montgomery's field goal would account for California's scoring. On offense, Washington's most dependable source of yardage was, no surprise, up the middle, with fullback Bill Hainsworth being hailed as the most consistent ground gainer. Oddly, the *Oakland Tribune* heaped gushing praise on right halfback Cy Noble as being a "battering ram [who] made consistent gains," while the *Daily* stated that he met his "Waterloo nearly every time he attempted to carry the oval."

Ernest Murphy, who Dobie called the brains of the team, was again in the backfield and called signals. Dobie had questioned Murphy's play calling after the Oregon State game over decisions to pass right at the goal line and by taking the glory of carrying the ball over the goal line after other players had done the hard work of getting the ball in scoring range. This statement found its way to the press, which could mean that either Dobie was about to make a change or this was done as a psychological ploy to get his athlete to shape up. Dobie, of course, if he fully intended to remove a player from the lineup, never gave this to the press. He would not publicly embarrass a player whose game was falling short. His messages aimed at players through the press had only one purpose—the team was made up of eleven equals.

In the third quarter California was forced to punt from their own 10-yard line. Fullback Fred "Fritz" Brooks did the punting for the Blue and Gold, but the kick was blocked with the ball ending up on the 5-yard line. Hainsworth then ran the ball in from scrimmage for the touchdown, and Ted Faulk kicked the extra point. A new addition to the Berkeley squad pulled off one of the most exciting plays of the afternoon. QB George Hicks had played exceptionally well in the two games prior and earned a starting spot on the team. When he went out to receive a pass thrown by right halfback Fred Brooks, he was blocked and fell to the ground, but before he got up the ball arrived, with Hicks catching it for a 10-yard gain.

In postgame interviews "luck" was reported in the *Oakland Tribune* to having played a big part in the outcome. Andy Smith stated, "With the breaks we'd have won. That's no alibi but a plain fact." He was satisfied with his boys' individual play, but as a team they made some "bad bloomers." Both team captains stated that breaks that fell in Washington's favor could have made the difference in the game. Ever the enigma and always for some intended purpose, Dobie was his outspoken self. As the game ended he jumped up in excitement with a genuine sense of joy for the victory. However, he also attributed the win to luck and reported, "We had the breaks in our favor and but for these same breaks I would have had a beaten team." His statement to the team was restrained, at best, considering this was a win on the road played before a huge crowd, but oh so typical of Dobie. Washington 13, California 3.

# CHAPTER TWELVE

## *Kings, Presidents, and Statesmen—1916*

"Coach Dobie was satisfied with the performance of his men. The coach deserves more credit than anyone else for the victory. His team was not a team of stars, and Dobie worked wonders with his material. If the report that the tall Scott is leaving is true, his going will be regretted. He will leave with the greatest record ever hung up by a football coach in the history of the gridiron game."

*Royal Brougham, Post-Intelligencer, December 1, 1916*

On-campus intrigue, controversy, accusations, confusion, and much drama took place this week, threatening a cancellation of the California game on University Field. In the eye of the storm was Bill Grimm, who had a sterling reputation as the youngest of the famous Grimm brothers of Centralia. He followed in the footsteps of the great Huber "Polly" Grimm, captain of the 1910 team, and Warren "Wedge" Grimm, Flaherty Medal winner of 1909. The conflagration erupted over Bill Grimm's getting caught cheating on a history exam.

The *Daily* on Thursday, November 23, 1916, one week before the Thanksgiving Day Big Game, screamed out in a full-page banner headline for all the world: "PLAYERS MAY BE EXPELLED," with a second subhead, "DRASTIC ACTION FOLLOWS TEAM'S DECISION AT NOON," and a third subhead, "Coach Dobie May Be Dismissed By Board." The page one banner headline in the *Post-Intelligencer* was just as dramatic: " 'U' FOOTBALL SQUAD GOES ON STRIKE"; second subhead, "SUSPENSION OF MEMBER IS RESENTED"; and third subhead, "Players Will Announce Their Decision Today." These were to announce the cascading events that followed the decision to suspend Grimm in an action by the student-run Board of Control from December 1, 1916 to December 1, 1917 which would allow him to play the Thanksgiving Day game. This recommendation was subsequently overruled by the faculty-run Athletic Committee to suspend him from November 20, 1916, to September 1, 1917, thus removing him from the California game on Thanksgiving. This was officially announced as a joint unanimous vote of the Board of Control and the Athletic Committee. By the faculty moving the suspension back from the end of next year's season to the beginning, this would allow Bill Grimm to play that year. This was a concession on the part of the faculty to gain acceptance of the students. The team felt they were being unfairly punished by taking a star out of a game for a matter they had nothing to do with. At noon in a meeting in Denny Hall, by secret ballot, the team voted 13-10 to go on strike (one player was absent who later voted with the majority). It was emphasized that this was a decision of the team that Coach Dobie had nothing to do with.

At that evening's practice, Dobie, Assistant Coach Sutton, and freshman squad coach Hap Miller all showed up. Dobie swore that it was his intention to be there for practice and that he would remain neutral and not put pressure on one side or the other. Three starters came out: Ben Mayfield, Bill Hainsworth, and Ted Faulk. Second-team players suiting up were Bob Abel, David Logg, Laurie Smith, and Malcolm Moran. In planning for the dismal eventuality that the others would not be joining the team, Dobie thought he could convert Ted Faulk from his end position to the backfield, but this effort failed.

To better understand just how this seemingly controllable affair could get so far out of hand as to threaten the biggest and most profitable game of the year, we need to first look at the rules governing the newly formed Pacific Coast Conference. This was its first year, and the stricter league rules were not always considered, nor were many fully aware that they even existed. If care had been taken to use these standards in making a ruling on the matter, the terrible disruptions and hard feelings that followed could have been avoided. These are the three rules that were germane to the matter before the school:

> <u>Article 1</u>. Each of the schools shall appoint an athletic committee to supervise and enforce rules regarding football and all intercollegiate athletics.

> <u>Article 7.</u> No athlete who is found by the faculty to be delinquent in his classroom work shall be permitted to play in any intercollegiate contests.

> <u>Article 8.</u> All games shall be played under student management exclusively.

As everyone knew, the Athletic Department in those days was run by the Associated Students organization and managed by a graduate manager. This highly charged mêlée was good preparation for current GM Arthur J. Younger, who later served in the U.S. House of Representatives from California for 1953 to 1957. A seven-member, student-run Board of Control functioned as the operating body. In their official review of the cheating infraction, they ruled 4-1 (two members were absent) that Grimm be suspended from all intercollegiate athletics from December 1, 1916, to December 1, 1917, allowing the star lineman to play in the big Turkey Day game.

Matters were further complicated by the absence of President Suzzallo, who was coming to the close of an extended tour of eastern universities. He was not due back until Tuesday, November 28, just two days before game day. He was only available by telegram, and this fact led to his misunderstanding of events and caused resentment among many of the students. The telegram that was sent to Suzzallo was incorrect in setting out the unfolding actions between the Board of Control and the faculty. The Board of Control was a body set up to investigate such matters and "suggest" punishment to the faculty. This interplay between student board and faculty is at the very heart of the confusion that followed, placing the game in jeopardy. Suzzallo was misled in the telegram in that it said Grimm was "declared ineligible for football by action of the Board of Control," without explaining that this was only after an action by the faculty to reverse the original decision of the students allowing him to play. The second and very damaging statement in the telegram stated that, "Team feels decision unjust, refuses to play Thanksgiving Game. Dobie with team." This leaves the obvious misimpression that the coach must have been a catalyst in the decision of the team to strike. It was reported in the press that Dobie's "sympathies were entirely with the team in their stand." Given this position of sympathy, the coach was on the side of his team but did not instigate the mutiny, which would have been reckless and unacceptable on his part.

An editorial in the *Daily* added fuel to the flames by correctly stating that the telegram to Suzzallo "gave no hint that the action of the Board of Control was overruled by the faculty." The editorial declared what most students and certainly the team members felt: that this was a matter for student self-government and shouldn't be overruled by faculty. This could be understandable, since the Athletic Department was a student-run organization. Before the founding of the current Pacific Coast Conference, these matters were not subjected to such careful scrutiny. Had the editorial writer referred back to the new league rules, he could easily see that the faculty was in control. A sober explanation of the lines of authority would have gone a long way towards reducing some of the heat that had built up. The Athletic Committee, under Article 1, was a faculty group and, in Washington's case, that year was headed by Dean A. R. Priest. The faculty's control in the matter was further augmented by Article 2 in disallowing any student to play who was "delinquent in his classroom work." Cooler heads did not prevail, and for two days chaos reigned.

Captain Seagrave was one of the team members who voted for the strike, and he was the primary team spokesman in advancing their grievances. Ernest Murphy was the other player who took a leading role in the talks. Seagrave and Murphy were the leaders of the movement to go on strike and later went on record declaring that Dobie had no complicity, whatsoever, in calling for the walkout. Murphy said that if Grimm were out of the game for any other reason, "we'd keep going till our tongues hung out." These efforts in no way were an attempt to take Grimm off the hook, and no apologies were given for his misconduct. The bone that stuck in the team's craw was their being punished as a team for something they had nothing to do with. At one point, Seagrave stated, "The matter of the supposed irregularity is something that does not affect the conference in the slightest degree and has no right in affecting the team." This statement would fly in the face of Article 2 of the new conference rules. Cheating on a test and thus not getting class credit would on its face disqualify a player. Further, in an open letter published on Thursday, November 23, by the joint committee of students and faculty, this point was laid out very clearly: "Our conference agreement would not permit us to play a man whom we should not wish to have played against us were the case reversed." If this fact was understood by the *Daily* editorial staff, Coach Dobie, the student protestors, and the striking team players, this whole nasty episode would never have happened.

There was one extenuating circumstance that cut in the favor of Dobie and the team. Grimm was one of the players called up for duty on the National Guard and did his military exercises at the camp set up at American Lake. This placed a severe strain on students, as guard duty took them out of class for three weeks. Dobie was able to obtain a car to transport his players to practice, and early on Dr. Suzzallo stated that it was his wish that guardsmen be given every consideration in making up their studies. Dobie and the team felt that this "wish" had not been acted on, and that professors were not allowing guardsmen time for "making up their studies," as Suzzallo's directive had authorized. The distance factor added greater pressures to the affected players. This is certainly a valid issue in that the highest-ranking authority at the university had taken this position, but it didn't seem to be acted on at the very place where needed—at test-taking time in the classroom. It's fair to question whether Grimm or his professor had discussed any special consideration and whether or not the student had been given some leeway. It is also fair to ask whether Suzzallo had taken sufficient effort to make the faculty fully aware of the need for special consideration to guardsmen. Judging by the action of the faculty in suspending Grimm for the game, it appears that this was not the case. If so, it would seem that some reference to this effect would have been made in their official announcement of the suspension.

There was talk that Washington would play the game if the players did not return. Even if it became necessary to cobble a team together from class intramural squads, Dobie, Student Body President Walt Shiel, and school officials were prepared to face the Golden Bears. There certainly was a matter of honor at stake, and the school didn't want to suffer the embarrassment of canceling a game of this magnitude. Of no minor concern was the very real issue of the $2,000 guarantee of expenses committed to the opposing team. If the game had to be cancelled after California made the long trip up the coast, this would place a huge strain on the ASUW budget.

The fourteen team members who signed on to the protest met with Dean A. R. Priest one at a time at noon in the president's office on Thursday, November 23. He carefully explained the gravity of their action should they not proceed with the game. In this meeting, the team held steadfast with their earlier pledge that they would not be suiting up for the game. Priest gave them a deadline of 9:00 that evening to officially notify him if this was to be final.

This was a busy day of buttonholing and immense pressure by all factions, including an impressive turnout of respected alumni. Former captain "Wee" Coyle from Dobie's inaugural team, Senator Ralph Nichols, former Graduate Manager and now State Representative Victor Zednick, and many others met with the players at 8:00 p.m. to aggressively lobby the team to end their walkout. The alumni ad hoc committee earlier in a downtown meeting had passed a resolution and presented this to the team with their request that the men return to practice. Bill Grimm himself spoke one on one to the fourteen strikers, pleading with them to remember the greater good, forget about him, and go out on the field and play the game. The College Club submitted a letter of resolution urging that the players change their position and return to the practice field. The final document presented to the players was the telegram dated November 23, from President Suzzallo:

"The honor and courage of the student board of control is superb. Glad faculty and administration have sustained them. Do not permit Grimm to play under any circumstances. The team is not a bunch of individuals, but a set of representatives. It must keep the university honor by complete fulfillment of the agreement with California."

HENRY SUZZALLO

The magnitude of support for the team coming from so many sides as it finally did was conclusive. The players decided to reverse their stand and take the field. Captain Seagrave, who was the first to volunteer to turn out, spoke of this having unified the team as never before. Picking up on the call to honor that was heard in both the statement of the Board of Control and President Suzzallo's telegram, he also advanced honor as being the team's justification in making this reversal. Seagrave stressed that their position on the action of the faculty to bar Grimm was unchanged. The team still felt that it was being punished because of something it had nothing to do with.

Dean Priest gleefully accepted the team's decision, even though it was delivered at 10:30, well past his deadline of 9:00. He said he expected all along that this is what they would do. Either he had lost faith in human nature or he was attempting to flatter by telling the team that this had restored his faith in the student body. It remained to be seen as just how well the team could do after this harrowing two days of roller-coaster emotions.

No practice, skipped meals, loss of sleep, and pressure heaped on from all quarters could take its toll.

The team's statement to the faculty, signed by every player, laid everything on the line as to their displeasure with the faculty's decision. Honor and duty to the students, alumni, and public served as the basis for their willingness to set aside the principle behind their original stance. There were two critical declarations placed in the document that must be examined in light of events that would soon unfold between Coach Dobie and President Suzzallo. Quoting from "The Team's Statement to Faculty" as it appeared in all reports of the press:

Statement that Coach Dobie had nothing to do with the strike: "It was the uncoerced action of the individuals of the squad, to which Coach Dobie was not a party."

Statement on President Suzzallo's absence: "The absence of President Suzzallo from the campus, whose presence we believe would have prevented the deplorable situation now brought to an end, has impelled us to overlook for the present the narrow-minded position of the faculty."

Though all were haggard and weary from the week's crisis, there was still a game to be played. They were already weakened by injuries to Gardner, Anderson, George Smith, and Mayfield, and now with Grimm's absence, together with starters Bud Young and Ross MacKechnie having pulled out at the season's opening, Dobie went into this game with less than half his starters at the beginning of the season. This was the varsity's fourth game in four successive weeks with two long trips involved. Missing two days of practice was not something that the coach could easily deal with, considering his meticulous and exacting game preparations. Observers of the time steeled themselves for gloom, foreboding, and the darkest of the dark projection for that week's game—particularly considering that California had a strong team much less impacted by injury than Washington's. The pregame opinion of the *Seattle Star* was accurate in summing up the Golden Bears: "A better looking bunch of athletes than the 21 members of the California crew that arrived from the south last night would be hard to find. The boys were in an altogether different spirit than the stage-frightened squad that came north last year to do battle with the local gridiron warriors." If anyone would ever have to agree with the dour Scot's forecast for calamity, this was the time. Who could argue that a reasonable review of all the things going against the Purple and Gold could only spell disaster?

The football world was set on its ear with Dobie's prediction for this, his sixty-second game over nine years at Washington: "We should win." At this time the "football world" had not taken into account Dobie's predictably contrarian positions at times like this. As we have seen, when all evidence points to a rough road ahead, he backs off from the gloom and lets the gloomy press do his work for him. Rather than acting out of character, as was widely reported at the time, according to the bible of standard practices as preached by Gil Dobie, this fell right in line with his belief system.

Even casual followers of the sport knew of Dobie's remarkable winning streak and his spotless record for often predicting catastrophe. There undoubtedly were legions reading this headline who thought this must be a misprint. Surely this had to be the quote of opposing Coach Andy Smith predicting the Bears' victory! Actually, Smith also predicted a win for Washington. In analyzing the tumultuous events leading up to the Turkey Day game and the fact that sportswriters and fans were just about unanimous in their negative assessment of the northerners' chances, we see just why the leopard changed his spots periodically over nine years. This was entirely consistent with how Dobie actually functioned. The attitude was unanimous from everyone close to him that he was smart and a master at the art of psychology. One of his favorite ploys was to get his players to focus their anger on him and get them into a mind-set that "I'll prove it to this pessimist that we can win." Here is the very best example of Dobie as master manipulator. This event offers a clear expression of his genius for sizing up a situation and getting his men hyped up to do battle. The whole world seemed to be doubters, so Dobie threw his arms around the team to build their fighting spirit. They didn't have to focus their anger on the coach, but just prove to the skeptics they didn't know what they were talking about.

### University of California

As the Thanksgiving game approached, there were no signs that the closed society of Dobie's day was opening up. A very talented African American tackle for California, Walter Gordon, was a starter for this game. He was described in the *Seattle Star* as being a "giant negroe" and to have size and weight to his advantage. Checking his stats in the game program, he was listed as 6 feet 2 inches, weighing 174 pounds. The reporter claiming him to be a giant was taking considerable license, as he actually weighed less than the average for the Bears' interior linemen. The game-day newspaper lineup showed that this so-called giant was the lightest interior lineman for either team, leaving one to conclude that every player must be a giant. It was announced in the Short Sport section of the *Daily* that "Washington fans will be treated to a novelty in college football…Gordon, right tackle for the Bears is colored, and is one of the few negroes playing big college football in the country." This would be the first time that a black player had played at University Field, and it would go unopposed by observers that such an event would be downgraded to mere "novelty" status. As we look back, this was an event to be celebrated, but as history shows, such a time was still decades away.

On the women's front there also weren't any signs of movement. Despite the state of Washington being well ahead of the national curve, having approved women's suffrage in 1910, societal standing still had a long way to go. Miss Ethel Hundley Coldwell, dean of women, made it abundantly clear that women were only to attend the football parade as spectators. She wanted women to uphold her desire "that they not be subjected to such publicity as a public spectacle of this sort would entail." This despite the fact that the men were now showing maturity in toning down what many considered their somewhat juvenile antics. The long-standing practice was to dress up as babies and men in drag (representing opposing players) as a means of mocking their manhood. Yell king Barrett Herrick announced that there would be no weird costumes or makeup or shirttail effects in this year's parade. Women were further marginalized repeatedly as being "feminine" and thus incapable of understanding a man's sport such as football. The *Daily*, just the day before the contest, clarified women's knowledge of the game in this condescending offering: "The feminine contingent may lack the technical knowledge, but it has enthusiasm to spare. In fact, a girl will scream her head off and jump up and down in ecstasy and then when the hubbub is over and the grandstand settled to its normal state of watchful waiting, she will turn to a sister and say, 'What happened?' " But, of course, she was handicapped in figuring out what was going on. We must remember that the young damsel was in the segregated "women's only" section of the stands and there wasn't a convenient, all-knowing, manly man around to assist.

Additional stands were set up and two thousand sideline, standing-only tickets were sold to accommodate the largest crowd to date at University Field. The nine thousand fans in attendance were treated to identifying player numbers, three announcers on megaphones, and upgrades to the scoreboard. The newly built scoreboard included a large clock at the top displaying the minutes remaining in the quarter, under that the number of the down and the yards to go, and the score at the bottom. It sounds rudimentary, but previous to this the down marker on the field hadn't shown the number of the down. For this game a new design was introduced with a box at the top of the staff, with each down shown in sequence. For those who got to the game early, fans enjoyed the added attraction of a 50-yard dash with a $10 wager attached between referee George Varnell and Plowden Stott. "Swagger sticks," as they were called, were created for one thousand women to carry to display the Purple and Gold. The women's rally committee instituted the tradition at Washington and reported that this design, which they created was an innovation on college campuses. Others had obviously worn their college colors, but this design was original, consisting of a pennant cane cut in half with purple and gold ribbons attached on the end, creating the forerunner to modern pom-poms. At this last game of Gil Dobie's at Washington, pom-poms were introduced to football.

**THE LINEUPS**

| No. | California | | Position | No. | Washington | |
|---|---|---|---|---|---|---|
| 5 | Willis "Brud" Montgomery | wt.171 | R.E.L. | 11 | Ted Faulk | wt.168 |
| 20 | Walter Gordon | wt.174 | R.T.L. | 34 | Ben Tidball | wt.180 |
| 10 | Claude Monlux | wt.190 | R.G.L | 14 | Julius Calkins | wt. 180 |
| 6 | Bill Russell | wt.176 | Center | 4 | "Sandy" Wick | wt.175 |
| 31 | Charles Bell | wt.185 | L.G.R. | 24 | Captain Louis Seagrave | wt.185 |
| 11 | "Midge" Madison | wt.201 | L.T.R | 20 | Clarence "Vic" Morrison | wt.186 |
| 7 | Douglas "Dug" Cohen | wt.154 | L.E.R. | 24 | Don Abel | wt. 165 |
| - | George Hicks | wt.152 | QB | 29 | Clark "Ching" Johnson | wt.174 |
| 3 | LeRoy Sharp | wt.148 | L.H.R | 26 | Ernest "Tramp" Murphy | wt.180 |
| 22 | Daniel "Danny" Foster | wt.175 | FB | 25 | Bill Hainsworth | wt.170 |
| 1 | Fred Brooks | wt.176 | R.H.L | 27 | Elmer "Cy" Noble | wt.170 |

Royal Brougham supplied this account of the matchup. "At the onset of the game and then again near the close, the boys from the golden state furnished the spectators with the unusual spectacle of a Washington team being outplayed. But without a doubt the best team won." California came into Seattle with the reputation as a master of the open style of play with a heavy dependence on passing. LeRoy Sharpe, the lightest man on the field at 148 pounds, kept Cal in the game with his brilliant open-field running. Dobie had just played them the week before, and despite the fact that his players were familiar with the Bears' style, he focused the shortened practice time he had on defense against the pass. It worked, as the varsity totally shut down the southerners' passing game. Washington's offensive game plan was classic

Dobie football: use a small number of plays, but execute with perfection and run the ball up the middle. The strategy was to gain shorter yardage but wear down the defense in the process.

The missing Bill Grimm had Washington loyalists on edge. It was bad enough that the team was short of practice time and their every move was being microanalyzed by an army of reporters from Berkeley to Seattle, but missing an anchor of their interior line was just too much to handle. With Seagrave holding down the right front and Grimm the left, this formed the nucleus of a line that had allowed but one breach of their goal all year. Fans were in heated exchanges over just who could fill the giant void left by Grimm's absence. Dobie settled the locals' anxiety with the choice of journeyman Vic Morrison, who was tagged to play both his normal left guard position on defense and assume Grimm's role on offense at right tackle. He did have some past experience at this tackle slot, so Dobie's choice was well founded. Julius Calkins, who was a bit lighter than Morrison, was picked to switch with his teammate when the ball changed hands.

It was a beautiful, dry, fall day which favored the faster Cal squad over UW's slower line-plunging collection. The visitors kicked off to the Varsity, who soon gave up the ball without making a first down. Known for his booming punts, Vic Morrison, with the weight of the world (and the Bill Grimm affair) on his shoulders, could only manage a trifling boot. The Golden Bears, given this gift of field position on their first play, a fake placekick, put the ball on the 20-yard line. On only their second play, with less than two minutes off the clock, they made another first down, advancing the ball to the 10 before the home crowd even settled into their seats. With a score seeming a certainty, Cal tried a pass over the middle of the line that was picked off by Ching Johnson. Washington still wasn't able to move the ball after this returned favor and had to punt again. The locals did collect themselves from this rugged start and, on this third try, were finally able to establish a ball-control game with line smashes up the middle. Noble, Hainsworth, Johnson, and Murphy all made solid contributions but couldn't score in the first half. California was less successful in moving the ball on the ground, but since the Varsity was only marginally better, this didn't cost the visitors. Left halfback LeRoy Sharp made their only first down by way of a line plunge, all of the others coming through the air.

In the second half the Bears continued to show multiple offenses, changing their lineups on almost every play as they had done the week before. The ends substituted often, and the backs and linesmen interchanged in an effort to confuse the defense. The passing game showed moments of brilliance interspersed with bad decisions allowing UW to step in front of Cal receivers. The team had progressed greatly over their 1915 blowout at the hands of Washington but Dobie's men showed that his meticulous emphasis on fundamentals accounted for their thin margin of superiority over this quicker eleven.

It was well into the third period before Washington got on the scoreboard. All of the backs were still effective, with unheralded Bill Hainsworth at fullback delivering the strongest performance. A fumble stopped this momentum, but when Washington got the ball back they were not rattled by the miscue and continued with strong gains right at the heart of Cal's line. A short pass from Cy Noble to left end Ted Faulk positioned the ball on the 20-yard line. First blood came on the best run of the day for the Varsity by QB Ching Johnson, who made a diagonal run across the field for the 20 yards to paydirt. In getting to the final chalk line, he fought off two tacklers upfield, and when he got to the goal line he was greeted by the ever-dangerous LeRoy Sharp. With his 26-pound weight advantage, which meant a great deal more in that day of much lighter players, the heavier Johnson won the battle for the score. Ted Faulk kicked the extra point to put the home team up 7-0.

Washington's second score came in the fourth quarter, set up by an intercepted pass by center Sandy Wick, who broke the hearts of hopeful Bears' fans by returning the ball to Cal's 20-yard line. Not the most original game plan ever developed by Dobie, but since the off-tackle line buck was working so well, he used his old standby to fight down to the 6-yard line. With everyone in the stadium and on the field expecting a run up the middle for the attempted score, they were all fooled with what Royal Brougham described as a "pretty forward pass Noble to Faulk" that put six more points on the board. It seems all too ironic for a team who had built their national reputation primarily by the run to win their last game on a pass play. Faulk also kicked the extra point, bringing the score to 14-0 for Washington.

If MVPs were selected in 1916, the smallest man on the team, California's LeRoy Sharp, would have won the honor without question. In the fourth quarter he took control of the game. On a punt by Sharp, he delivered a boot that rolled to Washington's 1-yard line. Since they held the lead, Washington wanted to take no chances and kicked the ball away, but on a terrific runback by the multi-talented Sharp, dodging tacklers all the while, he finessed his way to UW's 20-yard line. This one-man team then completed a pass to Captain Brud Montgomery, right end. The ball was now inside the 5-yard line on first down. On fourth down fullback "Dummy" Wells, in as a substitute for starter Danny Foster, plunged up the middle for the touchdown. Adding further to this game's reverse logic, Coach Andy Smith, who built his game around the pass, scored their only touchdown on an off-tackle line buck more fitting in Washington's playbook. Captain Montgomery kicked the final extra point of the game. Out of respect for the incredible football clinic put on by Sharp, the Washington crowd carried him off the field on their shoulders. Young boys mobbed him, anxious to meet a real hero.

Leading up to the game Dobie was shorthanded which greatly contributed to this as being one of the hardest fought games of his career. He had a team under stress from the past week's off-the-field drama and a terrible injury count in this hard fought contest placed an additional strain on his coaching skills. Murphy, in the first minutes of the game, suffered a severe gash to the head but returned and played out the game. Seagrave sprained his ankle and limped for a while and also returned. Morrison was laid out twice and, when his head cleared, returned. Only Hainsworth, who dislocated his wrist, had to leave the game for good. His replacement, a Canadian, Erroll "Sam" Briggs (#19), broke his nose. This guy was tough, staying in the game and later, in the locker room, laughing as the team doctor pulled the nose back into place. On the California side, Fred Brooks took a hit to the midsection in a collision with Hainsworth but finished the game. Late in the contest, Walter Gordon had to limp off the field. The players' strike took a toll on the Varsity's psyche, but considering how the drama played out and given Dobie's signal that they would win despite the dopesters predicting their demise, the scale tilted in Washington's favor. In a postgame interview the coach paid high tribute to the team for the win and their toughness in fighting through the heavy number of injuries they suffered.

Museum of History and Industry          Washington vs. California, University Field, Thanksgiving Game, Nov. 30, 1916

Dobie in his overcoat and hat is standing on the sidelines on the yardage marker, adjacent to the play, to gain the best view of the action of his men on the field. This would be his last game at Washington. This was the sixty-second game he coached in his nine-year undefeated run.

As the game ended, the field was flooded with wildly celebratory fans. This time Dobie enjoyed that he was being recognized by the appreciative undergraduates, who hoisted him on their shoulders. *Post-Intelligencer* sports reporter Conrad Drevick described the scene: "When they set him down on the steps of the gym, and roared their tribute, he took off his hat, waved it, and smiled and bowed in evident pleasure." The fans were demanding a speech, and as he said "Good-bye, boys, good-bye, boys," they wouldn't hear of this as they drowned him out. The players were equally appreciative of the football magician's work as they slapped him on the back and pushed him back into the crowd and also demanded a speech. With this he again tipped his hat and scrambled into the locker room.

This game served as a perfect bookend to Dobie's sixty-two-game career at Washington. It ended as it started. His 1908 early season was replete with huge coaching challenges, just as he faced in closing out the 1916 season. This year both Oregon and Washington went undefeated, but since the southern team had an ineligible man who played in two games, the first Pacific Coast Conference championship was awarded to Washington. Since Washington was still a member of the original Northwest Conference, they were also declared champions of that league.

As he closed out his Washington coaching term, he was being loudly praised across the land. Tom Thorp, sports reporter for the *Boston Morning Post*, placed him as his pick for number one in the nation: "By again proving the most formidable aggregation on the coast, Dobie's team earns the right to be classed with the best." He had it as a four-way tie for the top spot with Washington, Army, Pittsburgh, and Ohio State. Rounding out his next five slots were (2) Colgate, (3) Brown, (4) Yale, and (5) Harvard. In a flattering article wrapping up the season, the *New York Times* stated, "No football coach in the world has such a record as Gilmour Dobie." An article by H. C. Hamilton, a reporter for United Press International, was also lobbying to include Dobie in the company of his favorites at the top of the football world: Pittsburgh, Colgate, Brown, and Army. "Dobie's record stands as the most imposing in American football records. It would do the eastern eleven credit to do homage to such a football team while they rest from their own squabbles." It was with this background on the national stage that Dobie achieved the win over California, completing the remarkable record of sixty-two games with no defeats. Final score: Washington 14, California 7.

## The Undefeated Coach Leaves Washington

Coach Dobie's professional career was marked with spectacularly controversial events. For downright Shakespearean high drama, nothing can beat his departure from Washington. As if the team walkout over the cheating scandal wasn't exhausting enough, what was to follow elevated passions to even loftier heights. It should again be noted that the operational body of intercollegiate sports was the Student Board of Control. There were two sharply contrasting opinions as to their proper role in selecting a coach. Many felt that they should have a stronger voice in hiring, with others of the opinion that the faculty Athletic Committee should have total control. No matter what the feelings, the actual structure as was made clear in the Bill Grimm affair: the board "recommends" to the committee chaired by Dean A. R. Priest. It certainly was expected that the student board, at a minimum, would hold a formal meeting and vote, with this tally submitted through channels to the faculty for their decision. This was not done and became the central contributing factor setting off another campuswide firestorm.

When President Suzzallo returned to the campus, he studied the issues of the Bill Grimm firing. Having been gone, he was at a decided disadvantage in evaluating and weighing the evidence of all parties. These were: (1) the faction who held the archaic notion that there should only be student "player coaches" and no professionals (Dobie's contract became null and void if the conference did away with professional coaching); (2) members of the faculty who represented both pro and con positions on Dobie; (3) Bill Grimm's history professor from the class where the cheating incident occurred; (4) Bill Grimm; (5) the football team; (6) student leadership; (7) alumni leadership; (8) the Student Board of Control; (9) the Faculty Athletic Committee; and (10) Coach Dobie.

Since the Thanksgiving holiday intervened, and also since Dr. Suzzallo was reported to be recovering from his long trip, there wasn't sufficient time for either interviews with these parties or time to do a thorough investigation. Mrs. Suzzallo had also fallen ill, which understandably took the president away from his job in tending to her needs. Events moved at a rapid pace considering the little time between Suzzallo's return and his decision to dismiss Dobie and issue his public statement to this effect late on the evening of December 8, 1916. Given that Suzzallo had a busy catch-up schedule after having been gone for several weeks, this was only one of the matters facing him upon his return to Seattle on Tuesday, November 28. There were only nine calendar days (interrupted by Thanksgiving and the weekend) and four business days to vet this issue, Monday, December 4, through Thursday, December 7. Considering that there were ten parties, as noted above, who had legitimate reason to voice an opinion in a fair hearing, this short timeline did not allow for that.

Suzzallo held a conference with Coach Dobie, Captain Seagrave, and faculty members. This leaves seven other parties who should have been heard. A "conference" falls far short of the proper forum to get to the bottom of this critical matter. Both conferences and public hearings are what were called for. In this one conference, Captain Seagrave assumed responsibility for the team's actions and clarified that the strike did not originate with Dobie. Dobie reiterated that he had no part in instigating the strike but that he did stand by the men in their action. Dobie himself did not go on strike, as he and Assistant Coach Wayne Sutton held practice for those team members who showed up.

Suzzallo was sending out conflicting signals as to his leanings. On Wednesday, December 6, Royal Brougham reported in the *Post-Intelligencer,* "Dr. Suzzallo declared that the coach matter rested with the student board and Dobie himself." It was universally known across Seattle that the student board was in favor of keeping the coach, so this appeared to be a signal that Suzzallo was also favorably disposed. The next night a closed joint meeting was held by the Board of Control and the Faculty Athletic Committee. Two shocking matters occurred regarding this meeting, Suzzallo did not attend, and the Student Board of Control did not have an opportunity to submit a formal declaration of their recommendation. This clearly would have been in support of Dobie's rehiring. These are the only sanctioned bodies that have standing in the rehiring of the coach.

E. B. Stevens, Suzzallo's secretary who was in attendance at this meeting, made a statement that night which made it clear that Dobie's fate was already sealed. "The president deemed that Dobie's maturer judgment should have prevailed when the boys went on their strike, and that instead of upholding the players, he should have upheld the university." The question can be asked as to what purpose was served by calling a meeting between the official bodies authorized to take action on hires and rehires if the decision had already been sealed. Without allowing the joint body to respond through proper channels, Suzzallo took matters into his own hands rather than risk a contrary vote. Further evidence that the fix was in is supported by the fact that in this joint meeting, the Board of Control was not allowed to make a recommendation as its charter allowed. A decision to not allow the students' voice to be heard could only come from the president, who took the matter out of the faculty's hands. Remembering that the Athletic Department in this time was run by the students, this was a sensitive and volatile matter that the faculty committee would not dare make on their own unless they had the weight of the president's office behind them. We can see that Suzzallo's mind was made up. This placed the faculty between the proverbial rock and a hard place. If they went against the president, their jobs and/or promotions could be at risk. If they went against the students, as they did, they only risked the enmity of the majority of the student body, the alumni, and the downtown business community. A veritable no-brainer.

The signals were clear that Suzzallo had already made an intractable decision to terminate the coach. There was no consideration of allowing a hearing with his strong feelings being so firmly entrenched. Suzzallo had every right as president of the university to relieve Dobie of his duties. The events show that whether you agree with his decision or not, he miserably botched the handling of the process. He had just returned from a grueling fact-finding academic mission to gather useful ideas from eastern universities that he could implement at Washington—a laudable goal, and certainly more important than the football program. He was anxious to begin downloading these ideas to his faculty and the university community. To do otherwise he would have been derelict in administering his duties. There was no mistaking that this was a man of immense talent. He saw a clear course as to how he wanted to advance the institution, and with the tools he gathered in his exhaustive study of cutting-edge ideas, he was now ready to implement it.

There was one nagging problem standing in his way of launching his master plan for the future: Coach Gilmour Dobie. Dobie and Suzzallo were both charismatic, demanding leaders, of strong wills and strong personalities. Much has been written of the clash between these two. There are suggestions that Suzzallo resented the national press that Dobie received for his remarkable record. It could be galling for Dobie and the football program to receive so much public attention when Suzzallo's work was of greater importance. Both men deserved recognition for their accomplishments but football commanded the headlines, then as now. In these early days of collegiate sports, the mushrooming trend of reverence to college sports and academicians' consequent resentment of the large salaries paid to better coaches was much more than today. During Dobie's time, nonprofessional player coaches were still in existence. At Washington this was the case in basketball. Professors in 1916 were often outspoken against these overpaid newcomer upstarts who were hogging the spotlight.

In an interview I held in 2010 with Tom Morrison, the son of Dobie's talented interior lineman and punter Clarence "Vic" Morrison, he shed some light on what this firsthand witness of the time had to say. Tom reports that his father was quite outspoken in holding the opinion that Dr. Suzzallo was jealous of Dobie's star power and that he seized on this opportunity to unfairly eliminate the one person on campus that was getting more acclaim than he could garner. This was Dobie's ninth year as campus hero and only the second in Suzzallo's tour of duty, so it is understandable that the president could opt for such a chance to remove this thorn in his side. Football season had ended, and for added cover he had the benefit of the unseemly brouhaha over the Grimm affair.

Could Suzzallo have been one of the academics who harbored resentment toward professional coaches? He attended college in the late 1890s when player coaches were commonplace, so he was definitely aware of the developing movement that eventually supplanted them for professionals. The Gil Dobie episode was a forerunner to another inelegantly handled personnel matter by Suzzallo that followed not long thereafter during World War I. He later removed Professor H. L. Meisnest, as head of the German Department, who differed with him over the United States' entry into the war.

Most definitely Suzzallo was excited about getting back to his focus of implementing his vision for the university. Dobie's star status was a reality and being wary of this is understandable; or he may have felt that Dobie's transgression left him no alternative except termination. Despite evidence showing the matter was handled in haste, he did have a big job ahead of him on the academic side. The university was indeed a tiny place for two titans of such enormous professional stature. Driving more faculty to oppose Dobie was undoubtedly advanced when the players, in agreeing to break the strike, took a shot at the faculty committee calling their decision "the narrow minded position of the faculty." These were fighting words and certainly insubordination regardless of the circumstances.

If Suzzallo had allowed a totally transparent process of review and followed all of the procedures as set out by the university in handling this matter, there would have been a satisfactory resolution to the controversy that everyone could accept since it would have been a hearing of all parties. In the end, the final decision prevails to which there must be acceptance. While Dobie's behavior in the strike was immature, the behavior of Suzzallo in the firing can be characterized as petulant and, by subverting policy, disingenuous. Both can be rightly criticized. But since Dobie was never awarded due process before the Athletic Committee through Suzzallo's clumsy interference, the weight of blame rests on Suzzallo. A coach who served nine years without defeat and received such national acclaim for his achievements deserved better.

Dobie had gotten a jump on the situation, issuing his statement several hours before Suzzallo's official announcement. This statement was reported in the *Post-Intelligencer* by Royal Brougham the afternoon of December 9, 1916: "I'm tired of the job, and have positively coached my last team. I have fought for Washington for nine years on the field but have met with too much opposition in my own university to consider another year of it. I'm through for good." It would seem that it was Dobie who was the first in taking action and quit before he was fired. By the time the coach made this statement, it was clear to him and everyone else that all indicators pointed towards his firing. The afternoon statement was a face-saving gesture and likely an agreement between the two sides in a vain attempt to make it appear that Dobie's leaving was independently arrived at by both. There should be no mistake about how this sorry episode ended: Dobie was indeed fired.

Suzzallo's statement was reported in the same article:

> "Mr. Dobie will not be with us next year. That is now final. The chief function of the university is to train character. Mr. Dobie failed to perform to his full share of that responsibility on the football field. Therefore we do not wish him to return next year.

> "It has become quite apparent that Mr. Dobie and I disagree as to the functions of a university coach. He has not accepted in practice the obligation to be a vigorous moral force as well as an excellent technical instructor. In such a disagreement it is natural that we cannot utilize Mr. Dobie. Every part of the university organization must cooperate toward one end, character building."

This statement can be criticized from many directions. Suzzallo could be seen as not exhibiting "character" by his roadblocking a full hearing and for short-circuiting the rehiring procedures after the process had been set in motion. He does not identify the "we" who do not wish him to return. The majority of the student body, the Student Board of Control, the alumni association, a number of the faculty, the downtown chamber of commerce, and the football team all strongly expressed their desire to have Dobie come back the next year. Royal Brougham, the most respected sports journalist in the city, made it clear as to where he came down on the issue:

> "Will Gilmour Dobie, the greatest football coach of all time, be lost to Washington?" The president claimed that he had support for the decision, but there were few around who expressed agreement with his statement. The vast majority took an opposite position and were emphatic in wanting Dobie to stay. It should be noted that it was just one year ago in his farewell speech on Dobie's aborted attempt to split with the university that Suzzallo gave such effusive praise to the coach. He drew a direct bridge between athletics and academics, and it was Dobie's "principles" that were to be his guide: "It would be my purpose to carry into the academic life of the institution the principles the invincible coach has used in his remarkable success on the gridiron."

The finality of this announcement cast a pall over both the city and especially the university. There existed widespread disbelief throughout the Northwest that a coach who for nine years had never lost a game could be summarily dismissed. Students and his players were Dobie's greatest advocates and took no time in expressing their support; it was at 2:00 on Saturday morning, only hours after Suzzallo's bombshell that three hundred of them marched to Dobie's house. Reported as an "early morning protestation of faith," it did have all the trappings of religious zealotry. They hooted and shouted until Dobie came out on his porch in his bathrobe. At his first sighting by the throng, even louder shouts broke out for several minutes. They quieted down only after Dobie was able to be heard above the earsplitting din as he launched into a brief, impromptu speech.

Dobie was visibly moved by such an immediate outpouring of support coming in the middle of the night. He told the crowd that nothing had touched him so much as their showing of support. He stated that this would take away much of the bitterness over the events of the past week. He told them, "I only came back on the personal solicitation of Dr. Suzzallo. This action on his part I cannot feel as deserving." Showing a bit of outreach to his neighbors and this being wintertime, he finally had to beg their forgiveness and return to bed. This only served to raise the volume right back where it started. There were loud shouts to "Fight 'em, Fight 'em, Dobie," college yells, and more shouts of adoration. With undoubted negative offerings from Dobie's neighbors, the crowd marched back to the campus, putting on another demonstration before finally breaking up.

Coach Dobie, in his response, obviously sought to give a full public airing of his thoughts. He went to great lengths to give his side of the story, issued on Saturday, December 9. Here is Dobie's explanation in his pull-no-punches response of how he felt he and the team were wronged:

"Yes, I am through as football coach at the University of Washington. And while my regret in severing these relations is most keen, my greater regret is that I could not have stepped out of the position I have held for nine years with a feeling that the greatest goodwill existed between myself and the head of the great university and his faculty associates.

"At this time I am torn between conflicting emotions. I do not feel that publicity can do the situation a bit of good: while on the other hand, there are thousands of University of Washington students and alumni and thousands of friends of the institution who have kindly interested themselves in the matter, that it seems they are entitled to know briefly what has happened to place me in this position.

"It is unfortunate for the state university that a football coach should be given a distinction totally out of proportion to the relative position he should occupy in the scheme of things. I am placed through no fault of my own, in the position of being a 'big issue,' when as a matter of fact I am not entitled to it. I didn't want it. I am sorry, very sorry, it has happened.

"Briefly as possible, I am going to sketch what has happened to provoke from Dr. Suzzallo, head of the university, a statement to the effect that, 'Dobie will not be with us next year. The chief function of the university is to train character. Mr. Dobie failed to perform to his full share of that responsibility on the football field. Therefore we do not wish him to return next year.'

"This statement of mine must be considered only as an explanation due to those who have gone so far as to favor me with a vote of approval, which took the form of a movement to have me retained at the institution as a football coach. I am not seeking a further approval. I am simply explaining, with the assurance that it will be the last and only word from me on the subject.

"The statement issued last Friday night by President Suzzallo was based on an investigation conducted by him into the incidents of a so-called 'strike' on the part of the football team on the eve of the Thanksgiving day game with California, a 'strike' caused by the removal of a member of the team from participation in that game, the removal directed by the student board of control and the faculty.

"The incident of that 'strike' and its ultimate outcome—the squad returning to the game—are too fresh in mind to repeat here.

"Now the position of the football coach in that 'strike' has never been in doubt. The coach was 'for the team.' That attitude has cost the coach a public reprimand, as bound up in the statement of President Suzzallo last night.

"And yet that reprimand, administered publicly, be it justified or not, I can bear with equanimity; for, I believe that my support of the 'strikers' was justified, and that a great good has been accomplished. I cannot believe but that the strike revealed that the football players hold a weapon of defense that can be used when, in the future, they are similarly attacked.

"I did not suggest or incite the rebellion against a faculty authority, but I did stand with the players when they rebelled. I did it with a full knowledge of the responsibility I had to assume. I knew at that time— and long before—that I could no longer work as football coach under the conditions with which I had been surrounded.

"I felt that the football team was being grossly wronged by robbing it of a member whom I had approved as the best man in the defensive scheme of the team's existence; robbed of his services on the eve of the season's crucial game; taken out ten days after he had been adjudged guilty of an offense against college ethics; taken out after he had been already allowed to participate in another football game subsequent to his conviction; eliminated without having committed any breach of conference eligibility.

"If I can do a service for the man or men who come after me by preventing the possibility of making the football team suffer at the whim and caprice of outsiders, then I will be perfectly willing to accept all the abuse they can heap upon me.

"That was my attitude expressed at the time I took my step and came out into the open in support of the position of the 'strikers.'

"Neither the members of the football squad nor myself ever approved of the alleged offense of the player who was removed; but he had been placed in the position of being obliged to crowd two months' work into one month's study. This was due to his national guard service on the border and at American Lake encampment.

"Had there been any faculty mercy the student-player would have been allowed to make up his studies during the holiday vacation; had there been any co-ordination of spirit between the faculty and the student body this young man would never have been 'put under the guns.

"If he committed an offense it was so that he could remain with the team. Would it have been just for the men for whom he was fighting not to have stood by him when he was trying to do as much for them?

"The truth of the whole matter, in a nutshell, is that there are men close to the athletic situation at the University of Washington, who realize, as I have realized for years, that the student body has become settled in its smug satisfaction that 'Washington can't be beaten in football.'

"It's fatal—such an attitude—to the good of college spirit. These athletic authorities have felt that a beating would be a good thing for the school. It should shake everybody up. And I felt just exactly as these men felt; but we were approaching it from different angles—a solution of this problem. I felt that a defeat would be effective; but I wanted it to come through the course of the fortunes of war."

GILMOUR DOBIE

The main theme of the students who weighed in on the state of affairs was overwhelmingly that Dobie didn't get a fair hearing. Members of the Student Board weren't shy about expressing their disgust in the *Daily*. The matter that got their dander up was their complaint of this being a rush to judgment. The checks and balances built into the system were there just to prevent what happened. In matters of the Board of Control, they had always been permitted to hold hearings. Animosity over this was made clear in a *Daily* editorial that they were disgusted with the state of affairs. In these times rarely would an editor be so bold as to write a veiled trashing of the university president and the institution he led, but the editorial team pulled no punches: "Jealousies, conceit, hatred, petty politics, hypocrisy, and false pride, all were overcome. And of all the institutions peculiar to student and university life, football is the only one that to this time has stood free from influences. Dobie is the cause." Quite an indictment of the goings-on around campus. There's no mistaking that this was directed at the head of the university. Engagement in such matters as this were not typical of women in 1916, but passions were so heated that Hazel Jones, a member of the Board of Control, spoke out for herself and other women. "He was not given a square deal. He was sincere in his stand and should have been given more consideration...I think that the girls as a body are strongly in favor of him and regret his leaving." In calling on a familiar cliché, she probably best summed up the views of the vast majority of fans and students: "We all make mistakes, and in this instance a mountain was made out of a molehill."

Wee Coyle, star quarterback from Dobie's first team, who was now a respected lawyer and businessman speaking on campus for a humanitarian event, boldly went off subject to get in a plug for Dobie. For his tribute he received a resounding ovation lasting several minutes from the large crowd. "The man who is about to leave our midst has developed more character, more manhood, than any other member of the faculty except our beloved Professor Meany." Since President Suzzallo, who was scheduled as the main speaker, was home with his sick wife, it's unknown whether Coyle would have included the "developed more character" reference had Suzzallo been present. This was a direct slap at the president for his accusation in his statement of the firing that Dobie did not do his share to "train character."

On a cold, rainy, Monday night, December 11, a second rally was held to pay tribute to the departing coach. The crowd was described in the *Post-Intelligencer* as one thousand and in the *Daily* as eight hundred. The estimated number of women was one hundred to one hundred fifty (Roberta Hindley stuck her neck out with the observation that "woman has come into her own"), and there were a reported thirty to fifty faculty. The street was overflowing to the sidewalks, blocking traffic; men climbed up utility poles for a better vantage, and the women gathered on the porch. When they arrived at Dobie's house on the 4700 block of Fourteenth Avenue Northeast (today University Avenue), it was Captain Seagrave, in the midst of a deafening roar from the crowd, who was able to draw the humbled coach to the door. He called the recently retired mentor "the master wizard of them all." Dobie didn't disappoint in his soaring tribute to the students:

> "Kings, presidents, and statesmen have been greatly honored, but I know that they could have felt no greater honor than the honor I feel has been bestowed on me tonight. It is much to know that you students believe in me and have believed in me for nine years. I have returned year after year feeling that I was wanted and appreciated by the students. It pleases me more than I can say to see this last expression of your loyalty."

The downpour didn't dampen the crowd's spirits. The yell leaders led the crowd in school fight songs, and supporters yelled out "We're with you, coach," and "Dobie, we'll get you back again." The crowd of enthusiasts quite obviously agreed with this sentiment but Dobie quickly held up his hand in rejecting the thought of ever returning. It was unmistakable to anyone not so swept up in the emotions of the moment that he was through at Washington. He quieted the crowd long enough to give his parting remarks, speaking less rhetorically than earlier (taken from reports in both the *Daily* and *P-I*):

"I stayed at the end of my first year because I felt at least that I had made good with you people. When I came I never expected to remain for any length of time. I kept staying because I felt that the men and the students appreciated my efforts. If I have succeeded to this extent, then I am satisfied. I never expect to be again connected with athletics officially in the University of Washington.

"Remember this, college work at the University of Washington is not what it should be. The spirit of the university lies largely in the hands of its faculty. Students here have been made suspicious. They have learned to look underneath the outward results for underlying influences and causes. This pettiness is the cause for poor college spirit at Washington.

"My advice to you is to take your stand for or against intercollegiate athletics and stay there. Do not allow the fostering of intercollegiate athletics and then place every possible obstacle in the way of those who participate in them. Be reasonable. Make the University of Washington a desirable place for a student to attend—not an undesirable one. I have been a hard master to these football boys, and I know that my men are not quitters or disposed to expect easy treatment at the hands of the faculty."

The cheering would not stop, and seeing this, Dobie said good-bye to his adoring followers, halted to take in the moment, smiled, and went back inside. The supportive throng couldn't bring themselves to disburse. It must have been evident to them that when they left Fourteenth Avenue that night, this would be their last direct contact with the much-admired coach. They took up the most fitting salute possible: the university fight song, "Bow Down To Washington," with its rousing chorus "Dobie, Dobie, pride of Washington." Their singing lasted long after the coach had gone back inside. This would be the last official tribute to him, as the song would soon be modified. Pride in the coach will last forever, but in that line of work careers are fleeting. His success at Washington proved to be the greatest of his long career and elevated him to national prominence. Writing at the time of his dismissal, the *New York Times* was broadcasting to eastern schools his remarkable achievement: "No football coach in the world has such a record as Gilmour Dobie." The coach, who was fired by President Suzzallo but never lost a game, would launch the concluding stage of his long professional life on the East Coast. His achievements at Washington, together with his outstanding record at Navy, Cornell, and Boston College, place him in the top echelon of football coaches in the history of the game. It is ironic that exactly ten years later, Suzzallo's controversial firing as president would match the student clamor and public uproar following Dobie's firing.

Dobie can be criticized for his brash action of not stepping in to stop the team's standoff. He had their respect, and if he had asked them to resume practice, they would follow. While his nonaction led to his ultimate downfall, if these circumstances were repeated, he would follow exactly the same course. Throughout his career he showed unwavering predictability in every characteristic of his personality. Two of these personality traits were evident in the soap opera that led to his dismissal: his unwillingness to back down when his mind was made up, and fierce loyalty where his players were concerned. This trait was supported by his good friend George Varnell: "He still was a fine fellow who would battle anyone in the cause of any member of his squad." This is exactly what he did. His strong will would never allow him to abridge his core beliefs. He demanded strict loyalty from his players, and in supporting Bill Grimm and the team, he returned it in kind. Doing otherwise was not an option.

The *Argus* sports section had for years praised Dobie, but at season's end the editorial section, in an article dripping with cynicism, took a sharply different stance. "President Suzzallo has gotten the idea into his head that the educational functions of the university are of vastly more importance than the football team. This error of judgment, while regrettable, is excusable." The editor conceded that the school's football success belonged to Coach Dobie but couldn't resist still another derisive shot—this time at the team's fans. "Coach Dobie, assisted by such material as he was able to gather from the rolls of the University, has won victory after victory. And all this time the University has grown and prospered. Any football fan will tell you that this growth has been entirely due to the wonderful record which Dobie has achieved. There can be no question of this—in their minds." It is only right and is well deserved to commend Suzzallo for his success in advancing the university's academic standards. Dobie made numerous public statements placing academics above sports and never took a position that his players should shortchange class work for football. The editorial writers took a position against Dobie, which they had every right to do, but the final judgment of this case should be based on the actions of the parties and not on whether there was some overarching conflict between scholarship and athletics. For entirely different reasons than the editorial writers chose, both Dobie and Suzzallo are entitled to praise, just as both are deserving of criticism.

The clash of egos between the president and the coach was a predictable circumstance. Both of these hugely talented men could survive (indeed thrive) on their own, as their later careers proved. The fact that Dobie could have saved his job by backing down is immaterial. It is undeniable that there would have been another dust-up in the future causing Dobie to either be fired or quit. Could he have gone another year or two undefeated? It's certainly possible that the team could have lost its first game next season. Every team in the league was focused on beating Dobie, and either an off game, breaks not falling his way, or a superior opponent could blemish his otherwise spotless record. Weighing matters as a whole, this gave Dobie the opportunity to maintain an undefeated record at Washington. One more game could have taken this unprecedented achievement away. Since Suzzallo and Dobie would surely have tangled again, ending it all there at the conclusion of the 1916 season was best after all.

# CHAPTER THIRTEEN

## *National Champions*

"Gilmour Dobie will undertake the greatest task of his career, namely, that of defeating individual stars through the steadiness and efficiency of team play. Probably there is no coach whose predilections have been so strongly focused on just such a problem. Dobie's work on the coast has been so steady and consistent that his career has been marked by a succession of victories continuing not while a certain set of men were playing on his team but with whatever set of material he has on hand. The game he has originated has been one of a succession of steady consistent gains of comparatively small distance but eating up the ground so steadily as to retain possession of the ball. He has been able to teach this game, not to one of his men, but to succeeding sets until the victims of his teams have become very nearly hopeless and have been found on the defensive. The precision with which his men execute is admirable and he gets every man into it and thus has been able through the means of his coaching, to develop that steady consistent drive, which after all is the most discouraging thing that any team can be put up against.

*Walter Camp, 1917*

After Coach Dobie was fired, there was great resentment from many quarters that this decision was so ill conceived as to bring irreparable harm to Washington football. Hardly anyone with a passing interest in sports felt that firing a coach with nine undefeated seasons over such an issue was justified. As matters were sorted out, supporters of Dobie discovered that the Board of Control, had been totally usurped, which served to foment charges that the process was rigged. Missing in these eruptions of anger was an understanding of what was at the root of the whole unseemly episode—jealousy and the spotlight. The scandal was the opener that Suzzallo needed to bring an end to playing second fiddle. The facts of the case were straightforward in that cheating on an exam led to this fiasco. Neither of the principals comported themselves as would be required by men of their position, so the final result was inevitable. In the end, passion prevailed over professionalism.

The angst over the firing and lingering anxiety felt by Dobie's fans would soon be overtaken by much more serious matters than the firing of a football coach, never mind the circumstances. It was only four months later, on April 6, 1917, that the United States would enter World War I by declaring war on Germany. For good cause, all undercurrents of resentment towards Suzzallo for his handling of Dobie's termination were set aside. Loyalty to a winning coach runs strong, and at most any other time considering the drama of his termination, it would be typical for die-hard supporters to openly voice their discontent, thus prolonging the public debate. By the end of the war, both of the principals had greatly advanced their careers; thus, any lingering recriminations were rendered meaningless.

When Dobie left Washington, he surprised all the dopesters by taking the head coaching job at the University of Detroit. He was expected to accept a higher-level position at Wisconsin, California, Minnesota, or one of the big eastern universities. He was mistakenly reported to have been on the job working to assemble and train a team over the summer months, and in early August of 1917 an unsubstantiated announcement was made that he was dissatisfied with the small squad and, for this reason, took a position as head coach of the Naval Academy. Thirty-one years later, Bill Reid revealed the real story. During the summer of Dobie's arrival, he was hired as Athletic Director at Detroit.

Reid that fall received an offer from Colgate, his alma mater, and went to the administration and reported the opportunity; they were gracious enough to release him to accept the position at the New York school. He revealed that Dobie never actually reported for his job at Detroit as, in the meantime, he had received the offer to coach the midshipmen. On his way to assume the reins at Detroit, the Navy called, and he told Reid of his prior obligation to Detroit. The Naval Academy called Detroit and it stepped aside. Instead of Reid and Dobie working together, they would later become competitors when Dobie took over head coaching duties at Cornell. The two schools scheduled a four-game series, with Dobie running the table against his friend, winning all three that were contested while he was Cornell's coach.

The high-minded notion calling for pure amateurism in college sports still held sway in 1917. A crack in the system growing out of the more liberal substitution rules of 1910 and 1912 posed a risk to those desperate to hold onto this unrealistic ideal. The increasing complexity of the sport that so successfully opened up the game placed such a burden on the field general that many teams were trying to beat the system by having subs carry in intelligence from the coach. Purists were aghast as this took the contest out of the player's hands, and for this round the old-timers had their way. This year penalties were enacted placing a temporary brake on modernization. The argument against sideline support held that individual initiative was being taken from the players reducing the game to a contest of automatons. The only exception allowed a substitute quarterback to alert players to the signal for hiking the ball, but otherwise, dialogue between teammates and substitutes was disallowed. As the passing game grew in importance, the exposure of the receiver to danger was also of concern. That year a new pass interference rule penalized a player for roughing a receiver in the act of catching a pass by awarding the ball to the offended side at the point of the foul.

With only seven weeks to select and prepare the Midshipmen for the season ahead, Dobie hit the ground running, winning his first game against Davidson of North Carolina, 27-6. But on the second game, against West Virginia, the football world was set on its ear with the shocking news now reverberating from coast to coast: a Gilmour Dobie team lost a football game! It had been thirteen years going back to his high school coaching days in 1904 that his teams had gone unbeaten. Dobie's men went down to defeat by the unimaginable score of West Virginia over Navy, 7-0. For the rest of the season, the newly installed mentor went back to business as usual by winning the next six games, four of which were shutouts.

Late in December of 1917, Dobie quietly returned to Detroit. There was little fanfare of just why he was making the trip, but about the same time word came from out west that fiancé Eva Margaret Butler had caught a train heading east to marry Gilmour Dobie. The two met in Detroit and, in a low-key ceremony, were married by a minister on January 2, 1918. Eva, a stenographer, lived in the University District in Seattle, where the two met and became engaged but the couple had not revealed their wedding plans. Dobie went to great lengths to maintain a veil of privacy around his personal life, so he was able to pull off the wedding just as he wished, out of the prying eyes of the press. Their first child, Jane, was born in Maryland on October 25 of that year during Dobie's second year at Navy. She graduated from Simmons College and was voted "Most Bostonion" by her graduating class. She had the reputation of being quite poised and was a fashionable dresser like her father.

At Navy, just as with Washington, he immediately turned a team into winners that had been only so-so prior to his arrival. In 1918 Navy's loss to the Great Lakes Naval Training Base team, headquartered outside of Chicago, was a result of what Dobie described as "a play that will be remembered as long as football survives." The legendary George Halas, whose career spanned sixty years as player, coach, and owner of the Chicago Bears, was an end on the star-studded Great Lakes team. As it was one of the games that stood out in his mind, he wrote of this contest in his autobiography, *Halas by Halas*.

With less than seven minutes to play, the great Navy fullback and captain, Bill Ingram, fumbled as they were about to score from the 5-yard line, and just before he crossed the goal line, the ball popped into the hands of Lawrence "Dizzy" Eielson, who ran it back 90 yards. Jimmy Conzelman, who later was an early star and coach in the pros, and Halas provided downfield blocking duties.

Dobie said that all along he was excitedly yelling from the sidelines, " Tackle him, somebody tackle him. Only Saunders took my supplications literally and tackled the runner." The problem being that the tackler was William Hardin "Bill" Saunders, a Navy substitute who, coming off the bench, brought the runner down 5 yards short of the goal line.

A verbal melee that almost came to blows among coaches, players and referees erupted and carried out onto the field over this outrageous turn of events. The referees correctly called a penalty, and over the shouted protests of Great Lakes were about to step off the yardage of one-half the distance to the goal line. They wrongly were insisting that even though the ball hadn't crossed the goal they were entitled to a touchdown. In an effort to restore order, in marches Academy Superintendant Captain Edward Eberle, quite clearly upset at his own player's unseemly deed. The officials explained that the rules called for the penalty, but the belligerent captain would hear nothing of logic, insisted that the "ridiculous rule" didn't apply, and demanded that a touchdown be awarded. "It would have been a touchdown if that idiot hadn't run onto the field. I run this place, and a touchdown it is." The deciding extra point split the uprights, resulting in the second loss of Dobie's career.

Dobie, ever supportive of his players, took the blame for the horrible outcome. With both teams having undefeated seasons, B. O. Kendall, president of the Tournament of Roses in Pasadena was waiting for the outcome of the game to decide who to invite to play in the New Year's Day football gala against the Marine Corps team of Mare Island. By the slim margin of this game's final score of 8-7 in favor of Great Lakes, they got the nod. So, once again, Coach Dobie, through remarkable circumstances beyond his control, missed a bowl bid.

In 1918 Navy won four games, losing the controversial Great Lakes struggle, but many colleges cancelled football altogether because of the war, and the scheduling of games was even further curtailed by the worldwide flu pandemic that struck that year.

Dobie only had three losses in as many years and ended up with a record of 18-3. Most importantly, he reversed the annual dominance suffered at the hands of Army, beating the Black Knights of the Hudson in 1919 at the Polo Grounds. This would be the only time he ever faced them, winning by a razor-thin 6-0 on two field goals by Clyde King. It wouldn't have mattered if the Midshipmen had lost every other game, since they hadn't beaten Army since 1912. This alone was enough to elevate him to hero status.

As independent minded as Dobie was, the rigid structure of a military academy became too confining for him. For a man who was so strict and controlling in his own right, he hated it when others tried to rein him in using the same tactics. He was good at giving orders but not so good on the receiving end. He wasn't the least bit shy in expressing his discontent with a complaint that the admirals hanging out at the academy were encroaching on his turf in trying to run the football team when they should be at sea. His wish would be granted belatedly, as Captain Ederle in 1919 left the academy to command the battleships division of the Atlantic Fleet.

At this time the Cornell alumni's patience was wearing thin with the lackluster output of their football team. To make matters worse, it had been five years since they had beaten archrival Pennsylvania. By February 1920, word was on the street that the short list for a replacement coach was down to four, with Dobie on the inside track. Dobie's Naval Academy contract was still in force but, being unhappy with the testy relationship he had with high-ranking officers, his request to be let out of his contract didn't meet with much resistance.

A huge boost was given to his hiring by Cornell men who were at Annapolis during the war and saw the tall Scotsman in action. As soon as negotiations were settled, Dobie contacted his favorite player from Washington, Ray "Mike" Hunt, to be his assistant. The bond created when this shy and tongue-tied kid first approached Dobie eighteen years ago still ran deep. Along with the glowing praise Dobie received from Walter Camp, he also picked up an endorsement from Henry Lamberton, a star who played for Princeton and worked under Dobie as an assistant coach. The eastern establishment snubbed their noses at Far West football, but here we have a highly respected East Coast blueblood not just promoting Dobie but openly chastising eastern coaches for their blind spot against the West. He made a widely spread public declaration that Dobie, because of his teaching techniques, would make even a greater name for himself at Cornell. After the season, another easterner, the great Sol Metzger, who played for Pennsylvania before his coaching days, in his nationally syndicated column predicted that Cornell now "seemed to be on the verge of great events." Both of these predictions would come to pass far sooner than anyone could have imagined.

Dobie's opening act at Cornell absolutely thrilled the Big Red crowds at Schoellkopf Field. What he did in October must have had the hiring committee slapping themselves on the back and popping champagne corks in exalted glee. There were five Saturdays the month of October 1920, and every one of them had a home game scheduled. Dobie rolled over the competition, posting five victories with a combined score of 194-19. After having been blanked the last two games the previous season, the football-loving Cornellians knew they had found their man.

Moving to the East Coast, Dobie was brought front and center into the national limelight. His Washington record, along with his idiosyncratic personality, had for years made front-page news across the country, and the only question remaining was, could he keep up his winning ways? His fame was such that at Navy he had been hired to write a nationally syndicated column detailing his coaching techniques, and early in his time at Cornell he teamed up with Bob Zupke, head coach at Illinois, to teach a summer seminar on coaching. For the series of articles he was billed as "the world's most famous football coach." He also was invited into a group of the most élite company of football coaches in the country to write a second nationally syndicated column on "Supreme Football Strategies, Described by the Master Coaches." In addition to Dobie, this coaching Who's Who list included the likes of Fielding Yost, Amos Alonzo Stagg, John Heisman, Andy Smith, and Glenn "Pop" Warner.

If there ever was a golden age of college football, my candidate for the honor would most certainly have to begin with Dobie's taking over the reins at Cornell in Ithaca, New York, in 1920 and continuing through the 1924 season. His first year he posted a less-than-stellar 6-2-0 record and, even worse, the team was blanked in the annual showdown against Pennsylvania (as had been the case the last three times the teams met) by an embarrassing 29-0. But further to the west, twenty-five-year-old All-American halfback George Gipp, from his deathbed a few weeks after leading Notre Dame to their second straight undefeated season, made a request to his coach, Knute Rockne. "When the breaks are beating the boys, tell them to go in there and win just one for the Gipper." In this remarkable year for college football, there was an undefeated team from every region in the country: Boston College in the East, Notre Dame in the Midwest, Virginia Military Institute from the South, and California out West. California's sudden vault onto the national stage had come about in just five years from its 72-0 defeat against Washington in 1915. Dobie's legacy of elevating the level of football competition on the West Coast had now been realized.

The gloomy title naturally followed Dobie back east, but writers seemed a little less motivated to beat this drum with their former zeal. That monotony gave way to actual space dedicated to his skills as a coach. In an early eastern shift demonstrating respect for this upstart westerner, a widely read article went out on the national wire pitting Dobie against an established eastern coach—and it was the new kid on the block who got the praise. Columbia coach Frank "Buck" O'Neill had been ridiculing Dobie over his coaching techniques in 1921 even though the two were scheduled for a head-to-head contest in New York City on November 5. Dobie settled the matter on the football field, coming away with a 41-7 victory. And through it all he never raised an eyebrow over the criticism of his coaching methods. Quite the contrary, he was praised for being a cool cucumber no matter that others were throwing rocks. For this year Dobie's record ended up 8-0-0, with O'Neill's at 2-6-0. As the top team in the nation Dobie's team was honored with a Rose Bowl invitation but the nationally acclaimed coach was again denied as the Cornell faculty turned it down.

On June 5, 1921, Eva presented the family with their second child, a son they named Gilmour Jr. Nicknamed "Bud" he would later do his father proud at Bowdoin as a star halfback and member of the Polar Bear track team in the 1940s. Now in his second year at Cornell, Dobie's teams were being compared to his Washington elevens as being machines. This wasn't just thrown out to adopt a throwaway line from his earlier coaching days, but to pat him on the back for accomplishing this so decisively after taking over a team so oft described as "ordinary material." The obvious conclusion? The Dobie influence made the difference. Faithful followers of the Big Red will be quick to claim the national championships for 1921, '22, and '23, and it's a well-founded claim, since during this span they were unbeaten and untied. The NCAA, however, has never awarded an undisputed national championship. Since no playoff tournament exists, any claim of a national championship is based on mathematical rating systems. These are questioned as to their accuracy at best and fraught with subjective bias at worst.

The national rankings are far from what they appear on impressive archival lists or self-promoting team Web sites because of a little-known fact in their determination. The number crunchers creating the mathematical models in the early days rarely ever saw the games, hardly any of them. The reason for this is quite understandable: most of the systems were developed years or decades after the games of this early era were played. From 1921 to 1923, only Cornell and California went undefeated for the entire three years; however, California's record is diminished by a tie against Washington and Jefferson in the 1921 Rose Bowl and Nevada in 1923. Of the others, Illinois and Michigan were each 8-0-0 in 1923, Iowa was 7-0-0 for both 1921 and 1922, Princeton was 8-0-0 for 1922, and Lafayette was 9-0-0 in 1921. The record stands that there was only one undefeated and untied team for the entire period, and that was Cornell. Big Red advocates can lay claim to having the undisputed best record of any team in the country for these three years, but, considering there were other undefeated championship-nominated teams for specific years, the title must be shared. Another leg up for Cornell was its selection in the years 1921 and 1922 by the preeminent football historian, Parke Davis, who and made his choices by careful analysis of team schedules. Following this logic, Illinois must be given credit for 1923, as Parke Davis chose them that year.

After all these years, as enduring evidence of his compulsive nature, the tall, lean mentor still wore his dark overcoat to all games but traded his derby for what was described as a "queer little straight brimmed hat." For a coach who so purposely maintained a low-key profile, he clung to his uniform as a statement of authority. He had previously built stars out of seeming walk-ons, but in the glare of the eastern klieg lights of fawning press attention, he now found that his players were getting as much recognition as the coach. He never overtly sought to attract attention, but he did feel he needed a way to visually balance the scales. For this, nothing better than consistency of dress. His mantra for attention to detail could be applied no matter the venue.

For 1922 Cornell was led by quarterback George Pfann and the remarkable halfback Edgar "Eddie" Kaw. These all-time greats were the anchors on Dobie's second successive undefeated team. This was also the second year that Kaw was selected as an All-American. A movement was building that in no way diminishes the honors bestowed on this deserving athlete, but resentment to the long-simmering charge of an East Coast bias in such selections was now boiling over. Football was born on the more populous East Coast, and who could blame Walter Camp and the press for favoring the teams from the earliest years who were the best practitioners of the sport? But after 1910 and on into the 1920s, a groundswell of complaints built up arguing everything from favoritism to insularity and that football was now rightfully a national sport. In Dobie's time at Washington, only Polly Grimm and Louis Seagrave received All-American recognition, but both were on the third team. And yet Dobie had players who transferred to eastern teams and there made Camp's first team.

The year 1922 was the tipping point of disenchantment towards the Walter Camp picks, charging him with downright unfairness. In the East vs. West head-to-head competition, the West won 8, tied 1, and lost 2. In the selections of All-Americans, the East garnered nineteen of the thirty-three players on the three teams chosen, including seven out of eleven on the first team. While the East only managed to win 18 percent of their intersectional games against the West, the Walter Camp selection committee saw a remarkable level of individual talent in awarding 64 percent of the first-team spots to eastern teams. An AP article by Ross Tenney calling out this discrepancy was headed, "Walter Camp Soundly Scored For Poorest Team Ever Foisted on Public."

The extent of eastern bias is in the eyes of the beholder, but Cornell and Penn this year took a giant step in advancing the popularity of college football. The game took on historical consequences even beyond the legendary matchup of two of the greatest coaches of history, John Heisman against Gil Dobie. Up until now it was only through attending the games in person or reading the post game write-ups that a fan could get a firsthand account of the on-field action. But football would be changed forever at the Quaker's Franklin Field on November 30, 1922, with history's first radio broadcast of a football game. Playing before a wider audience on this day was particularly timely for Cornell, as this concluded their undefeated season 9-0. Bringing football into far-distant fans' homes was a large contributor in balancing the East/West dispute over regional supremacy.

In 1923 Cornell brought home another national championship and added two more All-Americans to its ranks, George Pfann and tackle Frank L. "Sunny" Sundstrom. Another of those enduring quotes for the ages came during this year of the golden age of football. Coach Dwight "Tad" Jones, in his pregame pep talk to motivate his team for their final game, offered this gem: "Gentlemen, you are about to play football for Yale against Harvard. Never in your lives will you do anything so important." His eloquent charge that lives on in the hearts of the Bulldogs' faithful served the purpose. That afternoon his gentlemen beat Harvard 13-0 for the first time in seven years, completing an undefeated season.

This marked fifteen years since Dobie's identity as being the perennial pessimist was first stamped on his forehead. As we have seen in these pages, his behavior earned him the title, and even with famous coaches such as Amos Alonzo Stagg of Chicago, Hugo Bezdek of Oregon, and Jock Sutherland of Pittsburgh being of like character, the label at the time was much more widely associated with the Scotsman. And even though he had long since been called out for his doleful predictions he hadn't yet totally given up on the effort.

The debate as to whether he was really a downcast sort or just putting on a show could also be counted on for a lot of ink, however it was diminishing in 1920s and '30s. With regularity his defenders still came out with effusive declarations of his intelligence and good nature in private settings. His players continued to support him time and again as the most important influence in their college lives. Sunny Sundstrom was one of the many players who expressed a debt of gratitude to the great coach's methods as being a factor for his success in life and kept in contact with the coach over the years. In a letter while serving as a United States Congressman from New Jersey he stated: "Outside of my own father, there was no man with whom I have associated or knew that I respected more." He acknowledged that to a large extent what success he had was owed to the "honest, forthright and sincere teachings" of Dobie and knowing the coach meant he had lived "a richer, fuller life."

He was praised as a coach's coach because of his summer seminars and the publishing of his plays as a teaching tool. A good friend of his explained that his idea was to show everyone else what he was doing and then to use the plays more effectively than anyone else. As he did in his earliest days at Washington, he also at Cornell would meticulously dissect his opponents' strategy and then apply the very same methods to beat them at their own game. In addition to the mandatory "gloomy," the other words long associated with Dobie, such as "perfectionist," "attention to detail," "obsessive," and "master of psychology," followed right along with him to the East Coast. There were many reasons for the success of his teams, but the favorite description that boiled everything down to one word continued to be "machine."

While the colorful aspects of Dobie's character made for entertaining reading, the reality that there was more to his personality than the attention-getting headlines gained wide exposure during his lifetime. One of the great all-time sports writers of history, Allison Danzig of the New York Times, played as a sub on Dobie's early Cornell teams. As Danzig expressed it, he was "Eddie Kaw's substitute's substitute." After playing for Dobie and being a firsthand observer of Knute Rockne, in his opinion both had very similar qualities and "knew how to develop winning football teams, as did few others." He felt that "they will be remembered for their personalities long after other winning coaches have faded into obscurity."

Many writers were now publishing articles to debunk the superficial legend and openly rebuked reporters who dealt in caricature over fact. There was an active movement of reporters who personally observed Dobie, were not "homers," and who dug into the story a few layers below the fun of painting Dobie as a hopeless pessimist living a hermit's life of doom and gloom. Two men of note who had no axe to grind for Dobie or Cornell were William Braucher, reporter for the *Lowell (Massachusetts) Sun*, and James Driscoll, publisher of the

*Connellsville (Pennsylvania) Courier*. Braucher had this observation: "Legend has it that of all the sour coaches of the western hemisphere, none is more sour and morbid than Gil Dobie of Cornell. There is no more misjudged man in football today. Dobie can smile, even in defeat, and he is a sportsman of the very highest caliber. He is a friendly man, with always a word of praise for players who have done well, whether they are his own or not." It should be added that such praise was used sparingly by Dobie. For his own players he mostly believed in withholding praise until the end of the season or until after their active playing days. This stemmed from what Braucher would have to agree was Dobie's "morbid" fear of a player becoming overconfident.

James Driscoll gave voice in print to what many knew: that Dobie was a man of depth as opposed to the superficial file copy portrayals so often recycled. "Some of the most colorful stories about Gilmour Dobie, head football coach at Cornell University, have been pounded out on typewriters far away from Cayuga's waters by sports writers who never talked to Cornell's coach and in some instances writers who never even saw him. An examination of a pile of clippings regarding Mr. Dobie shows him to be a tall man, a short man, a garrulous man, a silent man; an old time coach knowing no new football [and] a master of the new forward passing game." Driscoll, in researching Dobie in the 1920s, reports that he read the accounts of many writers who went to Dobie's games and also attended many practices. Their findings gave accounts far different from the wire service fillers. "Not given to praise, there was never a practice where Dobie did not leaven his criticism with a word of encouragement spread here and there for an exceptional piece of work. Swell head has ruined more football players than broken collarbones, and Dobie knows the psychology of the star better than most men." Here Driscoll paints the broader picture of the more mature and experienced Dobie. He indeed openly criticized his players, even those at the level of Pfann, Sundstrom, and Kaw, but he looked for those times where he could use this tool to cool off their overheated egos. He was known to slip in a pinch of sugar just when the recipe called for a little sweetener. He was sparing of praise, not devoid of praise.

Sundstrom, two years an All-American, tells of Dobie as still displaying a facility for both force and tenderness. "It was his way of being a practical psychologist with young men. One minute he'd have you hating him, and the next you'd feel as close to him as if he was your own dad. And somehow his method in the net never smacked of insincerity." When Dobie chose to use a broken leg suffered in practice by Bill Carey as an object lesson for keeping up the fight even in the face of adversity, Sundstrom tells of another episode of his rough but fatherly side. In ordering the stretcher to remove Carey from the field and have him taken to the hospital, Dobie's only emotion was that of strict efficiency. In the company of the men there was no hint of sympathy for the fallen soldier. It was five years later at a players' reunion before the team learned the full story. That night Dobie had gone alone to the hospital to explain to Carey that he used this incident to "make a sacrifice out of you for the sake of the whole squad. It was my way of trying to keep their morale intact to keep their fighting spirits up after seeing one of their teammates cut down as you were. I hope you will try to understand and try to believe you are my friend." Carey had tears in his eyes even five years later in telling how the man of iron had come so humbly to his bedside only hours after the incident to ask forgiveness in using him to toughen up the team.

On the personal front, 1924 was the year the Dobies completed their family with the birth of Mary Louise on November 14. She flew as a stewardess for Pan American Airlines in the late 1930s and served in the Marine Corps in World War II. She married J.J. Flanagan. Being stricken with Multiple Sclerosis, her sister Jane took on the full-time responsibility of caring for her until her death from the disease at age 41. The year 1924 also marked the turning point for Dobie's term at Cornell. After not losing a game for the last three years the team went 4-4 that year. This .500 record marked the coach's first nonwinning collegiate season in eighteen years. Never again would his teams climb to the heights of their former glory. For the rest of his coaching career he became a coach of more than respectable accomplishment, but the years of greatness were behind. There were other teams and younger coaches now moving to center stage.

It was in this year that my choice as the golden age of football came to an end. Notre Dame closed out my five-year span for twenty-four-carat football with yet another inspiring quote for the ages. Grantland Rice described Notre Dame's 13-7 victory over Army to complete their 10-0 season thus: "Outlined against a blue-gray October sky the Four Horsemen rode again. In dramatic lore they are known as famine, pestilence, destruction and death. These are only aliases. Their real names are: Stuhldreher, Miller, Crowley and Layden. They formed the crest of the South Bend cyclone before which another fighting Army team was swept over the precipice at the Polo Grounds this afternoon as 55,000 spectators peered down upon the bewildering panorama spread out upon the green plain below."

Cornell posted a respectable six wins and two losses for 1925. Continuing a dreaded trend, one of the losses was to Pennsylvania. In fact, the Quakers were the singular nemesis of all the teams Dobie opposed in his thirty-three-year college coaching career. He had beaten John Heisman two out of the three games he coached against him when he first took the reins at Cornell. But it was Lou Young of Penn who really had his number. Against him Dobie could only manage a record of 1-5-2. While at Ithaca he came up short against Penn with a dismal 6-9-1 overall profile. For opponents he met multiple times during his thirty-three-year career, only Young and Glenn "Pop" Warner (posting a 1-0-2 record) would come out ahead in the win column against Dobie. Coming as Young's defeats did at the hands of their archrival is one matter that the die-hard Cornellian will hold against the coach who otherwise brought them more wins than any other coach in history.

Collection of Dobie's granddaughter, Eva Zayha

This is a widely used professional portrait of Coach Dobie taken for the announcement of his unanimous election as the third president of the American Football Coaches Association. The selection was made in December of 1925 to be effective for the 1926 season. Well after his retirement from football, he was called in as an expert consultant on football matters coming before the association.

Dobie was unanimously elected president of the American Football Coaches Association for 1926 and, by posting a record of 6-1-1; he could hold his head high when conducting meetings with his peers. However, even though Cornell continued its winning ways, the tie that year with the Quakers was a wholly unsatisfactory conclusion to the Penn problem. There indeed appeared to be no solution to the one-sided affair against Penn. It wasn't until Coach Young mercifully had left Pennsylvania after the 1929 season that Dobie would break the chokehold they held over Cornell. The three games for 1927-28-29 weren't even close, with two shutouts, and only in the last game did the Big Red manage a not-so-big single touchdown.

On November 21, 1926 Eva would write a letter to her younger brother, Edgar "Ned," Butler with the tragic news that she had been diagnosed with cancer of the stomach and large intestine. She told him she wrote "to the folks in Seattle" but did not reveal how serious her illness was, because they "would worry themselves to death." Over the fall she had been checked by a total of five doctors, two of whom gave her one chance in fifty for survival. Eva was a woman whose physical beauty was only exceeded by her indomitable will and strength of character. In this most poignant of letters she expressed deep concern for the children but not a word for herself, even feeling anxious over her Christmas card with the children's pictures reaching her brother in time. There was no hint of self-pity for the inevitable fate soon to befall her.

The end came on June 25, 1927 after only nine and one-half years of marriage, leaving Dobie with three small children ages eight, six, and three. Jane, the eldest, was barely old enough to process the consequences of this heartbreaking event. She now had to assume a familial role even larger than her years would portend. As a husband and father, Dobie had been a good provider, and becoming a single parent, he pledged to double down to make sure the children were well cared for. Having come from poverty, he understood what it meant to be poor, and from this lesson it came naturally for him to lead a frugal life. Being a savvy investor, he was able to accomplish his objective in spades. Before the Depression he became wealthy from prudent stock investments. He did endure some financial anxiety from the Depression, but coaching provided him with steady work during this time, enabling the family to live comfortably. Dobie placed an emphasis on his children's education and made it a priority to set aside enough money to cover all the costs.

Cornell football could only be described as lurching along for 1927 and 1928, posting identical records of 3-3-2 for both years. Matters improved in 1929 with a record of 6-2-0, and, with Louis Young's retirement from Penn, this (sort of) brought an end to their dominance over the Big Red. From 1930 through Dobie's last year at Ithaca, the teams split down the middle, each posting 3-3 records. Looking on the bright side, this was phenomenal progress from Cornell's prior six years (1924-29), where all that could be mustered against this behemoth was a 10-10 tie against five losses.

The alumni were getting restless now that Cornell had fallen from the pinnacle of college football and were making noises that Dobie's coaching techniques and game strategy were not keeping pace with the modern game. He was still an advocate of off-tackle football and did coach an up-to-date game, but the most frequent complaint held that he should open up his game even more. There were charges that his methods were old-fashioned and only new blood could bring Cornell back to prominence. The riled-up alumni marshaled a highly vocal and visible front and made it known that they wanted change. It would be natural to hearken back to the three consecutive seasons of 8-0-0 football since this had been just five years back. The alumni raising the stink, after all, had been in the stands of Schoellkopf Field laying witness to the halcyon days.

The movement failed, and it failed for only one reason: the devotion of his players for their coach. Their personal lobbying mirrored the outpouring of support from his players when the news broke that Dobie was being shown the door at Washington. In some quarters this had been rationalized as stemming from his unprecedented record of never losing a game in Seattle and not for any bond developed with his men. However, this overlooks the fact that his players unabashedly expressed their respect for his leadership and character while at Washington and for decades after he left.

During this time of the late 1920s at Cornell, the teams were good and even had flashes of brilliance, but the fact remained that the current roster weren't in college during the glory years. The outspoken support campaign began with the team and spread to the students. Together they stopped the dump-Dobie campaign dead in its tracks. This movement grew to campuswide protest levels, even though the team had just completed back-to-back mediocre 3-3-2 seasons. In summing up the sentiment of the players, Warren Warden, John Anderson, and Fred Wrampalmeir wrote an open letter that spoke to the main issue for supporting the coach: "That there may be better football coaches we are not qualified to say, since we have only played under Mr. Dobie, and know football practically only as he has taught it to us, but that there aren't any coaches who are better influences on their men, we doubt.

"There has been much material sent around in the form of letters expected to poison the reader against Mr. Dobie. That those of us who know Mr. Dobie are hastening to bring the truth back into the discussion. If attacks are confined to technical points in coaching, we can only hope that something good for Cornell football will come out of the discussion, but if attacks are to be made on Mr. Dobie as a leader and a teacher for young men we rise up to combat them.

"Not the least valuable experience of four years at Cornell were the football seasons under Mr. Dobie. Face a problem squarely and work to make the most of it. Work for a thing if you want to get it; try hard. These are some of the things you learn besides tackling and kicking. Frankness and truth are Mr. Dobie's tactics with his team—let's use the same tactics when we discuss him. Needless to say, we like him." The rumors and innuendo as to Dobie's removal, as they were referred to by syndicated sportswriter Lawrence Perry, came to an end only three weeks after this moving tribute to him from his own players was published. The groundswell of opinion from students and players carried the day. Dobie took great pride in being described by his players as a leader and teacher over that of being their coach.

Another movement at Cornell and other campuses was boiling to the surface in the mid-to-late 1920s that extended on into the 1930s: the question of recruiting players as athletes first, students second. For as long as he coached Dobie had never hesitated in advocating for scholarship over athletics. This enlightened campaign was gaining traction but was unevenly applied from school to school. Dobie objected to this and was less than delicate in voicing his concerns. One of the most famous quotes claimed to have been uttered by him as he left Cornell at season's end was the line, "You can't win games with Phi Beta Kappas." Rather than springing this remark in seeming disgust as he left Cornell, he had been stating the obvious for years that there was a diminishing pool of players available to the schools who imposed higher academic standards. This left them with players that he called "Phi Beta Kappas" who had to compete unfairly with squads who were not restrained from recruiting the best athletes. An overstatement to make his point, but he was famous for such pointed talk, just as he derided his ego-inflated "All-Americans," to bring them down to earth. This pejorative dated back as far as his Washington days when he felt the need to knock back some of the self-importance built up in the minds of his stars.

Once Dobie's colorful usage of Phi Beta Kappa was cemented into the popular lexicon, it became a favorite topic in the press, never mind that he wasn't speaking out against scholarship. Once his remarks became a topic of public discussion, they stuck. What started it all was his observation on September 21, 1925. "They're just a lot of scholars dressed up as athletes with their minds on Phi Beta Kappa keys instead of interference." Coming as it did before the season started, this was garden variety Gil Dobie branding his team as hopeless for the year. While at year's end the team could hardly be described as phenomenal, they did win 75 percent of their games, ending up with a quite acceptable 6-2-0 record. Whether Dobie's goading of these Phi Beta Kappas did any good to motivate them to achieve can't be answered, but it can be seen that when he used such tactics, the team won far more than they lost.

Alan Gould, the originator of the AP Football Poll and a highly respected sportswriter of the time not given to passing along thinly documented stories, summed up the account of how the issue of scholarship versus athletics was finally settling down by 1931. He documented just how it was that Dobie first was drawn center stage onto the forefront of the debate. Gould stated, "Now that the noisy chatter about over-emphasis in college sports has died down, it becomes apparent that most of our principal institutions of learning and culture are going ahead with sane sensible programs designed to keep affairs on an even keel."

He went on to tell of Dobie having found himself on an uneven playing field with Cornell's archrival. "Pennsylvania, this year may find itself in the same position as Gil Dobie found himself a few years ago at Cornell. Gil's boys after three unbeaten seasons experienced a slump and a young coach, finding the veteran in a hotel lobby, was seeking an explanation.

" 'Mr. Dobie you must have had a pretty tough season,' ventured the young man.
" 'Yup,' responded Gil.
" 'Why, Mr. Dobie, even Williams beat Cornell—that certainly was a surprise. You can't be losing your grip, can you?'
" 'Nope.'
" 'But, Mr. Dobie, what is the explanation? How can such a thing have happened?'
" 'Well,' drawled Gil, 'we're playing our students now.' "

Dobie's angst only grew with the ever-more-complicated game that he saw developing, and he expressed his concerns in a speech to the American Football Coaches Association. His point was that the game had become "so big, so vast, so unwieldy it is almost impossible to do justice to their scholastic duties. We cannot go on expanding indefinitely. It is not the quality of the game but quantity that is undesirable. It consumes too much time and effort and is too expensive. We can junk half of it and still have more left than is sufficient for a college game."

His brand of football had always been a game with fewer plays in which he would drill his team to execute with exacting precision. Given his innate skill for detail and his meticulous practice regimen, the formula worked to famous ends. However, the overwhelming path of progress was towards complexity, which would inevitably lead to specialization. And in the end, the sport adopted the system of indefinite expansion that Dobie spoke out against. He sought to put the brakes on complicating the game, since, with the growing emphasis on scholarship, doing otherwise would further damage the game. As history has shown, the more complex game came out ahead and scholarship lost. Success in big-time college football now requires it to be a launching pad to the pros. Under Dobie's formula of making room for his Phi Beta Kappas, the game as played today would not exist. He was the last great advocate for maintaining a better balance between class standing and athletics. This meant not going totally over to what he termed a big, fast, unwieldy game. But big-fast-unwieldy won out and the student athlete came a cropper. Critics of today's giant-scale collegiate game can look back and wish Dobie had prevailed. The ardent football fan can only be glad that the Coaches Association didn't see it his way.

The 1930s saw the introduction of strict academic standards, together with rule changes that improved spectator appeal but accelerated the onset of player specialists. These conflicting objectives did not sit well with Dobie. He had always done best by reducing the fundamentals of blocking, tackling, kicking, and passing to rote tasks that good players could master. Each good player, when inserted into this painstakingly detailed system, helped elevate the team from average to outstanding. Now that recruiting was restricted because of higher standards of scholarship, many of the better players that Dobie previously had pulled in went elsewhere. Rather than adapt to the times, he never fully gained a footing in this new world.

It became a subject of considerable discussion that Dobie's tactic of pessimism that had been understood as a useful psychological tool in his winning days was now a severe detriment when Cornell no longer placed winning as a priority. Cornell had resolved itself to the reality that higher performance levels in the classroom meant fewer wins due to the narrowed recruiting base. Since Dobie lost in his campaign to maintain the less complex game of a bygone era, this meant his only salvation was to adapt, and this he could not do. Coaching at Cornell now had become more a game of motivating less-talented players to accomplish average results, rather than what he had always done—recruiting good athletes and demanding perfection with an eye towards achieving excellence. The new formula definitely was not Dobie's style, and his fans grew to recognize it.

The record for his last years at Cornell from 1930 to 1935 reflects a steady downward trend of almost mathematical precision. The overall record was marginal at best at 24-19-2, but the direction he was heading was disastrous. The year-over-year decline in the number of wins for the six seasons was 6-7-5-4-2-0. For Dobie to go winless for the 1935 season was not something within the realm of believability, but it did happen. Only an effete 7-7 tie with Columbia saved the team from a total washout. There were hardly any parades to note the fact, but at least the Big Red had gained parity with Pennsylvania, managing to level out at 3 wins, 3 losses each. Dobie's efforts to gain on the Quakers were made all the more difficult since Cornell came earlier to the practice of setting academic standards for athletes than did Penn.

Dobie's termination at Cornell became a race to the finish line as to whether he or the administration would be the first to pull the plug. During the years of triumph, the winning teams were exalted, but now that the team had plummeted to the depths he was losing one of his strongest constituencies, student support. As with Dobie, his former players weren't enamored with the restrictive academic standards, but it was hard for them to muster the strong support of earlier years given the team's performance of late. The deciding issue came down to an adjustment in attitude that winning was secondary to a "broad and healthy sports program." This meant a sports program that had resolved itself to nonchampionship status. Dobie's tool of using pessimistic forecasts was no longer a useful ploy but he nevertheless would predict defeat and, of course, would be proven right. This came to be seen as a defeatist attitude, the last thing loyal fans needed now that they had resolved themselves to accepting a .500 season as their lot in life. It was shown at Washington that Dobie would predict defeat when the rest of the world saw a win and would predict a win when everyone else saw a loss coming up. This contrarian attitude couldn't work now; Cornell was a real underdog rather than the make-believe underdog posited by Dobie in earlier days.

The end came with a harmonious meeting of the minds. Dobie submitted his resignation January 22, 1936. His contract had another two years to run, and with both parties wanting out, the university agreed to a buy out the contract. The termination theme expressed by both Director of Athletics James M. Lynah and Coach Dobie was to maintain a "sense of fairness." Both sides went out of their way to declare that this was accomplished. There also was praise for Dobie in taking the lickings he suffered of late just as quietly and with the same exhibition of good sportsmanship as he always demonstrated in his many years of winning teams. He left Cornell with an overall record of 82-36-7 (.684) as the winningest and longest-serving head coach in school history.

# CHAPTER FOURTEEN

## *Virtue of Perfection*

"Dobie was a contemporary of such famed football coaches as Fielding H. Yost, Knute Rockne, Percy Haughton, Dr. Harry Williams, Major Frank Cavanaugh, Bill Roper, Johnny Heisman, and Bob Folwell. There was a stretch of years when his name probably topped them all, but his string ran out. It happened to many of the others too. But there's no gainsaying the fact that from 1906 through 1923 Gil Dobie had the success formula almost monopolized."

*Henry J. McCormick, Sports Writer, December 26, 1948*

The ink was hardly dry on Dobie's termination agreement before he had signed on with Boston College. This announcement went out on the wires on February 4, 1936. Hiring a new coach from scratch takes a good bit of time, so the quick announcement showed that the two parties had engaged in talks before Dobie had officially concluded his affairs with Cornell.

In his first year at the Heights, Dobie suffered only one loss. That came in his second game when the Boston College Eagles faced the Temple Owls for the Birds of Prey Bowl (at least that's what it should have been called). To maximize attendance, this was BC's first game to be played at Fenway Park, where Dobie faced a coach that also became a legend in the sport, Glenn "Pop" Warner. These two coaching titans would meet three times in this final stage of Dobie's career, all being down-to-the-wire struggles. Dobie never broke into the winner's column against Warner. He lost this game 0-14 and the last two deadlocked at 0-0 in 1937 and 26-26 in 1938.

Dobie showed that he had learned something coming out of Cornell. He now toned down the gloomy predictions, but after thousands of articles where attaching the G-word to his name was an editorial requisite, the tag would follow him throughout his life. He appeared sincere in publicly expressing his respect for the caliber of men playing football at Boston College. They reminded him of his own upbringing in Hastings, Minnesota, a half century before. These weren't bluebloods from privileged backgrounds but hard workers who were solid and dependable. He also connected their football success to the fact that they didn't "carouse." He tossed an olive branch to the administration, praising them for the nonpolitical environment on campus with no "arguments or fussing." He attributed this more charitable attitude of the new Dobie to ageism. "When you get to be as old as I am, it is nice to settle down in the orderliness I have found here."

Dobie would have been the toast of Boston if for no other reason than his first-year win over the Eagles' chief foe, the Holy Cross Crusaders, coached by the famous Dr. Eddie Anderson. Dr. Anderson went onto later fame at Iowa and would return in 1950 to finish his joint medical and coaching careers at Holy Cross. He would lead the team until 1964. A man of enormous talents, he excelled in both coaching and medicine. He practiced as an eye, ear, nose, and throat specialist during the day and spent his late afternoons as a very successful football coach. Unfortunately, a biography of Coach Anderson is inaccurate in stating that Gil Dobie's student-fans hated him. The actual case was just the opposite. They grew to love him, and the documented accounts written at that time reflect numerous instances of students being his strongest advocates at Washington and Cornell. In researching *Pursuit of Perfection,* I reviewed over six hundred sources written during Dobie's time, and not one mentioned even a faint reference to any student showing personal animus towards Dobie. Such mistakes of history get into the record by relying on writings that cite dramatized legend over actual accounts written at the time. Joan Waugh, UCLA professor of history, in her biography of President Ulysses S. Grant titled *U.S. Grant, American Hero, American Myth*, brilliantly makes this point regarding her historically misrepresented subject. Myth eventually morphs into popularly conceived reality.

Boston College had suffered defeat the last two years to the dreaded Crusaders, providing the perfect scenario for Dobie to further burnish his reputation as a winner who could win when backed to the wall. The last game of the season was played at Fenway Park on November 28, 1936, on a windy and bitingly frigid day. For both fans and players, the nor'easter was a constant presence that afternoon, bringing unwelcome snow flurries along as it blasted the field. It was before this game that Dobie gave another of those oft-reported quotes that reporters closely following him would savor. Making casual conversation, a writer approached him and said, "Fine day, Gil." Without lifting his eyes from the ground, Dobie was quick to reply, "So far." In the multiple times this innocuous encounter on this cold and bleak day has been repeated in print, the setting has been "adjusted" by the writer to mesh with his or her take on Dobie's complex makeup. Be it a sunny day, before a win, at practice, during a game, or after a game—it would seem to the uninitiated that Dobie ran into this question everywhere he went. Repeating this chance encounter and placing it into manufactured circumstances, it could serve to drive home the writer's opinion that Dobie was indeed, hopelessly pessimistic. No interpretation even pays lip service to the obvious sarcasm Dobie employed because of the terrible weather as he was about to go into a critical game.

Both teams were enjoying successful seasons with the favored Crusaders coming into the game with an impressive 7-1-1 record against the Eagles' 5-1-2. Holy Cross appeared to be cruising to victory by scoring two first-half touchdowns but came up short on both extra-point tries, one being blocked and the other missed, which would prove critical to the outcome. They also suffered a huge setback when two of their stars, center Bob Mautner and tackle Hipolet Moncevick, had to leave the game with injuries.

Halfback Fella Gintoff scored a touchdown in the second quarter, but, this not being an ideal kicking day; BC also missed their extra-point attempt, bringing the score to 12-6 for Holy Cross. The third quarter was scoreless. Fella Gintoff's number was again called in the fourth quarter, and once more he put the ball over the plane of the goal on a short run for six points to tie the score. Then came time for the legendary quarterback, Tony DiNatalie, to go to work, and that he did. Honored in the annals of Boston College football for punting, it was for the one extra point he placed on the boards under these most dreadful conditions that won the day. With unsure footing caused by snow and slush, he booted the game winner through the uprights. Out of the four extra-point tries on this dreadful New England day, this was the only one to clear the minimum standard required to register a score. The most important game of the season was decided by this one kick; the game ended favoring Boston College, 13-12. Thus Dobie's hero status and champion's reputation, just as in his glory days, could be included among the greats at this, the final stop of his career. From his playing days at Minnesota through every coaching interlude along the way, his followers would remember him as a winner.

Four days after the game, Dobie and Frank Murdock, the coach of his freshman squad and former Cornell tackle, were seriously injured in a car accident when they hit a railroad abutment on Beacon Street near Boston's Kenmore Square returning from a year-end team celebration. Dobie's injuries were diagnosed as a fractured jaw, concussion, severe lacerations of the face, and shock. Murdock suffered a skull fracture, concussion, and a deep facial laceration. Both had a severe loss of blood and were found unconscious at the site. Hours later they were still semiconscious at the hospital. While Dobie's injuries were serious, they were not life threatening, but they would have lingering effects, coming as they did at fifty-eight years of age. He was released from the hospital on Christmas Eve, but Murdock's more serious injuries required that he stay another three weeks. This was the second injury Dobie had suffered that year, having broken his collarbone in spring practice when he was accidentally hit teaching his patented off-tackle line buck. Never one to sit on the sidelines, even in his late fifties Dobie would mix it up on the field with players thirty-five years his junior.

His successful inaugural year had caught the eyes of Syracuse recruiters, and the first-year Boston man was already being widely spoken of in connection with their vacant slot. It was well known that Dobie loved Ithaca and would favor the idea of returning to upstate New York. This would also give him a chance to settle a score with Cornell by scheduling a game with his old team. Dobie's accident didn't allow him to actively pursue the position that was ultimately given to Ossie Solem—who did beat Cornell the next year.

Even though Dobie posted a very good 6-1-2 record in his first year and had won the hearts of the Eagles' loyalists, his honeymoon was coming to a close in only his second year. The constant game of predicting defeat was passé, and Dobie recognized this and had laid it to rest, but alumni were now branding him as old school. Players told of his intense practices, and this, too, had fostered an image that the old wizard wasn't keeping pace with the modern game. There was no clamoring for his head, but the chatter in the background was heard by Dobie. The handwriting was on the wall despite the fact that he was still winning. There was no loss of faith that Dobie could coach effectively, it was just that a youth movement was growing that overcame all other considerations. Everyone that followed football knew full well that Dobie was not one to give any thought to changing his style.

The 1937 squad posted a lackluster 4-4-1 record that couldn't get anyone excited, but one item getting attention was the team's failure to score in three of the games, albeit one was a 0-0 tie with Pop Warner's Temple Owls. But worst of all was the 20-0 shellacking the Eagles took at the hands of Holy Cross, which hurt the most. This, coming as it did in a four-loss season, brought out the wolves.

For 1938 Dobie's team bookended their first year with another good 6-1-2 season. The one loss had special significance since it was against Holy Cross, who themselves had a spectacular 8-1-0 record, only losing by a razor-thin 7-6 margin to Carnegie Mellon. To the young-blood advocates, this sealed the deal. They could only look admiringly at the Crusaders' Eddie Anderson, a coach twenty-one years Dobie's junior. Well before the final agreement came to deny renewal of Dobie's contract that expired this year, word was on the street that the next coach was not going to be another veteran with a reputation. The UPI account summed it up based on what it claimed was to be coming from "trustworthy operatives at Boston…It's merely a reflection of the march of time. It's the ancient story of not being able to teach an old dog new tricks. And it is particularly tragic in the case of Dobie, who for years was publicized as the 'wizard' of the gridiron—one of the most advanced pigskin philosophers."

Weighing his options, the canny Scotsman by early December saw that his time was up. Naturally there were many who saw in Dobie a coach who had brought home a perfectly acceptable 6-1-2 season and would want to give him one more year. Dobie, being the negotiator that he was, always dealt from a position of strength. He now found himself in the unknown waters of only appearing lukewarm to the other side. He knew it was best for him to make a move. Rather than wait for what in all certainty was an announcement that his contract would not be renewed, he got in the first punch. He forwarded this announcement to the authorities: "I wish to advise that I am not a candidate to succeed myself as football coach at Boston College."

That year the football world seemed to have more than its usual shifting of coaches, with moves coming at universities that were satisfied with their leader. Notably, Holy Cross' Eddie Anderson was accused of turning his back on them after their fabulous 8-1 season, even abandoning the entire East Coast by landing in the far outpost of Iowa.

The appointment of Frank Leahy to replace Dobie was announced in late January of 1939. His hiring was a result of a call from the Holy Cross president to Coach Carl Snavely, who had replaced Dobie at Cornell. Snavely recommended Leahy for the job. He suggested that the young Catholic and Fordham coach would be an ideal replacement. The timing came just as Dobie turned sixty-one and was evidence of Boston College's determination by its modernistic alumni wing to bring in a "young fast-stepping coach." He was certainly worthy of replacing Dobie. He had played center and tackle at Notre Dame in the latter years of Knute Rockne's tenure and gained fame as the line coach at Fordham, developing the seven blocks of granite. In a bittersweet display of poetic coincidence, the new thirty-one-year-old coach was born on August 27, 1908—the exact day that, thirty-three years before, a young Gil Dobie launched the segment of his career that brought his greatest fame—his nine-year undefeated run at the University of Washington.

Upon retirement, Dobie retained his residence at Newton, Massachusetts, until later moving to Putnam, Connecticut. Comfortably situated from prudent investing, he devoted himself to supervising the higher education of his three motherless children. Gil Dobie Jr. followed his father's example and played college football. He made the 1940 Bowdoin University freshman squad at halfback and continued his junior and senior years in 1946 and '47 on the varsity. After the first year he enlisted in the army in 1942 and served throughout the war before returning to college. He was an above-average starter and was known as a dependable runner the team could count on. The Polar Bears hadn't beaten their ancient rival, Amherst, since 1940. It was Gil Jr. who did his father proud, picking up 28 yards in three carries and scoring the winning touchdown to cap off an 8-6 victory over the Lord Jeffs in 1947.

Dobie continued to maintain contact with his teams long after he left the schools where he coached. While living in the Boston area, he had ready access to Boston College, but he also traveled back to Ithaca, Annapolis, and Seattle for reunions with his teams. He was frequently called in as an honorary advisor to the Executive Committee of the American Football Coaches Association. At BC he would attend practices and observe from the sidelines, and, viewing games high up in the stadium, he still watched the play with total focus on every detail. Royal Brougham, who reported on Dobie's games at Washington, was still going strong when Dobie visited Seattle in 1940 for a huge reception and pointed out that Walt Shiel told him back a quarter-century earlier that he hated Dobie's "Simon Legree" practices until he could have killed him but now "the tall Scot is his idol." In 1960, twelve years after his death, the team held even another reunion in Dobie's honor and packed the ballroom of the Olympic Hotel, drawing virtually every big name from the glory days at Washington.

In a 1941 interview, AP reporter Steve O'Leary found that Dobie still retained his love of football and actively followed the game. Dobie confided that he did miss the action of full-time coaching but enjoyed the leisure of retirement. Much of his time was now devoted to his hobby of studying world history and current international affairs. His take on the game since his days on the sidelines focused more on the larger, more talented squads as the biggest difference since the old days when he was on top. "Forward pass?" Dobie asked. "Why, my Washington team back in 1909 used the forward pass pretty effectively. I'd use it whenever I had a good passer on the team." Rules were still changing, but the most dramatic adjustments in the game had been made in the 1906 to 1912 period. Most of the football world of Dobie's post-football days would single out his Cornell elevens of the early '20s as his greatest. Dobie, however, while conceding that his teams led by Kaw, Pfann and Sundstrom were fine, believed they were not as good as his UW teams of 1909 and 1914. He rated his all-time greatest as the 1909 squad captained by right halfback Melville Mucklestone with Wee Coyle at quarterback.

Gil Dobie, for his last five years, made his home in Putnam, Connecticut. In August of 1948, in failing health, the great coach was admitted to the Institute of Living in Hartford. He had never fully recovered from the serious injuries suffered in the Boston car accident twelve years earlier. Death came in his sleep at age seventy on the night of December 23, 1948. When he was first admitted to the hospital, there were initial reports that he was suffering from a nervous disorder, but his adult children reported the cause of death as coronary failure.

He worked hard in creating a dour public persona, but those who knew him personally were well aware that this perfectionist away from the spotlight had a mischievous sense of humor and warm personality. He considered it a mark of his professional responsibility to maintain a calm public demeanor before his players, no matter if he won or lost. This added to the perception of him being downbeat, which more accurately should be described as a man striving to project an even temperament to serve as an example in front of the team.

A winner at everything he set his mind to. His thirty-three year coaching record was 183-45-15 for a lifetime winning percentage of .784 placing him among the greatest of the game. Undoubtedly, the greatest mark of his many professional accomplishments was the near universal praise he received from the players he coached. Legions of his players lauded this intense man's methods of coaching and credited him for teaching them those all-important lessons in team sports that derive from working under a master's tutelage. Among his pallbearers were Ray Hunt, who so timidly walked into his life in 1912 and rose to renown at Washington, and All-American George Pfann, a star of his undefeated

Cornell teams from the early 1920s. His pallbearers were all selected from former players, and the honorary bearers were friends, neighbors, university officials, businessmen, and athletic staff members.

He was the coach who made "Far Above Cayuga's Waters" the ringing symbol of football prominence while he coached at Cornell, and it was there that he chose to be buried next to his wife, Eva. As with everything else in his life, even the final act of funeral and burial had been planned by him in detail. The service was to be simple. This was befitting a man who never sought attention for himself regardless of his spectacular record of accomplishment and the many accolades that followed. By never publicly revealing that his early childhood included living at an orphanage, no one really knew the enormous challenges he overcame to achieve his great accomplishments. The widower, devoted father, national championship and Hall of Fame coach, holder of the NCAA record for undefeated seasons that probably will never be surpassed, skilled teacher, successful businessman, lawyer by education, and leader of men was eulogized by the Reverend Dr. Walter A. Dodds. In paying tribute to Dobie's dual personal and professional qualities, Dodds most eloquently described Dobie's life's pursuit as "the virtue of perfection in doing all things."

# Sources

The Argus

(1) Victor Zednick. "Coach Dobie Is Idol Of University." Nov. 13, 1909. (2) Boyce, Bobby. "Coach Dobie Must Start Reform Movement." Nov. 7, 1908: 6. (3) Boyce, Bobby. "President Kane Of The University Of Washington Sustains The Argus Charges." Nov. 28, 1908: 7. (4) Bobby Boyce. "Mucklestone And Eakins Had Legitimate Right To Play On Washington Football Team." Dec. 5, 1908. (5) Victor H. Zednick. "Varsity Plays Second Practice Game Today." Oct. 16, 1909. (6) Victor H. Zednick. "Coach Dobie Is Idol Of State University." Nov. 13, 1909: 7. (7) Robert Watson Boyce. "The Premonition Of Disaster." Reprinted from *The Argus* in the *Post Intelligencer* titled "The Dreaded Specter." Oct. 4, 1914. (8) "Football." Nov. 4, 1916. (9) Robert Watson Boyce. "Making A Quarterback." Oct. 2, 1915: 16. (10) "Gilmour Dobie." Dec. 16, 1916.

The Washington Alumnus

(1) F.A. Churchill. "Dobie A Vignette." 1910. (2) Wee Coyle. "The Dobie System." Nov. 1914: 8,16. (3) "Retain Coach Dobie." Dec. 10, 1910: 3,4. (4) F.E. Jeffrey. "The New Football Rules." Sep. 1910: 8,9. (5) Allen M. Lacey. "The Whitman Game." Oct. 29, 1910: 9,10. (6) Allen M. Lacey. "Dobie Likes New Football Rules." Dec. 3, 1910: 10. (7) Allen M. Lacey. "The Athletic Situation." Nov. 5, 1910: 9-15. (8) Allen M. Lacey. "Dobie Likes New Football Rules." Dec. 3, 1910: 10. (9) Ralph Casey. "The Championship Game." Dec. 8, 1911: 14-16. (10) "Another Football Championship." Nov. 1912: 3,4. (11) "Five Years Of Championships." Nov. 1912: 9,10. (12) "Dobie Picks All-Time Team." Mar. 1913: 4. (13) "Coach Dobie Resigns Place; New Coast Conference Formed." "Dobie Feted By Seattle Alumni." Dec. 1915.

The Washingtonian

(1) Andy Eldred. "Why A Man Turns Out." Nov. 11, 1911: 11,12. (2) Gilmour Dobie. "A Word From Mr. Dobie." Dec. 1908: 18-20. (3) E.R. Hughes. "Maxwell Eakins." Nov. 1909: 41-44. (4) Neal A. Hawley. "A Football Review." Dec. 1909: 4-9. (5) Ralph Casey. "The Varsity As A Scoring Machine." Dec 13. 1910: 37-39. (6) Victor H. Zednick. "For A Fourth Championship." Oct. 1910: 7-9. (7) Clark Squire. "Gilmour Dobie, Wizard Coach." Dec. 1915: 16-18.

Seattle Post Intelligencer

(1) Royal Brougham. "The Morning After." Oct. 3, 1940. (2) "Men Who Figure In Opening OF 1908 Football Season Today." Sep. 26, 1908. (3)"Varsity Is Held By Lincoln High." Sep. 27, 1908. (4) "Washington May Lose Big Tackle." Oct. 3, 1908. (5) "Varsity Makes Weak Showing." Oct. 4, 1908. (6) "Star Tackle To Help Washington." Nov. 7, 1908. (7) "Washington And Pullman In Tie." Nov. 8, 1908. (8) "Dobie Offered To Fight The Whole Darned Squad." Nov. 23, 1916: 9. (9) "Washington Will Not Play Post-Season Game IN South." Oct. 17, 1909. (10) "Varsity Team Off For Idaho Gridiron Battle." Oct. 29, 1909. (11) "Washington Faces First Hard Game." Oct. 30, 1909. (12) "Idaho Defense Poor." Oct. 31, 1909. (13) "Championship Is At Stake Today." Nov. 25, 1909. (14) "Oregon Hopes Are High For Victory." Nov. 25, 1909. (15) Kiley H. Allen. "Washington Victorious Over Oregon In Northwest Championship Battle." Nov. 26, 1909. (16) "Fear Field Goals Will Decide Game." Nov. 5, 1910. (17) "Dobie's Champs Show Great Form." Nov. 6, 1910: 1,4. (18) "New Rules Harder On Officials Than Teams." Nov. 13, 1910: 3. (19) "Washington Downs Pullman Farmers." Nov. 13, 1910: 1. (20) "Dobie Prays For Bright Weather." Nov. 23, 1910. (21) "Dobie's Team Has Crucial Test Today." Nov. 24, 1910: 1. (22) "Seventh Annual Thanksgiving Game." Wash. Vs O.A.C. *Souvenir Program,* Nov. 24, 1910. (23) "Varsity Wins Championship." Nov. 25, 1910: 1,4. (24)"Varsity Easily Best Team In Northwest, Says O.A.C Coach." Nov. 25, 1910: 10. (25) Gilmour Dobie. "Varsity Coach Selects Star Team." Nov.25, 1910: 10. (26) "Close Gridiron Battle Expected." Oct. 13, 1911. (27) "Crucial Games At University Today."Oct. 14, 1911. (28) "Varsity Swamps Worden, 99 To 0. Oct. 15, 1911. (29) "Oregon Elevens Fast Shaping Up." Oct. 16, 1911. (30)"Varsity Beats U.P.S. 35 to 0" Oct. 22, 1911. (31) "Wonder If Team Was Under Wraps." Oct. 23, 1911. (32) "Stiff Practice For Dobie's Men." Oct. 24, 1911. (33) "Dobie Is Wrapped In Pall Of Gloom." Oct. 27, 1911. (34) "Washington And Dobie Are Ready." Oct. 28, 1911. (35) "Varsity 11 Downs Idaho On The Grid." Oct. 29, 1911. (36) "Dobie Beginning Blackboard Work." Nov. 3, 1911. (37) "Washington Easily Beats O.A.C. Team." Nov. 5, 1911: 1,2. (38) U. Of W. Defeats Oregon Aggies By Lop-Sided Score. " Nov. 11, 1911: 1,4. (39) Bradford. "Washington Team Mystifies Oregon By Trick Plays." Nov. 19, 1911: 28. (40) Ralph Casey. "Oregon Downed By Washington 29 To 3." Nov. 19, 1911. (41) "Pullman Team On Edge For Struggle." Nov. 30, 1911: 1. (42) Ralph Casey." How Dobie's Men Won Fourth Consecutive Championship—Stars." Nov. 1, 1911: 1. (43) "Varsity Machine On Lowest Gear." Sep. 29, 1912: 2. (44) "Varsity Eleven Defeats P.S.U." Oct. 13, 1912. (45) "Navy In Annual Clash With Dobie." Oct. 19, 1912. (46) "Navy Puts Up Stubborn Fight." Oct. 20, 1912. (47) "Dobie Is Hoping For Dry Field." Oct. 25, 1912. (48) "Dobie Is Hoping For Dry Field." Oct. 25, 1912. (49) "Varsity Eleven In Hard Game Today." Oct 26, 1912: 10. (50) "Varsity Defeats Moscow Eleven. " Oct 27, 1912: 1. (51) "Washington And Oregon Will Settle Supremacy On Grid This Afternoon." Nov. 16, 1912. (52) Ralph Casey. "Dobie's Machine Beats Oregon U." Nov. 17, 1912. (53) Sidney Brunn. "Great Finish Makes Battle Spectacular." Nov. 17, 1912. (54) "Gilmour Dobie, Washington's Great

Football Genius, Sought By Penn Alumni." Nov. 18, 1912. (55) "Pullman Plans To Trim Washington." Nov. 27, 1912. (56) "Washington And W.S.C. To Battle For Title Today. Nov. 28, 1912. (57) "Crowd of 7,000 Sees Washington Win Championship." Nov. 29, 1912: 1,8. (58) Sidney Brunn. "City Chaps Too Much For Pullman Farmers." Nov. 29, 1912: 9. (59) "Washington Has Even Chance To Win Thursday, Says Dobie." Says Dobie. Nov. 26, 1913. (60) "Washington Gets Plenty Of Action." Oct. 4, 1914. (61) Conrad Brevick. "Washington And Aggies Quit With Honors Even." Oct. 31, 1914. (62) "Oregon Football Squad On Way To Lick Dobie." Nov. 12, 1914: 9. (63) "Washington And Oregon Ready For Big Contest." Nov. 14, 1914: 9. (64) Conrad Brevick. "Oregon Beaten By Washington In Close Game." Nov. 15, 1914: 1. (65) "Washington Football Season Comes To Close Today." Nov. 26, 1914: 8. (66) Conrad Brevick. "Pullman Buried By Dobie's Champions." Nov. 27, 1914: 1. (67) "Southern Team Determined To Put Up Battle." Nov. 13, 1915: 8. (68) Portus Baxter. "Yesterday's Contest Was A Thriller From Whistle To Whistle." "California Team Springs Surprise And Almost Ties." Nov. 14, 1915: 1,2. (69) "Washington Just Wins By 13 To 7, In Last Minute." Nov. 14, 1915: 15. (70) "Washington To Face Oregon In Crucial Battle." Nov. 4, 1916. (71) "Washington And Oregon Elevens Battle To Tie." Nov. 5, 1916: 1. (72) Conrad Brevick. "Washington Runs Up Score On Oregon Aggies." Nov. 12, 1916: 1. (73) Royal Brougham. "O.A.C. An Easy Prey To U. OF W." Nov. 12, 1916: 1. (74) "Berkeley Bunch Plans Surprise For Dobie's Men." Nov. 13, 1916: 5. (75) "California Dangerous Because They Play The Open Game, Coach Says." Nov. 22, 1916: 9. (76) " 'U' Football Squad Goes On Strike." Nov. 23, 1916: 1,3. (77) "Football Strike Declared Off." Nov. 24, 1916: 1,3. (78)Conrad Brevick. "Game Was Stubbornly Contested All The Way." Dec. 1, 1916: 8. (79) Royal Brougham. "Washington Men Coast Champions For Ninth Time." Dec. 1, 1916: 1,8. (80) Royal Brougham. "Friends Of Washington Start Movement To Keep Dobie At The University." Dec. 8, 1916. (81) "Gilmour Dobie Is Through At The University." Dec. 10, 1916. (82) "Football Followers Of City And On The Campus Regret Dobie's Leaving." Dec. 10, 1916. (83) "Retiring Coach Is Given Ovation By Thousand Friends." Dec. 12, 1916.

Seattle Times

(1) Wee Coyle. "The Spell Of Gil Dobie". Coyle Calls Roll Of Scot's Star Performers." Jan. 8, 1949: 6. (2) Wee Coyle. "40 Years Ago In Sports. Zednick Also Had His Problems With Dobie." Jan. 13, 1949. (3) "Washington Victor In First Big Game." Oct. 18, 1908: 16. (4) "Varsity Prospects Looking Up." Oct., 19, 1908: 12. (5) "Varsity Eleven In Bad Way." Nov. 4, 1908: 13. (6) "Pullman Not Very Confident." Nov. 5, 1908: 17. (7) "Varsity Eleven In Bad Shape." Nov. 6, 1908: 17. (8) "Washington Plays Pullman Tie." Nov. 8, 1908: 17. (9) "Oregon No Match For Washington." Nov. 15, 1908. (10) "Oregon Aggies To Meet U. Of W." Nov. 25, 1908: 11. (11) "Varsity Undisputed Championship." Nov. 27, 1908: 17. (12) "Dobie Goes Over Past Season." Nov. 29, 1908: 15. (13) Wee Coyle. "The Spell Of Gil

Dobie", Coyle Recalls Years Under Immortal Coach." Dec. 30, 1948: 15. (14) Wee Coyle. "The Spell Of Gil Dobie". 'The Toughest Players Ate Out Of His Hand.'" Dec. 31, 1948: 8. (15) Wee Coyle. "The Spell Of Gil Dobie". His Psychology Brought Stunning Grid Upsets." Jan. 1, 1949: 9. (16) Wee Coyle. "The Spell Of Gil Dobie". One Fumble Outweighed 23-5 Victory With Gil." Jan. 2, 1949: 36. (17) Wee Coyle. "The Spell Of Gil Dobie". Tall Scot Didn't Use Signal to call plays." Jan. 3, 1949. (18) "Dobie Driving Men Hard For Whitman Game." Nov. 4, 1909: 10. (19) "Washington Whips Whitman By 17 To 0 Score." Nov. 7, 1909: 24. (20) "Dobie Quits Washington After This Year." Nov. 15, 1909. (21) "Want Dobie To Stay With An Increase In Pay." Nov. 18, 1909. (22) "Washington Students Banking On Dobie." Nov. 19, 1909. (23) "Dobie Re-Elected But May Not Stay." Nov. 19, 1909. (24) "Coach Dobie Expects Hard Game Thursday." Nov. 21, 1909: 21. (25) "Oregon Will Spring Some Tricks In Thursday's Game." Nov. 23, 1909. (26) E.R. Hughes. "Both Colleges Right On Edge For Game." Nov. 24, 1909: 10. (27) "U. Of W. Whips Oregon In Great Game." Nov. 26, 1909: 2. (28) "Dobie Declares He Will Stay Another Season." Dec. 16, 1909. (29) "The Spell Of Gil Dobie". Players Believed In The Coach And Won Again." Dec. 5, 1949. (30) "Coach Dobie To Get Increase In Salary For Great Work." Nov. 30, 1910. (31) "Coach Dobie Signs Up With Washington For Three Years." Dec. 9, 1910. (32) "Washington Football Men Are Still Limping." Oct. 22, 1909. (33) "Facts About Saturday's Game." Oct. 23, 1911. (34) "Washington Play Simply Amazes Portland Folk." Nov. 20, 1911: 3. (35) "Where Did Sutton Get The Ball?" Nov. 21, 1911. (36) "Pullman Will Be Worthy For Washington On Turkey Day." Nov. 26, 1911. (37) Wee Coyle. "The Spell Of Gil Dobie". Scot Planned Super-Secret Surprise For Oregon." Jan. 6, 1949. (38) Wee Coyle. "The Spell Of Gil Dobie". Ducks Didn't Even See T.D. On Famous 'Bunk' Play." Jan. 7, 1949. 22. (39) John B. Foster. "Foster Gives Plays That May Be Made Under New Rules." Oct. 29, 1912. (40) "Washington Eleven Has No Trouble Beating Everett Eleven." Sep. 29, 1912. (41) "Washington Wins In Romp Over Puget Sound Eleven." Oct. 13, 1912. (42) "Washington Team Has Easy Time Winning From Husky Sailors." Oct. 20, 1912: 24. (43) "Idaho Eleven Comes Here Confident Of Victory."Oct. 25, 1912: 20. (44) "Idaho's Backs Fail To Pass Washington's Alert Forwards." Oct 27, 1912: 23. (45) "Idaho's Highly Touted Team Completely Outclassed." Oct. 27, 1912: 28. (46) "Football Experts Are Loud In Praises Of Coach Gil Dobie." Oct. 28, 1912. (47) "Washington Wins Game In Last Three Minutes Of Play." Nov. 10, 1912. (48) "Varsity's Bungled Up Bunch To Play Whitworth Tomorrow." Oct. 17, 1913: 25. (49) "Washington Scores Century In Game With Whitworth." Oct. 19, 1913: 28. (50) "Oregon Aggies To Play On Denny Field Tomorrow." Oct. 25, 1913. (51) Ted Cook. "Dobie's Boys Dazzle Aggies And Win By Big Margin." Oct. 26, 1913: 28. (52) By Hank. "Cheerful—Cheerless Gil Dobie, Coach." Oct. 26, 1913. (53) Ted Cook. "Whitman Gets Jump On Varsity, But Loses Game." Nov. 2, 1913. (54) "Washington Only Eleven Conference Eleven So Far Undefeated." Nov. 3, 1913: 15. (55) "Washington Eleven Leaves For Oregon This Afternoon." Nov. 14, 1913. (56) "Tricks Of Bezden (sic) Cause Varsity Its Only Worry." Nov. 15, 1913. (57) "Washington Beats Oregon But Has Real Fight To Win."

Nov. 16, 1913: 1. (58) "Pullman Sure To Fight Hard Against Washington Eleven." Nov. 26, 1913. (59) "Washington Beats Pullman By Playing Better Football." Nov. 28, 1913. (60) Ralph Benjamin. "Washington Defeats Oregon In Desperately Played Game." Nov. 15, 1914. (61) "Berkeley Ready For Opponents." Nov. 4, 1915. (62) "Washington Is On Scene Of Battle." Nov. 5, 1915. (63) Douglas Erskine. "Only G. Dobie Is Pessimistic." Nov. 6, 1915: 7. (64) "Washington Team Run To Death At California; Heated Up, They Could Do No More Than 72-0." Nov. 7, 1915: 1,10. (65) "Critics Blame It On Coaching." Nov. 8, 1915. (66) "Dobie's Flock Is Back Home." Nov. 9, 1915. (67) "California Meets Varsity Tomorrow." Nov. 12, 1915. (68) "Rival Aggregations Are Evenly Matched For Big Contest Scheduled Today." Nov. 13, 1915. (69) "No Goal Crossed Until Last Period." "California Eleven Throws Scare Into Dobie." Nov. 14, 1915. (70) "Dobie's Men Hold Oregon To Zero Tie." Nov. 5, 1916: 1,15. (71) "Oregonians Plan Open Style Game With Dobie Team." Nov. 10, 1916: 25. (72) "Dobie's Machine Continues March Towards Pennant." Nov. 12, 1916: 1,2. (73) "Bears Fearing Dobie's Attack." Nov. 17, 1916. (74) "Washington Wins Speedy Game From California; 13 To 3." Nov. 19, 1916. (75) "Today's Game Means Much In History Of Athletics On Coast." Nov. 30, 1916. (76) "Washington Wins Thrilling Game With California." Dec. 1, 1916: 18. (77) "Dobie Comes 'Home,' Visits Old Haunts, Vets To Meet Him." Oct. 1, 1940. (78) "Gil Dobie Honored By Grid Vets." Oct. 3, 1940. (79) Wee Coyle. "The Spell Of Gil Dobie". U of W Coach Lets Team Teach Itself a Lesson." Jan 4, 1949.

The Pacific Daily Wave

(1) "Squad Out For First Practice." Sep. 15, 1908. (2) "Coach Dobie Talks To Football Squad." Sep. 16, 1908: 1-2. (3) "Open Practice This Afternoon." Sep.23, 1908. (4) "First Football Game Tomorrow." Sep. 25, 1908. (5) "Coach Dobie Will Not Definitely Pick Men Until Tonight." Sep. 26, 1908. (6) "Faculty And Co-Eds Neglect To Support Football." Oct. 5, 1908. (7) "Faithful 200 See Scrimage." Oct. 8, 1908. (8) "Three Veterans Report To Dobie." Oct. 13, 1908: 1. (9) "Whitworth Coach Grows Pessimistic." Oct. 14, 1908. (10) "Ducked For Violating Rule Prohibiting First Year Men From Taking Co-eds To Functions." Oct. 14, 1908. (11) "Washington Fears First Big Game." Oct. 16, 1908. (12) "Washington In Champion Class." Oct. 20, 1908. (13) "Will Eakin[s] Play In Whitman Game." Oct. 23, 1908. (14) "Varsity Defeats Fast Eleven." Oct. 24, 1908. (15) "Victor H. Zednick Raps Outside Knockers." Oct. 28, 1908. (16) "Board May Select Dobie For Next Year." Nov.1, 1908. (17) "Eakins Is Back On Varsity Team." Nov. 4, 1908. (18) "Pullman Game Will Be Battle Of The Giants." Nov. 6, 1908. (19) "Hard Luck Cheats Team Of Victory." Nov. 10, 1908. (20) "Varsity Must Fight To Win." Nov. 13, 1908. (21) "Oregon Loses To Washington." Nov. 17, 1908. (22) "Pullman Admits Playing Ringers." Nov. 19, 1908. (23) "Injuries Will Keep Eakins Out Of Championship Game." Nov. 24, 1908. (24) "Dobie Doubts Washington's Ability To Win From O.A.C." Nov. 25, 1908. (25) "Souvenir Program Will Be A Beauty." Nov. 25, 1908. (26) "Varsity Men Are Again Champions." Dec. 1, 1908. (27) "Four Varsity Men On All-Northwest." Dec. 1, 1908. (28) "May Not Play

W.S.C. Any More." Dec. 2, 1908. (29) "Dobie Believes "W" Rules Are Too Rigid." Dec. 3, 1908. (30) "Is Not At Home To State College." Dec. 3, 1908.

<u>The Daily</u>
(1) "Last Efforts To Train Team Are Expended." Nov. 24, 1909: 1,2. (2) "Gilmour Dobie." Oct. 24, 1910. (3) Street, Jimmy. "Dobie's First Victory Greatest." Dec. 11, 1913. (4) "Greater Washington." Oct. 13, 1909. (5) "University Plays Erratic Football." Oct. 17, 1909. (6) "Varsity Exhibits Small Improvement." Oct. 18, 1909. (7) "Spokane Newspapers Boost Big Game." Oct. 26, 1909. (8) "Zednick Favors Numbering Players." Oct. 28, 1909. (9) Victor H. Zednick "All Spokane Calls Washington Winner." Oct. 30, 1909. (10) "Varsity's Showing Surprises Dobie." Nov. 1, 1909. (11) "Washingtonians Put It All Over Grogan's Men." Nov. 2, 1909. (12) "Whitman Player May Make All-American." Nov. 4, 1909. (13) "Whitman Arrives And Rests Ready For Big Battle." Nov. 5, 1909. (14) "Vincent Borleske A 'Made' Player." Nov. 5, 1909. (15) "Washington Holding Championship Place." Nov. 8, 1909. (16) "Give Football Team Ringing Farewell Rally." Nov. 11, 1909. (17) "O.A.C. Will Use Reorganized Team." Nov. 12, 1909. (18) "Varsity Colors Go Steadily On To Championship." Nov. 15, 1909. (19) "Times Froths At The Mouth Again." Nov. 16, 1909. (20) "Coach Dobie Breaks Silence Of Two Years." Nov. 17, 1909. (21) "Number Players In Thanksgiving Game." Nov. 18, 1909. (22) "Average Weight Of Oregon 178 Pounds." Nov. 22, 1909. (23) "Student Body Goes Wild Over Gilmour Dobie." Nov. 24, 1909: 1. (24) "Last Efforts To Train Team Have Been Expended." Nov. 24, 1909: 1,2. (25) "Purple And Gold Wave In Triumph On Pacific Coast." Nov. 29, 1909: 1,4. (26) "Coach Dobie Reviews 1909 Football Season." Dec. 1, 1909. (27) "Dobie Shakes Up Backfield Trio." Oct. 5, 1910. (28) "Disciples Of Dobie Trounce Lincoln High." Oct. 10, 1910: 1,4. (29) "Rules To Digest Before Next Saturday's Game." Oct. 10, 1910: 4. (30) "Dobie Analyzes Rules At Smoker." Oct. 10, 1910. (31) "Pigskin Pedagogue Relegates 'Wee' Coyle To Lamb Position." Oct. 13, 1910. (32) Ora P. Willis. "Varsity Rolls Up Tall Score On Stony Field." Oct. 17, 1910. (33) Archie M. Major. "Varsity Undismayed To Fight Heavy Odds." Oct. 21, 1910. (34) Archie M. Major. "One Bill Cook Saves Day In Whitman Game." Oct. 24, 1910: 1,4. (35) Archie M. Major. "Capt. Polly Grimm Will Watch Game." Nov. 2, 1910. (36) "Idaho Comes To Wallop Our Crippled Team." Nov. 3, 1910: 1,4. (37) "Varsity Anxiously Awaits Tomorrow." Nov. 4, 1910: 1. (38) Archie M. Major. " Varsity Overwhelms Idaho." Nov. 7, 1910: 1,4. (39) "Parting Varsity To Get Royal Sendoff." Nov. 9, 1910: 1. (40) Archie M. Major. "In Fierce Game Varsity Beats State Farmers." Nov. 12, 1910: 1. (41) Archie M. Major. "Team Returns Amid Shouts Of Glad Acclaim." Nov. 14, 1910: 1,4. (42) Victor H. Zednick. "Why 'U Of W' Will Not Play Oregon." Nov. 16, 1910: 1. (43) "Oregonian Says Varsity Afraid To Play Oregon." Nov. 17, 1910. (44) "Pullman Explains The Mystery Of Their Defeat." Nov. 22, 1910. (45) "Championship Roosts Again With Varsity. Nov. 28, 1910: 1. (46) "Dobie Heads Program For Y.M.C.A. Mixer." Sep. 22, 1911. (47) "Dobie Picks Men To Start Game With Lincoln High." Sep. 28, 1911. (48) "Varsity Beats Lincoln

High Team Easily." Oct. 2, 1911. (49) Fred A. Woeflen. "Fort Worden Has Fast Aggregation." Oct. 3, 1911. (50) Fred A. Woeflen. "First Team Players On Second Eleven." Oct. 5, 1911. (51) Fred A. Woelflen. "Freshman Guard Leaves The Gridiron." Oct. 6, 1911. (52) Fred A. Woeflen. "Worden Soldiers Have Fast Team." Oct. 9, 1911. (53) "Varsity Makes Record Score Against Army." Oct. 16, 1911: 1,3. (54) "Varsity Without Pullen And Patten." Oct. 17, 1911. (55) "Varsity Veterans Fired To Scrubs." Oct. 19, 1911. (56) "Varsity Attack Against U.P.S. Surprises Fans." Oct. 1911. (57) "Oregon Team To See Idaho Game." Oct. 25, 1911. (58) "Coach Says Hard Scrap Due Eleven." Oct. 26, 1911. (59) "Varsity Eleven Wins 17-0 Victory In Idaho Contest." Oct. 30, 1911. (60) "Washington In Bad Shape To Meet O.A.C. Stars." Nov. 1, 1911: 1,4. (61) "Washington Team Speeds Up On Eve Of Game." Nov. 2, 1911. (62) "Seven Seniors On Varsity Football Team Who Play Last College Game Tomorrow, Nov. 29, 1911. (63) "Washington Crushes Oregon Mercilessly." Nov. 20, 1911. (64) "Football Rules O.K. Contends Coach Dobie." Nov. 29, 1911: 4. (65) Gilmour Dobie. "Coach Dobie Picks All-Star Team For Daily." Dec. 5, 1911: 1. (66) "Will Inscribe History On Famous Hook." Dec. 5, 1916. (67) "Dobie Faces Task With Grim Smile." Sep. 18, 1912: 1. (68) "Varsity To Play Everett Eleven." Sep. 27, 1912. (69) "Varsity Shows Well Against Bagshawites." Sep. 30, 1912. (70) "Methodists Eager To Slaughter Dobieites." Oct. 10, 1912. (71) "Varsity To Meet U.P.S Tomorrow." Oct. 11, 1912. (72) "Varsity Backs Lack Championship Form." Oct. 14, 1912. (73) "Dobie Shakes Up First Backfield." Oct. 15, 1912. (74) "Varsity To Meet Tars Tomorrow." Oct. 18, 1912. (75) "Varsity Fans Expect Humiliation By Idaho." Oct. 23, 1912. (76) "Rooters' Club To Be Noisy Tonight." Oct. 23, 1912. (77) "Students Allowed To Watch Team Tonight." Oct. 24, 1912. (78) "Untried Varsity To Play Idaho In Critical Match." Oct. 25, 1912. (79) "Varsity Easily Downs Idahoans." Oct. 28, 1912: 1. (80) "Hook In Danger." Nov. 8, 1912. (81) "Washington, Better Team In Pinch, Beats Oregon Aggies, 9-3." Nov. 11, 1912: 1,3,4. (82) "Washington Wins In Early Period." Nov. 18, 1912: 1,4. (83) "Looks For No Cinch In Pullman Contest." Nov. 19, 1912. (84) "Anxious Gil Dobie Ejects Old Stars." Nov. 24, 1912. (85) "Varsity Takes Fifth Conference Pennant." Dec. 2, 1912. (86) "Football Eleven To Be Banqueted." Dec. 4, 1912. (87) "Football Prospects Are Gloomier Than Ever Before, Says Coach Dobie." Sep, 7, 1913: 1. (88) "Dobie Coaches Behind Closed Gates While Oregon Aggies Boldly Assert They'll Win." Sep. 23, 1913: 1,4. (89) Frank Gibb. "Washington May Not Play Game With Michigan." Sep. 25, 1913: 1. (90) "Dobie Experiments With New Line-Ups." Sep. 30, 1913: 1. (91) Jimmie Street. Dobie's Men Make One Sad Showing." Oct. 6, 1913: 4. (92) "Husky Tars Planning Overthrow Of Dobie." Oct. 10, 1913: 1. (93) "Sailor Eleven Gives Varsity Hard Game." Oct. 13, 1913: 1,4. (94) "Quarterback Job Still Undecided." Oct. 16, 1913: 1. (95) "Dobie's Men Facing Hard Game With Whitworth." Oct. 17, 1913: 1,4. (96) "Dobie's Machine Makes Fricassee Of Whitworth." Oct. 20, 1913: 1. (97) Jimmy Street. "O.A.C. Will Win From Varsity Asserts Coach." Oct. 21, 1913: 1. (98) Jimmie Street. "Dobie's Squad Works Hard To Defeat O.A.C." Oct. 22, 1913: 4. (99) "Oregon Aggie's Refuse To Abide By

'Ringer' Rule." Oct. 23, 1913: 1. (100) "Aggies Game Will Be Played Under Protest." Oct. 24, 1913: 1. (101) "Washington Tramples On Heavy O.A.C Eleven." Oct. 27, 1913: 1. (102) "Washington Team In Bad Shape For Game." Oct. 29, 1913: 4. (103) Jimmie Street. "Is Dobie Kidding About Whitman?" Oct. 30, 1913:1. (104) Jimmie Street. "Fighting Whitman Eleven To Play Varsity Tomorrow." Oct. 31, 1913: 1. (105) Jimmie Street. "Whitman Scores On Varsity But Loses By Score Of 41-7." Nov. 3, 1913: 1,3. (106) "Dobie's Men Make Sad Showing In Practice." Nov. 6, 1913: 4. (107) "Reservations Made For Loyal Rooters." Nov. 6, 1913: 1. (108) "Willamette Issues Challenge To Dobie." Nov. 7, 1913:1. (109) "Dobie Will Talk To Football Assembly Tomorrow Morning." Nov. 11, 1913: 1. (110) Jimmie Street. "Dobie Sees Oregon Play Tie With O.A.C." Nov. 10, 1913: 1,4. (111) "Squad Put Through Real Stiff Workout." Nov. 11, 1913: 4. (112) Farnsworth Wright. "Two More Days As Football Champs Says Coach Dobie." Nov. 12, 1913: 1,2. (113) Jimmie Street. "Dobie Will Name Team Tomorrow For Oregon Game." Nov. 13, 1913: 1. (114) "Girls Should Go On Portland Trip." Nov. 13, 1913: 4. (115) "Varsity Team Is All Ready For Struggle On Multnomah Field." Nov. 14, 1913: 1,2. (116) Gilmour Dobie. "A Wonderful Game." Nov. 17, 1913, 1. (117) "Washington Wins Over Oregon Team In Terrific Battle." Nov. 17, 1913, 1,4. (118) Jimmie Street."Dobie Putting Team Through Last Hard Scrimmage Practice." Nov. 25, 1913: 1, 4. (119) "Coeds To Occupy West Grandstand." Nov. 25, 1913: 1. (120) "Board Will Offer Coach Dobie Another Contract." Nov. 26, 1913: 1,3. (121) "Coach Dobie—Champion." Dec. 1, 1913. (122) "Charlie Smith, Varsity's Plucky Quarterback." Dec. 5, 1913. (123) Louis Seagrave. "Chances Good For 1914 Championship Under Coach Dobie." Dec. 5, 1913: 1. (124) Conrad Brevick. "Football Prospects Look Dark To Dobie." Sep. 14, 1914. (125) "Varsity Will Have Ex-Captain Anderson." Sep. 16, 1914. (126) "Football Conditions Look Much Brighter." Sep. 17, 1914. (127) "1914 Football Rules Show Many Changes." Sep. 18, 1914. (128) "Coach Hugo Bezdek A Gloomy Mentor." Sep. 21, 1914. (129) "Dobie Sends Out Spectators And Also 'Bear' Story." Sep. 21, 1914. (130) "Dobie Weeds Out His Raw Material." Sep. 22, 1914. (131) "The Sword Of Dobocles." Sep. 22, 1914. (132) Roscoe Fawcett. "Oregonian' Sporting Editor Says Dobie In For Hard Rub." Sep. 29, 1914. (133) "Varsity Shows No Improvement In Second Preliminary Contest." Oct. 5, 1914. (134) Conrad Brevick. "R.V.A.C. Is No Match For Varsity Machine." Oct. 12, 1914. (135) Conrad Brevick. "Broken Wrist Puts Ed Leader Out For Season." Oct. 19, 1914. (136) "Open Conference Season With Whitman Saturday." Oct. 20, 1914. (137) Conrad Brevick. "Dobie Must Hustle To Win From Hahn." Oct. 22, 1914. (138) Conrad Brevick. "Washington Football Team Starts Fight For Seventh Championship." Oct. 23, 1914: 1,4. (139) Conrad Brevick. "Fawcett Forecasts Washington's Defeat." Oct. 23: 4. (140) "Washington Wins But Fails To Show Class Against Lighter Team." Oct. 26, 1914: 1,4. (141) " 'Get That Hook' Is Battle Cry Of One Thousand O.A.C. Noise Makers." Oct. 28, 1914. (142) Conrad Brevick. "Stewart's Aggies Expect To Mar Washington's Brilliant Record." Oct. 30, 1914: 1,4. (143) " 'Fight Is Key To Success' – Stewart." Nov. 10, 1914. (144) "Oregon Aggies

Give Washington Great 0 To 0 Battle On Wet Field." Nov. 11, 1914: 1,4. (145) "Varsity Not Up To Form For Battle With Oregon." Nov. 12, 1914. (146) "64 Mile Wind Plays Havoc On Campus." Nov. 12, 1914: 1. (147) Alfred Campion "Graduates Revive Old Washington Spirit For Tomorrow's Game." Nov. 13, 1914: 1. (148) Conrad Brevick. " Both Contenders For Championship Weakened By Injuries To Lineup." Nov. 13, 1914: 1,4. (149) "Championship Lovers Get One Rare Treat." Nov. 14, 1914. (150) Jimmy Street. "Compares Dobie's Team To Williams." Nov. 24, 1914. (151) "Dobie Given Boost By Chicago Critic." "Washington May Get No Games At Home." "Washington Sets New 'Win' Record." "Bender Praises Work Of Varsity Quarter." Nov. 30, 1914. (152) "California Hits Hot Pace In Work On Gridiron." Sep. 21, 1915. (153) "Dobie Gives Men Strenuous Work." Sep. 23, 1915. (154) "Adds Fancher To Coaching Staff." Sep. 24, 1915. (155) "President Approves Co-Ed Independence." "Dobie Grooms Team For Practice Game." Sep. 27, 1915. (156) "Trick Plays And California's Team." "Noble Kept Out By Severe Injury." Sep. 30, 1915. (157) Clark Squire. "Dobie's Men Fail To Show Ability Against Ballard." Oct. 4, 1915: 1,3. (158) "Dobie Wants More Speed From Players." Oct. 5, 1915. (159) "Offer Good Prizes For Songs And Yells." "Roberts Whispers Into Dobie's Ear About California." Oct. 6, 1915. (160) "Respect Traditions President Advises." "Dobie Working Men Hard These Nights." "Brother of Grimms Fast On Gridiron." Oct. 7, 1915. (161)"Without A Pivot, Varsity Team To Tackle Clubmen." Oct. 8, 1915. (162) "Dobie Demands Speed Of Backs." Oct. 9, 1915. (163) "California Maintains She's Still In Race." Oct. 27, 1915. (164) "Borleske Has Chance OF lifetime To Beat Dobie." Oct. 28, 1915. (165) "Consistent Work Wins For Varsity." "Song That Won Daily Contest." Nov. 1, 1915. (166) "California Maintains She's Still In Race." Oct. 27, 1915. (167) "Washington Team Leaves For Game With California." "Telegraph Report Of Game Downtown." "Schaffer Closes Field To Students" Nov. 3, 1915: 1,4. (168) "Blue And Gold Students Fear Varsity Eleven." Tomorrow Will Be U. Of W. Day at Fair." Nov. 4, 1915. (169) "Rival Teams Ready For Great Fight On Berkeley Field." Nov. 5, 1915. (170) "Dobie's Men Win With Ease From Washington Park. Oct. 11, 1915. (171) "Expect To Send Bandmen South." Oct. 12, 1915. (172) "Blue And Gold Lack Effective Defense." Oct. 13, 1915. (173) "Defensive Strength Is Object Of Coach." Oct. 15, 1915. (174) "Gonzaga Aches To Whack Dobie." Oct. 16, 1915. (175) "Gonzaga Game To Open Big Season." Oct. 19, 1915. (176) "Ernest Murphy Hurt In Final Scrimmage." Oct. 21, 1915. (177) "Bronson On Squad After Three Years." Slowness Fault Of Dobie Machine." "Gonzaga Scores On Dobie Squad In Slow Contest." Oct. 25, 1915. (178) "Varsity Crushes California 72-0." "Dobie Given Boost By Eastern Critic." Nov. 8, 1915. (179) "Rooters Return From Excursion Tired But Happy." Nov. 9, 1915. (180) "Mighty Ovation Greets Victors." Nov. 9, 1915. (181) "Washington And W.S.C. Best On Pacific Coast." Nov. 10, 1915. (182) "Schaffer Quits Place As Coach." "California Crowd Will Reach Here On Friday Evening." Nov. 11, 1915. (183) "Bears Stronger, Declares Dobie." "Dobie Really Hopes To Beat California." "Big Game Program Is Like Real Football." Nov. 12, 1915. (184) "California Men Upset All Dope." Nov. 15, 1915: 1,4. (185)

"California Greets Her Varsity Wildly." Nov. 18, 1915: 1. (186) "Two Governors Will Talk At Big Rally." Nov. 20, 1915. (187) "Game With Colorado Worries Washington." Nov. 22, 1915. (188) "Washington Adopts The Freshman Rule." Rooters Rally To Back Eleven." Coach Dobie May Resign." Nov. 15, 1915. (189) "A Gloomy Thanksgiving." Nov. 28, 1915. (190) "Varsity Makes 8-Year Record." "Time Turns Spotlight Off Four Football Warriors." Coach Dobie Decides To Quit Gridiron." Nov. 29, 1915. (191) "Coach Committee May Act Today." Jan. 28, 1916. (192) "Dobie May Speak At Special Rally." Feb. 8, 1916. (193) "MacKechnie Will Not Join Varsity." Sep. 19, 1916. (194) "Bud Young Leaves School To Teach." Sep. 21, 1916. (195) "Few Take Interest In Open Practice." "Dobie Baffles With Backfield Formation." Sep. 26, 1916. (196) "Poor Form Shown In Opening Game." Oct. 2, 1916. (197) "Fast Back Who Is Holding Own Is Holding On Dobie's Team." Oct. 3, 1916. (198) "Rooters Can See Team In Practice." Oct. 4, 1916. (199) "Mars Inhabited Says Scientist." Oct. 9, 1916. (200) "Yell King To Form Girls' Song Staff." "Field Rally Is Success." "Dobie Losing Form, He Says So Himself." Oct. 10, 1916. (201) "Coach Unrelenting; Changes Hold Good." Oct. 12, 1916. (202) "Gloom Clouds Shift A Little When Dobie's Men Play Navy." Oct. 16, 1916. (203) "Dobie Launches Football Bark On Perilous Sea." Oct. 27, 1916. (204) "Whitman Victory Is Costly To Varsity." Oct. 30, 1916: 1. (205) "Same Old Line Of Bunk" - Borleske, "Lacks Washington Punch" - Varnell. Oct. 31, 1916. (206) "Oregon's Coach Has Best Chance Of Four Years." Nov. 3, 1916. (207) "Washington Wins In Supreme Test Of Sportsmanship." Nov. 6, 1916: 1,3. (208) "Denny Field Passes Into Mere Memory" "Dobie May Stop Rallies On Field." Nov. 6, 1916. (209) "Parsons Is Ruled Out By Officials." "Old Fear Of Defeat Is Felt Over Game Tomorrow." Nov. 10, 1916. (210) Kirby Torrance. "Dismal Failure Of Forward Pass Surprise Of Game." Nov. 13, 1916: 1,3. (211) "California Paying $12,000 In Effort To Beat Washington." Nov. 13, 1916. (212) "Bears Expect To Win Big Game Of Year." Nov. 14, 1916. (213) "Varsity Off For Southland After The Golden Bear." Nov. 15, 1916. (214) "We've Got A Chance Is California's Watchword." Nov. 17, 1916. (215) "Varsity Men Give Out A Little First-Hand Dope On Big Game In Southland." Nov. 20, 1916. (216) "Players May Be Expelled." Nov. 23, 1916. (217) "Faithful Seven Show Class Though They Need Not Play 'Bears' This Year." Nov. 24, 1916. (218) Kirby Torrance. "Men Decide To Play When Old Grads Present Plea." Nov. 24, 1916: 1,2. (219) " Team's Statement To Faculty." "Doctor Suzzallo Upholds Actions Of Board." Nov. 24, 1916: 1. (220) "Women Will Attend Parade Only As Spectators." Nov. 28, 1916: 1. (221) "Women Will Carry Swagger Sticks At Game." Nov. 29, 1916. (222) "Dobie's Twelfth Year Ends With No Defeat." Dec. 2, 1916. (223) "Wheels Set In Motion To Retain Gilmour Dobie." Dec. 8, 1916. (224) "Farewell Dobie", An Editorial. Dec. 11, 1916. (225) "Football Honors Go To Smith And Noble." "Will Pay Tribute To Dobie." "Statements Of Principals In Coaching Situation." Dec. 11, 1916. (226) "Plea Made For Aid Of Student War Prisoners." Dec. 11, 1916. (227) "Members Of Board Make Statements On Student Government And Coach Situation." Dec. 12, 1916. (228) "Gilmour Dobie Freed By Board." Dec. 1, 1915. (229) "Cy Noble's Laurels."

Dec. 1, 1915. (230) "Managers Form New Conference." Dec. 3, 1915. (231) "Dobie Will Never Accept Contract." "Dobie Touched By Gift Of Gold Watch." Dobie Will Be Honored At Alumni Luncheon." "Search Begun For Dobie's Successor." Dec. 9, 1915. (232) "Great Ovation Given To Ex-Coach Dobie." Dec. 13, 1915. (233) "Committee Cannot Reach Decision On New Coach." Jan. 1, 1916. (234) "Many Coaches Would Wear Dobie's Shoes." Jan. 3, 1916. (235) "Coach Applicant Has A Brilliant Record." Jan. 10, 1916: 1. (236) "Dobie May Not Take Wisconsin Position." Jan. 18, 1916. (237) "Coach Selection Again Put Off." Jan. 16, 1916. (238) "Dobie Stays With Washington; Will Hold Former Contract." Feb. 7, 1916. (239) Robert Hindley. "And Their Tribute Won Dobie's Smile." Dec. 12, 1916. (240) George Varnell. "Varnell Deplores Loss Of Coach Dobie." Dec. 13, 1916. (241) Tom Thorpe. "Washington Eleven Placed At Top Of List By Eastern Sport Writer." *Boston Morning Post,* Reprinted in *The Daily,* Dec. 14, 1916. (242) "Former Washington Coach Returns To Visit Campus." Oct. 2, 1940.

Oakland Tribune

"East Vs. West Passing Techniques." Nov. 19, 1915. (2) "Washington Pilot Is Pessimistic Despot." Oct. 10, 1915: 29. (3) "20,000 Await Gridiron Clash At U.C. Tomorrow." Nov. 5, 1915. (4) "Vast Assemblage Sees Game, Surprises Sprung By Rooters." Nov. 6, 1915. (5) Billy Fitz: "Operation A Success But The Patient Died." Nov. 7, 1915. (6) "Golden Bear Crushed Beyond Recognition By Dobie's Indians." "U.C. Licked In Bleachers As Well As On Grandstand." Nov. 7, 1915. (7) Hazel Pedlar Faulkner. "To Blooms, Tunes And Stunts, Old Game Comes Back." Nov. 7, 1916: 39. (8) "California Is Asking For An Explanation." Nov. 8, 1915. (9) "Washington Squad Boots Pigskin At California Field." Nov. 17, 1916: 14. (10) "U.C. Wins Over Three Northwest Colleges." Dec. 3, 1915. (11) "Gil Dobie To Again Coach Washington." Feb. 8, 1916. (12) "Gilmour Dobie Is Out With Usual Hard Luck Wail." July 27, 1916. (13) "Washington Squad Boots Pigskin At California Field." Nov. 17, 1916. (14) "Highlights Of The Big Game." Nov. 19, 1916. (15) "Washington University Wins From California 13 To 3 In Desperate Battle." Nov. 19, 1916: 46. (16) Daniel M. Daniel. "Dobie Sings Grief Just To Fool Boys." Oct. 26, 1926: 24.

Seattle Sun

(1) "Mike Hunt, End, Joins 'U' Squad." Sep. 18, 1914: 8. (2) By Gee. "University Of Oregon Faces Hardest Schedule In Its History." Sep. 19, 1914: 8. (3) "Bud Young 'Out' For 1914 Season." Sep. 22, 1914: 8. (4) "Washington 'U' Opens Football Season Today." Sep. 27, 1914: 1. (5) "Zednick Would Like To See New Conference." Dec. 8, 1914. (6) "In The Old Days At 'U' Faculty Urged By Big Men To Play Football." Dec. 22, 1914.

University of Washington Tyee

(1) Volume X. May 1, 1909: 113-129. (2) Volume XI: May 6, 1910: 117-122. (3) Volume XII. 1910:106-117. (4)Volume XIII. 1911: 86-109. (5) Volume XIV. 1912:

102-112. (6) Volume XIII. 1913: 112-126. (7) Volume XIV. 1914: 97-107. (8) Volume XV. 1915: 47-58, 95. (9) Volume XVIII. May 1916 to April 1917: 70-81. (10) "Trophies" *University Of Washington Tyee  1922.* Edition: 243.

The New York Times
    (1) "Terse News Of Sports." Dec. 17, 1915. (2) "Rally To Support Dobie." Dec. 12, 1916. (3) "Outlook Is Bright For Navy Football." Sep. 22, 1918. (4) "Gil Dobie Injured In Auto Accident." Dec. 2, 1936.

Syracuse Herald
    (1) "Dobie Among Coaches Whom Cornell Seeks." Feb. 25, 1920: 13. (2) "Dobie Has Praise For Rochester." Oct. 5, 1920: 18. (3) "George Pfann To Help Dobie As Grid Coach." *Syracuse Herald,* Jan. 6, 1924: 9. (4) Joe Williams. "Sports Roundup." Feb. 8, 1933: 17. (5) "Gil Dobie Quits Cornell Football." Feb. 2, 1936: 3-B. (6) "Gil Dobie Is Gravely Hurt In Auto Crash." Dec. 2, 1936: 13. (7) "Dobie Changes To Optimist Role." March 4, 1917. (8) "Dobie Buried As He Planned At Ithaca." Dec. 29, 1948: 5.

Lowell Sun
    (1) William Braucher. "Hooks And Slides, Justice To Gil." Dec. 1, 1930: 13. (2) "Columbia Fears Cornell Eleven." Sep. 7, 1932: 8. (3) Bernard Freeman. "Dobie Splits Boston College Candidates Into Five Elevens." Sep. 2, 1937: 17.

Other Media
    (1) "Mattson Will Captain Varsity Eleven." *Seattle Star.* Dec. 3, 1908. (2) "Board Of Control At The University With Dobie." "Dobie Leaves Gridiron Machine For New Coach." "Dobie's Machine Wins Another." *Seattle Star.* Nov. 26, 1915. (3) "Noble Played Entire Game." *Centralia Chronicle Examiner.* Nov. 16, 1914. (4) "Noble May Land End Position." *Centralia Chronicle Examiner.* Sep. 25, 1913. (5) "Cy Noble Again Reported Killed." *Centralia Daily Chronicle.* Oct. 29, 1918: 1. (6) Alan J. Gould. "Sport Slants." *Centralia Daily Chronicle.* Aug. 24, 1929: 6. (7) "Believe Juneau Will Be Retained." *Janesville Daily Gazette.* Dec. 1, 1915. (8) "Pat O'Dea Praises The Work Of Coach Dobie." *Janesville Daily Gazette .* Dec. 15, 1915. (9) "Gil Dobie Due For Walking Papers At Boston College." *Wisconsin State Journal.* Dec. 5, 1938: 2. (10) Edwin J. McCormick. "Playing The Game." *Wisconsin State Journal.* Dec. 26, 1948. (11) "Football Game. Washington Vs. California" *Souvenir Program.* Nov. 13, 1915. (12) "Football. Washington Vs. California." *Souvenir Program.* Nov. 30, 1916. (13) Gilmour Dobie. "Fundamentals Of Football." *Fort Wayne Sentinel.* Oct. 20, 1917: 20. (14) "Grid Coach Is Unbeaten In 10 Years; Gives Credit To Mothers Of Players." *Fort Wayne Sentinel.* Oct. 27, 1915: 8. (15) Emil E. Hurja. "A Pessimist On The Gridiron." *Sunset, The Pacific Monthly.* Nov. 1914: 86-88. (16) "Captain OF Grid Team Has No Snap." *Lincoln Daily Star.* Dec. 25, 1917: 3. (17) "Dobie's Unique Gridiron Record Draws Comment." *Cornell Daily Sun.* Nov. 26, 1923: 8.

(18) Allison Danzig. *The History of American Football.* 1956: 183-184, 244-248. (19) Wee Coyle. "Coyle Defends Gilmour Dobie As Sportsman." *Olympian.* Sep. 23, 1914. (20) "Cy Noble Is Coming Back." *Daily Chronicle Examiner.* Aug. 29, 1914. (21) "16 Make Varsity Letter." Three Washington Men On All-Star Team." *Seattle Times.* Nov. 26, 1915. (22) "Washington/Oregon. Championship Game." *Souvenir Program Thanksgiving Day.* Nov. 25, 1909. (23) "Football Washington Vs. Washington State." *Fifth Annual Souvenir Program.* Nov. 30, 1911. (24) "Gilmour Dobie Is A Remarkable Coach." *San Antonio Light.* Nov. 7, 1915. (25) "Ships Of The Redwood Coast." *Stanford University Press.* 1945: 88,89. (26) "Dobie Is The Favorite." *Daily Northwester.* Dec. 10, 1915. (27) "Dobie For Coach Is Newest Gossip." *Racine Journal-News.* Jan. 27, 1916: 7. (28) "Is The Entire World Against Coach Dobie?" *University Journal.* June 28, 1916: 4. (29) *H. C. Hamilton.* "Dobie's Washington Record Of Nine Defeatless Years Is A Password Of Gridiron." *United Press, La Cross Tribune.* Dec. 20, 1916. (30) Walter Camp. "Army-Navy Game Still Undecided." *Indianapolis Sunday Star.* Nov. 4, 1917: 4. (31) "West Is Far Ahead Of East In Football" *La Crosse Tribune And Leader-Press.* Dec. 25, 1917: 10. (32) "Dobie Takes Blame For Player's Tackle Says Game Official." *New Castle News.* Dec.7, 1918: 10. (33) "Navy Coach Drills Plebe Grid Material." *Washington Post.* Aug. 17, 1919. (34) Jack Keene. "Sports And Snap Shots." *Olean Evening Herald.* Dec. 9, 1919. (35) Sol Metzger. "Princeton And Cornell Will Be Dangerous." *Waterloo Times Tribune.* Dec. 5, 1920: 16. (36) "Gil's Buster Keaton Of Gridiron." *Ironwood Daily Globe.* Nov. 11, 1921: 10. (37) "Gilmour Dobie Once More Looms As Wonder Man As Cornell Coach." *Logansport Morning Press.* Nov. 16, 1921: 2. (38) "Two Famous Coaches Will Expound Theories At Illinois." *Logansport Pharos-Tribune.* May 22, 1923. (39) Ross Tenney. "Football Dean Is Accused Of Favoring East." *Des Moines Capital.* Dec. 31, 1922. (40) "Gilmour Dobie – Some Facts And Fancies About Why He Gets Results." *Cornell Alumni News.* Nov. 1, 1923: 67,68. (41) "Gil Dobie, Cornell Coach, Is Miracle Man Of The Gridiron." *Wisconsin Rapids Daily Tribune.* Dec. 15, 1922: 8. (42) "Gil Dobie Hands Palm To Eckersall." *Sunday Star Journal, Lincoln.* Sep. 7, 1924: 7,8. (43) "Gil Dobie Has Fine String Of Fast Backs Who Hope To Shatter Dartmouth's Line." *Bridgeport Telegram.* Nov. 14, 1924: 18. (44) "Cornell Eleven Not Impressive." *Morning Herald.* Sep. 22, 1925: 9. (45) Frank G. Menke. "'Doleful" Dobie, Cornell, Unique Character On Grid." *Charleston Gazette.* Nov. 7, 1926: 10. (46) "Mrs. Gilmour Dobie." *Cornell Alumni News.* July, 1927: 12. (47) James Driscoll. "Close-Up Of Gilmour Dobie." *Daily Courier, Connellsville.* Dec. 11, 1928: 7. (48) "Warden, Kin Of Olean Man, Defends Dobie" *Olean Herald.* June 6, 1929: 9. (49) Lawrence Perry. "Dobie Will Remain Coach At Cornell." *Charleston Daily Mail.* June 20, 1929: 10. (50) Alan J. Gould. "Sport Slants, Playing Students." *Daily Mail, Hagerstown.* Mar. 30, 1931: 8. (51) "Langford Likely To Be Named Grid Rules Committee Head." *Abilene Daily Reporter.* Dec. 28, 1932: 2. (52) Edwin Pope. "Gloomy Gil Dobie Had Eleven Perfect Seasons." *Abilene Reporter News.* Oct. 21, 1937. (53) "Boston To Give Dobie Release." *Daily Messenger, Canandaigua, N.Y.* Dec. 13, 1938: 7. (54) Steve O'Leary. "Gloomy Gil Dobie Thinks His Grid

Record Is Safe." *Evening Independent, Massillon, Ohio.* March 26, 1941: 10. (55) "Football's Famed Gil Dobie Dies." *San Mateo Times.* Dec. 24, 1948. (56) Whitney Martin. "Gil Dobie, Jock Sutherland Alike In Coaching Methods." *Lincoln Journal.* Dec. 27, 1948. (57) Professor G. Thomas Edwards. "A Sketchy History Of Whitman Football: Excitement And Controversy." Presentation given on Oct. 18, 2008. (58) "Public record: A very sad case of suicide," *Hastings Gazette,* May 22, 1886. (59) "Public record: Matter of George and Gilmour Dobie, a matter of admission to public school," *Hastings Gazette,* Dec. 8, 1886. "Gil Dobie Into State's Sports Hall Of Fame, *Hastings Gazette,* April 18, 1963.

Birth records researched by Dave Lilja of Dakota County, Minnesota in book 1, page 92, line 145 lists Dobie's birth date as January 31, 1878. The Draft Registration Card, serial number 808 signed by Dobie and showing his correct address gives his birth date as "1– 31– 1878." Most non-official reporting of his birth incorrectly reflects a year of birth as 1879.

8939211R1

Made in the USA
Lexington, KY
15 March 2011